THE WISDOM OF SOLOMON

VOLUME 43

THE ANCHOR BIBLE is a fresh approach to the world's greatest classic. Its object is to make the Bible accessible to the modern reader; its method is to arrive at the meaning of biblical literature through exact translation and extended exposition, and to reconstruct the ancient setting of the biblical story, as well as the circumstances of its transcription and the characteristics of its transcribers.

THE ANCHOR BIBLE is a project of international and interfaith scope: Protestant, Catholic, and Jewish scholars from many countries contribute individual volumes. The project is not sponsored by any ecclesiastical organization and is not intended to reflect any particular theological doctrine. Prepared under our joint supervision, THE ANCHOR BIBLE is an effort to make available all the significant historical and linguistic knowledge which bears on the interpretation of the biblical record.

THE ANCHOR BIBLE is aimed at the general reader with no special formal training in biblical studies; yet, it is written with the most exacting standards of scholarship, reflecting the highest technical accomplishment.

This project marks the beginning of a new era of co-operation among scholars in biblical research, thus forming a common body of knowledge to be shared by all.

William Foxwell Albright
David Noel Freedman
GENERAL EDITORS

THE ANCHOR BIBLE

THE WISDOM OF SOLOMON

A New Translation
with
Introduction and Commentary

by

DAVID WINSTON

DOUBLEDAY & COMPANY, INC.
GARDEN CITY, NEW YORK
1979

Library of Congress Cataloging in Publication Data

Bible. O. T. Apocrypha. Wisdom of Solomon. English.
Winston. 1979.
The Wisdom of Solomon.

(The Anchor Bible; vol. 43)
Bibliography: p. 70.
Includes indexes.
1. Bible. O. T. Apocrypha. Wisdom of Solomon—
Commentaries. I. Winston, David. II. Title.
III. Series.
BS192.2.A11964G3 vol. 43 [BS1753] 220.7'7s
[229.'3'077]

ISBN: 0-385-01644-1
Library of Congress Catalog Card Number 78–18148

To Irene
who has enabled me to pursue Sophia
without interruption

THE APOCRYPHA

The term Apocrypha (or "Deuterocanonical Books" in Roman Catholic usage) is popularly understood to describe the fifteen books or parts of books from the pre-Christian period that Catholics accept as canonical Scripture but Protestants and Jews do not. This designation and definition are inaccurate on many counts. An apocryphon is literally a hidden writing, kept secret for the initiate and too exalted for the general public; virtually none of these books makes such a claim. Not only Roman Catholics but also Orthodox and Eastern Christians accept these books, wholly or partially, as canonical Scripture. Roman Catholics do not accept all of them as canonical Scripture, for I and II Esdras and the Prayer of Manasseh are not included in the official Catholic canon drawn up at the Council of Trent (1545–1563). Many Protestant churches have no official decision declaring these books to be non-canonical; and, in fact, up to the last century they were included in most English Protestant Bibles. What is certain is that these books did not find their way into final Jewish Palestinian canon of Scripture. Thus, despite their Jewish origins (parts of II Esdras are Christian and Latin in origin), they were preserved for the most part in Greek by Christians as a heritage from the Alexandrian Jewish community and their basic text is found in the codices of the Septuagint. However, recent discoveries, especially that of the Dead Sea scrolls, have brought to light the original Hebrew or Aramaic texts of some of these books. Leaving aside the question of canonicity, Christians and Jews now unite in recognizing the importance of these books for tracing the history of Judaism and Jewish thought in the centuries between the last of the Hebrew Scriptures and the advent of Christianity.

PREFACE

Many scholars have zealously sought to dissociate the author of the Wisdom of Solomon as far as possible from the Philonic corpus and the Hellenistic philosophical tradition generally, in order to claim him as a representative of traditional Jewish religious piety, but the evidence, in my opinion, weighs heavily against them. With a few exceptions, however, I have generally avoided polemic confrontation, preferring to allow the evidence to speak for itself. Of the innumerable commentaries on Wisd, I have benefited most from the following: Grimm, Deane, Gregg, Goodrick (despite his singularly perverse approach to the book), Stein, and Fichtner. In translating the text from the Greek, I have derived much inspiration from the spirited versions of the Jerusalem and New English Bibles.

I am most grateful to various friends for reading all or parts of this book and making many useful criticisms: Baruch Bokser, John J. Collins, John Dillon, Gerd Lüdemann, E. P. Sanders. I owe a special debt of gratitude to Albert Henrichs, who kindly placed his vast erudition at my service, saving me from a number of errors, and considerably enriching my commentary. Thanks are also due to Martin Schwartz who was always ready to discuss with me matters Iranian. I have also derived much benefit from the careful critique of Anchor Bible editor David Noel Freedman, and wish to thank Robert Hewetson and Eve Roshevsky for their skillful preparation of the work for publication. The flaws that remain in spite of all this help are those of the writer.

I wish to thank the Institute for Advanced Studies of the Hebrew University of Jerusalem for the grant of a fellowship in 1976 which enabled me to start on the book, and my teacher and friend Saul Lieberman, who invited me to be with him at the Institute and whose consummate scholarship has ever been my guide and inspiration. I am equally grateful to the National Endowment for the Humanities for granting me a fellowship for the year 1978 which enabled me to put the finishing touches to the commentary. I am indebted to Claude Welch, President and Dean of the Graduate Theological Union at Berkeley, who provided the funds for the typing of my manuscript. I should also like to express my appreciation to

Barbara Saylor Rodgers, who did a magnificent job of typing, and to my graduate assistant Dan Rothwell who saved me much time by procuring books and Xeroxing articles. I could never have completed this work without the understanding patience and encouragement of my wife Irene, who also helped with the indices, and to whom it is dedicated.

CONTENTS

TRANSLATION and NOTES

PRINCIPAL ABBREVIATIONS

AB	Anchor Bible
AJP	*American Journal of Philology*
AJSL	*American Journal of Semitic Languages and Literature*
AJT	*American Journal of Theology*
AnBib	Analecta Biblica
ANET	*Ancient Near Eastern Texts,* ed. J. B. Pritchard, 2d ed. Princeton, 1955
ANRW	*Aufstieg und Niedergang der römischen Welt,* Philosophie und Wissenschaften, ed. W. Haase. Berlin, 197?
AP	*Anthologia Palatina,* eds. H. Stadmüller and F. Bucherer, 1906
Apoc.	Apocalypse
APOT	*Apocrypha and Pseudepigrapha of the Old Testament,* ed. R. H. Charles, 2 vols. Oxford, 1913
ARN	*Abot De-Rabbi Natan,* ed. S. Schechter. New York, 1945. English trans. by J. Goldin, *The Fathers According to Rabbi Nathan.* New Haven, 1955
ARW	*Archiv für Religionswissenschaft*
ATA	Alttestamentliche Abhandlungen
AWJEC	*Aspects of Wisdom in Judaism and Early Christianity,* ed. R. L. Wilken. Notre Dame and London, 1975
A.Z.	*'Aboda Zara*
BA	*Biblical Archaeologist*
BBB	Bonner biblische Beiträge
BDF	F. Blass and A. Debrunner, trans. and edited by R. W. Funk, *A Greek Grammar of the New Testament.* Chicago, 1961
Ber.	*Berakoth*
BHT	Beiträge zur historischen Theologie
BibLeb	*Bibel und Leben*
BIFAO	*Bulletin de l'institut français d'archéologie orientale du Caire.* Cairo
BJRL	*Bulletin of the John Rylands University Library of Manchester*
BR	*Bereshith Rabbah,* ed. J. Theodor, with additional corrections by C. Albeck. 3 vols. Jerusalem, 1965
BT	*Babylonian Talmud*
BVC	*Bible et vie chrétienne*
BZ	*Biblische Zeitschrift*
BZAW	*Beihefte zur Zeitschrift für die Alttestamentliche Wissenschaft*
CAH	*Cambridge Ancient History,* 12 vols. 1923–39
Cat.Cod.Astr.	*Catalogus Codicum Astrologorum Graecorum,* 1898*ff*

CB	*Cultura biblica*
CBQ	*Catholic Biblical Quarterly*
CD	*Codex Damascus* or *Damascus Document* (older designation: CDC) *Cairo Damascus Covenant*
CG	*Corpus Gnosticum*
CH	*Corpus Hermeticum*
CIG	*Corpus Inscriptionum Graecarum*, 1828*ff*
CIL	*Corpus Inscriptionum Latinarum*, 1862*ff*
CNRS	Centre National de la Recherche Scientifique
CRAI	*Comptes rendus des séances de l'académie des inscriptions et belles-lettres.* Paris
DK	H. Diels and W. Kranz, *Die Fragmente der Vorsokratiker*, 8th ed. 3 vols. Berlin, 1956. (Pagination remains the same in later editions.)
Dox.	*Doxographi Graeci*, ed. H. Diels. Berlin, 1958
EJ	*Encyclopaedia Judaica.* 16 vols. Jerusalem, 1972.
Ency.Bib.	*Encyclopaedia Biblica.* 7 vols. so far. Jerusalem, 1955*ff.* Hebrew
Epigr.Gr.	*Epigrammata Graeca ex lapidibus conlecta*, ed. G. Kaibel. 1878
Ep.Jer.	*Epistle of Jeremiah*
ERE	*Encyclopaedia of Religion and Ethics*, ed. J. Hastings. 12 vols. and index volume. New York, 1908*ff*
ETL	*Ephemerides theologicae Lovanienses*
ExpT	*Expository Times*
FGH	*Die Fragmente der grieschischen Historiker*, ed. F. Jacoby. Berlin and Leiden, 1923*ff*
FPG	*Fragmenta Pseudepigraphorum Quae Supersunt Graeca*, ed. A. M. Denis. Leiden, 1970. Pseudepigrapha veteris testamenti Graece, eds. A. M. Denis and M. de Jonge, vol. 3
FRLANT	Forschungen zur Religion und Literatur des Alten und Neuen Testaments
GRBS	*Greek, Roman, and Byzantine Studies*
Ḥag.	*Ḥagigah*
HR	*History of Religions*
HSCP	*Harvard Studies in Classical Philology*
HTR	*Harvard Theological Review*
HUCA	*Hebrew Union College Annual*
IDB	*Interpreter's Dictionary of the Bible.* 4 vols. Nashville, 1962
IEJ	*Israel Exploration Journal*
IG	*Inscriptiones Graecae*, 1873*ff*
IGR	*Inscriptiones Graecae ad res Romanas pertinentes*, ed. R. Cagnat. Paris. vols. 1–4. 1911–1927. (vols. 1 and 2 bound together)
IIJ	*Indo-Iranian Journal*
IPE	*Inscriptiones Orae Septentrionalis Ponti Euxini*, ed. V. Latyshev, 1890–1901
ITQ	*Irish Theological Quarterly*
JAAR	*Journal of the American Academy of Religion*

JAOS	*Journal of the American Oriental Society*
JB	*Jerusalem Bible*
JBL	*Journal of Biblical Literature*
JCS	*Journal of Cuneiform Studies*
JE	Jewish Encyclopaedia. 12 vols. Ktav reprint, New York, n.d.
JEA	*Journal of Egyptian Archaeology*
JHS	*Journal of Hellenic Studies*
JQR	*Jewish Quarterly Review*
JRAS	*Journal of the Royal Asiatic Society*
JSJ	*Journal for the Study of Judaism in the Persian, Hellenistic, and Roman Period*
JTS	*Journal of Theological Studies*
JUB	Jubilees
KBG	R. Kühner, *Ausführliche Grammatik der griechischen Sprache,* rev. by F. Blass and B. Gerth. 4 vols. 3d ed. Hannover, 1890–1904
LAB	Pseudo-Philo's *Liber Antiquitatum Biblicarum,* ed. G. Kisch. Notre Dame, 1949. English trans. by M. R. James, *The Biblical Antiquities of Philo.* Reprint New York, 1971, with prolegomenon by L. H. Feldman
LSJ	H. G. Liddell and R. Scott, *A Greek-English Lexicon* (1843), 9th ed., rev. by H. S. Jones. Oxford, 1948
LXX	The Septuagint
M.	*Mishnah*
MAMA	*Monumenta Asiae Minoris Antiquae,* eds. W. M. Calder and J. M. Cormack. Manchester, 1928ff
Mek.	*Mekilta De-Rabbi Ishmael,* eds. H. S. Horovitz and I. A. Rabin. Jerusalem, 1960. English trans. by J. Lauterbach. 3 vols. Philadelphia, 1933
MGWJ	*Monatsschrift für Geschichte und Wissenschaft des Judentums*
Mid.Teh.	*Midrash Tehillim,* ed. S. Buber. Reprint, New York, 1947
MRS	*Mekilta De-Rabbi Shimeon ben Yoḥai,* eds. J. N. Epstein and E. Z. Melamed. Jerusalem, 1955
MT	*Mishneh Torah*
MVAG	Mitteilungen der vorderasiatisch (-ägyptsch)en Gesellschaft
NEB	*New English Bible*
Nid.	*Niddah*
NRT	*La nouvelle revue théologique*
NTS	*New Testament Studies*
Num.R.	*Numbers Rabbah*
OGIS	W. Dittenberger, *Orientis Graeci Inscriptiones Selectae.* 2 vols. Leipzig, 1903–05
Pap.	Papyrus (*P.* when specific edition cited)
	P. Corn. Greek Papyri in Cornell University Library, eds. W. L. Westermann and C. J. Kraemer; New York, 1926
	P. Fay. Fayûm Towns and their Papryri, eds. B. Grenfell, A. Hunt, and D. Hogarth. 1900
	P. Lond. Greek Papyri in the British Museum, eds. F. G. Kenyon and others. 1893ff

	P. Mag. Leid. W. Leiden Magical Papyrus W., ed. A. Dieterich, *Abraxas.* Leipzig, 1891.
	P. Oxy. The Oxyrhynchus Papyri, eds. B. Grenfell and A. Hunt. 1898*ff*
	P. Tebt. The Tebtunis Papyri, eds. B. Grenfell, A. Hunt, and others. 1920*ff*
Par.Jer.	*Paraleipomena Jeremiou*
Pes.R.	*Pesikta Rabbati,* ed. M. Friedman. Reprint, Tel-Aviv, 1963. English trans. by W. G. Braude, Yale Judaica Series, XVIII:1. 2 vols. New Haven and London, 1968
PG	J. Migne, *Patrologia graeca*
PGM	*Papyri graecae magicae,* ed. K. Preisendanz. 2 vols. Berlin, 1928
Phil.Woch.	*Philologische Wochenschrift.* 1921*ff*
PL	J. Migne, *Patrologia latina*
PRE	*Pirke De-Rabbi Eliezer,* ed. D. Luria. Vilna, 1837. English trans. by G. Friedlander, 2d ed. New York, 1965
PRK	*Pesikta de Rav Kahana,* ed. B. Mandelbaum. 2 vols. New York, 1962. English trans. by W. G. Braude and I. J. Kapstein. Philadelphia, 1975
Ps-	Pseudo
PT	*Palestinian Talmud*
PW	A. Pauly and G. Wissowa, *Real-Enzyklopädie der classischen Altertumswissenschaften.* 1892*ff*
1Q	First Cave, Qumran
	1QH Qumran *Hôdāyôt* (Hymns of Thanksgiving)
	1QM Qumran *Milḥamot* (Wars between the Children of Light and the Children of Darkness)
	1QpHab Qumran *Pešer* (Commentary) on Habakkuk
	1QS Qumran *Serek* (Manual of Discipline)
RAC	*Reallexikon für Antike und Christentum*
RB	*Revue biblique*
RBén	*Revue bénédictine*
REG	*Revue des études grecques*
REL	*Revue des études latines*
RevThom	*Revue thomiste*
RHR	*Revue de l'histoire des religions*
RivB	*Rivista biblica*
RL	*Religion in Life.* New York
RSO	*Rivista degli studi orientali*
RSPT	*Revue des sciences philosophiques et théologiques*
RSR	*Recherches de science religieuse*
RSV	*Revised Standard Version*
RV	*Revised Version*
Sanh.	*Sanhedrin*
Sed.'OlamR.	*Seder 'Olam Rabbah*
S.H.A.	*Scriptores Historiae Augustae,* ed. E. Hohl, 1927

Shab.	*Shabbath*
ShR	*Shemoth Rabbah*
ŠHŠR	*Shir Ha-Shirim Rabbah*
Sib Or	*Sibylline Oracles*
Sifre Deut.	*Sifre on Deuteronomy,* ed. L. Finkelstein. Republished by Jewish Theological Seminary. New York, 1969
Sifre Num.	*Siphre d'be Rab, Siphre ad Numeros,* ed. H. S. Horovitz. Jerusalem, 1966
SIG	*Sylloge Inscriptionum Graecarum,* ed. D. Dittenberger, 3d ed. 4 vols. Leipzig, 1915–24
Smyth	H. W. Smyth, *Greek Grammar,* rev. by G. M. Messing. Cambridge, 1956
ST	*Studia theologica*
Suk.	*Sukkah*
SVF	*Stoicorum Veterum Fragmenta,* ed. H. von Arnim. 4 vols. Reprint, Stuttgart, 1964
Swete	H. B. Swete, *The Old Testament in Greek according to the Septuagint,* Vol. 3. Cambridge, 1912
Ta'an.	*Ta'anith*
Tanḥ.	*Midrash Tanḥuma.* Reprint, Jerusalem, 1965. ed. S. Buber. 2 vols. Reprint, New York, 1946
Targ.Yerush.	*Targum Yerushalmi*
TDNT	*Theological Dictionary of the New Testament,* eds. G. Kittel and G. Friedrich. Trans. and ed. G. W. Bromiley. 10 vols. Grand Rapids, 1964–76
Test.XII	*Testaments of the Twelve Patriarchs.* Translated and edited by R. H. Charles. Oxford, 1908. (Cited individually as e.g. *Test.Gad*)
TGF	*Trierer Grabungen und Forschungen*
TGl	*Theologie und Glaube*
TLZ	*Theologische Literaturzeitung*
Tosef.	*Tosefta,* ed. M. S. Zuckermandel. Reprint, Jerusalem, 1963
TrGF	*Tragicorum Graecorum Fragmenta,* ed. B. Snell, Göttingen, 1971
TTZ	*Trierer theologische Zeitschrift*
TU	Texte und Untersuchungen zur Geschichte der altchristlichen Literatur
TZ	*Theologische Zeitschrift*
UF	*Ugarit-Forschungen*
VC	*Vigiliae christianae*
VD	*Verbum domini*
VT	*Vetus Testamentum*
Wayyik.R.	*Wayyikra Rabbah,* ed. M. Margulies. 3 vols. Jerusalem, 1972
Yeb.	*Yebamoth*
ZAW	*Zeitschrift für die alttestamentliche Wissenschaft*
ZKG	*Zeitschrift für Kirchengeschichte*

ZKT   *Zeitschrift für katholische Theologie*
ZNW   *Zeitschrift für die neutestamentliche Wissenschaft*
ZPE   *Zeitschrift für Papyrologie und Epigraphik*
ZWT   *Zeitschrift für wissenschaftliche Theologie*

GREEK AND LATIN AUTHORS

Albinus *Did.   Didaskalikos*
Alexander of Aphrodisias=Alex.Aphr.
Aristotle *EN   Ethica Nicomachea*
Augustine *Civ.Dei   De civitate Dei*
Cicero *Fin.   De Finibus Bonorum*
         ND   De Natura Deorum
         Off   De Officiis
         Tusc.   Tusculanae Disputationes
Clement of Alexandria=Clem.Alex. *Prot.   Protrepticus*
                                  Strom.   Stromata
Diogenes Laertius=D.L.
Epicurus *K.D.   Kyriai Doksai (Principal Doctrines)*
Eusebius *HE   Historia Ecclesiastica*
         PE   Praeparatio Evangelica
Hesiod *Op.   Opera et Dies*
Hippolytus *Haer.   Refutatio omnium Haeresium*
Irenaeus *Adv. Haer.   Adversus Haereses*
Josephus=Jos. *Ag.Ap.   Against Apion*
              Ant.   Antiquities
              J.W.   The Jewish War
M. Aurel.=Marcus Aurelius
Philo *Abr.   De Abrahamo*
      Aet.   De Aeternitate Mundi
      Agr.   De Agricultura
      Cher.   De Cherubim
      Conf.   De Confusione Linguarum
      Congr.   De Congressu Eruditionis Gratia
      Cont.   De Vita Contemplativa
      Decal.   De Decalogo
      Det.   Quod Deterius Potiori insidiari soleat
      Deus   Quod Deus sit Immutabilis
      Ebr.   De Ebrietate
      Flac.   In Flaccum
      Fug.   De Fuga et Inventione
      Gig.   De Gigantibus
      Her.   Quis Rerum Divinarum Heres sit
      Hypoth.   Hypothetica

Jos. De Josepho
LA Legum Allegoriae
Legat. Legatio ad Gajum
Mig. De Migratione Abrahami
Mos. De Vita Mosis
Mut. De Mutatione Nominum
Op. De Opificio Mundi
Plant. De Plantatione
Post. De Posteritate Caini
Praem. De Praemiis et Poenis
Prob. Quod omnis Probus Liber sit
Prov. De Providentia
QE Quaestiones et Solutiones in Exodum
QG Quaestiones et Solutiones in Genesim
Sacr. De Sacrificiis Abelis et Caini
Sobr. De Sobrietate
Somn. De Somniis
Spec. De Specialibus Legibus
Virt. De Virtutibus
Plato *Rep.* Republic
    Symp. Symposium
    Tim. Timaeus
Pliny the Elder *NH* Naturalis Historia
Plutarch *Is. et Os.* De Iside et Osiride
Seneca the Younger *Ep.* Epistulae
Sextus Empiricus=Sext.*Math.* Adversus Mathematicos
Virgil *Ecl.* Eclogues
Xenophon *Mem.* Memorabilia Socratis

TRANSLATIONS OF CLASSICAL TEXTS

All translations from the following classical authors are cited from the Loeb Classical Library (LCL): Anacreontea, Pseudo-Aristotle, St. Augustine, Cicero, Diodorus of Sicily, Pseudo-Demosthenes, Diogenes Laertius (D.L.), Epictetus, Hesiod, Horace, Hymn to Athena, Josephus (Jos.), Marcus Aurelius (M. Aurel.), Menander, Philo, Plato, Plutarch, Sextus Empiricus (Sext.), Seneca, Propertius, Tacitus, Virgil.

Lucretius is cited from Cyril Bailey's translation (Oxford, 1947); Sophocles from R. C. Jebb (7 vols. Cambridge, 1924); and Plotinus from S. MacKenna, 4th rev. ed. (London, 1964).

Translations from the following pseudepigrapha have been cited from *The Apocrypha and Pseudepigrapha of the Old Testament* (*APOT*), ed. R. H. Charles, 2 vols.: Assumption of Moses, II Baruch, IV Ezra, I and II Enoch, Sibylline Oracles, Testaments of the XII Patriarchs.

Translations from Pseudo-Aristeas and IV Maccabees are from M. Hadas'
editions in the Dropsie College series published by Harper. (II Maccabees is
cited from S. Tedesche's translation in the same series.)

Translations from Justin Martyr, Clement of Alexandria (Clem.Alex.), and
the Clementina are from three volumes of *The Ante-Nicene Fathers* (Grand
Rapids: Eerdmans, vols. 1 and 2 reprints, 1967; vol. 8, 1951). Theophilus of
Antioch *Ad Autolycum,* is cited from R. M. Grant's translation in the Oxford
Early Christian Texts (1970).

Translations of the *Mishnah* are from P. Blackman (New York: Judaica
Press, 1964). All translations from the *Babylonian Talmud* (*BT*) are from the
Soncino edition. Translations from the Pentateuch, Isaiah, Psalms, and the five
Megilloth are from the new Jewish Publication Society (JPS) translation.
Translations from the Qumran scrolls except where otherwise noted are from
G. Vermes, *The Dead Sea Scrolls in English* (Penguin Books: Middlesex,
1968).

INTRODUCTION

The Wisdom of Solomon* is an exhortatory discourse written in Greek by a learned and thoroughly hellenized Jew of Alexandria, after that city's conquest by Rome in 30 BCE, when the earlier optimism of the Alexandrian Jewish community for a growing rapprochement with the Greeks and for social and cultural acceptance by them, had been replaced by a mounting sense of disillusionment and disappointment. The new Jewish mood was reflected in III Maccabees (ca. 24/23 BCE), where the conception of the Jewish diaspora as a temporary exile (*paroikia*, 6:36) was the obverse side of the attempt by the Greek community to classify the Jews among them as "strangers" whose religion was absurd and whose manners were odd and barbarous. The author of III Macabbees had abandoned the struggle of the Alexandrian Jews for civic rights, and considered the acquisition of Greek citizenship as treason to Judaism. In contrast to Pseudo-Aristeas' mild criticisms of heathen cults, the author of Wisd's wrathful exhibition of the innumerable crimes and corruptions connected with pagan idolatry and his unrestrained attack on Egyptian theriolatry (worhip of animals), is an unmistakable sign of the complete rupture which had in his time sundered the Jewish community from the native Egyptians and Greeks (see Tcherikover-Fuks 1. 74–75). We shall later argue more specifically for the reign of Gaius 'Caligula' (37–41 CE) as the political setting which best explains the distinctive historical traits of Wisd.

The dating adopted by us makes Wisd roughly contemporary with Philo of Alexandria, the famous Hellenistic Jewish thinker who radically transformed biblical thought by forcing it into the mold of a mystical Middle Platonism. We shall find that our author was similarly steeped in this philosophical tradition so influential at that time in Alexandria. Indeed, much of the earlier misapprehension of Wisd's philosophical views may be attributed to the fact that, until recently, our knowledge of Middle Platonism has not only been exceedingly sparse but virtually inaccessible to the non-specialist. J. Dillon, who has contributed greatly to our understanding of this tradition, has well described the situation:

[This period in the history of Platonism] seems fated to remain in the position of those tedious tracts of the Mid-Western United States through

*Shortened throughout to "Wisd"—Ed.

which one passes with all possible haste, in order to reach the excitements of one coast or the other. In Platonism, likewise, one tends to move all too hastily from Plato to Plotinus, with, at most, a perfunctory glance at those vast tracts of Academic scholasticism that lie between the two, and which were of such basic importance in the intellectual formation of the latter (1977:xiii).

The reader will find that the philosophical sophistication of Wisd is considerable, and that in consequence Parts VII.8 and VIII of our Introduction are somewhat more technical than would ordinarily be expected in a book of this kind; he may therefore be well-advised to read the text before turning to the extensive philosophical analysis at VII.8 and VIII, below.

I. CONTENTS

The Wisdom of Solomon is readily divided into three parts: A. Wisdom's Gift of Immortality (1 – 6:21); B. The Nature and Power of Wisdom and Solomon's Quest for Her (6:22 – 10:21); C. Divine Wisdom or Justice in the Exodus (11–19), with two excursuses, one on Divine Mercy (11:15 – 12:22), the other On Idolatry (13–15).

A. *Wisdom's Gift of Immortality* (1 – 6:21). The author begins by addressing to the pagan rulers of the earth an exhortation to justice, with the added warning that those who pursue immoral ends will ultimately be exposed and convicted by the Divine Wisdom which scrutinizes all (1:1–11). He admonishes those who invite death through a deviant way of life and insists that God is not responsible for their eventual destruction (1:12–16). The wicked are now allowed to speak for themselves. Convinced that life is chance, and death final, they inevitably conclude that one ought to derive maximum enjoyment from the pleasures at hand without regard for moral scruple. The man of integrity, who boasts close kinship with God, must be brutally exterminated as posing a standing threat to their own frankly amoral way of life (2:1–20). Blinded by their own malice, they are ignorant of God's mysteries, and thus pass up the prize of immortality. Harking back to his earlier statement concerning those who have convenanted with Death, the author points out that though God had indeed created man as an immortal image of his own proper being, through the devil's envy, Death has nevertheless entered into the cosmic order, to be experienced by his devotees (2:21–24).

An attempt is now made to deal with various facets of the problem of reward and retribution. The suffering and death of the just, we are told, are in reality only brief episodes of trial in the immortal destiny of righteous souls which will bring them peace, future glorification, rulership over nations, and a special divine illumination (3:1–12). The barren woman whose life has been pure shall be fruitful at the great assize of souls, and the righteous eunuch will receive a delectable portion in the [heavenly] temple of the Lord. Bastard offspring, on the other hand, will be cut off, so that even childlessness is to be preferred, if it be accompanied by virtue (3:13 – 4:6). Moreover, early death is not necessarily an evil, since it may actually signify early removal to safety through divine providence, and true length of life is in any case not to be measured chronologically but by the degree of wisdom attained (4:7–20). A portrait is now provided of the just man's ultimate vindication, which apparently involves his elevation to heaven to be among the angelic host, and of the wicked's final remorse when they come to the full realization of their former folly. There follows a lively description of the divine judgment, in which the cosmic elements join battle in order to crush the all-encompassing power of wickedness (5:1–23). The author concludes this part of his work with a second exhortation, this time to Wisdom, which from this point on becomes the explicit theme of the book, usurping the place of the various synonyms earlier employed in conjunction with her. The lords of the far corners of the earth [the reference is probably to Roman rule under Augustus or one of his early successors] are to take note of the fact that their sovereignty is God-given, and that their criminal acts will be relentlessly scrutinized and punished. It therefore behooves them to seek Wisdom so that they may keep the divine ordinances (6:1–11). This task, we are assured, offers no insuperable obstacles, for Wisdom actually anticipates her lovers, and graciously seeks out those worthy of her. Employing the *sorites,* a standard chain syllogism frequently found in Hellenistic philosophical writings, the author eloquently argues that the desire for Wisdom leads to sovereignty (6:12–21).

B. *The Nature and Power of Wisdom and Solomon's Quest for Her* (6:22 – 10:21). In this part of the book, which constitutes its core, we find the author at his best. With engaging imagery he describes his unwavering search for the great passion of his life, and with an unbridled exuberance he limns the exalted attributes of his beloved Wisdom. Without mentioning Solomon by name, in accordance with a stylistic feature of certain genres of Hellenistic literature (see NOTE on 4:10), he nevertheless now clearly identifies himself with that illustrious king (cf. M. Smith:210).

In the opening section, the author promises to reveal what Wisdom is, tracking her from her first beginnings (6:22–25). Identifying himself now indirectly in a first-person address as King Solomon, he emphasizes that kings too are mortal, and therefore in need of divine wisdom (7:1–6). He informs us that he loved Wisdom and desired her above all else, though he quickly discovered that all other good things too are eventually acquired along with her (7:7–14). The sole source of Wisdom, however, is God, and her scope includes the entire range of ancient knowledge (7:15–21). Wisdom's twenty-one attributes are enumerated, followed by an elaborate fivefold metaphor (exhalation, effluence, effulgence, mirror, image) describing her essence and unique efficacy. She is pictured as entering generation by generation into holy souls, rendering them friends of God and prophets. She surpasses even the celestial lights, and nothing can prevail over her (7:22–30). She is God's companion, and Solomon sought to make her his bride, knowing that through her he would have immortality and also win the admiration of all (8:1–16). Though naturally well-endowed, Solomon knew that he could not otherwise gain possession of her, unless God graciously bestowed her (8:17–21). There follows a very moving prayer in which the king, acknowledging his feebleness and ephemeral nature, beseeches his Lord to send forth from the holy heavens his throne-companion, Wisdom, who was present at the world's creation and through whom man himself was created, to be his guide and guardian (9:1–12). Mortal reason is at best precarious, weighed down as it is by a perishable tent of clay, so that man can barely make inferences concerning what is on earth, let alone what is in the heavens. It is only God's holy spirit of Wisdom descending from on high which has taught men what is pleasing to Him, and has brought them salvation (9:13–18). Part two [B] concludes with a detailed recitation of Wisdom's saving power in history from Adam through Moses and the Exodus (10:1–21).

C. *Divine Wisdom or Justice in the Exodus* (11–19). In an elaborate *synkrisis* or 'comparison,' the author now proceeds with a series of antitheses in order to illustrate the theme that Egypt was punished measure for measure, whereas Israel was benefited by those very things whereby Egypt was punished. The first antithesis contrasts the turning of the Nile water into blood for the Egyptians with the supply of water for the Israelites from the flinty desert rock. The brief trials of the Israelites are explained on the pedagogical ground that it was necessary for them to receive a taste of their enemies' punishments so that they would realize how compassionate God's discipline was in their own regard, being in the nature of a fatherly reproof, whereas the torments of the Egyptians, on the other hand, were inflicted by a stern king passing sentence. By the same token, when the Egyptians learned that the Israelites were actually benefited through their own punishments, they took note of the Lord (11:1–14).

This leads the author into an excursus on the nature of God's mercy. The supreme power of the deity which created the world out of formless matter could readily have destroyed the Egyptians with one swift blow, but it is this very omnipotence which is the source of the compassion he exercises with a view to man's repentance (11:15–12:2). This also explains God's mercy toward the Canaanites, whose loathsome practices included sorcery, licentious mystery rites, infanticide, and cannibalism. Though their seed was evil and their viciousness innate, they, too, were nevertheless judged gradually to afford them a chance for repentance (12:3–18). God's mercy thus serves as a model lesson for Israel, to teach them humanity, and at the same time instill in them confidence in their own relationship with the deity (12:19–22). In a transition passage leading to his second excursus, the author points out that the Egyptians, who had taken the most despicable of loathsome beasts as their gods, were tormented with their own abominations. Punished by means of the very creatures whom they deemed gods, they came to recognize the true God (12:23–27).

The author is thus led to his second and rather long excursus on the nature of idolatry. Those who worship Nature are chided for not pressing their search beyond visible reality, which, for all its beauty and dynamic character, only points to its supreme author. Though not entirely culpable, since they are at least searching for the deity, neither are they to be excused, for if they were resourceful enough to infer the 'Universe,' they should certainly have discovered its Master (13:1–9). More blameworthy, however, are the wretches who worship images manufactured of gold and silver or carved out of crooked wood streaked with knots, addressing their prayers to lifeless objects that are entirely impotent (13:10–19). The author now seeks to explain the origin of idolatry, which he claims did not exist from the beginning but came into the world through the empty illusions of men. A father consumed with untimely grief made an image of the child so suddenly taken from him, honoring as a god what was once a corpse, and handed down to his descendants mysteries and initiation rites. Again, when men were unable to honor their ruler in his presence because of the remoteness of his dwelling, they honored his image in order to flatter the absent one as though present. The artists, in their desire to please the ruler, skillfully forced his likeness into a more beautiful form, and the masses, charmed by the workmanship, mistook for an object of worship him who was but lately honored as a man (14:12–31). This turned out to be the one great trap of human life, for idolatry is the source of every moral corruption. Worst of all, however, is the malicious manufacturer of clay figurines, who, for monetary gain, makes cheap clay counterfeits of gold and silver idols (15:7–13). But the blindest of all are the Egyptians, Israel's oppressors, for they worship hateful beasts, who compared for brutishness are worse than all the rest, and whose appearance is without the slightest trace of beauty (15:14–19).

There now follow six further antitheses between the Egyptians and the Israelites (16:1 – 19:8). In the second antithesis, the first of this group, the Egyptians are depicted as being unable to eat because of the hideousness of the beasts sent against them, while Israel, after briefly suffering want, enjoys exotic quail food (16:1–4). In the third antithesis, the Egyptians are described as being slain by locusts and flies, while Israel survives a serpent attack through the agency of the bronze serpent, interpreted by the author as a symbol of God's salvation which was to remind them of the commandments of the Law. The Israelites are said to have been prodded sharply and delivered quickly to keep them from falling into complacency through God's kindness (16:5–14). In the fourth antithesis, the Egyptians are described as being plagued by thunderstorms in which fire was marvelously the most dynamic force, so that the cosmic order itself can be seen to have been championing the righteous. The Israelites, on the other hand, were spoonfed with angel food from heaven, equivalent to every pleasure and suited to every taste. This ice-like manna did not melt in the fire, which forgot its own power so that the righteous could be fed. Creation, serving its Maker, thus tensed itself for punishment of the unrighteous, and relaxed into benevolence on behalf of those who trusted in Him (16:15–29). In the fifth antithesis, the lawless Egyptians who had thought that they could remain unnoticed in their secret sins, are described as being appropriately shackled by the darkness of a long night, during which they were terrified by crashing noises and grim-faced apparitions. Though the darkness which gripped them was in reality powerless, since it came from the powerless infernal realm, the Egyptians were paralyzed by the betrayal of their own minds, overwhelmed by a sudden and unexpected fear. Having kept God's sons captive, through whom the imperishable light of the Law was to be given to the world, they well deserved to be deprived of light. For Israel, in contrast, there was light supreme (17:1 – 18:4). In the sixth antithesis, we are told that on the same night that the Egyptian firstborn were destroyed, Israel was summoned to God and glorified, while to the chant of their praises of the fathers there echoed the discordant cries of their enemies. It was at the stroke of midnight that the all-powerful Divine Logos leaped forth out of the heavens, from the royal throne, bearing God's unambiguous decree as a sharp sword. It touched the heavens, yet stood poised upon the earth, and filled all things with death. The righteous, too, however, had to be touched by an experience of death, and suffered a mass slaughter in the wilderness. Still, the divine anger did not long abide, for a blameless man, Aaron, interposed with prayer and atoning incense. On his full-length robe there was a representation of the entire cosmos, and the glories of the fathers upon his four rows of carved stones (18:5–25).

In the seventh and last antithesis, the Egyptians, while still engaged in their mourning, are depicted as adopting one last mad scheme, to pursue the fugitives whom they had beseeched to leave. For a condign fate drew them on to this denouement, so that they might fill in the one penalty still lacking to their torments, and bring upon themselves a bizarre death. The miracle at the Red Sea is described as involving the refashioning of the whole of creation in its original nature, so that God's children might be preserved unharmed (19:1–8). For as the notes of a psaltery vary the beat [key] while holding to the melody, so were the elements transposed, land animals becoming aquatic, and things that swim migrating to shore. Similarly fire retained its force in the water, whereas flames did not waste the flesh of perishable creatures that walked among them, nor was the ice-like manna dissolved (19:18–21). In order to emphasize the culpability of the Egyptians, the better to justify their terrible punishments, the author adds that they were even more blameworthy than the Sodomites. The latter refused to welcome strangers who visited them, but the Egyptians enslaved guests and benefactors, and after a festal welcome, oppressed with hard labor men who had already shared with them equal rights (19:13–17). The book concludes with the conventional doxology: "For in every way, O Lord, you exalted and glorified your people, and did not neglect to assist them in every time and place" (19:22).

II. STRUCTURE

Although many earlier scholars had cavalierly carved Wisd up into a confusing disarray of units (see III. AUTHORSHIP, below), recent scholarship has succeeded in demonstrating the structural unity of the book and the skill with which it was put together. Fichtner (1938), Mariès, and Pfeiffer had already noted some of its repetitions of vocabulary, but J. M. Reese (1965) was the first to recognize the author's skillful use of the rhetorical device of *inclusio* or *kyklos* (the name given by ancient rhetoricians to the figure by which a sentence returns to its opening word or words at the close: see Denniston:90) in order to mark off many sections of his book, and to have attempted to structure the book on that basis. A. G. Wright, following in Reese's footsteps, applied this method systematically, though somewhat exaggeratedly, in an attempt to establish the structure of the entire work. According to Wright,

> The use of systematic arrangement, announcement of subjects, *mots crochets,* and inclusions is attested in biblical and extra-biblical literature alike. Up to now, the systematic use of all of these indices of structure in a single work has apparently been observed only in the Epistle to the Hebrews. (See A. Vanhoye, *La structure littéraire de l'épitre aux Hébreux* [Paris-Bruges, 1963]:60–63.) To that work can now be added the Book of

Wisdom, and one may be permitted to speculate whether this structural characteristic was an occasional feature of Alexandrian rhetoric and another instance of Alexandrian contact in the Epistle to the Hebrews. (1967:184)

Though Wisdom can readily be divided into three parts (designated here as A, B, and C), there is not always complete agreement on their exact limits, much less as to the various subdivisions of each part. An outline of the book's structure that I have adopted follows:

A. Wisdom's Gift of Immortality (1 – 6:21)
        I. Exhortation to Justice which brings immortality (1:1–15) (*dikaiosynē* forming an *inclusio*)
       II. Speech of the wicked who have covenanted with Death (1:16 – 2:24) (*tēs ekeinou meridos* forming an *inclusio*)
Problems of Reward and Retribution (III–V)
       III. Sufferings of the immortal just only a trial (3:1–12)
       IV. Sterility of the virtuous will ultimately be converted to fruitfulness (3:13 – 4:6)
       V. Early death a token of God's solicitous care (4:7–20)
       VI. Vindication of the just and Final Judgment (5:1–23) (*stēsetai/ antistēsetai* forming an *inclusio*)
       VII. Exhortation to Wisdom which is easily found and brings immortality and sovereignty (6:1–21) (*basileis/ basileusēte* forming an *inclusio*)

Part I [A] teaches that man's true being is destined for immortality, though the latter may be forefeited by the abandonment of Wisdom. By means of pointed contrasts between the just and the wicked, consisting, as Reese (1965, 391–399) has pointed out, of five sections arranged in chiastic order (A B C B' A'), the author depicts their opposing life-paths and ultimate fate.

B. The Nature and Power of Wisdom and Solomon's Quest for Her (6:22 – 10:21)
       VIII. The nature of Wisdom and her mysteries will be revealed (6:22–25)
Solomon's Speech (IX–XI)
       IX. Solomon is only a mortal (7:1–6) (*isos hapasin/ pantōn isē* forming an *inclusio*)
       X. Solomon prefers Wisdom above all else (7:7–14)
       XI. God is sole source of all-encompassing Wisdom (7:15–22a)
       XII. Nature of Wisdom: her twenty-one attributes (7:22b–24)
       XIII. Fivefold metaphor describing Wisdom's essence and her unique efficacy (7:25 – 8:1)
       XIV. Solomon sought to make Wisdom his bride (8:2–16)

XV. Wisdom a sheer gift of God's Grace (8:17–21) (*kardia/ kardias* forming an *inclusio*)

XVI. Without Wisdom no human enterprise can succeed (9:1–6)

XVII. Without Wisdom Solomon could not reign (9:7–12)

XVIII. Divine Wisdom brought men salvation (9:13–18)

An Ode to Wisdom's Saving Power in history (XIX–XX) (By anaphora Wisdom is introduced six times with the emphatic pronoun *hautē*.)

{
    XIX. From Adam to Moses (10:1–14)
    XX. The Exodus (10:15–21)

C. Divine Wisdom or Justice in the Exodus (11–19). (An elaborate *synkrisis* employing seven antitheses): with Excursuses on the Divine Mercy (11:15 – 12:22) and on Idolatry (13 – 15)

XXI. First Antithesis: Nile water changed to blood, but Israelites obtained water from the desert rock (11:1–14). Introductory Narrative 11:1–4 (*edipsēsan/dipsēsantes* forming an *inclusio*)

Excursus I: Nature and Purpose of the Divine Mercy (XXII–XXIV)

{
XXII. God's Mercy toward the Egyptians and its causes (His Might the source of His Merciful Love) (11:15 – 12:2)

XXIII. God's Mercy toward the Canaanites and its causes (12:3–18)

XXIV. God's Mercy a model lesson for Israel (12:19–22)

XXV. Return to theme of measure for measure and transition to second Excursus (12:23–27)

Excursus II: On Idolatry (XXVI–XXXI)

{
XXVI. Mindless nature worship (13:1–9) (*ischysan eidenai* forming an *inclusio*)

XXVII. Wretched wooden-image making (13:10 – 14:11)

XXVIII. Origin and evil consequences of idolatry (14:12–31)

XXIX. Israel's immunity from idolatry (15:1–6)

XXX. Malicious manufacture of clay figurines (15:7–13) (*gēn/ geōdous* forming an *inclusio*)

XXXI. Folly of Egyptian idolatry (15:14–19)

XXXII. Second Antithesis: Egyptians hunger through animal plague, but Israel enjoys exotic quail food (16:1–4) (*ebasanisthēsan/ebasanizonto* forming an *inclusio*)

XXXIII. Third Antithesis: Egyptians slain by locusts and flies, but Israel survives a serpent attack through the bronze serpent, symbol of salvation (16:5–14) (particle *gar* used seven times) (*epēlthen/ekselthon* forming an *inclusio*)

XXXIV. Fourth Antithesis: Egyptians plagued by thunderstorms, but Israel fed by rain of manna (16:15–29)

XXXV. Fifth Antithesis: Egyptians terrified by darkness, but Israel illuminated with bright light and guided through desert by a pillar of fire (17:1 – 18:4) (*katakleisthentes/katakleist-ous*, and *skotous/skotei* forming inclusions)

XXXVI. Sixth Antithesis: Egyptian firstborn destroyed, but Israel protected and glorified (18:5–25) (A digression, vv. 6–9, pictures the liturgical enactment of Jewish fidelity to law and covenant. The Egyptians and Israelites are each set off by an *inclusio: apōlesas/apolōntai; peira/peira*)

XXXVII. Seventh Antithesis: Egyptians drowned in the sea, but Israel passes safely through (19:1–9)

XXXVIII. Retrospective review of God's wonders through which Nature was refashioned for Israel (19:10–12)

XXXIX. Egypt more blameworthy than Sodom (19:13–17)

XL. Transposition of the elements (19:18–21)

XLI. Concluding doxology (19:22)

III. AUTHORSHIP: SINGLE OR COMPOSITE

The history of the critical literature dealing with Wisd parallels to some extent that dealing with the Homeric question. By the middle of the seventeenth century we begin hearing the voices of those who, like the *chōrizontes* or ancient grammarians who ascribed the *Iliad* and *Odyssey* to different authors, sought to carve the book up and assign its various parts to different authors. The first to attack its unity was Charles F. Houbigant, a priest at the Paris Oratory. Chapters 1–9, he argued [in the preface to his 1753 edition of Wisd], were of authentic Solomonic origin, whereas the rest was added by a Greek writer. In 1795, the year in which F. A. Wolff's *Prolegomena ad Homerum* was published, J. G. Eichhorn, on better grounds, separated the first ten chapters from the rest, explaining the disharmony between the two parts, either by attributing the second part to another writer, or considering it a product of the earlier years of the author of the first part, an idea which had already been broached by J. F. Kleucker. A few years later, J. C. C. Nachtigal presented his bizarre view that Wisd was a mosaic, to which no fewer than seventy-nine wise men had contributed. He divided the work into two main parts (1–9; 10–19), and saw in them two Israelite wisdom collections. C. G. Bretschneider (1804) went further than Eichhorn by suggesting that the oldest part (1:1 – 6:8) was the fragment of a work composed by a Palestinian Jew of the Maccabean age, that chaps. 6:9 – 10:21 were composed in Greek about the time of Christ by an Alexandrian Jew, and that the third part (12–19) also came from that period. (Chapter 11, he claimed, was inserted by the editor of the whole.) All these attempts, however, were soon demolished by Carl Grimm's great commentary of 1860, which demonstrated that the unity of Wisd was guaranteed by the uniformity of language and style characterizing the whole. At the turn of the century, R. Siegfried could speak of "now forgotten hypotheses which assigned various parts of the book to different hands," without mentioning even one of them. After a hundred-year gap, however, the search for multiple authorship revived. In 1903, L. Lincke argued that 1:1 – 12:8 was written by a Samaritan, whereas 12:19 – 19:22 was the product of an Alexandrian Jew. A year later, W. Weber postulated four authors (one, Book of Eschatology: 1–5; two, Book of Wisdom: 6–11; three, Book of Divine Method of Punishment: 11:2–13, 15, 18–19; four, Book of Idolatry: 13 – 15:17), and E. Gärtner adopted the same position. F. Focke divided the book into two parts (1–5; 6–19), but suggested that the author of the second part may also have been the translator of the Hebrew original of the first part. (Peters, Speiser, and M. Stein [1936] accepted Focke's view that the first part was a translation from Hebrew.) Others, like Gregg, Goodrick, Feldmann (1926), Fichtner (1938), and Pfeiffer, continued to maintain unity of authorship, and this is now the consensus. (See Focke 1913:1–16; Purinton:276–278; Grimm 1860:9–15.)

Focke's arguments for attributing chaps. 1–5 and 6–19 to two different authors (one Palestinian, the other Alexandrian), seem at first sight quite plausible and must therefore be examined in detail. He claims that Greek philosophical terminology is absent in chaps. 1–5; that Wisdom, who plays a central role in chaps. 6–19, is of minor significance in chaps. 1–5; that there is nothing of God's mercy in chaps. 1–5, but always only the strict judge, unlike chaps. 6–19, where much emphasis is placed on the attribute of mercy; that the God-concept in chaps. 1–5 is purely ethical, but in chaps. 6–19 nationalistic; that there is an implied doctrine of resurrection in chaps. 1–5, whereas in chaps. 6–19 the body is denigrated and the soul's immortality emphasized; that chaps. 1–5 contrasts Sadducees and Pharisees, while chaps. 6–19 Israelites and heathen. Now, the argument that Greek philosophical terminology is absent from chaps. 1–5 is palpably false. One need but cite the following words or phrases: *to synechon ta panta* (1:7), *sōtērioi hai geneseis tou kosmou* (1:14), *rhembasmos epithymias* (4:12), and *sbesthentos* (2:3), which are Stoic formulations; *aphtharsia* (2:23), an Epicurean term; *diaskedasthēsetai* (2:4) and *poreia* (3:3), echoes from Plato's *Phaedo; athanasia* (3:4), used by Plato, Aristotle, and Epicurus; *polia de estin phronēsis anthrōpois* (4:9), a common theme in Greek diatribe. Moreover, it is hard to believe that chaps. 1–5 contain an implicit doctrine of resurrection, since that teaching, which had taxed the credulity of even the staunchest believers of the ancient world,[1] would have required explicit formulation on the part of the author

---

[1] See Winston 1966:210–211.

with the likely accompaniment of supportive arguments. The argument that
Wisdom plays only a minor role in 1–5 would be neutralized if we are correct in seeing 6:1–21 as the conclusion of part I [A]. The claim that 1–5
contrasts Sadducees and Pharisees must be branded purely speculative,
since the characteristic doctrines of these sects are nowhere attested in the
text.

The arguments concerning the nationalistic conception of God and the
emphasis on his mercy which characterize 6–19 but are lacking in 1–5
carry little weight once it is realized that part I was probably designed as a
broadside against asssimilated Alexandrian Jews who had turned their
backs on their spiritual heritage (cf. Philo *Mos.* 1.31), some ultimately resorting to apostasy, and those pagans (either Alexandrians or Romans or
both) who were hostile to Judaism. In this case, the emphasis was bound
to be on the divine wrath which the author was convinced would finally
overtake the enemies of his people, both internal and external. In part II
[B], on the other hand, in the course of a historical retrospect in which
the author surveys the saving power of God in Jewish history in order to
comfort and encourage his fellow Jews, he naturally turns his attention to
the questions of divine mercy and God's special relationship to Israel. Finally, Focke points out that in 1–5, the *parallelismus membrorum* is never
abandoned, whereas in 6–19 there are many passages which read as prose.
In 6–12:18, the Hebraising poetry is predominant, along with some
prose; 12:19–19:22, however, is largely prose, with scattered parallelisms. He therefore suggests that the author of part II wrote his own work
in close connection with part I, which he had already found complete before him. He tried at first to imitate its Hebraic form, although his own poetic art burst the bounds he had set for it, and with 12:19 he finally, un-
willingly and apparently unconsciously, abandoned it, allowing it to appear
only here and there. It is difficult to believe, however, that an author
whose style is as elaborate as that of the author of Wisd did anything un-
willingly or unconsciously. I prefer to think that he had carefully planned
the writing of the whole, employing a variety of styles in its sundry parts
(note the elaborate similes even in part I [5:10–21]) in order to heighten
the rhetorical effect. In sum, Focke's arguments for composite authorship
turn out to be either unfounded or at best inconclusive.

IV. LANGUAGE AND STYLE

The strongest argument for the unity of Wisd may be drawn from its language and style. In spite of some Hebrew coloring, such as *parallelismus*

membrorum, Hebraisms,[2] the simple connection of clauses by conjunctions such as *kai, de* (less frequently *te*), *dia touto, dio, gar,* and *hoti,*[3] Grimm has correctly pointed out that the author's Greek was on the whole rich and spontaneous,[4] and that St. Jerome's judgment that his style was "redolent of Greek eloquence"' (*Preface to the Books of Solomon,* Migne *PL* XXVIII. 1242) was completely justified. Thus the author of Wisd is quite capable of constructing sentences in true periodic style (12:27; 13:11–15), and his fondness for compound words[5] is almost Aeschylean. His manner at times has the light touch of Greek lyric poetry (17:17–19; 2:6–9; 5:9–13), and occasionally his words fall into an iambic or hexameter rhythm.[6] He employs *chiasmus* (1:1,4,8; 3:15), *hyperbaton,*[7] the

[2] E.g. *haplotēs kardias* (1:1); *meris* and *klēros* (2:9); *triboi* (2:15; 5:7; 9:18; 10:10); *logizesthai eis ti* (2:16); *plēroun chronon* (4:13); *thentes epi dianoia* (4:14); *hosioi tou theou* (4:15); *hyposteleitai prosōpon* (6:7); *heuriskesthai* (7:29; 8:11); *eks holēs kardias* (8:21); *euthytēs psychēs* (9:3); *huioi anthrōpōn* (9:6); *ariston en opthalmois tinos* (9:9); *aiōn* (13:9; 18:4); *plēttein aorasia* (19:17); *stenochōria pneumatos* (5:3); *diadēma tou kallous* (5:16). See Grimm:5; Reider 1957:24, n.118.

[3] It should be noted, however, that paratactic structure was also characteristic of the early (i.e. Hellenistic) Greek diatribe. See Wendland:41; *RAC* 3.993.

[4] For detailed studies of Wisd's vocabulary, see Gärtner:102–229; Reese 1970:1–31. For the author's supposed misuse of the words *metalleuō* (4:12) and *philopsychos* (11:26), see NOTES. It is difficult to believe that a writer who, as Speiser:469 noted, "had enough insight into the language to form new words after the regular manner, could be charged with not knowing a verb (*metalloioō*) that was used at that period by much inferior writers (Ps-Aristeas 17)." As for richness of language, it has been pointed out that the entire book contains only 6,952 words, but employs a vocabulary of 1,734 words, of which 1,303 appear only once (Reese 1970:3).

[5] *Hypermachos* (10:20; 16:17); *homoiopathēs* (7:3); *gēgenēs* (7:1); *polychronios* (2:10; 4:8); *oligochronios* (9:5); *polyphrontis* (9:15); *petrobolos* (5:22); *pantodynamos* (7:23; 11:17; 18:15); *panepiskopos* (7:23); *philanthrōpos* (1:6; 7:22; 12:29); *prōtoplastos* (7:1; 10:1); *kakotechnos* (1:4; 15:4); *adelphoktonos* (10:3); *splangchnophagos* (12:5); *dysdiēgētos* (17:1); *genesiourgos* (13:5); *nēpioktonos* (11:7); *teknophonos* (14:23); *genesiarchēs* (13:3); *kakomochthos* (15:8); *brachytelēs* (15:9); *metakirnasthai* (16:21); *eidechtheia* (16:3); *anapodismos* (2:5); *eudraneia* (13:19); *autoschediōs* (2:2). (Grimm:6; Palm:39, 43, 79–81.)

[6] Iambics: *ek ponōn errysato* (10:9); *psychōn miasmos, geneseōs enallagē* (14:26); *eidos spilōthen chrōmasin* (15:4); *pothei te nekras eikonas . . . hōn opsis aphrosin eis oneidos erchetai* (14:5); *kakōn erastai* (14:6). Hexameters: *synapōleto thymois* (10:3); *aiōni didosthai* (18:4). See Gregg 1909:xv. Thackeray has attempted to show that a similar rhythmical principle (the mutual assimilation of beginnings and endings of sentences) runs through both the Epistle to the Hebrews and Wisd, but although Blass accepted it, Wilamowitz's judgment in this regard was negative (see Focke 1913:54, n.1). (According to Cicero, sentence endings or *clausulae* are rhythmically most important, though the rest of the sentence is not to be neglected.)

[7] "In contrast to the LXX version of Isaiah," writes Reese, "which has only eight examples of this figure, and the Psalter, which has only three, Wisdom contains 240 examples of hyperbaton, an average of more than one for each five stichs. The figure is more frequent in the last nine chapters, which show more freedom and poetic im-

Sorites (6:17–20), antithesis,[8] accumulation of epithets (*accumulatio; synathroismos*) (7:22–23), alliteration,[9] assonance,[10] *homoioteleuton,[11] paranomasia,[12] isokōlia* (balance of clauses), *litotes,[13] anaphora* (c. 10), and Greek philosophical terminology.[14]

These characteristics, in addition to the author's many favorite 'theme' words and expressions which recur throughout the work,[15] argue for unity

---

agery, but many examples appear in the early part of the work. This feature of style argues for a Greek original; it also offers confirmation for the unity of the work" (1970:26–27).

[8] *oliga paideuthentes megala euergetēthēsontai* (3:5); *katakrinei de dikaios kamōn tous zōntas asebeis* (4:16); *mia de pantōn eisodos eis ton bion eksodos te isē* (7:6); *ta en chersin . . . ta de en ouranois* (9:16); *sōtēria men dikaiōn, echthrōn de apōleia* (18:7).

[9] *Presbytou . . . polias polychronious* (2:10); *barys . . . kai blepomenos* (2:14); *krinousin . . . kratēsousin* (3:8); *tekna . . . atelesta* (3:16); *periklasthēsontai klōnes* (4:5); *belous blēthentos* (5:12); *korytha krisin anypokriton* (5:18); *hosiōs . . . hosia hosiōthēsontai* (6:10); *dikaios . . . dikaiōs . . . katadikasai* (15:15); *lamprō . . . katelampetō* (17:20); *dynatoi de dynatōs* (6:6).

[10] *ous-throus* (1:10); *empaigmon . . . paigniois* (12:25–26); *nosousēs . . . enosoun* (17:8); *en opsei . . . tēn opsin* (14:17); *idios . . . idiotētos* (2:23); *eumathōs . . . euprepōs* (13:11); *adolōs . . . aphthonōs* (7:13); *asebous . . . chnous* (5:14); *panoplian . . . hoplopoiēsei* (5:17).

[11] *agapēsate . . . phronēsate . . . zētēsate; en agathotēti . . . haplotēti* (1:1); *apanastēsetai . . . elengchthēsetai* (1:5); *apobēsetai . . . diachythēsetai . . . epilēsthēsetai* (2:3–4); *ēgapēthē . . . metetethē* (4:10).

[12] *stenochōrian . . . stenaksontai* (5:3); *atrapon . . . tropios* (5:10); *potamoi . . . apotomōs* (5:22); *prodosia . . . prosdokia* (17:12–13); *adranestaton . . . eudraneia* (13:19); *parodeusō . . . synodeusō* (6:22–23); *arga . . . erga* (14:5).

[13] Found seventeen times (1:2; 19:22; 1:11; 3:11; 11:7; 12:9,10,13). Many examples involve the use of alpha-privative formation; the same feature of style is characteristic of Diodoros of Sicily (Palm:154; Reese 1970:30).

[14] In addition to the terms referred to above in part III [C], we may note: *eustatheia* (6:24); *systasin kosmou, energeian stoicheiōn* (7:17); *pneuma noeron, polymeres, lepton, eukinēton, tranon* (7:22); *akōlyton, philanthrōpon, bebaion, asphales* (7:23); *kinētikōteron, diēkei de kai chōrei dia pantōn* (7:24); *aporroia eilikrinēs* (7:25); *apaugasma, eikōn* (7:26); *metabainousa* (7:27); *diateinei, dioikei* (8:1); *syngymnasia, phronēsis* (8:18); *euphyeis, mimēma* (9:8); *barynei, brithei, skēnos* (9:15); *alogōn zōōn* (11:15); *amorphou hylēs* (11:17); *epieikeia* (12:18); *technitēs* (13:1); *analogōs* (13:5); *pronoia* (14:3); *kenodoksia* (14:14); *oreksis* (16:3); *epiteinetai . . . kai anietai* (16:24); *prosdokia* (17:12); *phantasmatōn* (17:14) (Gregg 1909:xv).

[15] *apotomos* (5:20–22; 6:5; 11:10; 12:9; 18:15); *eksetazein, eksetasis, eksetasmos* (1:9; 4:6; 6:3; 11:10); *metalleuō* (4:12; 16:25); *synkrinesthai, synkrisis* (7:8,29; 15:18); *skolioi logismoi, asynetoi logismoi, logizesthai ouk orthōs* (1:3,5; 11:15; 2:1); *parodeuein* (1:8; 2:7; 5:14; 6:22; 10:8); *ekbasis* (2:17; 11:14; 8:8); *entrepesthai* (2:10; 6:7); *parapiptein* (6:9; 12:2); *syngnōstos* (6:6; 13:8); *en cheiri theou* (3:1; 7:16); *triboi* (2:15; 5:7; 9:18; 10:10); *katadynasteuein* (2:10; 15:14; 17:2); *enedreuein* (2:12; 10:12); *eutelēs* (10:4; 11:15; 13:4; 15:10); *knōdala* (11:15; 16:1; 17:9); *homothymadon* (10:20; 18:5; 5:12); *kibdēlos* (2:16; 15:9); *peirazein* (2:24; 12:26); *okseōs* (3:18; 16:11); *episthasthai tini* (6:5,8; 19:1); *thēriōn thymoi* (7:20; 16:5); *eukinētos* (7:22; 13:11); *diepein* (9:3, 12:15); *thronoi* (9:4,12; 18:15); *euergetein* (3:5; 11:5,13; 16:2); *diodeuein* (5:7; 11:2); *anypokritos* (5:18; 18:16); *phthanein+inf.* (4:7; 6:13); *tēkesthai* (1:16; 6:23); *dioikein* (8:1;

of authorship, and make the hypothesis that Wisd is a translation of a Hebrew original virtually untenable.[16] Significant, too, is Wisd's quotation in 2:12 of the LXX of Isa 3:10, which is radically different from the Hebrew, and of Isa 44:20 and Job 9:12,19 (in 15:10 and 12:12), a fact

---

12:18; 15:1); *tauta elogizanto, tauta logisamenos* (2:21; 8:17); *arneisthai ton theon eidenai* (12:27; 16:16).

[16] Church Fathers like Clement of Alexandria (*Stromata* 6.11 and 14), Tertullian (*De Praescriptione Haereticorum* 7: "What indeed has Athens to do with Jerusalem? . . . Our instruction comes from the 'porch of Solomon' who had himself taught that 'the Lord should be sought in simplicity of heart' "), Cyprian (*De Mortalitate* 23), and Lactantius (*Divinae Institutiones* 4.16), having ascribed Wisdom to Solomon, naturally assumed a Hebrew original. The same view was held by some medieval rabbis. Naḥmanides, in a lecture dealing with Ecclesiastes which he delivered in Gerona in 1266 or 1267, asserts: "We find another book called *The Great Wisdom of Solomon* which is written in difficult Aramaic and the Christians have translated it from that language. I believe that this book was not arranged by the men of Hezekiah, the king of Judah [cf. Prov 25:1], but that it went with the Jews to Babylon orally and there they fixed it in their language, for it only contains sayings of wisdom and has not been written by inspiration." (See Marx:60. Cf. Gedaliah ben Joseph ibn Yaḥya, *Shalshelet Ha-Kabbalah* (Venice, 1587; Warsaw, 1882) 46b; [after ascribing Wisd to Philo, he writes]: "Others say that King Solomon wrote it".) The theory of a Hebrew original was also held by many Catholic theologians, several Protestant mystics (see Grimm:17), and even by the Jewish Haskalah poet and exegete N. H. Wessely, who began his literary career with the translation of Wisd (from Luther's German rendering) to which he appended a brief commentary, later elaborated into a full-length exegesis, *Ru'aḥ Ḥen* (Berlin, 1780); see the introduction to his translation.

The first Hebrew translation made directly from the Greek was that of Edmund Menahem Stein, in A. Kahana's *Ha-Sefarim Ha-Ḥitzonim* (Tel-Aviv, 1936). The earlier Hebrew version of Isaac Seckel Fraenkel included in his translation of the Apocrypha into Hebrew, entitled *Ketuvim Aḥaronim* (Leipzig, 1830) is a free paraphrase made from the German. According to Y. M. Grintz (*EJ* 15. 120): "Recently a 16th-century manuscript was found (now in Hechal Shlomo in Jerusalem) which is a translation of the whole apocryphon, seemingly from the Latin, into a corrupt Hebrew."

An early nineteenth-century advocate of a Hebrew original for Wisdom was C. G. Bretschneider, who even emended the text that he had retroverted. Later, D. S. Margoliouth's bizarre effort (1890) on behalf of this hypothesis was easily demolished by J. Freudenthal (1891). Margoliouth's retroversion is into a language he calls New Hebrew, and which, as F. Zimmermann puts it, "in reality is no more than an amalgam of Hebrew and Aramaic expressions, even rabbinic constructions, not found before or since." A more recent and sophisticated attempt to defend this position was that of Speiser (1923–24), who, like Bretschneider before him, had emended his own retroversions from the Greek (see Zimmermann 1966:4, 11).

The Aramaic hypothesis has also had its advocates. The Renaissance Jewish Italian scholar Azariah dei Rossi (ca. 1511–ca. 1578) long ago suggested that Solomon had composed his book in Aramaic in order to send it to some king in the distant East (*Meor 'Einayim, Imre Binah,* chap. 57), and in recent years a similar suggestion has been made by Zimmermann, who believes that the book was composed in the first quarter of the first century CE in Antioch on the Orontes, a third of whose population was Jewish. "It was written in Aramaic because it was the language of the Jews in the Syrian Diaspora, and addressed to Jews. Naturally, there was a quick demand to have the Aramaic translated into Greek because of the bilingual character of the Syrian population" (1966:133–134). His retroversions, like those of Speiser, are highly speculative, and have failed to convince the majority of scholars.

which compelled Margoliouth to conclude that the Greek translators of Isaiah had utilized the Greek text of Wisd. As Pfeiffer (321) has correctly indicated, "if any part of Wisdom was translated from the Hebrew, the rendering was so free and so rhetorically Greek that it amounts to an original work with only the vaguest resemblances to its supposed prototype." In short, although it is possible to maintain that the author may have used an earlier Hebrew document or documents deriving from Palestine in the composition of chaps. 1–10, we should nevertheless have to admit that they were not simply translated by him but rather served as the raw material for a new literary production.

V. GENRE

The literary genre employed by the author of Wisd, as Focke had already noted (1913:86), is the *logos protreptikos* or exhortatory discourse.[17] According to the *Rhetorica ad Alexandrum* (1421b21), "exhortation (*protropē*) is an attempt to urge people to some line of speech or action," and "one delivering an exhortation (*protreponta*) must prove that the courses to which he exhorts are just, lawful, expedient, honorable, pleasant and easily practicable" (cf. Wisd 6:12; 8:7,10,16,18). The protreptic was a union of philosophy and rhetoric and originated with the Sophists, whose sham productions were criticized in Plato's *Euthydemus,* which has preserved for us the earliest example of the genre (278E–282D).[18] Socrates' questioning of Cleinias in that section of the dialogue which serves as an illustration of what he desires a hortatory argument to be, leads to the following conclusion: "Since you think wisdom is both teachable and the only thing in the world that makes man happy and fortunate, can you help saying that it is necessary to pursue it and that you intend to do so?" For a better understanding of the structure and style of a protreptic discourse, however, we must turn to Aristotle's *Protrepticus,* which (at least in the view of some) has been plausibly reconstructed by scholars,[19] and is a eulogy on the life of reason, exhorting men to "exercise moral virtue for the sake of wisdom, for wisdom is the supreme end" (B21, Düring; cf. B85–86; Wisd 6:15), and "everything exists for the sake of reason"

---

[17] For a detailed discussion, see Reese 1970:117–121.

[18] See Hartlich:224–229; Gaiser:25, Düring:19. For the pseudo-Platonic *Epinomis* as a protreptic to the purer and happy life, see Tarán:66*ff;* Festugière 1973:101–156; and for an example of protreptic discourse found in the Arabic summary of Galen's *Peri ēthōn* (end of the second book), see Walzer:164–174.

[19] See W. Jaeger 1948:54–101; and especially Düring, and the bibliography cited there.

(B23; cf. Wisd 8:4). Happiness is not determined by external goods but depends on the condition of the soul (cf. Wisd 7:8–10). Since man is not born to wisdom, which comes only through learning,[20] one should pursue philosophy unhesitatingly (B2 ξ 5; cf. Wisd 6:12). Wisdom should be chosen "not for the sake of anything else, but for itself" (B44), and "of thoughts those are free which are pursued for their own sake" (B25). Moreover, in the other arts and crafts men do not take their tools from what is primary (*autōn tōn prōtōn*), but at second or third hand, basing their reasonings on experience. The philosopher alone copies from that which is exact; for what he looks at is the exact itself, not copies (*mimēmatōn*) (B48; cf. Wisd 9:8). Consequently, just as a builder should use the rule (*kanoni*) rather than any existing building as his standard for straightness, so the philosopher-statesman cannot expect to create good laws if he uses as his standard the existing laws of some state, for an imitation of what is itself neither divine nor stable (cf. Wisd 7:23) cannot be stable either. It is clear, then, that to the philosopher alone belong laws that are stable, for he alone lives with his eye on nature and the divine, and like a good sea captain moors his life to that which is eternal and unchanging (B49–50; cf. Wisd 6:24).[21] The conjunction of soul with body, says Aristotle, is reminiscent of the Etruscan custom of torturing captives "by chaining dead bodies face to face with the living" (B107; cf. Wisd 9:15).[22] The exhortation ends on the note that wisdom is man's only immortal possession, and is alone divine (B108; cf. Wisd 6:18; 8:13,17), "for 'Reason is the god in us,' and 'Mortal life contains a portion of some god'" (B110; cf. Wisd 7:25–27; 2:23). The anonymous exhortation *To Demonicus,* which Jaeger believes to be a rejoinder to Aristotle's *Protrepticus,* similarly concludes by promising a share in immortality to those who pursue virtue with devoted toil (46, 50).[23]

[20] That virtue can be taught is one of the key elements of protreptic discourse, and appears in Plato's *Euthydemus* 282CD quoted above, and in Posidonios' lost work of this genre (Frag. 2, Kidd. The only other certain piece of information we have of this work, Frag. 1 asserts that disagreement is no reason for abandoning philosphy). We know that among the Stoics ethical philosophy included the theme of "inducements to act or refrain from acting" (*protropōn te kai apotropōn,* D.L. 7.84). For a list and discussion of authors of protreptics, see Burgess:89–261, esp. p. 234.

[21] This is in sharp contrast with Aristotle's view in *EN* 1094b12*ff* and 1095a30*ff.*

[22] Aristotle's earlier view of the soul may be gleaned from the fragments of his lost dialogue *Eudemus* which contained a series of arguments for the immortality of the soul. In this work he also "apparently argued that the soul is in its true and natural state when it is separated from the body. Cicero (Frag. 1, Ross) reports a story which implies that Aristotle concurred in the view that when a man dies his soul returns to its true home, and a passage in Proclus (Frag. 5) suggests that he compared the soul's existence without the body to health, and its life in the body to disease. Finally, two of our sources (Frags. 5 and 11, Ross) suggest that the soul has certain visions in its disembodied state" (see Lloyd 1968:29–30; Jaeger 1948:39–53).

[23] See Jaeger 1948:58.

Although it is clear that the author of Wisd has shaped his work in the form of a protreptic discourse it is equally clear that his argumentation, unlike that of Aristotle's *Protrepticus,* is largely rhetorical rather than demonstrative. On the other hand, there is considerably more close-knit argumentation and philosophical reasoning in Wisd than, say, in Isocrates' Cyprian discourses, where, as the author expressly states elsewhere (*Antidosis* 68–69),[24] he merely wishes to give advice, not to connect his argument so as to prove a thesis. If we had a large selection of examples from the genre under discussion we should undoubtedly find a model for Wisd which would come much closer than any of those available. In any case, although the protreptic is not a formal philosophical treatise, but a highly charged appeal designed to persuade a large audience to succumb to the charms of the philosophical life, there must have been considerable variety in its mode of presentation, with different authors varying the doses of demonstrative reasoning or rhetorical flourishes to be lavished on their readers.

The protreptic discourse readily lent itself to the incorporation of diatribe, the popular moral invective so characteristic of the Hellenistic period,[25] and Wisd contains a number of diatribal features. We may note the following: personified abstractions (1:4–6,8,16; 7–10; 18:15); speeches of an imaginary adversary (2 and 5); imaginary objections of the adversary accompanied with answers (13:6–9); simple paratactic style (1–6); parallelism,[26] *isokōla,* and antitheses (1–10); *accumulatio* (7:22–23; 14:25); evocation of mythological heroes or wise men (4:10; 10); elaborate similes (5:10–12); protreptic conclusion with monitory imperatives aimed at deflecting the evildoer from his path (6:1–11); invective (13–15).

VI. Date

No consensus has thus far emerged regarding the date of Wisd, and various scholars have placed it anywhere between 220 BCE and 50 CE.[27] There

[24] "I detach one part from another, and breaking up the discourse, as it were, into what we call general heads, I strive to express in a few words each bit of counsel which I have to offer."

[25] On the diatribe, see the following. Burgess:234–240; Wendland:39–50; *RAC* 3. 990–1010; Wallach; Kustas; Reese 1970:90–116; Bultmann. For the influence of the diatribe on rabbinic midrash, see Marmorstein:48–71.

[26] The paratactic style and use of parallelism are undoubtedly due in this case to biblical influence, but they coincide with characteristics of the diatribe with which the author was quite familiar.

[27] D. S. Margoliouth (1900), arguing that Isaiah made use of Wisdom, ascribed the book to King Solomon.

is virtual agreement that the author made use of the LXX version of Isaiah which would carry us at least to the end of the third century BCE (see NOTES on 2:12 and 15:10).[28] Zeller, however, had already suggested that the address to the rulers of the four corners of the earth (6:1) referred to the period of Roman rule, and that the reference to the remoteness of the rulers' dwelling in 14:17 indicated more specifically the age of Augustus.[29]

Although many commentators have interpreted Wisd 14:16–20 as referring to the period of the Ptolemies, such a view, in my opinion, is untenable. First, the reference to the remoteness of the rulers' dwelling readily applies to Egypt under Augustus (and his immediate successors), who organized it not as a province under designated military authority, but as his own private domain, and ruled it in absentia through a prefect chosen from the knights. As Nock put it, "Asia had been delivered from bondage but Egypt had merely passed into the hands of absentee landlords who

[28] For Pfeiffer, it brings us to ca. 150 BCE, when, in his view, Isaiah was translated into Greek. Holmes argues that "if the line in I Enoch 5:7 is the source of Wisd 3:9 the book must be later than the translation of Enoch into Greek, which was probably undertaken as a whole, seeing that the fragments which survive include chap. 89. The latest part of Enoch consists of chaps. 37–71 and the date of this according to Charles is 94–79 BCE. We may suppose Enoch to have been translated at some date between 70 and 50 BCE and adopt this period as the *terminus a quo*" (APOT: 1. 520. The second part of the book, he dates between 30 BCE and 10 CE). On the Greek version of Enoch, see now Milik:70–78. Unfortunately, as Milik points out, "There are no studies of the dates of the translation of the various Enochic writings —studies that should take as their starting-point a comparison of the vocabulary and phraseology of the Greek Enoch with those of classical texts, and more especially, with the language of the papyri and of the Hellenistic and Roman periods." Grimm (:32–35) dates the book between 145 (the date of the accession of Ptolemy Euergetes II, with whose name is connected the first attempt at Jewish persecution in Hellenistic Egypt [Jos. *Ag.Ap.* 2.53–55. The same story is attributed to Ptolemy IV Philopator in the legendary account of III Maccabees] and 50 BCE (since Wisd shows no knowledge of Philo's Logos doctrine). According to Focke (1913:78–84), chaps. 1–5 were written in Palestine during Alexander Janneus' massacre of his Pharisaic opponents (88–86 BCE), whereas chaps. 6–19 were composed when Ptolemy Soter II (89–80), upon his return from his war with Janneus in 88–87, persecuted the Jews of Alexandria (this is based on an ingenious reconstruction by H. Willrich [*Hermes* 39 (1904) 244–258] of the data in III Maccabees and Jos. *Ag.Ap.* 2.51–56). In an interesting variation of Focke's 1913 theory, Ruppert has proposed that Wisd 2:12–20 and 5:1–7 originally constituted an apocalypticizing dyptich on the theme of the suffering just (based on Isa 52:13 – 53:12), composed in Palestine ca. 100–75 BCE in Hebrew under the impact of Alexander Janneus' persecution of the Pharisees in 86. It was translated in Egypt relatively early into Greek by the author of Wisd, and served as a fillip for the composition of his own book (Ruppert:70–105).

[29] In the first edition of his *Die Philosophie der Griechen*, E. Zeller suggested on the basis of 6:1 the period of the Second Triumvirate (43–31 BCE), but later, on the basis of 14:17, he altered his view to the time of Augustus (vol. 3.2 [reprint, Hildesheim 1963]:295 n.1). The latter view was accepted by Bousset (31); and Holmes, in APOT: 1.521; Motzo, 1924:31–66; Graetz 3. 611–613; Goodrick 1913:13–17; and Scarpat also opted for the Roman period, but specified the reign of Caligula. On the grounds of its inimical attitude to the religion of the pagans, V. A. Tcherikover places Wisd in the early Roman period (1957, 1. 75).

kept strict bailiffs" (*CAH* 10. 486). More important, however, is the fact that the Ptolemies had openly and explicitly proclaimed themselves gods (*theoi*), and had established a full dynastic cult, centrally organized with a hierarchy of provincial priests appointed by the crown,[30] whereas our passage envisages a process which only gradually led to the idolatrous worship of rulers, a situation which can only apply to the Augustan period. "Octavian's portrait appeared on Egyptian monuments in the guise of the Pharaohs (at Dendera, Philae, Dendur and other sites) and his statue was probably erected in all the temples of the land" (L. R. Taylor 1931:143). In Alexandria the temple that Cleopatra had begun as a shrine of Antony was completed as a temple of Octavian, where he received the cult name *Epibatērios,* as protector of seafarers. Philo described this Sebasteum as "fitted on a scale not found elsewhere with dedicated offerings, around it a girdle of pictures and statues in silver and gold" (*Legat.* 151). Yet the living Caesar was never raised officially to the level of a deity, and not even in Egypt was he officially designated *theos.*[31] In spite of his official reserve in this matter, Augustus was undoubtedly for his Eygptian subjects a divine king with the attributes of the Pharaohs of old. It is only in this context that one can make any sense at all out of Wisd's theory that it was the desire on the part of subjects to flatter a distant ruler which ultimately led to idolatry.[31a] If this analysis is correct, it appears certain that the word *kratēsis* in 6:3 refers to Augustus' conquest of Egypt (see NOTES on 6:3; 14:20, for the significance of the word *sebasma;* and 14:16).

Although attention has often been drawn to certain words and usages which are first attested in Wisd and do not appear in secular Greek literature before the first century CE, no comprehensive study of this aspect of the book's vocabulary has so far been made.[32] My own analysis reveals that there are some thirty-five such words or usages and that they are fairly well distributed throughout the book (fourteen appear in chaps. 1–10, and twenty-one in 11–19).[33] This provides additional confirmation

---

[30] See Fraser 1. 213–246.

[31] See Blumenthal; Taylor:240, 244; Bell 1957:56–58.

[31a] I am well aware that the author's theory concerning the origin of idolatrous worship is undoubtedly etiological in nature, but the form an etiology takes is generally shaped by the social and historical context in which the author finds himself. cf. NOTE on 14:15.

[32] The most detailed studies so far have been those of Scarpat and Reese (1970:1–25), but they have provided only a very small sampling of such words.

[33] I list them in the order of their occurrence: *autoschediōs (2:2); anapodismos (2:5); ekbasis (2:17); aneksikakia (2:19); epitimia (3:10); *akēlidōtos (4:8); *epibasis (5:11); *anypokritos (5:18); akatamachētos (5:19); dekamēniaios (7:2); *en synkrisei (7:8); genetin (7:12); amolyntos (7:22); panepiskopos (7:23); *apaugasma (7:26); lythrōdēs (11:6); splangchnophagon (12:5); genesiarchēs (13:3); genesiourgos (13:5); *diereunaō (13:7, in sense of 'search, examine'); *syngnōstoi (13:8, used of persons); emmeletēma (13:10); apoblēmata (13:12); eudraneia (13:19); *anatypoō (14:17); *thrēskeia (14:18); pēlourgos (15:7); chrysourgos (15:9); synolkē (15:15); indalmasin (17:3); eulabeia (17:8, in bad sense); proüphestōtos (19:7);*

for the unity of the book, but more important, it is very strong evidence that the date of Wisd cannot be earlier than the Augustan age, and that very likely (though by no means decisively) it was written in the first half of the first century CE. Although much of the literature of the first century BCE has been lost, a fact which virtually converts our inference into an argument from silence,[34] the occurrence of so large a number of such words within so small a compass is not likely to be due to chance. When used in conjunction with the evidence for dating adduced above, it makes the beginning of the Roman period in Egypt (30 BCE) the only acceptable *terminus post quem* for the composition of the book.

There are further considerations, however, which point to the reign of Gaius 'Caligula' (37–41 CE) as the likeliest setting for Wisd. The apocalyptic vision in which the author describes the annihilation of the wicked with such ferocious passion (5:16–23) could only be called forth by a desperate historical situation in which the security of the Jewish community of Alexandria (and for a short while even that of Palestine) was dangerously threatened by a power against which it was hopeless to put up any serious resistance. The riots which broke out in Alexandria in 38 CE involved the demolition of many synagogues in areas where few Jews lived, the rendering unfit of synagogues in the two "Jewish districts" by placing portraits of Gaius in them (Philo *Legat.* 133–134), and above all a proclamation by the Roman prefect A. Avillius Flaccus declaring the Jews "aliens and foreigners" (*ksenoi kai epēludes;* Philo *Flac.* 54) in Alexandria. This measure, as Smallwood (240) puts it, "degraded them from their legal status of resident aliens, on which the existence of the

---

anadysis (19:7, in sense of 'emergence'); *dieskirtēsan* (19:9); *achanei* (19:17). It may also be noted that *prytaneis kosmou* applied to the sun and moon is first attested in our author (13:2). I have omitted the words *katalalia* (1:11) and *prōtoplastos* (7:1) also first attested in Wisd, since they occur again only in Jewish or Christian writings or both (whither they may presumably have found their way from Wisdom itself), but do not appear in secular Greek literature. (Words with an asterisk before them are also attested in Philo.)

[34] It should be pointed out that the author of Wisd is very fond of neologisms and that there are twenty-seven *hapax legomena* (five are *hapax* only in the peculiar sense in which they are used in Wisd in the book. This may somewhat diminish the force of our argument above, but does not, I think, seriously damage it. I list these neologisms in the order of their occurrence: **rhembasmos* (4:12); **metalleuei* (4:12, in sense of 'change'); *hoplopoieō* (5:17, in sense of 'make or use as a weapon'); **phriktōs* (6:5, adverbial form only here); **aneklipēs* (7:14; 8:18); **pantodynamos* (7:23; 11:17; 18:15 [*pandynamos* is found in Plotinus]); *hairetis* (8:4); **katabasion* (10:6); **nēpioktonos* (11:7); *synektripsai* (11:19); *myriotēs* (12:22); *teknophonos* (14:23); **skiagraphos* (15:4); *kakomochthos* (15:8); **brachytelēs* (15:9); **argyrochoos* (15:9); **chalkoplastēs* (15:9); **eidechteia* (16:3); **enkentrizō* (16:11, in sense of 'spur on'); *antiparēlthen* (16:10, in sense of 'come up and help'). **metekirnato* (16:21); **diastraptō* (16:22); **dysdiēgētos* (17:1); **periekompoun* (17:4, in sense of 'sound round about'); **proanamelpontes* (18:9); *prosodyromenoi* (19:3); **misoksenia* (19:13); **heortasmatōn* (19:16). (Words with an asterisk before them occur in Patristic literature.)

politeuma depended, to that of aliens without the right of domicile. Legally they could now all be expelled." Although Flaccus was soon executed, "the situation remained unstable and the Jews lacked security for a further two years and a half, until their rights were officially and explicitly re-established by Claudius in 41" (Smallwood:242). Moreover, in his famous letter to the Alexandrians, Claudius, as V. A. Tcherikover has correctly noted, hardly reveals himself as a 'philo-Semite.' Far from enlarging the civic rights of the Jews or at least facilitating their acquisition of such rights, his measures had the opposite tendency. He forbade Jews to participate in gymnastic contests, thus depriving them of gymnasium education which was a prerequisite to citizenship. His order for Jews to be satisfied with their situation and not to aim at the acquisition of new rights, culminates with the ominous threat that if they should prove recalcitrant, he would "by all means take vengeance on them, as fomenting something like a general plague for the whole world." The Jewish tendency toward 'emancipation' which had undoubtedly intensified after Augustus' imposition of the *laographia,* or poll tax, was thus brought to an end (Tcherikover-Fuks 1. 73–74). In this tense atmosphere, saturated with frustration and disappointment, the author of Wisd's disguised[35] invective against the Alexandrians and Romans, and probably also the renegade Jews who supported them, finds its appropriate setting.[36]

[35] See Graetz:612, where the 'just' man of chaps. 2–5 is identified with Israel. It may also be noted that the title 'son of God,' which in 2:18 is applied to the 'just' man, is in 18:13 applied to Israel. Cf. III Maccabees, where Augustus is disguised as Ptolemy IV. See the article by A. Tcherikover referred to in fn. 36, below, and M. Hadas' edition (1953):18–23. For Philo's political polemic "in code" or "by innuendo," see Goodenough 1967:21–63. It should also be noted that the single-minded intensity with which the author describes the Egyptian plagues in part C with its concluding doxology of the Lord who "did not neglect to assist [his exalted people] in every time and place" (19:22), clearly implies his confident hope that God will soon overwhelm Israel's present enemies with a similar series of plagues. Cf. the Apocalypse of Abraham 29–30, where we are told that God "will bring upon all creatures of the earth ten plagues," which are then enumerated in detail. See also PRK, *Wayehi Baḥaṣi Hallaylah,* Mandelbaum:133; and *Tanḥ.* Buber 2. 22a.

[36] Another period of troubles for Alexandrian Jews came in 66 CE, when riots again erupted, and the prefect Tiberius Julius Alexander, a renegade Jew, let his legions loose on the "Delta" quarter with permission to burn and loot Jewish property as well as to kill the rioters. The death toll was put at fifty thousand (Jos. *J.W.* 2.487ff). It is unnecessary, however, to move the date of Wisd that far up, and it is also less likely that a book as spirited as Wisd, which in spite of its hostility to the pagan world, was still aiming at a Jewish Hellenistic synthesis, would have been produced in that bleak age. Nickelsburg (90–91) accepts Motzo's attempt to show that Greek Esther was dependent on III Maccabees, and since Bickerman dated the former before 78/77 BCE (A. Tcherikover preferred 114/13), he concludes that that date may serve as the *terminus ante quem* for III Maccabees. He then goes on to suggest that III Maccabees was dependent on Wisd, thus requiring a date for the latter before 78/7, but surely Motzo's arguments (1924:274) were based on his assumption that III Maccabees was to be dated ca. 100 BCE, whereas Tcherikover's researches later demonstrated that the book should be dated ca. 24/23 BCE, so that its relationship with Greek Esther must necessarily be reversed (see Tcherikover 1945). Hadas (1953) arrved at the same date as did Tcherikover, and Smallwood (1976:

Most commentators have assumed an Egyptian provenance for Wisd, and in this they are undoubtedly correct. The intensity of the author's hatred of the Egyptians can only reflect the persecution of the Jewish community in Alexandria at the hands of the Greeks aided and abetted by the native Egyptians. It is difficult not to see an allusion to contemporary conditions in Egypt in the manner in which the author imputes greater blame to Egypt than even to Sodom (19:13–17, see NOTES ad loc.), and there may even be an allusion at 17:16 to the phenomenon of *anachōrēsis* especially characteristic of Egypt in the Roman period (see NOTE ad loc.).

It is interesting to note that Jewish hatred for the Egyptians and Romans which is still carefully disguised in Wisd, finds explicit and much sharper expression in a later Alexandrian Jewish writing, the fifth Sibylline Oracle (finally redacted between 115 and 132 CE). Three of the six oracles of the book deal with woes to come upon Egypt, and, in particular, the sibyllist revels in the expectation of the destruction of the shrines of Isis and Sarapis (484*ff*). The outburst against Rome is especially bitter:

Woe unto thee all unclean city of Latin land, frenzied and poison-loving. . . . Didst thou not know what God can do and what are his designs? But thou hast said, I am unique, and none shall bring ruin on me. But now God whose Being is forever shall destroy thee and all of thine (162–78). (See Collins 1974:76–80.)

The earliest stages of the Sibylline Oracles (3.175*ff.*, 350*ff.*) contain oracles directed against Rome, but as Collins 1974:78 has correctly noted, these oracles were part of the general opposition of the Near Eastern world to Rome and were not indicative of any specific quarrel between Rome and the Jews.

VII. RELIGIOUS IDEAS

1. *Preexistence and Immortality of the Soul*

It has been suggested by a number of commentators that, in his attempt to point out the superior endowments of young Solomon, the author of Wisd was led to the designation of the body as the personal subject which receives the soul, inasmuch as he was referring to the origins of his existence (8:19: "I was, indeed, a child well-endowed, having had a noble soul fall to my lot"). Since, however, in his view, it was with the soul rather than with the body that the personal 'I' is to be connected, he proceeded to correct his initial formulation in v. 20 ("or rather being noble I entered an undefiled body"), which nevertheless went somewhat beyond his origi-

232), too, has accepted it. As for the claim that Paul had already made use of Wisd, one can only say that the evidence for this is inconclusive, since most of the similarities involve common Hellenistic themes. (See Larcher 1969:14–20, who takes the same position, though adding that in his opinion it is at least very likely that Paul did have knowledge of Wisd; and Keyser.)

nal intention (Larcher 1969:273–274). The preexistence referred to here is therefore not to be taken in its Greek philosophical sense but to be understood only as consisting in the creation of the soul immediately before its "coming" into a determinate body, as in the case of Adam (Larcher:277). It seems to me, however, that had the author merely wished to emphasize the primacy of the soul in the identity of the personal 'I', his initial formulation would have been completely apt, and in need of no further revision. For once having asserted that the body-soul complex constituting the child Solomon could be called "well-endowed" merely by virtue of its being allotted a noble soul, he had already thereby clearly indicated the primacy of soul over body. (Larcher's statement that *pais* apparently refers to the "état embryonnaire" is unwarranted.) Since he was not indeed satisfied with his initial formulation, and felt constrained to correct it, we must conclude that the words "I entered an undefiled body" are meant to suggest the preexistence of souls of varying spiritual capacities, and that in the case of Solomon it was a noble soul that had taken the initiative of entering an undefiled body. In this the author was plainly associating himself to some extent with Platonic doctrine, though at the same time suppressing the major elements of Plato's myth about the procession of souls and the fall of some of them into bodies. (That this is so may be further inferred from the fact that in 9:15, he reproduces the distinctive Platonic dualism regarding body and soul, replete with verbal echoes from the *Phaedo*.) According to the myth of Er, Lachesis, the daughter of Necessity, addresses the souls marshaled before her as follows:

> Souls that live for a day, now is the beginning of another cycle of mortal generation. . . . Let him to whom falls the first lot first select a life to which he shall cleave of necessity. . . . The prophet placed the patterns of lives before them on the ground, far more numerous than the assembly. They were of every variety, for there were lives of all kinds of animals and all sorts of human lives, for there were tyrannies among them . . . and there were lives of men of repute for their forms and beauty and bodily strength otherwise and prowess and the high birth of their ancestors. (*Rep.* 617E–618B).

It is essential at this point to emphasize those elements in Plato's theory of soul which are conspicuously absent in Wisd. We have already alluded to the author's suppression of the conception of the soul's "fall." This particular omission, however, is neither surprising nor really at variance with Middle Platonism. Although in the *Phaedrus,* the incarnation of souls seems to be the result of an intellectual 'fall,' in the *Timaeus,* the soul seems to be destined from the beginning to give life to a body. Mortal creatures came into being so that the Heaven or universe not be imperfect (*atelēs*), which would be the case if it did not contain all the kinds of living being (41BC; cf. Plotinus 4.8.1). Middle Platonists had already noted this inconsistency in Plato's writings and attempted to resolve it by emphasizing one or the other of these positions, the majority apparently opting for the pessimistic rather than the optimistic view. Taurus was one of the few who adopted the optimistic attitude. We read in Iamblichus' *De Anima* (ap. Stobaeus 1.378, 25*ff*, Wachsmuth):

The Platonists 'about' Taurus[37] say that souls are sent by the gods to earth, either, following the *Timaeus,* for the completion of the universe, in order that there may be as many living things in the cosmos as there are in the intelligible realm; or declaring that the purpose of the descent is to present a manifestation of the divine life. For this is the will of the gods, for the gods to reveal (*ekphainesthai*) themselves through souls; for the gods come out into the open and manifest themselves through the pure and unsullied life of souls. (Dillon's translation:245.) (Cf. Festugière 1950: 3.219 and 63–96.)

In his discussion of this issue, Albinus enumerates four reasons (unfortunately highly compressed) for the soul's descent, two of which (*Did.* 25.6, Louis: "either awaiting their numbers, or by the will of the gods" cf. Dörrie 1957:414–435) appear to be similar to those given by Taurus. The other two are 'wantonness' (*akolasia*), i.e. sinful willfulness on the part of the soul, and 'love of the body' (*philosōmatia*), which indicates a nattural affinity or weakness for embodiment. "Body and soul have a kind of affinity towards each other," writes Albinus, "like fire and asphalt" (*Did.* 25.6). To judge from Iamblichus, it was the theory of 'wantonness' that Albinus favored, thus taking the pessimistic view (*De Anima* 375.10–11; Dillon:246). Philo seems to allude to all four of Albinus' explanations. At *Somn.* 1.138, he speaks of souls that are "lovers of body" (*philosōmatoi*) (cf. Didymus *Comment. on Job:* 56, 24–27); at *Her.* 240, of souls "unable to bear the satiety (*koron*) of divine goods" (a variation of Albinus' *akolasia*); at *QG* 4.74 (cf. *Op.* 135; *Somn.* 1.147) he suggests that the reason for descent might be in order that even terrestrial things might not be without a share in wisdom to participate in a better life (this is similar to Taurus' second reason, "the will of the gods to reveal themselves" cf. Didymus *Comment. on Job:* 56, 28–29); and at *Plant.* 14, we are told that some souls enter into mortal bodies and quit them again according to certain fixed periods (*kata tinas hōrismenas periodous*). (Cf. *Somn.* 1.138, where we hear of souls selected for return according to the numbers and periods determined by nature: *kata tous hypo physeōs hōristhentas arithmous kai chronous;* Origen *Contra Celsum* 8.53: *mechri an tais tetagmenais periodois.*) This emphasis on numbers and periods implies that the incarnation of souls is part of the mathematical structure of the universe and is thus similar to Taurus' first reason, "for completion of the universe" and Albinus' "souls awaiting their numbers" (*arithmous menousas*). At

[37] According to Dillon (245), "it is possible that Iamblichus is simply recording two different views of Taurus himself, whom he may well not have consulted at first hand, and making somewhat eccentric use of the common periphrasis 'those about X.'"

QG 4.74, Philo even suggests a fifth reason, namely, "in order that it might be akin to created beings and not be continuously and completely happy." Undoubtedly regarding this matter as an impenetrable mystery, Philo vacillates and simply retails to his readers the various explanations which he found before him in the Middle Platonic tradition. As for Plotinus, as Armstrong 255 has pointed out, he "firmly resolves the contradiction which appears in Plato's thought between the ideas of embodiment as a fall of the soul and as a good and necessary fulfilment of its function to care for body, by maintaining that it is both. It is in accordance with the universal order, which requires that everything down to the lowest level should be ensouled, that souls descend, and appropriate bodies and lower selves are prepared for them. But they want to descend, and are capable of descending, only because they have already a weakness, a tendency to the lower, which seems to be a development of the original *tolma* which carried Soul outside Intellect" (cf. Plotinus 4.8.5). It is thus evident, that in suppressing the pessimistic view of the soul's 'fall,' the author of Wisd, though clearly under the influence of Jewish tradition, was not necessarily being innovative even from the Greek point of view, but was simply aligning himself with that Middle Platonic position which was most congenial to his own way of thinking. The Jewish attitude toward this question is well illustrated in a late midrash:

> The angel immediately fetches the soul before the Holy One blessed be He, and when she arrives she bows forthwith before the King of Kings, whereupon the Holy One blessed be He commands the soul to enter into the drop of semen contained in so and so; but the soul replies, "Lord of the universe, sufficient for me is the world in which I have dwelt from the moment you created me, why do you wish to install me in this fetid drop, since I am holy and pure and hewn from your glory?" The Holy One blessed be He answers, "The world into which I am about to place you will be more lovely for you than the world in which you have dwelt hitherto, and when I created you, it was only for this seminal drop that I created you." The Holy One blessed be He then immediately installs her against her will (*Tanḥ. Pĕkûdê* 3).

On the other hand, there is no allusion in Wisd to Plato's elaborate doctrine of metempsychosis, which involves certain souls over a period of ten thousand years in a series of reincarnations according to their order of merit, with some transmigrating into animal bodies,[38] though souls of philosophers escape the "wheel of birth" after three thousand years. It should be noted, however, that there is also no mention of this doctrine in two

---

[38] Migration into animal bodies is briefly referred to in *Phaedrus* 249B, expanded on in *Rep.* 620, but ignored in *Laws* 904A–905A. Although prevalent among Middle Platonists (e.g. Albinus *Did.* 178, 29*f*), and followed also by Plotinus (3.4.2; 4.3.12), it was rejected by Neoplatonists from Porphyry on.

Ciceronian treatises, *Tusculan Disputations* I and *The Dream of Scipio,* which contain an elaborate theory of immortality presented along Platonic lines, though with Stoic characteristics. (See Dillon:96–102.) Nor is there any reference to Plato's doctrine of *anamnēsis,* according to which the acquisition of knowledge during one's earthly existence is seen as a process of recollecting the knowledge which the soul had once attained through its partial vision of true Being during its preexistent state (*Phaedrus* 247C–248E).[39] As to the parts of the soul, although there is no reference to the formal Platonic tripartition into rational, spirited, and desiderative (*Rep.* 4), there may be a passing allusion in Wisd 4:12 ("the giddy distraction of desire perverts the guileless mind") to two parts of the soul, reflecting either the actual bipartition of the soul into rational and irrational common in Middle Platonism[40] (*epithymia* representing the irrational and *nous* the rational; similarly, in 4:11, *dolos* may represent the irrational soul and *psyche* the rational [cf. Philo *LA* 3.161; *Her.* 55]), or the Stoic division of the unitary soul into the ruling element (*hegemonikon* or *nous*) and its seven physical faculties (all of which, including the passions, represent various states of the same psychic *pneuma*).[41]

Although it is usually claimed that the author of Wisd never speaks of the immortal nature of the soul as such, as Greek philosophers do, and makes immortality depend on the practice of justice, this assertion thus baldly stated is incorrect. In the first place, Wisd 2:23, according to which God created man for immortality, and made him an image of his own proper being, clearly implies that man's immortality derives from the fact

[39] In Philo, too, however, there is no "suggestion of recollection in the Platonic sense of the recollection of ideas. There are only three references to recollection in his writings (*Mut.* 100; *Praem.* 9; *Mos.* 1.21), and none of them is used in that Platonic sense" (Wolfson 1948:2. 8).

[40] Even in Plato himself, the basic stress in the *Timaeus* is upon the soul's bipartition into mortal and immortal parts. As for the so-called tripartition itself, "it is in fact more fairly described as bipartition with a further subdivison within it." In the *Laws,* tripartition is never mentioned at all. See T. M. Robinson:120–125. (There appears to be no reference to bipartition of the soul in rabbinic literature.)

[41] A third possibility is that he is following the Platonic view in the *Phaedo* which had banished *epithymia* from the soul altogether and had assigned it to the body. What makes it especially difficult to determine the author's view, is both his apparent unconcern with such details and the fact that in Middle Platonism, Stoic and Platonic terminology could be readily conjoined without any sense of contradiction. Thus Philo, for example, usually employs the bipartite division of the soul (*LA* 2.5; *Det.* 82, 91–92; *Conf.* 111, 176; *Sacr.* 112; *Her.* 132; *Spec.* 1.201, 333; 3.99; cf. Cicero *Tusc.* 1.80, 4.10–11, 2.47: Albinus *Did.* chap. 24), sometimes the tripartite division of Plato's *Republic* (*Spec.* 49.2: *Mig.* 66–67; *LA* 1.70, 3.115), and at other times, the Stoic division (*Op.* 117; *Her.* 232; *Mut.* 111; *Abr.* 29, where, for exegetical reasons, there are seven instead of eight parts). In response to certain biblical passages, Philo can even distinguish two different souls, a lower blood soul and a higher rational soul: *QG* 2.59; *Det.* 82–83. In *Her.* 55, however, he says that blood is the substance of the soul as a whole, whereas the divine breath or spirit is that of its most dominant part. See Dillon:174–175; Billings:50–52.

that his soul is an image of the Divine Wisdom, the "proper being" of the Deity. Second, even according to some versions of the Platonic myths concerning the soul, we are told that some souls are "judged incurable because of the enormity of their crimes and are hurled into Tartarus, whence they never more emerge" (*Phaedo* 113E; cf. *Gorgias* 525C; *Rep.* 615E). Nevertheless, it is true that for Plato, the majority of souls are eventually purified through a process of purgation and thus have a natural claim to immortality, and that the Platonists usually offer proofs for immortality from the very nature of soul[42] whereas the author of Wisdom places the emphasis not on this natural claim but on whether or not one has lived a life of righteousness. In so doing, however, he may (if our dating is accepted) have been following in the footsteps of Philo, who implies that only the souls of the wise enjoy immortality (*QG* 1.16; *Op.* 154; *Conf.* 149). Both he and Philo were undoubtedly influenced at this point by biblical tradition, but at the same time could claim to be following the Stoic view adopted by Chrysippus, though without the latter's limitation on the preservation of wise souls only until the next *ekpyrōsis* or world conflagration (*SVF* 2. 809,811).

One of the distinctive features of the Greek concept of immortality which acquires a new emphasis in the Ciceronian treatises mentioned above and again in Seneca, is equally characteristic of Wisd, although there is only a brief allusion to it in the eschatological section of the book. Plato had already described in glowing terms the region above the heavens where with varying degrees of success the souls attempt to obtain a vision of true Being, many of them being sucked downward in the process and suffering incarnation. After a series of purgations, however, they ultimately return to their heavenly home and presumably achieve the vision which had largely eluded them heretofore. This luminous goal comes into sharper focus in Cicero *Tusc.* 1.47:

> Surely objects of far greater purity and transparency will be discovered when the day comes on which the mind is free and has reached its natural home. For in our present state, although the apertures which are open from the body to the soul, have been fashioned by nature with cunning workmanship, yet they are in a manner fenced in with a compound of earthy particles: when, however, there shall be soul and nothing else, no physical barrier will hinder its perception of the true nature of everything.

---

[42] See, for example, Cicero *Tusc.* 1.55: 'The soul then is conscious that it is in motion, and when so conscious it is at the same time conscious of this, that it is self-moved by its own power and not an outside power, and that it cannot ever be abandoned by itself; and this is proof of eternity." Cf. Plato *Phaedo* 72*ff*; *Rep.* 10.608–611; *Phaedrus* 245C. Proofs for immortality take up most of chap. 25 of Albinus' *Didaskalikos*. Philo, on the other hand, like the author of Wisdom, is unconcerned with the presentation of elaborate proofs for the immortality of the soul.

(Cf. 1.45: What, pray, do we think the panorama will be like when we shall be free to embrace the whole earth in our survey, its situation, shape, and circumference? *Somnium Scipionis* [*De Re Publica*] 6.16).

Seneca's eloquent description of the soul's future knowledge reaches the heights of religious rapture:

> Some day the secrets of nature shall be disclosed to you, the haze will be shaken from your eyes, and the bright light will stream in upon you from all sides. Picture to yourself how great is the glow when all the stars mingle their fires; no shadows will disturb the clear sky. The whole expanse of heaven will shine evenly; for day and night are interchanged only in the lowest atmosphere. Then you will say that you have lived in darkness, after you have seen, in your perfect state, the perfect light (*Ep.* 102.28).

The author of Wisd similarly promises the immortal righteous: "In the moment of God's gracious dispensation they will blaze forth. . . . They will judge nations, and hold sway over peoples. . . . Those who have put their trust in Him shall attain true understanding" (3:7–9; cf. I Enoch 5:8). There are passages in the Qumran *Hôdāyôt* that breathe a spirit similar to that which had moved Seneca, and which recall the author of Wisd's passionate eloquence when he speaks of his beloved Sophia. We read in 1QH 3.19–23:

> I give thanks unto Thee, O Lord, for Thou hast freed my soul from the pit, and drawn me up from the slough of hell to the crest of the world. So walk I on uplands unbounded and know that there is hope for that which Thou didst mold out of dust to have consort with things eternal. For lo, Thou hast taken a spirit distorted by sin, and purged it of the taint of much transgression, and given it a place in the host of the holy beings, and brought it into communion with the sons of heaven. Thou hast made a mere man to share the lot of the Spirits of Knowledge, to praise Thy name in their chorus.

Here the writer is convinced that he already enjoys eternity and walks with the angelic hosts. His fervor soon reaches an even higher pitch:

> For Thou hast made them to know Thy deep, deep truth, and divine Thine inscrutable wonders . . . to be one with them that possess Thy truth and to share the lot of Thy Holy Beings, to the end that this worm which is man may be lifted out of the dust to the height of eternal things, and rise from a spirit perverse to an holy understanding, and stand in one company before Thee with the host everlasting and the spirits of knowledge and the choir invisible [literally, "Those versed in concerted song"], to be forever renewed with all things that are (1QH 11.9–14, Gaster 1976).

Like the composer of the *Hôdāyôt,* and like Philo (for whom mystical experience of God is obtainable in this life), the author of Wisd experiences the raptures of Divine Knowledge in his present existence (chap. 7) and already enjoys his prize of immortality.[43]

The centrality of Wisd's theory of immortality represents a new emphasis in the history of Jewish tradition, although it must be seen as part of a continuous development in Jewish Hellenistic thought. According to I Enoch 102:5, the spirits of the righteous descend to Sheol, but at the judgment will ascend to a life of joy as companions of the hosts of heaven (103:3–4; 104:6). Jubilees 23:31 ("and their bones will rest in the earth, and their spirits will have much joy") seems to presume an immediate assumption of the spirit,[44] and in *Test.Asher* 6:5–6, the soul of the righteous is led by the angel of peace into eternal life. Finally, in IV Maccabees, a book which may be roughly contemporary with Wisd, the patriarchs are already in heaven ready to receive the souls of those who have died for the sake of God (7:19; 13:17; 16:25; cf. 7:3; 9:22; 14:5; 15:3; 16:13; 17:12; 18:23; cf. Luke 16:22, and see E. W. Saunders, *IDB*, s.v. "Abraham's Bosom;" also Pseudo-Phocylides 105–108 [*FPG*:152]. Wisd's doctrine of preexistence, on the other hand, may be the earliest attestation of this teaching in Jewish literature (see NOTE on 8:19).

2. *Eschatology*

The author's eschatological descriptions form a sort of chiaroscuro, lacking any clear definition. He moves fitfully through alternating patches of darkness and light, almost deliberately blurring the points of transition. The picture which emerges is somewhat confused, but its broad outlines are nevertheless not difficult to draw. The just souls, after passing through the crucible of suffering during their earthly existence, are portrayed as being in the hand of God and perfectly at peace (either in some neutral zone in Hades, or more likely in Heaven). Conversely, the wicked who had oppressed their weaker brothers with apparent impunity, become ignominious carcasses, eternal objects of outrage among the dead. The picture is now abruptly transposed to the "moment of God's gracious dispensation," when the just will blaze forth, and in contrast to their formerly passive though peaceful state, will be rendered eminently active. Taking

[43] There is a similar emphasis in Plato *Tim.* 90BC: "But he who has seriously devoted himself to learning and to true thoughts, and has exercised these qualities above all his others, must necessarily and inevitably think thoughts that are immortal and divine, if so be that he lays hold on truth, and insofar as it is possible for human nature to partake of immortality, he must fall short thereof in no degree; and inasmuch as he is for ever tending his divine part and duly magnifying that daemon who dwells along with him, he must be supremely blessed." Cf. Philo *Spec.* 1.207. Similarly, according to the Muslim philosopher Alfarabi (d. ca. 950), a man at the stage of "acquired" intellect enters into the state of immortality even before the death of his body, and herein consists "supreme happiness." (*Al-Madīna al-Fāḍila*, ed. F. Dieterici [Leiden, 1895]:46, 4–65).

[44] See Nickelsburg:32–33, 198.

his indignation as full armor, and employing the elemental forces of nature as his weapons, God will now devastate and smash the lawless kingdoms of the earth, thus inaugurating a new, trans-historical era of divine rule. Screened by the divine power, and in receipt of royal insignia of the highest majesty, the just souls (now clearly among the angelic hosts) will, as God's agents, judge the nations of the world, while enjoying an unsurpassed vision of the truth (cf. NOTE on 3:8–9). But what was a gracious dispensation for the just will constitute the day of reckoning for the souls of the wicked, who are pictured as coming forward cringing to be convicted to their face by their own criminal acts. As is common in Jewish apocalyptic literature, the wicked and the just are thought to be able readily to witness each other's reversed roles under the new divine dispensation (see NOTE on 5:2). The righteous are therefore pictured as taking their stand with poised confidence to outface their former oppressors, who, in turn, are pictured as full of remorse and given to long self-deprecating monologues. It is not clear, however, whether the wicked face a double judgment, one immediately after death, and a second one at the time of the gracious visitation of the just, or whether they are at first automatically hurled speechless into the depths of Hades, only later to face formal charges in the presence of their former victims (cf. Nickelsburg:88–89).

3. *Torah and Sophia*

As we approach the core doctrines of the book, it becomes immediately apparent that its subtle blending of heterogeneous conceptions has inevitably entailed a degree of ambiguity in their formulation which makes it difficult to determine which elements are primary and which are secondary. Moreover, the author's habit of frequently alluding in passing to various doctrines, often of considerable significance, without any subsequent elaboration, adds to one's sense of uncertainty. He fleetingly refers, for example, to the view of the Zoroastrians concerning the origin of death and their peculiar notion of *khrafstra,* the emanation of Wisdom from God, the creation of the world out of formless matter, the cosmological and teleological proofs for the existence of God, the preexistence of souls, the mutual interchange of the elements, and the Stoic theory of *tonos.* If we add to this the fact that his argumentation is largely rhetorical rather than demonstrative, we soon realize that much in our interpretation will ultimately depend on what we sense to be the general drift of his thought and the special ambience in which it was formed. The latter, it is unmistakably clear, was the philosophical sphere of Middle Platonism, whose boundaries stretch from ca. 80 BCE to ca. 220 CE. The Stoicising Platonism of Wisd is the characteristic trademark of Middle Platonic scholasticism, and it is undoubtedly misleading to brand this philosophical mode as 'eclectic.' Eclecticism has a use, but, as Dillon has correctly noted, it surely implies the assembling of doctrines from various schools on the basis of the personal preferences of the thinker concerned, rather than on the basis of any coherent theory as to the historical development of philosophy, and it is thus not, I think, a fair word to use for what the Middle Platonists, from Antiochus on, were doing. Antiochus, as I shall try to show, thought he had a coherent view of how philosophy had developed, and that view may not have been quite as perverse as it now appears to us. He and his successors felt justified in appropriating from the Peripatetics and the Stoics such doctrines and formulations as seemed to them to express better what Plato had really meant to say. At most, they were 'modernizing' Plato. The rationale of their procedure was clear and consistent, and it does not seem to me to be profitable to characterize it as eclectic (p. xiv; cf. Früchtel:129).

When placed in its proper philosophical context, Wisd no longer appears to contain a pastiche of Greek philosophical doctrines used merely for ornamental decoration. The remarkable similarity of its teaching on many points with that of Philo of Alexandria [see part VIII, below], whose writings were roughly contemporary with it, only reinforces the view that its philosophical orientation is Middle Platonist.

The central figure which strides across the book is Sophia or Dame Wisdom, appearing at first under a variety of names (chap. 1), then gradually coming into sharper focus, until she begins to dominate the stage completely (6:12ff), but then again receding into the background and merging almost imperceptibly with the deity, only suddenly to emerge one last time in full power under one of her alternate titles (18:15). She is no innovation of the author of Wisd, but had already made her appearance as a cosmic force in Proverbs (8:22ff; 1:20ff), and Job (28:12ff) under the guise of a charming female figure playing always before Yahweh, after having been created by Him at the beginning of His work (Prov 8:30), and having obvious roots in ancient Near Eastern myth. She is undoubtedly a 'hypostasis' as that term was very broadly defined by Oesterly and Box, i.e. "a quasi-personification of certain attributes proper to God, occupying an intermediate position between personalities and abstract beings" (:169).[45] Hu and Sia, for example, are in Egyptian tradition the creative word and the understanding of the high god Re-Atum, personified and separated from their originator. Mythologically expressed,

[45] For Prov 8:1–36, see R. B. Y. Scott's commentary: AB 18, 69–71. Cf. Job 15:7ff where Wisdom is conceived as a kind of independent entity, which it is possible to detach from God to such an extent that somebody else can seize it. In Proverbs and Job, however, as also in Ben Sira, Wisdom is not yet an 'hypostasis' in the sense quoted above, since according to these texts she is clearly only the first creation of God. In Philo and Wisd, on the other hand, where Sophia is considered to be an eternal emanation of the deity, we undoubtedly have a conception of her as a divine hypostasis, coeternal with him. See G. Scholem, *Elements of the Kabbalah and its Symbolism* (Jerusalem, 1976):260–262 (Hebrew). For the significance of Job 28, see Weinfeld:257–260.

they are, as Ringgren has put it, "the first begotten children of Re-Atum and his assistants in the creation of the world. They follow him on his journey in the sun-barque, aiding him in his capacity as the ruler of the world, thus personifying his intelligence and his command. Later on, they attain so high a degree of independence that they can be associated with any other god" (Ringgren 1947:27). Similarly, Egyptian Maat is a personification of the concept *maat* or 'right order in nature and society' (originally a function of the high god) who became the daughter of Re, and was vouchsafed a cult of her own. She protects the sun-god, destroys his enemies, and embraces him day and night. As a guardian of moral life, the highest judge calls himself the priest of Maat and wears an image of her on his breast (cf. Prov 1:9; 3:22). According to one text, "Re has created Maat, he rejoices over her, he delights in her, he loves her, his heart is joyful when he sees her."[46] An example from the Akkadian sphere are Mešaru and Kettu, Righteousness and Right, who were sometimes conceived only as qualities of the sun-god or as gifts granted by him, and sometimes in a more concrete way as personal beings, even independent deities (cf. Ps 85:11–14. See Ringgren 1947:53–58). So, too, the divine word is praised in several Sumerian and Akkadian texts as an independent physical cosmic potency. Dürr has shown that the hypostatization of the word proceeds via its character of breath and wind (*šaru*). Thus it is conceived as something concrete, nearly material, which, having left the mouth of the deity, acquires an independent existence (Ringgren 1947:65–68). We also have an early Semitic reference (sixth century BCE) to Wisdom who is dear to the gods in *The Words of Ahiqar* 94–95 (found at Elephantine): "For all time the kingdom is hers. In heaven is she established, for the lord of holy ones has exalted her" (*ANET*:428).[47]

Wisdom appears again in The Wisdom of Ben Sira (ca. 180 BCE), a Jewish Palestinian work which, having been translated into Greek, left a distinct mark on Wisd. Both books, for example, use virtually identical images to describe their authors' ardent pursuit of Wisdom, and both place a similar emphasis on God's mercy.[48] Like Proverbs 8, Ben Sira describes Wisdom as having been created from the very beginning (1:4; 24:9), and as having been infused into all of God's works (1:9). She is further described as traversing the entire cosmos, but finally, at the divine behest,

[46] In an Egyptian Coffin text we read: "Nun said to Atum: kiss your daughter Maat, after placing her at your nose, then will your heart live." See Ringgren 1947:49–52; Kayatz:93–119. See also Keel:63–74.

[47] Hengel writes: "Donner derives his conception from the Egyptian doctrine of maat. . . . However, we cannot exclude the possibility that this *ḥokma* dwelling with God in heaven at the same time represents a transformation of the Semitic mother goddess and goddess of love who had even been set alongside Yahweh as *parhedros* [coadjutor] by the Jews at Elephantine, under the name of 'Anatyahu" (1. 154).

[48] Cf. Wisd 6:12–24; 7:7–14 with Sir 15:2; 51:26; 13; Wisd 11:23; 12:16 with Sir 18:11–13 (also Wisd 3:16 with Sir 23:25).

making her home in Israel, in God's beloved city of Jerusalem
(24:3–12). More important, going beyond the Book of Deuteronomy
which had identified the laws of the Torah with wisdom (4:6), Ben Sira
identified Wisdom with Torah (24:23), "as a result of which both were
conceived together as a heavenly element which descended from heaven to
take up its abode among the children of Israel" (Weinfeld:256). The author thereby reached the uneasy compromise of a Divine Wisdom
which pervades the cosmos, yet maintains its concentrated focus in Zion
and in the teachings of the Torah, which thus achieves a new universal
significance.[49]

At almost the same time as Ben Sira, we find a highly developed Wisdom doctrine in Aristobulus' *Interpretations of the Holy Laws* (ca.
175–170 BCE).[50] Aristobulus wishes the reader to understand the Torah
"truly" (*physikōs*), i.e. philosophically, and "not slip into the mythological
mode," for "those who are capable of thinking rightly, are amazed at
Moses' wisdom and divine spirit, by reason of which he has won fame as a
prophet" (*FPG:*217–218). The goal of Aristobulus' allegorical exegesis is
to demonstrate the rationality of the Torah, and, like Philo, he chides
those who cling to the letter (*tō graptō*) for their lack of strength and insight, and for providing a reading of the Torah in the light of which Moses
fails to appear to be proclaiming great things. Moreover, if anything unreasonable (*alogian*) remains in the biblical text in spite of his interpretations, says Aristobulus, the cause of this must be attributed not to
Moses, but to his own inability to describe correctly what Moses meant
(*FPG:*218). He then proceeds to identify the number seven with wisdom
and light:

> God created the world, and, because life is troublesome for all, he gave us
> for rest the seventh day, which in reality (*physikōs*) could also be called
> the prime source of light, through which all things are comprehended. The
> latter could also be metaphorically transferred to Wisdom, for all light
> comes from her; just as some members of the Peripatetic school say that
> wisdom has the role of a beacon-fire, because those who follow her
> unremittingly will remain undisturbed their whole life through. But one of
> our forefathers, Solomon, said more clearly and more beautifully that Wis-
> dom existed before heaven and earth (*FPG:*224).

The Pythagorean Philolaus had already associated the number seven with
wisdom and light (DK, A.12), and Philo later made a similar identifica-

[49] See Rylaarsdam:18–46; Hengel 1. 157–162. Hengel concludes: "Without question
there is an inner logic in this development in Jewish wisdom speculation, but we
should ask whether a movement in this direction would have developed at all if it
had not been furthered by the necessity to ward off foreign influences. We must
therefore agree with J. Fichtner, who sees the decisive motive force in the 'contro-
versy with Hellenism.'"

[50] On Aristobulus, see Walter: esp. 124–171; Hengel 1. 164–169; Gutman 1.
186–220.

tion, asserting that "the reason why the man who guides himself in accordance with the seventh and perfect light is both blessed and holy is that the
formation of things mortal ceases with the seventh day's advent" (*LA*
1.16–18; cf. *Deus* 12; *Spec.* 2.59: seven is the light which reveals as completed what six has produced; *Her.* 216). Aristobulus' luminous Wisdom
is also further identified with the Logos, when he asserts that the seventh
day is "a symbol of the seventh logos [probably, the *nous hēgemōn,* as in
Philo *Abr.* 28–29, which in turn is an inseparable fragment of the Logos]
through which we have knowledge of human and divine things," and that
"the entire cosmos revolves through sevens" (*FPG*:225).[51] Thus, according to Aristobulus, Preexistent Wisdom or Logos, which is identical with
the Primordial Light (the Archetypal Sun or intelligible *phōs* of Philo)
and symbolized by the number seven, gives the true Sabbath rest to those
who follow Her.

In the light of this tradition of Wisdom speculation, it is no longer
difficult to understand why the author of our text chose the Wisdom figure
as the mediator of his own message to his contemporaries. She was the
perfect bridge between the exclusive nationalist tradition of Israel and the
universalist philosophical tradition which appealed so strongly to the Jewish youth of Roman Alexandria. Moreover, as Reese and Mack have
recently shown, the author of Wisd skillfully adapted the Isis aretalogies
for his own use in describing Sophia.[52] The cult of Isis and Sarapis was
one of the most popular of the oriental religions from the fourth century
BCE to the fourth century CE, though its peak of popularity was reached in
the second century CE. It should also be noted that Gaius, who had
decorated a room (the *Aula Isiaca*) in his palace on the Palatine with
paintings depicting numerous Egyptian religious symbols, had built a
temple to Isis, and had instituted Isiac mysteries in which he is said to
have participated himself while dressed in female garb (Jos. *Ant.* 19.1.5
and 11). Köberlein has suggested that he had even created his own
"Mysteries," called *Hēgemonika* (Philo *Legat.* 56), which dealt with his
own person and the Imperial House, and which included 'Hymns' cele-
brating his *aretai* or great accomplishments (Dio Cassius 59. 29.6;
Suetonius *Caligula* 16.4; cf. Philo *Legat.* 144ff and NOTE on 10:1. See
Köberlein:24–25; 32–38. The Philonic evidence for these so-called
Hēgemonika, however, is by no means unambiguous, and as E. M. Smallwood has indicated (in her note ad loc.), the language of the Mysteries

---

[51] A similar interpretation is found in Philo *Abr.* 28–29: The Sabbath is so called
because the number seven is always free from factions and war. This is attested by
the faculties within us, for six of them wage ceaseless and continuous war, namely
the five senses and speech. But the seventh faculty is that of the dominant mind,
which after triumphing over the six, welcomes solitude and accepts a life of calmness
and serenity. Cf. *Her.* 225, where the Divine Logos, the Archetypal Sun, is designated as standing over the six parts (3 × 2) of the soul as the seventh; *LA* 1.19.

[52] Reese 1970:36–50; Mack:63–107. These parallels were already seen by Knox
1937:230–237; 1939:55–89; cf. Conzelmann:225–234.

at *Legat.* 56 is probably metaphorical.). It was only fitting that the author of Wisd reclaim the falsely appropriated *aretai* for 'Her' to whom they truly belonged.

4. *Logos and Sophia*

The most remarkable feature about the author's description of Sophia is that he depicts her as an effluence or emanation of God's glory. Most Middle Platonists (at least those of whom we have any knowledge) seem to have avoided such a conception, but it was apparently adopted by some of the Neopythagoreans, and was clearly implied by Philo, who often 'Pythagorizes,' though in this case he may very well have gotten the notion from the Middle Stoa (see NOTE on 7:25). Since, according to the writer, Wisdom pervades the entire cosmos and yet at the same time enjoys intimacy with God (7:24; 8:1,3), it may be said that there is an aspect of God's essence in everything, including the human mind, which remains inseparable from God. The only thing comparable to this view in ancient Jewish thought is Philo's similar notion of an all-penetrating Divine Logos which reaches into each man's mind, thus converting it into an extension of the Divine Mind, albeit a very fragmentary one (*Det.* 90; *Gig.* 27; *LA* 1.37–38; cf. M. Aurel. 8.57; *CH* 12.1). Like Philo, too, the author of Wisd evidently teaches that God created the world by means of Wisdom. Although his statement that "God made all things by his 'word' (*logō*), and through his 'wisdom' (*sophia*) formed man" (9:1–2) is in itself ambiguous, since it is by no means clear that 'word' and 'wisdom' here refer to Logos-Sophia, the matter is, I think, settled by the description of Wisdom as "chooser of God's works" (8:4), which clearly implies that Wisdom is identical with the Divine Mind through which the Deity acts. In the light of this, the assertion that "with you is Wisdom who knows your works and was present when you created the world" (9:9) must signify that Wisdom contains the paradigmatic patterns of all things (cf. 9:8) and serves as the instrument of their creation.

The author further specifies that God created the world "out of formless matter" (11:17), and we must now further inquire whether he believed that this formless matter was itself created by God, thus espousing a double creation theory, or whether he considered it to be eternal. There is considerable evidence, both internal and external, which makes it unmistakably clear that the latter alternative is the correct one. First, since no explicit theory of creation *ex nihilo* had heretofore been formulated in either Jewish or Greek tradition,[53] we should expect an emphatic and unam-

---

[53] See Winston 1971:185–191. There is no evidence that the normative rabbinic view was that creation was *ex nihilo*. Rabban Gamaliel's formulation in *BR* 1.9, Th-Alb:8 came only under the impact of a polemic with someone who was undoubtedly a Gnostic. In the context of such a confrontation, it would only be natural for the rabbi to counter with the notion that even the apparently primordial elements to

biguous statement from the author in this matter, if that were indeed his position. Second, as Grimm had already pointed out long ago (in his 1860 commentary on 11:17), it was the author's object to adduce as great a proof as possible of the power of God. Since creation *ex nihilo* would be an even greater marvel than that of conferring form on an already existent matter, he could hardly have failed to have specified the former had he thought it possible. Third, in his account of some of the miracles performed by God on behalf of the Israelites (especially the splitting of the Red Sea), the author employs a Greek philosophical principle in order to make the notion of miracles more plausible (see NOTE on 19:6), but had he held the doctrine of *creatio ex nihilo,* he could hardly have been troubled by lesser miracles and sought a philosophical principle to explain them, for *creatio ex nihilo* is the miracle of miracles. It quickly became the paradigm for God's miraculous powers, and its denial was taken to betoken the undermining of revealed religion (cf. Maimonides, *Guide* 2.22, 25; Albo *Iqqarim* 1.12.1; Abravanel *Mif'alot Elohim* 6a). It is true that Eudorus of Alexandria (fl. ca. 25 BCE), alone among the Middle Platonists, held the view, under the influence of Neopythagoreanism, that the One or Supreme God is the cause both of the 'Ideas' and of matter, but unfortunately we lack further information as to how this was understood by him (Simplicius *In Aristotelis de Physica Commentarii* 181,10ff, Diels; Alex.Aphr. *In Metaphysica* 988a 10–11, Hayduck; Dillon:126–128). If, as is likely, he conceived of the One as emanating both the Monad and the Dyad (see NOTE on 7:25), it would be difficult to imagine that the author of Wisd could be comfortable with such a notion.[54] To conceive of Wisdom as part of God's essence is one thing, but to allow that the material principle is itself also part of the divine essence would probably have been too much for him to swallow. In any case, the concept of creation *ex nihilo* formed no part of Greek philosophical thought or of Jewish Hellenistic or rabbinic thought, and its first explicit formulation appeared in second-century Christian literature, where (undoubtedly under the im-

---

which the Gnostic ascribed a dynamic cosmogonic function were created by God. Nothing may be inferred from this discussion as to the common rabbinic view of creation. Indeed, there is a passage in the *Mekilta* (*Shirta* 8), which provides strong prima facie evidence that the rabbis did not subscribe to the notion of creation *ex nihilo*. Ten examples are given there for the uniqueness of God's acts in contrast with those of man. The best example of all: that God can create *ex nihilo,* is not given. Moreover, example six states that to make a roof man requires wood, stones, dirt, and water, whereas God, on the other hand, has made of water a roof for his world (cf. *BR* 4.1, Th-Alb:25). In other words, when he created the heavens, he used water. (I owe this reference to the kindness of Prof. J. Goldin.)

[54] Like Philo, his Stoic use of materialistic language in describing Wisdom (7:22–24) was probably metaphorical. (For Philo, cf. *Gig.* 22, and see Billings:54–56.)

petus of the Gnostic challenge) the argument for a double creation is made on the grounds that creation out of an eternal primordial element would compromise the sovereignty of God (Tatian *Oratio ad Graecōs* 5; Theophilus *Ad Autolycum* 2.4,10 ad fin.).

Finally, we must raise the question of the author's conception of the nature of God's creative act. Did he conceive of it as temporal or as eternal? The author nowhere addresses himself to this issue and all we can do is indicate what his answer would be if he were a consistent Middle Platonist. With the exception of Plutarch and Atticus, the Middle Platonists denied that Plato had taught the temporal creation of the world, maintaining that the description given in the *Timaeus* was only for the sake of "clarity of instruction." Since the temporal interpretation of Plutarch and Atticus was based on their dualistic notion of a Maleficent Soul which (at least in Plutarch's version), before God created the cosmos proper, had itself created a dim prefiguration of the cosmos, which was then brought to completion by Logos,[55] it is plain that the monotheistic author of Wisd could not have followed in their footsteps. For most Platonists, there could be no adequate explanation of why God should wait before beginning to improve the eternal formless matter. Moreover, since the author of Wisd conceives of Sophia as a continuous emanation of the Godhead, and since it contains the paradigmatic forms of all things and is the instrument of creation, it would be reasonable to presume that its creative activity is also continuous. The fact is, however, that there are no grounds for assuming such philosophic consistency in a writer who seeks boldly to bridge two diverse traditions and must constantly maintain a delicate balance between them (and who, we might add, is more of a rhetorician than a philosopher). Even the redoubtable Philo falters on this issue, and although asserting a theory of eternal creation in his treatise *On Providence* (*De Providentia* 1.6–9), elsewhere he adopts the formula that "there was a time when the world was not" (*Decal.* 58).[55a] But while in the case of Philo, it might perhaps not be unreasonable to brush aside those passages which adopt the biblical idiom of temporal creation, we could feel no such confidence with regard to our author, and so, I think, the question must be left unresolved.

5. *Pursuing Wisdom*

In depicting Sophia, the author is all aglow with a burning enthusiasm that fills the verses dealing directly with her with a luminous and passionate intensity. His confident words convey a conviction, evidently confirmed by his personal experience, that Wisdom is easily found by those who seek her, to the point of even anticipating them in their search (almost like the

[55] Plutarch *Is. et Os.* 373C. See Dillon:203–204.
[55a] See Winston, "Philo's Theory of Eternal Creation," in the forthcoming American Academy of Jewish Research Jubilee Volume.

woman who pursues a man until he catches her) (6:12–16). He speaks of his love for her and his seeking to make her his bride so that he might live with her (8:9; 7:28; 8:16). It is noteworthy that the terms of the description of Wisdom's union with God correspond very closely to those of the description of the student's union with Wisdom.[56] This undoubtedly implies that man's ultimate goal is union with God, which may, however, be achieved only through union with His Wisdom, which is but one of His aspects (see Wilckens in *TDNT* 7. 499). This union with Sophia is possible because of man's kinship with her (8:17), through his possession of a rational mind, which is permeated by the intelligent spirit of Wisdom (7:23–24). But if Wisdom is already present in man's mind, as she is indeed in every part of the universe, what is the significance of man's hot pursuit of her and the need for special supplication to the Lord to send her down from his heavenly throne (9:10)? We have already seen that Wisdom is both immanent and transcendent (she pervades the universe, yet remains in unbroken union with God), so that both forms of description may easily be interchanged depending on the particular focus of the writer. Seneca employs a vivid simile (which probably stems from the Middle Stoa, and, incidentally, recurs later in Ḥabad Hasidism) in order to explain this double aspect:

> When a soul rises superior to other souls . . . it is stirred by a force from heaven. A thing like this cannot stand upright unless it be propped up by the divine. Therefore, a greater part of it abides in that place from whence it came down to earth. [Cf. Wisd 7:27.] Just as the rays of the sun do indeed touch the earth, but still abide at the source from which they are sent; even so the great and hallowed soul, which has come down in order that we may have a nearer knowledge of divinity, does indeed associate with us, but still cleaves to its origin; on that source it depends, thither it turns its gaze, and strives to go, and it concerns itself with our doings only as a being superior to ourselves (*Ep.* 41.5).[57]

The Neoplatonist Proclus later provides a concise expression of this bifocal perspective: "The gods are present alike to all things; not all things, however, are present alike to the gods, but each order has a share in their presence proportioned to its station and capacity, some things receiving them as unities and others as manifolds, some perpetually and others for a time, some incorporeally and others through the body" (*Elements* 142). From the human viewpoint, the Divine Wisdom enters man and departs; from the eternal perspective of God, however, it is ever present to man,

---

[56] Wisdom is God's throne-companion: cf. 9:4 with 6:14. For Wisdom's intimacy with God: cf. 8:3 with 8:9,16; and 9:9 with 6:23; 7:28; 8:18; 9:10. That God loved her: cf. 8:3 with 6:12; 7:10; 8:2, 18.

[57] Cf. Philo *QG* 2.40; *Det.* 90; M. Aurel. 8.57; Justin *Dialogus cum Tryphone Judaeo* 128.3–4; Tertullian *Apologeticus* 21.10–13; Lactantius *Divinae institutiones* 4.29, 4–5.

though its consummation in any particular case is conditioned by the fitness of the recipient.[58] Hence our author speaks in no uncertain terms of "desire for instruction" (6:17), "training in Wisdom's society" (8:18), and the need for pre-dawn vigilance on her behalf (6:14–15).

There appears to be good reason, then, to conclude that the author's highly charged language concerning the pursuit of Wisdom and her promised gifts, may allude to a mystical experience through which, he believes, man is capable of some measure of union with the Deity, at least under his aspect of Sophia. The road to this mystic consummation, however, is not through the attainment of some esoteric disclosure, or through the efficacy of special modes of prayer (from the mystic's viewpoint, prayer is in reality God's address to man), but rather through passionate and unremitting devotion to the acquisition of wisdom. Nowhere, however, does the author describe, as Philo and Plotinus do, the various traits which characterize the experience of mystical union, so that we may speak of his writing as containing at best an incipient movement along the road to mysticism.

6. The Nature and Efficacy of Wisdom

As the Divine Mind immanent within the universe and guiding and controlling all its dynamic operations, Wisdom represents the entire range of natural science (7:17–21). She is also the teacher of all human arts and crafts, including shipbuilding and the art of navigation (7:16; 14:2). She is skilled in the intricacies of logic and rhetoric, and having unsurpassed experience of both past and present, she also infers the future and possesses the key to the divinatory arts (8:8). Moreover, she is the source of all moral knowledge (8:7), is man's counsellor and comforter, bringing rest, cheer, and joy, and bestows riches and glory on her own, though her greatest boon is the gift of immortality (8:9–13). Above all, she is synonymous with Divine Providence, controlling historical events, and in each generation guiding the friends of God and inspiring his prophets (7:27; 14:3). It is significant that the author, unlike Ben Sira, nowhere explicitly identifies Wisdom with Torah[59] ("the keeping of her laws" in 6:18 is ambiguous, since it could refer to the statutes of natural law), although he refers to Israel's mission of bringing the imperishable light of the Law to

---

[58] Cf. Philo Op. 23; CH 10.4; Plutarch De Genio Socratis 20,589B; Plotinus 6.5.11 fin.; 6.9.8; Ps-Dionysius De Divinis nominibus 3.1. This was also the teaching of many Hasidic masters. "Where is the dwelling of God?" asked the Rabbi of Kotzk (1787–1859). Answering his own question, he said: "Wherever man lets him in." See Buber:175–176. Dodds (1963:274) notes that this is a favorite doctrine of the Cambridge Platonists, e.g. Benjamin Whichcote, Discourses (Aberdeen, 1751) 3. 102: "It is the incapacity of the subject, where God is not . . . for God doth not withdraw himself from us, unless we first leave Him: the distance is occasioned through our unnatural use of ourselves."

[59] Moreover, unlike Ben Sira, he makes no mention of the sacrificial cult.

the world (18:4), and says that Wisdom is the source of prophecy (7:27). (He is indeed confident that idolatry will ultimately disappear: 14:13–14.) Very likely he believed with Philo that the teachings of the Torah were tokens of the Divine Wisdom, and that they were in harmony with the laws of the universe and as such implant all the virtues in man (cf. Jos. *Ant.* 1. Proem 4.24); Ps-Aristeas 161; IV Macc 1:16–17; 5:25; Philo *Op.* 3; *Mos.* 2.52), but when he concentrates his attention on Wisdom, it is philosophy, science, and the arts that are uppermost in his mind. Wisdom is conceived by him as a direct bearer of revelation, functioning through the workings of the human mind, and supreme arbiter of all values. She is clearly the Archetypal Torah, of which the Mosaic Law is but an image. When he insists that unless God send his Wisdom down from on high men would not comprehend God's will (9:17), he is certainly implying that the Torah is in need of further interpretation for the disclosure of its true meaning, interpretation which Wisdom alone is able to provide. Once again the author closely approaches the position of Philo of Alexandria, in whose view, even before the Sinaitic Revelation, the Patriarchs were already constituted *nomoi empsychoi* or living embodiments of Divine Wisdom. (Similarly, in Wisd 10, Sophia had already served as a personal Guide to six righteous heroes who lived before the Sinaitic Revelation.) An echo of this notion may later be found in the statement of Rav Avin (fourth century) that the Torah is an incomplete form (*nōbelet*, literally, the fruit falling prematurely off the tree) or image of the Supernal Wisdom (*BR* 17.5; 44.12, Th-Alb:157, 239).

7. Universalism and Particularism

Although the substantive *philanthrōpia* never occurs in Wisd, the adjective *philanthrōpos* 'humane, benevolent' appears thrice. Twice Wisdom is described as philanthrōpos (1:6; 7:23), and in 12:19 we are told that God's mercy is a model-lesson for Israel, teaching them that the righteous man must be humane. God loves all that exists, loathing nothing that he has created (11:24), and as the lover of all that lives, he spares all, for his imperishable spirit (*aphtharton pneuma*) is in them all (11:26; 12:1). We have here a faint intimation of the Middle Stoic doctrine of *philanthrōpia*, or 'humanity,' which is fully elaborated in the writings of Philo. The special kinship between God and man, based on the notion of a Divine Logos at once immanent and transcendent, led inevitably to the concept of the unity of man. The Stoics spoke of the common community of gods and men: "The world is as it were the common house of gods and men, or the city belonging to both; for they alone make use of reason and live according to right and law" (Cicero *ND* 2.154; *SVF* 2. 527–528). The early Stoics, however, still emphasized the dichotomy between the wise and the foolish, and Zeno insisted that only the wise are capable of concord and unity (D.L. 7. 32.3; *SVF* 3. 672,674,725). The Cynics had gone so far as to say that the non-wise are not men (D.L. 6.41, 60). It was only in the Middle Stoa, in the writings of Panaetius and Antiochus (through a fusion of the Stoic concept of *oikeiōsis* and the Peripatetic doctrine of *oikeiotēs*),[60] that an all-embracing doctrine of human unity took shape. Panaetius focused his attention on the ordinary man, and thus produced an ethical ideal suited to the capacity of all (Seneca *Ep.* 116.5; Cicero *Off.* 1.46, 99). Going beyond the negative formulation of justice which forbids man to injure another, he advances the positive definition of it as an active beneficence which forms the bond of society (Cicero *Off.* 1.20–22). The fundamental principles on which this is based are elucidated as follows:

> We must go more deeply into the basic principles of fellowship and association set up by nature among men. The first is to be found in the association that links together the entire human race, and the bond that creates this is reason and speech, which by teaching and learning, by communication, discussion, and decision brings men into agreement with each other and joins them in a kind of natural fellowship (*Off.* 1.50).

Philo similarly writes: "All we men are kinsmen and brothers, being related by the possession of an ancient kinship, since we receive the lot of the rational nature from one mother" (*QG* 2.60; cf. *Decal.* 41, 132–134; *Det.* 164; *Spec.* 4.14; 1.294, 317; *Praem.* 92). Following Panaetius, Philo, too, emphasizes the positive aspect of justice as an active beneficence (*Virt.* 166ff). This quality is epitomized by him in the word *philanthrōpia*, a term which apparently came into philosophical prominence in the writings of Panaetius and Antiochus, and later in those of Epictetus' teacher Musonius Rufus, and with especial emphasis in those of Plutarch (see Hirzel 1912:23–32). In a section of his treatise *De Virtutibus* devoted to *philanthrōpia* (51–174), Philo points out that it has *eusebeia* or piety as its sister and twin, for the love of God involves the love of man, inasmuch as man, "the best of living creatures, through that higher part of his being, namely, the soul, is most nearly akin to heaven . . . and also to the Father of the world, possessing in his mind a closer likeness and copy than anything else on earth of the eternal and blessed Archetype" (*Decal.* 134). Moreover, in practicing *philanthrōpia*, man is imitating God. "For what one of the men of old aptly said is true, that in no other action does man so much resemble God as in showing kindness, and what greater good can there be than that they should imitate God, they the created, Him the Eternal?" (*Spec.* 4.73; cf. 1.294; *Congr.* 171). Here, indeed, we touch upon the formula which for Philo constitutes the best way to describe the *telos* of man's life, *homoiōsis theō* (imitation of God), and in adopting

---

[60] See Baldry:177–203.

this Platonic goal he was following, as Dillon has pointed out, in the footsteps of Eudorus of Alexandria.[61]

Many commentators find the "undisguised particularism" of part III [C], of Wisd, where God appears "as partial to the Jews and inimical to their enemies" (Reider 1957:41), and the verses regarding the innate viciousness of the Canaanites and their primal accursedness (12:10–11), irreconcilable with the universalism which we have found encapsuled in the adjective *philanthrōpon*. It seems apparent, however, that the ancient Egyptians and Canaanites merely served the author as symbols for the hated Alexandrians and Romans of his own day, upon whom he visited an apocalyptic vengeance in chap. 5. The intense hatred breathed in part III can only be understood in the light of contemporary conditions. Finding himself in similar circumstances, Philo, who has a much more elaborate doctrine of *philanthrōpia* and is always at great pains to tone down Jewish particularism (see NOTE on 18:4), is nevertheless quite capable not only of depicting the future divine punishment of Israel's enemies, but also of setting God's people apart as the special concern of the Deity who employs the Romans (not mentioned by name) as pawns in his larger historical plan:

Everything will suddenly be reversed, God will turn the curses against the enemies of these penitents, the enemies who rejoiced in the misfortunes of the nation and mocked and railed at them, thinking that they themselves would have a heritage which nothing could destroy. . . . In their infatuation they did not understand that the short-lived brilliance which they had enjoyed had been given them not for their own sakes but as a lesson to others, who had subverted the institutions of their fathers, and therefore grief—the very painful feeling aroused by the sight of their enemy's good fortune—was devised as a medicine to save them from perdition. . . . But these enemies who have mocked at their lamentations, proclaimed public holidays on the days of their misfortunes, feasted on their mourning, in general made the unhappiness of others their own happiness, will, when they begin to reap the rewards of their cruelty, find that their misconduct was directed not against the obscure and unmeritable but against men of high lineage retaining sparks of their noble birth, which have to be but fanned into a flame, and from them shines out the glory which for a little while was quenched. (*Praem.* 169–72; cf. *Mos.* 1.69–70; *Praem.* 96–97: "He promises to marshal against them to their shame and perdition, swarms of wasps [cf. Exod 23:28] to fight in the van of the godly.")

[61] See *Fug.* 63, where he quotes Plato's *Theaetetus* 176AB; *Op.* 144; *Virt.* 8, 168, 204–205; *Spec.* 4.188; *Decal.* 73; *LA* 2.4. Cf. Plato, *Tim.* 90A*ff; Laws* 716B. For Eudorus, see Dillon:115–135. The idea of *imitatio Dei* was, of course, also distinctively Jewish. See *Mek. Shirta* 3, Lauterbach 2. 25; *BT Shab.* 113b; *Sotah* 14a; and Marmorstein 1950:106–121; Schechter 1936:199*ff.*

This is not to deny that there is a certain degree of tension between the universalist and particularist tendencies both in Philo and in Wisd, but it is not distinctly more pronounced in the latter than it is in the former.

8. *Freedom and Determinism**

In a monotheistic creed there is almost an ineluctable tendency to fault the Omnipotent Deity for human sin. A late midrash, for example, put the following critique into the mouth of Cain:

> Master of the world, if I have killed him, it is thou who hast created in me the Evil Yeṣer [i.e. Instinct, Drive]. Thou watchest me and the whole world. Why didst thou permit me to kill him? It is thou who hast killed him . . . for if thou hadst received my sacrifice I would not have become jealous of him (*Mid.Tanḥ.Gen.* 9; cf. *Midrash Hagadol* on Gen 4:9).

That this form of critique was taken seriously even in earlier rabbinic literature is made clear by the statement of R. Simeon b. Yoḥai:

> It is a thing hard to say, and it is impossible for the mouth to utter it. It is to be compared to two athletes who were wrestling in the presence of the king. If the king wills, he can have them separated; but the king wills not; in the end one overwhelmed the other and killed him. And the dying man shouted: Let my case be examined before the king (*BR* 22.9, Th-Alb:216).[62]

In a more pointed attempt to locate the source of human motivations in God, the rabbis plead in favor of the brothers of Joseph, "When thou didst choose, thou didst make them love; when thou didst choose thou didst make them hate" (*BR* 84.18, Th-Alb:1022). Elijah, too, spoke insolently toward heaven saying to God, "Thou hast turned their heart back again," and God later confessed that Elijah was right (*BT Ber.* 31b; cf. *Sanh.* 105a) (see Schechter:264–292). A similar critique is voiced with almost consistent monotony by the author of IV Ezra: "This is my first and last word; better had it been that the earth had not produced Adam, or else, having once produced him, (for thee) to have restrained him from sinning" (7:116, *APOT* 1; cf. 3:8,20–22; 7:47–48; 8:42–44). The author of the Apocalypse of Abraham is equally exercised over the divine license for evil to invade the human psyche: "O Eternal, Mighty One! Wherefore hast thou willed to effect that evil should be desired in the hearts of men, since Thou indeed art angered over that which was willed by Thee" (23,

---

* This section is an expanded version of Winston 1973.

[62] The midrashic parable of an athletic contest seems to be drawn from Greek Sophistic discussions. Plutarch, for example, tells us that a certain athlete had hit Epitimus the Pharsalian with a javelin, accidentally, and killed him, and Pericles wasted an entire day discussing with Protagoras whether it was the javelin or rather the one who hurled it or the judges of the contests, that ought to be held responsible for the disaster (*Pericles* 36).

Box). Even in the polytheistic ambience of Homeric man we find an analogous attempt to put the burden of sin on Zeus. "Not I was the cause of this act," cries Agamemnon,

> but Zeus and my portion and the Erinys who walks in darkness: they it was who in the assembly put wild *atē* [i.e. folly] in my understanding, on that day when I arbitrarily took Achilles' prize from him. So what could I do? Deity will always have its way (*Iliad* 19.86*ff*).

That this is no idiosyncratic whim of Agamemnon is attested by the understanding response of Achilles:

> Father Zeus, great indeed are the *atai* [i.e. follies] thou givest to men. Else the son of Atreus would never have persisted in rousing the *thymos* [i.e. will] in my chest, nor obstinately taken the girl against my will (*Iliad* 19.270*ff*).[63]

In a sense, the Bible itself encouraged this feeling that God is ultimately responsible for man's wicked deeds. A distinct complex of historic events is explicated in Scripture through the primitive but potent concept of psychic invasion. God directly intervenes in Pharaoh's inner deliberations, "hardening his heart" in order to demonstrate ultimately his divine might (Exod 10:1; cf. Sir 16:15). He similarly hardens the heart of Sihon, king of the Amorites (Deut 2:30), and applies the same divine strategy to the Canaanites (Josh 11:20: "It was the Lord's purpose that they should offer an obstinate resistance to the Israelites in battle, and that thus they should be annihilated without mercy and utterly destroyed, as the Lord had commanded Moses"). Inversely, God does not permit Abimelech, king of Gerar, to sin with Abraham's wife Sarah (Gen 20:6; cf. *BR* 52.6, Th-Alb:548). In an encounter with Saul, David suggests that it may have been the Lord who has incited Saul against him (I Sam 26:19), and when the Lord's anger is kindled against Israel, we are told that he incites David to count them (II Sam 24:1; and for a contrary view, see I Chron 21:1). God prevented Eli's sons from taking their father's admonitions seriously, because he wished to slay them (I Sam 2:25), and in order to fulfill his word to Ahijah the Shilonite spoken to Jeroboam (I Kings 11:31), he induced Rehoboam to refuse the people's request that he lighten their yoke

---

[63] Cf. Herodotus 1.45: "But it is not you that I hold the cause of this evil [says Croesus to Adrastus], save in so far as you were the unwilling doer of it: rather it is the work of a god, the same who told me long ago what was to be"; *Odyssey* 1.32–34: "Look you now [says Zeus], how ready mortals are to blame the gods. It is from us, they say, that evils come, but they even of themselves, through their own blind folly, have sorrows beyond that which is ordained." See Dodds 1959:3; Theiler:46–103; Wust:95; Pohlenz 1966:124–160. For similar notions in Egypt and Mesopotamia, see S. Morenz and D. Müller, *Untersuchungen zur Rolle des Schicksalls in der ägyptischen Religion* (Berlin, 1960); A. L. Oppenheim, *Ancient Mesopotamia* (Chicago, 1964): 198–206; S. Morenz, *Egyptian Religion* (London, 1973): 57–80.

(I Kings 12:15). Isaiah takes up the same theme: "Make the heart of this people fat, and their ears heavy, and shut their eyes; lest they see with their eyes, and hear with their ears, and understand with their hearts, and turn and be healed" (Isa 6:10; cf. 29:10). Finally, both Jeremiah and Ezekiel foresee God's direct future intervention in order to transform the human psyche and redeem it from its congenital evil (Jer 31:30–33; 32:39–40; Ezek 36:16–30; 20:32–44; cf. Deut 30:6; Jub 1:23; 5:12).[64]

In the light of this background of ideas, in addition to the deterministic elements running through ancient Near Eastern wisdom literature, it is not difficult to see how Jewish wisdom and apocalyptic writings came to emphasize the decisive importance of God's prior gift of wisdom for the determination of a man's moral character. What baffles the reader of this ancient literature, however, is the easy coexistence in it of two apparently contradictory strands of thought, namely, an emphasis on God's ultimate determination of all human action coupled with an equally emphatic conviction that the human will is the arbiter of its own moral destiny. We shall begin our analysis of this problem with an examination of the Wisdom of Ben Sira and the Qumran scrolls, where the free will dilemma becomes immediately apparent.

Ben Sira clearly states that God has predetermined man's character from birth.

> To fear the Lord is the beginning of Wisdom,
>> And with the faithful was she created in the womb.
> With faithful men is she, and she hath been established from eternity;
>> And their seed shall she continue (1:14–15, APOT 1).

This is but a part of the larger cosmological picture which the author depicts.

> When God created His works from the beginning,
>> After making them He assigned them (their) portions.
> He set in order His works for ever,
>> And their authority unto their generations.
> They hunger not, neither are they weak,
>> And they cease not from their works.
> Not one thrusteth aside his neighbour,
>> They never disobey His word (Sir 16:26–28, APOT 1).

---

[64] See Lütgert; Kaufmann 3. 2, 438, 560–561. Cf. also II Chron 25:20; I Kings 22:20–23; Ps-Philo Liber antiquitantum biblicarum 12:3: "And when Aaron said this, they hearkened not unto him, that the word might be fulfilled which was spoken in the day when the people sinned in building the tower, when God said: 'And now if I forbid them not, they will adventure all that they take in mind to do, and worse.'" For the Greek notion of psychic intervention, see Dodds 1959:10ff (and for the Greek notion of atē as a deliberate deception which draws the victim on to fresh error whereby he hastens his own ruin, the grim doctrine that Quem deus vult perdere, prius dementat, see Dodds:38–39). For the similar Muslin notion of 'sealing' (Qur'an 2:5–6; 7:92–99), see Watt:15–16.

The notion of portions recurs throughout the book. "Praise is not seemly in the mouth of the wicked, for it hath not been apportioned him by God" (15:8, *APOT* 1; cf. 40:1; 38:1; 17:7; 41:3; 11:22; I Enoch 67:1; Ps Sol 5:6). A more detailed account of God's fashioning of man spells out the polar plan of creation which provides for two antithetical categories of people.

> Likewise also all men are made from the clay,
>   And Adam was created of earth.
> In His great wisdom God distinguished them,
>   And differentiated their ways.
> Some He blessed and exalted,
>   And others He hallowed and brought nigh to Himself;
> Some He cursed and abased,
>   And overthrew them from their place.
> As the clay is in the power of the potter,
>   To fashion it according to his good pleasure;
> So is man in the power of his creator,
>   To make him according to His ordinance
> [cf. Isa 45:9; Jer 18:6; *Test.Naphtali* 2:2–7; 1QH 1:21; 3:23; 4:29; Rom 9:20; *Amen-em-opet* 25, *ANET*:424].
> Over against evil (stands) the good, and against death life;
>   Likewise over against the godly the sinner.
> Even thus look upon all the works of God,
>   Each different, one the opposite of the other
> [Sir 33:10–15, *APOT* 1; cf. I Enoch 41:8].

Moreover, the hopeless condition of the sinner is explicitly related to his genetic endowment.

> (As for) the wound of the scorner [i.e. his lack of wisdom],
>   there is no healing for it,
> For an evil growth is his plant [Sir 3:28, *APOT* 1].

How can we now reconcile this stark predestinarianism with the equally emphatic teaching of Ben Sira concerning man's freedom to choose his life path?

> Say not: 'From God is my transgression,'
>   For that which He hateth made He not.
> Say not: '(It is) He that made me to stumble,'
>   For there is no need of evil men.
> Evil and abomination doth the Lord hate,
>   And He doth not let it come nigh to them that fear Him.
> God created man from the beginning,
>   And placed him in the hands of his *Yeṣer* [i.e. Instinct, Drive].
> If thou (so) desirest, thou canst keep the commandment,
>   And (it is) wisdom to do His good pleasure.

Poured out before thee (are) fire and water,
    Stretch forth thine hand unto that which thou desirest.
Life and death (are) before man,
    That which he desireth shall be given to him
    [Sir 15:11–17, *APOT* 1].

The dilemma under scrutiny confronts us even more poignantly in the Qumran scrolls. The author of the *Hôdāyôt* or thanksgiving psalms, for example, is acutely conscious of God's overwhelming and all-regulating power.

I know through the understanding which comes from Thee that right-eousness is not in a hand of flesh, that man is not master of his way and that it is not in mortals to direct their step. I know that the inclination of every spirit is in Thy hand; Thou didst establish all its ways before ever creating it, and how can any man change Thy words? Thou alone didst create the just and establish him from the womb for the time of good-will. . . . But the wicked Thou didst create for the time of Thy wrath, Thou didst vow them from the womb to the Day of Massacre, for they walk in the way which is not good. . . . Thou hast ordained them for great chastisements before the eyes of all Thy creatures . . . that all men may know Thy glory and Thy tremendous power (1QH 15.12–21).

Only God and his elect are privy to the "mysteries" of his predestined plan for the ages:

By the God of Knowledge is everything wrought. Before they occur He has set down all their designs; and when they come into being for the fulfilment of their functions they carry out their activity according to His glorious design, without any deviation. . . . He created the spirit of light and darkness, and upon them He founded every work and every action (1QS 3.15*ff;* cf. 1QH 1.21; 2.13; 10.2–5; 11.10; 1QS 9.18).

Yet in spite of the inevitability of the divine plan with its prior determi-nation of every human psyche for all time, we find alongside it a recurrent emphasis on man's voluntaristic action. We find reference, for example, in 1QS 6.13 to: "every man, born of Israel, who freely pledges himself to join the Council of the Community" and again in 1QS 5.1: "And this is the Rule for the men of the Community who have freely pledged themselves to be converted from all evil and to cling to all His commandments according to His will" (cf. 1QS 1.7, 11; 1QM 7.5; 10.5). The depth of feeling involved is clearly manifest in 1QH 15.10: "I have loved Thee freely and with all my heart and soul." The covenanter of Qumran must identify his will with that of God: "He shall freely delight in all that befalls him and nothing shall please him save God's will. He shall delight in all the words of His mouth and shall desire nothing except His commands" (1QS 9.23–24).[65]

Before attempting to resolve the riddle before us, we must briefly survey the development of the free will problem in Greek philosophy. Even a cursory reading makes it at once evident that before Epicurus the well-known polemics concerning freedom and determinism are absent from Greek thought. Plato and Aristotle seem to be content with a notion of relative free will,[66] but their virtual unconcern with the classical dilemmas which came to characterize the later debates over this issue has caused modern commentators no little trouble in elucidating their positions. Unfortunately, the objective cool with which the Classical period was able to approach this question gave way in the Hellenistic age to an earnest and impassioned anxiety. A feeling of helpless fatality begins to take hold of men, and Epicurus, whose major concern was the liberation of man from the grip of myth and superstition, could no longer ignore the new challenge to man's freedom. In Epicurus, for the first time in Greek philosophy (according to one interpretation),[67] we encounter the concept of absolute free will. The absence of primary sources, however, makes it difficult to determine the exact nature of Epicurus' doctrine of the atomic swerve. If we follow the Giussani-Bailey interpretation,[68] according to whom Epicurus posited an atomic swerve for every instance of free action, it would be necessary to classify Epicurus' doctrine as one of absolute free will. The latter teaches that voluntary motion is uncaused, and that no fixed inner structure of the will determines action. We find a similar doctrine in the

[65] See Licht; cf. Ringgren 1963; Merrill.
[66] See Wolfson 1948: 1. 430; Furley:210–226; Winston 1974–75:49–50 (and literature there cited); Loening: chap. 18; Allan:325–340.
[67] The expression *libera potestas* occurs first in Lucretius 2.256. See Huby. (Pohlenz, on the other hand, thinks that Epicurus dealt with the free will problem under the impetus of Zeno. See his 1955: 1. 59–60.) Huby's explanation, however, of the Epicurean preoccupation with this problem, as a reaction to the thoroughgoing determinism of Democritus, seems to me inadequate. In addition to the fillip imparted by the encroaching forces of astrological fatalism, I should like to point to an inner motivation for Epicurus' free will doctrine. The soteriological thrust of Epicurus' teachings required a clear hope for human salvation grounded in the theoretical principles of his atomic system. Since, on the one hand, the infinite causal atomic chain could easily be misconstrued by the common man as precluding even the slightest possibility of achieving happiness by special human efforts, and since the realistic limitations of human character, on the other, would dampen the prospects of any substantial success on the part of Epicurus with most men, it suddenly became essential to find a way to guarantee the effectiveness of the atomic world view in securing human happiness. The atomic swerve allowed the new teaching to break through the causal nexus which shaped man's character and moral destiny from an infinitely remote past and permitted the Epicurean philosophy to espouse a hopeful and confident meliorism.
[68] See Bailey:432–437; Giussani.

writings of Alexander of Aphrodisias (an early third century CE commentator on Aristotle), according to whom free will depends upon uncaused motion (*anaitios kinēsis*) and this in turn depends upon an admixture of non-being. Non-being destroys uniform and consistent action and accounts for the fact that persons of similar endowments and breeding frequently differ from one another.[69] If, on the other hand, we follow Furley's interpretation (pp. 161–237) which is by far the more likely, according to which Epicurus taught that the motions of the psyche are not determined *ab initio* because of the discontinuity brought about by the atomic swerve[70] which allows new patterns of motion to emerge which cannot be explained by the initial constitution of the psyche, we should have to classify his doctrine as a relative free will theory of the 'modified causal' type. The latter teaches that man's volitional motion, though unconstrained by an external force and thus relatively free, is a product nonetheless of man's own psyche, which is not a completely autonomous agent. In the causal variety of this doctrine, the soul is itself a part of the universal causal chain and fully determined by it (Stoicism), whereas in its 'non-casual' variety the soul is autonomous though limited by the irrational motions of the body, which is a part of the universal causal chain (Plato, Middle Platonism, Neoplatonism), and in its predestinarian variety, it is God who ultimately determines its nature (Ben Sira, Qumran scrolls, rabbinic thought). In the 'modified causal' version of the Epicureans, although the atomic soul cluster is a part of the causal nexus, the latter can be broken through and hence training and conditioning in the light of the Epicurean teachings could more or less rectify improper proportions in the soul and thus secure the ultimate sovereignty of reason in the life of man (Lucretius 3.307–322).

According to the causal variety of relative free will taught by the Stoics, voluntary motion is caused both by *Heimarmenē* or the universal causal

---

[69] *De Anima in Alexandri Aphrodisiensis praeter commentaria scripta minora. De Anima liber cum mantissa*, ed. Ivo Bruns (*Supplementum Aristotelicum II* [Berlin, 1887–92]:170–171; 22–27. Cf. Pack:418–436. The only example of such a doctrine in Arabic philosophy seems to be that of Thumama b. Ashras (d. 828), from the school of Baghdad, who taught that generated effects have no author at all (see Fakhry:67–68). For a modern example, cf. the Russian Orthodox thinker Nicholas Berdyaev who developed the notion of 'meontic' freedom (see Nucho:37–40; cf. also Shestov:218).

[70] For the atomic swerve, see Lucretius 2.216–250: If the atom were always falling perpendicularly downwards through the void at uniform speed, worlds could never have formed since the atoms would never have met. Hence arises the need for a minute swerve of atoms which takes place "at no fixed time and at no fixed place" (293). Moreover, "if every motion is always linked on, and the new arises from the old motion in order determined, nor by swerving do the first-beginnings make a certain start of movement to break through the decrees of fate, so that cause may not follow cause from infinite time; whence comes this free will for living things all over the earth?" (251–256). Cf. Cicero *De Fato* 22–23; Plutarch *Moralia* 764C.

chain (frequently identified with God), as well as man's inner character, which in turn is also a part of that chain.[71] They maintained, however, that our choices are within our power (*eph hēmin*) by distinguishing between the proximate cause (*prokatarktikē aitia*) and the principal cause (*autotelēs aitia*), and asserting that Heimarmenē provides only the proximate causes of man's actions, while man himself provides the principal causes thereby participating in the process which initiates action (Cicero *De Fato* 41).[72] Since the principal causes provided by man are themselves "the gift of *Heimarmenē*" (*SVF* 2. 991), one has two options in describing human acts. Objectively, man's mind is but an extension of the Divine Mind, and therefore all its activities are in reality the activities of God; subjectively, the *logos* fragment constituting each human mind is that of the individual who deploys it and exemplifies his very own power of thought and deliberation. This readily accounts for the varying degrees of emphasis in both the Stoic and Philonic writings on either man's activity or his passivity.[73] The paradoxes which result from this double conception are elegantly exemplified by the Persian mystic Bayazid of Bistam: "I went from God to God, until they cried from me in me, 'O thou I'" (Nicholson 1963:17).

The 'non-causal' variety of relative free will is represented by Carneades, Pseudo-Plutarch, Albinus, Apuleius, and Alexander of Aphrodisias in his *Peri Heimarmenēs*.[74] These thinkers denied that there was a universal causal chain which encompassed even acts of will and insisted that voluntary motion was its own cause. According to Albinus, for example, acts of will belong to the category of the 'possible' (*dynaton*) which is 'indeterminate' (*aoriston*), and the soul is its own master (*adespoton*).[75] It is unlikely, however, that the Middle Platonists would have disagreed with Plato that the soul is subject to contamination by the body and that if the latter is radically diseased, the soul might not always succeed in becoming sufficiently decontaminated to restore it to complete health. Albinus, for example, writes that involuntary evils may be committed either through ignorance or passion, but that these are conditions that can be removed by reason, good traits, and training (*Did.* 31.2, Louis). But this statement is probably only meant to emphasize that education and

---

[71] Diels:322: *en hē symplokē kai to par hēmas, hōste ta men heimarthai, ta de syneimarthai.* Cf. Cicero *De Fato* 30; *SVF* 2.979, 991, 1000.

[72] An excellent analysis of the Stoic position is given by Long 1971:173–199. See also Rieth:134–168; Reesor:288–297; Pohlenz 1940:105–108; 1955: 1. 101–106.

[73] For Philo, see Winston 1974–75:47–70.

[74] See Albinus *Did.* 26.3; Louis; Apuleius *De Platone* 1.12; Ps-Plutarch *De Fato*, ed. E. Valgiglio (Rome, 1964). On Alexander, see Verbeke 1968:73–100; Long:247–268. For Calcidius, see the annotated edition by den Boeft. A detailed discussion of this problem in the Middle Platonists will be found in Dillon.

[75] Similarly, according to Calcidius, "the soul is free and acts according to its own authority" (*In Timaeum* 180b). For the term *adespoton,* cf. Plato *Rep.* 617E; Epicurus *Epistulae* 3.133.

training can have a decisive influence on one's moral actions, and not to deny that there may be some residual recalcitrance in a soul encased in a body diseased by heredity and environment which cannot be completely overcome. Calcidius explicitly acknowledges that though the moderate are supported by the happy amalgamation of body fluids, the extravagant or immoderate suffer from the disharmonious mixture of these fluids, and that in the mind of the moderate man deliberation always has the upper hand, whereas the weakness of the immoderate man supports the defective parts of his mind (the desiderative and spirited) against reason (*In Timaeum* 181–184). These very debates, however, between reason and the defective parts of the soul, he argues, are proof of our freedom, although he concedes that when "excited or perverted by passion, we are not capable of judgment" (184b). It is clear, then, that the most Calcidius is arguing for is a relative freedom, since he allows that the *logistikon* may be thwarted by certain bodily conditions. The Middle Platonists would not deny that the human soul, as part of the World Soul, was ultimately determined either by that cosmic entity, or by the Supreme God who ordered and governed it. They could, thus, under no circumstances maintain an absolute free will doctrine. It appears, however, that most of them would, like Plato, have further restricted the soul's freedom by allowing for its partial contamination by body. Still, in spite of this restriction, the soul's freedom was in their view guaranteed if it could be shown that although it was capable through association with the body of being affected by 'Fate' or the causal chain of the physical universe, it was nevertheless, as an absolutely transcendent entity, not subject to its control.[76] Their disagreement with the Stoics was thus not over the relative character of human freedom, but whether or not to subject the soul to 'Fate.' Indeed, what unites Carneades, Alexander of Aphrodisias, and the Middle Platonists, is their common polemical thrust against the Stoic doctrine of the universal causal chain. Alexander, for example, felt that the subtle distinctions made by the Stoics would undoubtedly be lost on the average man, who would easily succumb to the so-called 'lazy argument' (*argos logos*) and resign himself to Fate (*On Fate* 16). He claimed that the Stoic causal chain theory was too rigidly conceived and needed to be modified to allow for the contingent and the possible (*On Fate* 22–24). Not even the gods, he argued, would be able to predict the future completely, but would "foreknow possible things (*ta endechomena*) only as possible." (For Carneades'

---

[76] Philo, on the other hand, seems deliberately to avoid the Platonic notion that the soul may become diseased through the body (*Virt.* 13; *Spec* 3.10–11). He thus apparently held that a healthy soul can essentially overcome the diseased conditions of the body and that even when sick (i.e. when the *eukrasia* of its three faculties is defective), it still functions autonomously since its sickness is in no way caused by anything external (i.e. Philo seems to have believed it was defective when it entered the body). (Cf. *Her.* 294ff.)

similar view, see Cicero *De Fato* 14.32–33.) Aiming at practical results (a fact which is further indicated by his dedication of the treatise to the emperors Septimius Severus and Caracalla), Alexander's polemic seriously misrepresented the Stoic position, and the popular character of his argumentation becomes emphatically clear when he proceeds at one point to defend his free will theory by claiming after the manner of Pascal's famous 'wager' that "men would not err in their actions by reason of the conviction of free will (even if it did not exist). But, on the other hand, supposing that some power of free will does exist . . . if we are persuaded that we have no control over anything, we shall let many things go that should be done by us" (*On Fate* 21). What especially irritated the critics of the Stoa was the severity and explicitness of their theory of causality.

Although Aristotle probably did not believe that there was an element of absolute contingency in nature (the matter has been much debated), unlike the Stoics, he did not provide his readers with a clearly articulated doctrine of universal causality. Chrysippus, on the other hand, allegedly asserted that "*Heimarmenē* is a natural order of the whole by which from eternity one thing follows another and derives from it in an unalterable interdependence" (Aulus Gellius *Noctes Atticae* 7.2.3), and Cicero provides us with a Stoic statement which virtually anticipates Laplace: "If there were a man whose soul could discern the links that join each cause with every other cause, then surely he would never be mistaken in any prediction he might make" (*De Divinatione* 1.125–128): cf. Sambursky:58. It was these stark formulations which aroused the philosophical ire of their antagonists, even though the position of almost all parties on human freedom was substantially the same.

It is not at all surprising that the Stoic formulation appears to be reflected in Jewish literature, since both traditions were similarly motivated. Both taught an emphatic doctrine of Divine Providence, yet were at the same time keenly concerned with the ethical responsibility of the individual. Although loyal to traditional Judaism, Ben Sira often absorbs Hellenistic ingredients which are thoroughly assimilated to his own thinking. It has been correctly pointed out, for example, that the polarity principle which he uses to good advantage is a characteristically Greek pattern of thought,[77] that his statement that God is all (43:27) bears a distant echo of Stoic terminology, and that his doctrine of the purposefulness of all created things was common Stoic teaching.[78] It is therefore not unlikely that in dealing with the free will problem, which by that time had begun to become troublesome, he made use of the well-known Stoic line of argu-

[77] See Lloyd 1966.
[78] See Pautrel; Hengel:146–147; Marböck; Middendorp. For the question of freedom and determinism in Ben Sira, see Maier; Hadot.

ment. Hence he could maintain the wisdom tradition which emphasized predestinarianism, and still admonish his readers not to attribute their sins to God. If we turn to rabbinic discussions of this issue, we find a similar set of parameters. Although the statement of R. Ḥanina b. Ḥama (a Palestinian Amora of the first generation) that "everything is in the hand of Heaven except the fear of Heaven" (*BT Ber*. 33b) has often been taken to imply an absolute free will doctrine, it is most unlikely that this interpretation is correct. The rabbi probably only meant to imply that whereas God's Providence in every other aspect of human life involves direct guidance and at times even intervention, this does not apply to man's moral deliberations which ultimately depend upon the spiritual endowments initially bestowed upon him by God. On the other hand, the famous paradox of R. Akiba which asserts that "everything is foreseen (by God), yet man has the capacity to choose freely" (*M. Aboth* 3.15) is clearly a Jewish version of the well-known Stoic paradox, adapted to a predestinarian framework, in the same manner as the later version of St. Augustine, who could say paradoxically that man sins freely even though his sinning is predetermined by his irresistible concupiscence.[79] This predestinarian emphasis is made explicit in the following passage from the *Mekilta, Pisḥa* 16 (Lauterbach, 1. 134):

> We find that the names of the righteous and their deeds are revealed before God even before they are born, as it is said, "Before I formed thee in the belly I knew thee" (Jer 1:5). We thus learn that the names of the righteous and their deeds are revealed before God. How about those of the wicked? Scripture says: "The wicked are estranged from the womb" (Ps 58:4).

The splitting of mankind by God into two rival camps (as in Ben Sira and the Qumran scrolls) is also clearly stated in *BR* 3.8, Th-Alb:23:

> From the beginning of the world's creation God foresaw the deeds of the righteous and the deeds of the wicked. . . . "And God separated the light from the darkness," between the deeds of the righteous and the deeds of the wicked.[80]

---

[79] See Wolfson 1951:158–176.

[80] Cf. *Tanḥ Wayyeŝeb* 4: "So, too, said Adam before the Holy One blessed be He, Lord of the universe, Two thousand years before you created your world, the Tora was beside you, like a master workman, and in it is written, 'This is the procedure: when a person dies in a tent.' Had you not decreed death for man, would you have thus written in it? But you have come to hang the libel ['alilah] on me. This is meant by 'He is terrible in his doing ['alilah] toward the children of men.' [Ps 66:5]." (See Urbach: 227–253.) With this one may compare Al-Bukhari *Qadar* b.11: "The prophet of God said that Adam and Moses maintained a debate before God, and Adam got the better of Moses who said: Thou art that Adam whom God created and breathed into thee his own spirit, and made the angels bow down before thee, and placed thee in Paradise; after which, thou threwest man upon the earth, from the fault which thou didst commit. Adam replied: Thou art that Moses, whom

Although we need not look for Stoic influence in the Qumran scrolls, it will be instructive to compare their view with that of the Stoa.[81] The sectarians of Qumran, like the Stoics, accented the all-controlling hand of omnipotent Providence and tended to view all things from the divine perspective. Neither wished thereby to deny man's relative freedom, but their sharp focus on the divine rather than the human pole, made a harsh impression on their contemporaries. The Qumranites were prone to see man's spiritual capacities as the sheer gift of divine grace, without which he would be bereft of all power and of all good. Thus, even when emphasizing man's voluntary decision they couple it with the notion of its complete assimilation to the will of God. In much the same way, the Stoics, too, said in effect that man has freedom to the extent that he can consciously participate in the rational process of the cosmos, and that the height of that freedom is achieved when he consciously and voluntarily accepts his appointed lot within the scheme of things. The prayer of Cleanthes (*SVF* 1. 527; cf. 2. 975; 3. 191; M. Aurel. 5.27) is an expression of one who has achieved that supreme stage of freedom which marks the upper limit of man's rational activity. Precisely this sentiment is expressed by the Sufi mystic Rumi, when he says that freedom in the full sense of the term belongs only to the man who loves God so perfectly that his will is one with the divine will: "The word 'compulsion' makes me impatient for Love's sake, 'tis only he who loves not that is fettered by compulsion" (Nicholson 1950:162).

In short, within the framework of a theory of relative freedom, the concepts of determinism and predestination may freely coexist with that of voluntarism. God could be envisaged as predetermining man's nature to include the power of deliberative choice, though as its sovereign author he also determined its mode of operation and consequently all that resulted from it. It did not particularly bother most ancient writers, however, that God was thus ultimately responsible for man's moral delinquencies and the punishments that followed. They simply accepted this hard reality as part of the divine mystery. It was only under the impact of extraordinary

---

God selected for his prophecy and to converse with, and he gave thee twelve tablets. . . . Then how long was the Bible written before I was created? Moses said: forty years. Then said Adam: Didst thou see in the Bible that Adam disobeyed God? Yes. Dost thou reproach me on a matter which God wrote in the Bible before creating me?" (see E. Sell, *The Faith of Islam* [London, 1880] 173). The great mystical poet Ibn 'al-Farid of Cairo (1182–1235) cites the *Hadith* [a tradition associated with the prophet Muhammad] that when Allah created Adam, he drew forth his posterity from his loins in two handfuls, one white as silver and one black as coal, and said: "These are in Paradise and I care not; and these are in Hell and I care not" (*Ta'iya* 746).

[81] Cf. Hengel 1. 231.

catastrophes that their concepts of freedom and predestination became unglued and required new and more subtle interpretations to put them together again. Much of the perplexity of modern critics at the seeming contradictions discussed above has been occasioned by their attempt to view the ancient documents through the lenses of later theological conceptions and needs.

In the light of all this, the apparent contradictions[82] which are found in Wisd can be quickly dismissed. According to the author of Wisd the impious summoned 'Death' themselves and made a covenant with him (1:16) because they are worthy to be of his portion (2:24). The idea of being worthy of either Death or Wisdom occurs more than once. Wisdom goes about seeking them that are worthy of her (6:16). Grace and mercy belong to God's chosen. In contrast to the wicked, the righteous were found by God to be worthy of himself (3:5). Wisdom takes the initiative in making herself known (6:13), and without her no one can comprehend God's plan or will (9:13,17). Furthermore, were it not for divine grace (8:21), even one who possessed the best natural endowments (8:19–20) would be of no account and would be rejected from among God's children (9:4,6). For even the best body is perishable and it weighs down the mind by encumbering it with distracting cares. Hence, only when God sends his Wisdom down from its heavenly abode can man's paths upon the earth be made straight and salvation be achieved (9:17–18). Moreover, the children of the impious are wicked and their generation is accursed (3:12). Of the Canaanites, the author asserts that their seed was evil and their viciousness innate, and that their mode of thought would in no way vary to the end of time (2:10–11). Finally, we are told that a condign fate (*anangkē*) drew the Egyptians to their destruction (19:4). On the other hand, training, instruction, and pre-dawn vigilance seem to be prerequisites for the attainment of Wisdom (6:17; 8:18; 6:14–15), and men must seek her in prayer (8:21). The world's rulers are exhorted to seek wisdom if they do not wish to go astray (6:9). "The gift of grace," as Rylaarsdam puts it, "is thus not irresistible" (:97). The answer to these apparent inconsistencies is once again that man's freedom is only relative, and that from the higher perspective, it is God who in reality makes certain individuals worthy of Wisdom, and destines others for 'Death.' As in the Qumran scrolls, mankind is seen as split into two camps, those sought out by Wisdom and those who belong to the portion or party of Satan (3:24). But though relative, man's freedom enables him to participate actively in the divine plan, and from the more limited human perspective, it may be said that he chooses his own life-path (cf. Amir:329–335).

[82] See, for example, Dalbert:85.

VIII. WISDOM OF SOLOMON AND PHILO OF ALEXANDRIA

A glance at our commentary will quickly reveal a considerable degree of similarity in many of the literary and religious themes discussed both by Wisd and Philo, including a number of striking linguistic parallels. The most natural conclusion to be drawn is that the one is dependent on the other, but it is difficult to determine which of the two has the priority, nor can it be ruled out that both are drawing on common sources. Much depends on the date of Wisd, and we have already seen that this is a much debated issue. I have attempted to demonstrate that Wisd was written sometime between 30 BCE and 50 CE, and have further conjectured that it was likely to have been composed ca. 37–41 CE. If this dating should turn out to be correct, then we must conclude that (barring dependence on common sources) it was the author of Wisd who was deeply influenced by Philo rather than the other way around. In the absence of any degree of certainty with regard to the dating of Wisd, the best we can do is to show that the author of that book shares most of the major themes of Philo's philosophy, at the same time indicating those Philonic ideas which either make no appearance at all in his work or to which he only alludes. It need not, of course, surprise us if in a brief protreptic discourse such as Wisd, the author should have made his own selection from the vast Philonic corpus, omitting whatever did not particularly appeal to him or did not readily fit his purpose, and emphasizing those thoughts which did. In any case, pending ultimate decision of the issue of priority, it will be useful to provide a brief summary of those ideas shared by Wisd and Philo, so that the intimate connection between them may readily be ascertained.

The central figure of Wisd is Sophia, described as an 'effluence' or 'effulgence' of God's glory, and his agent in creation (7:25–6; 8:4; 9:1–2). Philo similarly speaks of Sophia as streaming forth from God (*Somn.* 2.221), and acting as the agent of his creation (*Her.* 199; *Det.* 54).[83] Wisd implies that Sophia contains the paradigmatic patterns of all things (9:9; cf. 9:8), a basic doctrine in Philo's cosmology. Both describe Sophia as 'bright' (*lampros*) (6:12; *LA* 3.35, 171; *Op.* 30; *Plant.* 40), and insist that she is more radiant than the sun (7:29; *Mig.* 40). Both employ sexual imagery in connection with the pursuit of Sophia, calling her 'bride' or 'spouse' (8:2; *Congr.* 74; *QG* 3.21; *Post.* 79), and speak of 'liv-

---

[83] In *LA* 1.63, Philo explicitly identified Sophia with Logos. Cf. Plato *Philebus* 30C. For a resolution of the apparent contradictions in Philo's descriptions of Logos and Sophia, see Drummond 2. 207–211; Wolfson 1948 1. 258–261; Früchtel:177–178. Wilckens points out that *sophia* is used by Philo over two hundred times, and *sophos* some three hundred times (*TDNT* 7. 500).

ing with her' (*symbioun*) (8:3,16; *Cont.* 68; *Ebr.* 30; *Congr.* 5) and enjoying 'kinship' (*syngeneia*) with her (8:17; *Op.* 14.5–6; *Spec.* 4.14; *QG*
2.60). Sophia anticipates those who desire her (6:17; *Congr.* 122–123;
Virt. 185), and those who seek her will not weary (6:14; *Deus* 160). She
has no fellowship with pining envy (6:23; *Prob.* 13–14; *Congr.* 13, 122–
123; *Spec.* 1.320–321; *QG* 4.103), and must be wooed guilelessly (7:13;
Ebr. 49; *Virt.* 62). Without Sophia man is nothing (9:6; *Post.* 136; *LA*
1.82) and all his words and thoughts are in God's hands (7:16; *Cher.*
71). She spans the whole range of scientific knowledge (7:17–21; *Det.*
87–88), *Congr.* 14–19), and is the source both of morality and prophecy
(8:7; 7:27; *LA* 1.63–65; *QG* 3.9; *Gig.* 23). Man must make his soul a
proper abode for Sophia (1:4; *Somn.* 1.149; 2.251; *QE* 2.51; *Virt.* 188;
Sobr. 62; *Praem.* 123), but the godless, inviting Death, make a pact with
him (1:16; *Her.* 45; *Deus* 56; *LA* 2.18; *Mig.* 16). True age is not shown
by length of days, but through wisdom and perfection (4:8; *Cont.* 67; *Abr.*
271; *Fug.* 146; *Her.* 290; *Sobr.* 7; *Deus* 120; *Plant.* 168). Sophia is a direct bearer of revelation, functioning through the workings of the human
mind, and supreme arbiter of all values (9:17; chap. 10; *Op.* 3; *Mos.*
2.52; *Abr.* 3–6, 34, 275–276; *Prob.* 62; *Virt.* 194).

The Wisd and Philo also have virtually identical theories of creation. God
created the world out of primordial matter (11:17; *Prov.* 1.22, Aucher;
Op. 8; *Spec.* 4.187; *Mos.* 2.267; *Spec.* 2.225), and Sophia, the agent of
creation, pervades it through and through (8:1; 1:7; *Conf.* 136; *Plant.* 9;
Mig. 181; *Deus* 35–36; *Mut.* 28; *Det.* 90). She is, however, both immanent and transcendent, and while pervading all things, yet remains in
unbroken union with God (7:24; 8:1,3; *Det.* 90; *Gig.* 27; *LA* 1.38).
Teleological and cosmological arguments are employed to demonstrate the
existence of God, the supreme artificer (*technitēs*) (13:1–9; *Spec.*
3.187–189; 1.33; *Praem.* 41–42; *Decal.* 60; *Abr.* 71; *LA* 3.97–103; *QG*
2.34; *Fug.* 12; *Post.* 28, 167; *Mut.* 54). All created things possess an inner
drive to preserve their being (1:14; *Aet.* 35; *Op.* 44), and the entire universe is held together by a continuous outward-inward pneumatic motion
or tension (8:1; 16:24; *Conf.* 136; *Plant.* 9; *Mig.* 181; *Deus* 35–36; *Mut.*
28; *Det.* 90). The universe is governed by mathematical law (11:20;
Somn. 2.193; *Prov.* ap. Eusebius *PE* 7.21.336b; *Her.* 152, 143) and certain miracles may be explained as due to a transposition of the elements
through the mathematical manipulation of their pneumatic tension
(19:18; *Mos.* 2.266–267). Creation itself serves as God's weapon in his
punishment of the wicked (5:17–23; *Mos.* 1.96).

The doctrine of immortality plays a central role in both Wisd and Philo.
The just live forever (5:15; *Jos.* 264); their souls, after death, are in
God's hands (3:1; *Abr.* 258; *QG* 1.85–86; 3.11; 1.16; *Her.* 280; *Fug.*
97). The godless, on the other hand, are spiritually dead even while physi-
cally alive (1:11; 3:24; *Det.* 49; *Fug.* 55; *Spec.* 1.345). The soul is a pre-

existent spiritual entity (8:19–20; *Somn.* 1.133–143; *Gig.* 6–9; *Plant.* 11–14), and its descent into a body has an oppressive effect upon it (9:13–18; *Gig.* 31; *LA* 3.152; *Det.* 16; *Spec.* 4.114; *Plant.* 25; *Her.* 295).

The fundamental principles of Wisd's ethical theory also find their analogues in Philo. Four cardinal virtues are enumerated (8:7; *LA* 1.71–72), and we are told that a man's true glory is his virtue (3:15; *Abr.* 31; *Deus* 117–118). There is an allusion to Virtue's contest (*agōn*) and her victory, undoubtedly meant to contrast the sage's contest for virtue with 'unholy' athletic contests (4:2; *Agr.* 113, 119; *Mut.* 106; *Abr.* 48). One should seek Wisdom for her own sake, but external goods will later follow in any case (7:7–11; *Her.* 285–286). Sophia is described as *philanthrōpos,* and God's mercy is a model-lesson for Israel, teaching them that the righteous man must be humane (1:6; 7:23; 12:19; 11:24,26; 12:1; *QG* 2.60; *Decal.* 41, 132–134; *Det.* 164; *Spec.* 4.14,73; 1.294,317; *Praem.* 92; *Congr.* 171). Without natural endowments, the mind cannot be brought to its fullness (8:19; *Her.* 212; *Fug.* 138; *LA* 3.96; *Sacr.* 7; *Congr.* 71, 122; *Mut.* 212; *Gig.* 2; *Cher.* 101; *Mos.* 1, 9, 15, 18), but training with Sophia is indispensable (8:18; *Congr.* 141). The wicked are in anguish because of their own conscience (17:11; *Det.* 22–23; *Fug.* 117–118, 131; *QE* 2.13; *Deus* 50, 126, 135–138, 182–183; *Decal.* 17; *Op.* 128; *Post.* 59; *Virt.* 206; *Jos.* 47–48). Man's freedom is only relative, and from the higher perspective, it is God who in reality makes certain individuals worthy of Wisdom, and destines others for 'Death', though, unlike the Qumran scrolls, both Wisd and Philo insist that God is not the *direct* author of either death or evil (2:24; 6:16; 3:5; 6:13; 9:13,17; 8:21,19–20; 9:4,6,17–18; 3:12; 2:10–11; 19:4; 6:17; 8:18; 6:14–15; 8:21; 6:9; *Deus* 47; Frag. 8, Harris; *Cher.* 128; *LA* 3.136; *Somn.* 2.253; and NOTE on 1:12.).

Finally, we may note several particularly striking similarities involving linguistic parallels. Both present elaborate critiques of idolatry (including the Mysteries), which follow the same pattern and employ similar vocabulary (13–15: see especially introductory NOTE to chap. 13; *Decal.* 52ff; *Spec.* 1.13ff; *Cont.* 3ff; *Congr.* 133; 12:3–18; *Spec.* 1.319–25). Both are equally exercised to justify the Israelites' conquest of Canaan (12:3–18; *Hypoth.* 356), and their despoiling of the Egyptians (10:17; *Mos.* 1.140–142), and both, again using similar language, accuse the Egyptians of practicing hostility toward strangers (19:13–14; *Mos.* 1.36). As we have pointed out in the commentary, however, these themes were commonplaces in Jewish-Hellenistic literature.

In spite of all the parallels noted, it is clear that the author of Wisd has omitted a number of characteristic Philonic conceptions. He makes at best only vague allusions to the Platonic theory of "Ideas" (cf. NOTE on 13:7), a core doctrine in Philo's thought, and makes no mention of God's "Powers." He completely ignores Philo's doctrine of the unknowability of

God's essence, and makes no attempt to correlate the Mosaic commandments with the philosophic virtues, or provide an explicit formulation of natural law (although there are hints that he may have held such a doctrine (see Introduction VII.6). There are vague references to 'spirits' (7:20,23), but nothing like Philo's elaborate doctrine of 'daemons' or 'angels' (*Somn.* 1.133–143; *Gig.* 6–9; *Plant.* 11–14). There is only a bare hint that he knows the Stoic doctrine of *eupatheiai* or rational emotions (8:16), which forms an important part of Philo's ethical theory. His emphasis on union with Sophia implies a preference for the contemplative over the practical life (see Introduction VII.5), but, unlike Philo, he does not describe the characteristic traits of the experience of mystical union. The closest he comes to Philo's concern with proselytism is his brief reference in 18:4 to Israel's mission to spread the teachings of the Torah to the rest of the world. More important, however, is the fact that he makes no use of Philonic 'allegory' proper, although he is fond of symbolic interpretations (10:7, Lot's wife is a symbol of the untrusting soul; 16:5–7, the bronze serpent is a symbol of salvation; 16:28, gathering the manna before the sun melted it, points to prayer at the crack of dawn; 17:21, the Egyptian darkness is equivalent to hell; 18:24, Aaron's robe is a symbol of the entire cosmos; cf. introductory NOTE to Section XXXV, 17:1 – 18:4). It may very well be that he considered allegory too farfetched a method of exegesis, and therefore deliberately avoided it.[84]

The reader of our commentary will also have noticed a great number of rabbinic parallels to many of the themes employed both by the author of Wisd and Philo, and may wonder to what extent rabbinic literature may have influenced these two authors. Unfortunately, it is virtually impossible to date much of the rabbinic material and it is exceedingly difficult to establish the extent of the penetration of Palestinian traditions into Alexandria around the turn of the first century CE. Lieberman, however, has pointed out (1968:29–31) that the "twelve questions" (*BT Nid.* 69b; *Tosef. Nega 'im,* end) which the Alexandrians put to R. Joshua b. Hananiah (first–second centuries CE) prove that they were great rabbinic scholars, and were familiar with rabbinic customs.[84a] It is therefore likely that Palestinian traditions had already penetrated into Alexandria during the period of Philo and the author of Wisd, and it should occasion no surprise if these authors had some knowledge of them. On the other hand, it must

[84] Cf. the detailed discussion of the relationship between Wisd and Philo provided by Larcher 1969:151–178. Larcher concludes that in spite of the many striking parallels between the two, there is no evidence that the author of Wisd knew and utilized the writings of Philo. It should also be noted that Wisd has a clear conception of a divine covenant with the Patriarchs (12:20–22; 18:20–25), whereas Philo either understands the *diathēkē* of the LXX as "testament," or has allegorized it to mean "grace" or "Logos." (See Jaubert 1963:375–442).

[84a] See also Lieberman in *The Jewish Expression,* ed. J. Goldin (New Haven and London, 1976): 119–133.

be remembered that it is unlikely that either Philo or the author of Wisd knew Hebrew, and whatever knowledge of Hebrew sources they acquired must have been through secondary channels. Moreover, many of the parallelisms noted may simply be due to similar modes of exegesis of the biblical text.

Finally, in assesssing Wisd's connections with earlier Jewish literature, it should be noted, that, as our commentary makes clear, there is a close affinity between Wisd's eschatology and that of I Enoch (esp. chaps. 91–104, mediated through a Greek translation) and the Dead Sea scrolls. Moreover, there is in Wisd a continuous reflection of ideas from Jewish-Alexandrian literature, such as Pseudo-Aristeas, the Testament of Orpheus, Aristobulus, Demetrius, Artapanus, Ezekiel the Tragedian, the third Sibylline Oracle, and III Maccabees. (For a detailed analysis, including an assessment of Wisd's dependence on Scripture, see Larcher 1969:85–151).

IX. PURPOSE

Although we have already alluded to the author's purpose in writing the book, and the audience for which it was intended, we can now spell it out in greater detail. The author is primarily addressing his fellow Jews in an effort to encourage them to take pride in their traditional faith. He seeks to convince them that *their* way of life, rooted in the worship of the One true God, is of an incomparably higher order than that of their pagan neighbors, whose idolatrous polytheism has sunk them into the mire of immorality. Moreover, he attempts to justify their present suffering through the promise of immortality as a reward for their steadfast perseverance in the pursuit of righteousness. His accusing finger is especially pointed, however, at the pagan kings (i.e. the Roman rulers) who have abandoned the principles of divine justice and who will therefore suffer the consequences of their lawlessnesss. Following the philosophy of Greco-Roman kingship tracts, he insists that the king, above all, must pursue wisdom (6:21,24). According to Diotogenes, for example, the king

> must excel the rest in virtue and on that account be judged worthy to rule, but not on account of his wealth, or power, or military strength. . . . He must separate himself from the human passions, and draw himself up close to the gods, not in arrogance, but in high-mindedness and in the exceeding greatness of his virtue. . . . Royalty is an imitation of divinity (Goodenough 1928:70–73). (Cf. Sthenidas of Lokri: The king must be a wise man, for so he will be a copy and imitator of the first God [Goodenough:73–74].)

At the same time, the author naturally tones down the divine nature to which the pagan writers sought to assimilate the king. Ecphantus had written:

> Accordingly the king, as a copy of the higher king, is a single and unique creation, for he is on the one hand always intimate with the one who made him, while to his subjects he appears as though he were in a light, the light of royalty. . . . And the one who thus lives in royalty ought to share in its immaculate nature, and to understand how much more divine he is than the rest (Goodenough:76–77; cf. NOTE on 7:1).

Wisd emphasizes instead the king's lowly and mortal origins (7:1–5; 9:5). Moreover, the Greco-Roman doctrines of kingship, as indeed all the high philosophic ideals of Greek thought, are identified by the author with the teachings of Judaism (cf. Pseudo-Aristeas 187–294). The Torah, as we have already seen, has been refracted through his sharp philosophical lense, with the result that it has taken on the appearance of a Middle Platonist world view with mystical overtones. In the author's mind, undoubtedly, the process is reversed, and he would prefer to say that the Platonic philosophy is in reality nothing but the traditional teachings of Moses. By presenting Judaism in intellectually respectable terms, he sought to shore up the faith against hostile anti-Semitic attacks from without and gnawing doubts from within, and through a determined counterattack against the immoral pagan world which he threatened with divine retribution, he attempted to revive the flagging spirits of his hard-pressed people. The philosophical sophistication of his discourse is cloaked by the omission of elaborate demonstrative argumentation or technical detail. Although the style is highly wrought, it is not until we reach the third part of the book that the author's rhetorical prowess is fully displayed. The writing is intense and frequently passionate, but also highly allusive, allowing those possessed of a wider range of learning to enjoy the full thrust of its intent. The audience addressed was thus considerably wider than could be reached by a narrow technical treatise, although it must have comprised a somewhat restricted and highly literate group of readers. Finally, it must be said that in addition to the social and political factors which stimulated the author to write the book, we must reckon above all with his unbounded love and enthusiasm for wisdom, which verged on the mystical, and lent to his writing (at least to its central part) an extraordinary degree of intellectual excitement as appealing today as when the book had first left its author's study.

X. MANUSCRIPTS AND VERSIONS

The basis for our translation is the text published by Joseph Ziegler as part of the Göttingen LXX in 1962. It is the first critical edition of Wisd established on the basis of the whole of the pertinent recorded evidence in manuscripts, citations, and versions, and is furnished with a full apparatus detailing that evidence and an introduction evaluating it. The text of Wisd is well preserved, in whole or in part, in five uncial Manuscripts: A or codex Alexandrinus (London, British Museum), fifth century; B or codex Vaticanus (Rome, Vatican Library), fourth century; C or codex Ephraemi Syri rescriptus (Paris, Bibliothèque Nationale), fifth century (a palimpsest written over by St. Ephraem in the twelfth century, and containing only a part of Wisd; the original was restored by a chemical process); S or codex Sinaiticus (the "Leningrad" text, now in British Museum), fourth century; V or codex Venetus (Venice, Library of St. Mark), eighth century (important for its witness to many Origenic readings). According to Ziegler, the original form of the text of Wisd is best transmitted through the uncials B and S (which are so closely related that Ziegler treats them as a single witness, B-S) and A. When these manuscripts agree and are followed by most of the minuscules, we may be certain of the correct reading of the text. The later uncials C and V are secondary, C mostly because it contains large gaps, and V because it has many variants due to scribal errors. The cursive manuscripts or minuscules are of later age and inferior (forty-five are listed by Ziegler). There are also several papyrus fragments (Antinoopolis Papyrus 8, third century; Vienna, Nationbibliothek, Sammlung Erzherzog Rainer, Litt. theol. 5, fourth–fifth centuries; and a fragment from Khirbet Mird), and two Greek commentaries (one by Malachias Monachus, from the fourteenth century, in the Escorial, which is important because he makes use of Greek manuscripts no longer available today; the other by Matthaeus Cantacuzenus, from the sixteenth century, in the Vatican Library, has no special significance).

The book is known as the *Wisdom of Solomon* in Manuscripts A, B, S, and V (B: *Sophia Salōmōnos;* A and V: *S. Solomōntos;* S: *S. Salomōntos*). In the Syriac Peshitta version, it is known as the "Book of the Great Wisdom (*Ḥakmeta Rabba*) of Solomon, son of David," and in the Arabic, as the "Book of the Wisdom of Solomon, son of King David, who ruled over the children of Israel." In the Vetus Latina, it is simply *Liber Sapientiae,* "Book of Wisdom." Cyprian, who quotes Wisd frequently, habitually refers to it as "Solomon," or the "Wisdom of Solomon," while Clement and Origen call it the Divine Wisdom. Epiphanius and John of Damascus call it *panaretos,* "[The Wisdom of Solomon] which comprises all virtues." (See Gregg 1909:ix–x; Ziegler 1961:17.)

For textual criticism, the most useful of the versions is the Vetus Latina, originating in Africa in the second half of the second century (and left untouched by Jerome when he redid the rest of the Bible). The monks of San Girolamo collected all the Manuscripts available for a new edition of the Vulgate and Ziegler was able in March 1957 to collate all this material for the Göttingen LXX. The importance of the Vetus Latina lies in the fact that it represents the reading of Greek manuscripts earlier than any that have come down to us. Of the Coptic translations, we have the complete text of Wisd only in the Sahidic dialect, transmitted through two good manuscripts from the sixth–seventh centuries, and published respectively by Paul de Lagarde and Sir Herbert Thompson. According to W. C. Till, this translation did not aim at a faithful rendering, but sought only to reproduce the sense of the original. In the Bohairic dialect we possess only the four lections from the liturgy of Holy Week, and it is clear that this version is dependent on the Sahidic. There are also three Syriac versions: (1) The Peshitta, found in Brian Walton's *London Polyglot* of 1657 (a reprint from Le Jay's Paris Polyglot of 1645). The latest edition is that of J. A. Emerton (Leiden, 1959). According to Holtzmann, this is hardly an exemplary translation. It is marked by many misunderstandings, unsuccessful etymological derivations, incorrect connections between single words and sentences, and false interpretation of ideas. These faults, however, are not sufficiently numerous to rob the translation of all value. (2) A Syro-Palestinian translation, of which only a few fragments survive. It is frequently dependent on the Peshitta and its text-critical value is slight. (3) Syro-Hexaplar translation, an important witness for the Origenic recension of the LXX (the fifth column of the Hexapla). The great value of the Hexaplaric minuscule 253 was first recognized by Nestle and Klostermann. Fragments of this translation are also available in citations made from it by Mar Išoʻdad of Merw (ca. 850). The Old Ethiopic (Geʻez) translation (published by Dillmann in 1894) conscientiously follows the word order and sentence structure of the Greek, often doing violence to Ethiopic idiom. In spite of this, many difficult words of the Greek are rendered freely. The Arabic translation (found in the *London Polyglot*) is often very free in its rendering of chaps. 10–19, but it alone has preserved the original reading of 5:7a. The Armenian version generally follows the uncials S and A (as against B). It is generally a good translation, with few additions or omissions. Still, Feldmann's assessment of it ("It follows the Greek word for word and reproduces it with great fidelity" 1902:34) is too favorable. Because of its free renderings, the Armenian version must be used with great caution for establishing conjectural readings on its basis. For more information, see Ziegler's introduction to his 1962 edition of Wisd.

XI. Status and Influence

In the Sinaitic and Alexandrian codices, Wisd stands between the Song of Songs and Ben Sira (in the Vaticanus, Job stands before it), with the prophetic books following. The sapiential books thus hold an intermediate position between the historical and prophetic. St. Jerome recognized that Wisd was a pseudepigraphon and placed it among those books formally excluded from the Canon (*PL* 28: 1241*ff*. See Larcher 1969:58). St. Augustine, who quotes Wisd close to eight hundred times, at first attributed it to Ben Sira but later declared the author to be unknown. In his *De Praedestinatione sanctorum* 14.26–29, he nevertheless came out in favor of the canonicity of Wisd, citing apostolic, liturgical, and traditional evidence. (See La Bonnardière:56–57.) The Council of Trent (1545–63) decided the issue of canonicity raised by the reformers by decreeing the book's canonical status. For the Greek Church, the Synod of Jerusalem in 1672 introduced Wisd and other deuterocanonical books to a place in Holy Scripture. "There appears to be no unanimity, however, on the subject of the canon in the Greek Orthodox Church today. Catechisms directly at variance with each other on this subject have received the Imprimator of Greek Ecclesiastical authorities and the Greek clergy may hold and teach what they please about it" (Metzger:195). From the time of the Reformation, Protestant Churches, following the example of Luther, separated the so-called Apocryphal books from the rest of the Scripture (Deane:37–39).[85]

The oldest reference to Wisd appears to be in Clement of Rome's *Epistle to the Corinthians* 27 (end of first century): "Who shall say unto Him, what hast thou done? or who shall resist the power of His strength?" (cf. Wisd 11:21 and 12:12). Irenaeus, in *Adv. Haer.* 4.38.3, alludes to Wisd 6:19 (cf. Eusebius *HE* 5.8.8), and according to Eusebius (*HE* 5.26) he mentioned, in a book now lost, Hebrews and Wisd, quoting passages from both. On the other hand, Wisd is explicitly mentioned in the *Muratori Canon* (a catalogue of the New Testament writings with comments on each of them published in 1740 by Muratori from an eighth-century palimpsest manuscript which he found in the Ambrosian Library in Milan. The catalogue originated in Rome ca. 200, and was originally composed in Greek and then translated into a barbarous Latin, with the result that much of it remains unintelligible): "Further an epistle of Jude and two with the title John are accepted in the Catholic Church, and the Wisdom written by friends of Solomon in his honor" (68–70. See E. Hennecke and W. Schneemelcher, *New Testament Apocrypha*, tr. and ed. by R. McL.

---

[85] "Among the several Protestant Churches today, none of which regards the Apocrypha as the Word of God, various degrees of respect are shown the Apocryphal books. The Church that accords them the greatest degree of consideration is the Anglican or Episcopal Church. The latest revision of the Lectionary used by the Anglican Church in Great Britain contains 44 Lessons from the Apocrypha, and the latest revision of the Lectionary used by the Protestant Episcopal Church in America contains 110 such Lessons" (Metzger:203). For a detailed discussion, see Metzgr:175–204; and Larcher 1969:63–84.

Wilson [Philadelphia, 1963] 1. 44–45).[86] In the African Church, the first explicit use of Wisd is in Tertullian *Adv. Valentinianos* 2.2, where the Sophia of the Valentinians is contrasted with the true Sophia of Solomon in Wisd.

R. M. Grant has suggested that Wisd 7:25 "was in the mind of the apologist Athenagoras, writing about the year 177 perhaps at Alexandria, when he first quotes Prov 8:22 and then states that the Holy Spirit which spoke in Proverbs is called by Christians 'an emanation of God, flowing forth and borne along as a ray of the sun' (*Legatio ad Graecos* 10.4). The mention of the sun's ray conceivably reflects a text of Wisd which, like that underlying the Armenian and Ethiopic versions, read *aktis* instead of *atmis.*" Clement of Alexandria treated Wisd as Scripture (*Strom.* 5.108.2) and says that it was written by Solomon (6.93.2). Although in his major writings he never alludes to Wisd 7:25–26, of which later Alexandrians made much use in their christological speculations, he does seem to refer to it in a fragment from his lost *Hypotypōses* (Frag. 23, Stählin, 3:202), where it is said that "the Son is also called Logos, but is a certain power of God such as an emanation of his Logos." According to Photius, Clement tried to demonstrate the truth of his statement by using "some expression of scripture," and he could have found *aporroia,* 'emanation,' only in Wisd 7:25.

Origen admits that Wisd "is not held by all to have authority" (*De Principiis* 4.4.6), but he himself uses it freely. Although he sometimes quotes it with the skeptical formula *hē epigegrammenē tou Solomōntos Sophia* (*In Iohannem Commentarius* 20.4; *Contra Celsum* 5.29), he also quotes it almost as frequently as a work of Solomon. Moreover, in *De Principiis* 1.2.9ff, he provides an elaborate explanation of the christological meaning of Wisd 7:25–26 (cf. *In Iohan. comment.* 13.25; *In Matt. comment.,* Klostermann:375–376). Similarly, Dionysius of Alexandria (third century), a pupil of Origen, appeals to Wisd 7:26 to prove a point: "Since Christ is 'radiance of eternal light,' he is absolutely eternal. For since the light always exists, obviously there is always radiance . . ." (*Refutation and Apology,* Feltoe:186, 11). And "since God is spirit . . . analogously Christ is also called 'vapor'; for, it says, he 'is a vapor of the power of

---

[86] The placing of Wisd among the writings of the New Testament is certainly surprising, and various efforts have been made to explain this anomaly. It has been suggested that, given the feeble abilities of the Latin translator, the text here probably represents an original Greek version which read as follows: *kai hē Sophia Salōmōnos hypo Philōnos eis doksan autou gegrammenē* ("The Wisdom of Solomon written by Philo in his honor"). (Already suggested by Tregelles [1867:53] and Bishop Fitzgerald, and later accepted by T. Zahn, M. J. Lagrange, G. Bardy, and B. Motzo. See Larcher 1969:40.) The author of the Canon thus placed Wisd among the writings of the New Testament, following a tradition according to which Philo had been converted to Christianity (Eusebius *HE* 2.17.1; Jerome *De Viris Illustribus* 11; Photius *Bibliotheca* 105. Cf. Motzo 1924:34; Bruns 1973:141–145).

God [Wisd 7:25]' (cf. 187, 17–21; Quasten 2. 105–106). So, too, Theognostus (most probably the successor to Dionysius as head of the school of Alexandria, which he directed from ca. 265 to 282) utilized Wisd in a fragment first published (in 1902) by Diekamp. There he says that the Logos is also called the radiance of the glory of God [Heb 1:3] and an unspotted mirror [Wisd 7:26]. In another fragment preserved by Athanasius (*PG* 25, 460c) he writes: "The *ousia* of the Son originated from the *ousia* of the Father like radiance from light, like vapor from water [Wisd 7:25–26]." (See Grant:70–82. For a detailed discussion of the use of Wisd in Patristic literature, see Larcher 1969:36–63).

Finally, we must note the close affinities that exist between the *Teachings of Silvanus* (late second or early third century), the only non-Gnostic document in Codex VII of Nag Hammadi, and Jewish wisdom literature, particularly The Wisdom of Solomon. Schoedel has pointed out that Silvanus is dependent on three main literary genres: classical Jewish wisdom, the Stoic-Cynic diatribe, and the Hellenistic hymn. We have already seen that these three literary strands are characteristic features of Wisd. In one of Silvanus' hymns we have an explicit allusion to Wisd 7:25–26: "For he [the Logos] is a light from the power of God, and he is an emanation of the pure glory of the Almighty, and he is the spotless mirror of the activity of God, and he is the image of his goodness. For he is also the light of the Eternal Light" (The *Teachings of Silvanus* 113. Robinson 1977:359).[87]

---

[87] There are other echoes of Wisd in Silvanus. At 114, for example, he writes: "But no one prevents him [God] from doing what he wants. For who is stronger than he that he may prevent him? (cf. Wisd 12:12; 11:21). There is also a reference to the symbolism of the High Priest's garment at 89: "I am giving you a high-priestly garment which is woven from every kind of wisdom" (cf. Wisd 18:24). At 115 we read: "Only the hand of the Lord has created all these things. For this hand of the Father is Christ, and it forms all" (cf. Wisd 11:17; 7:12). (There is a sorites at 108. Cf. Wisd 6:17–20.) Schoedel has also correctly noted that "it is only in writings like the *Wisdom of Solomon* and the *Teachings of Silvanus* that reasons regularly support exhortations in a way that goes beyond the older wisdom. The frequent repetition of the conjunction *gar* 'for' both in Silvanus and Wisd is quite different from the usage in classical Jewish wisdom. Not experience but a metaphysic determines the sentiments." See Schoedel:169–199.

SELECTED BIBLIOGRAPHY

Adinolfi, M.
1966 "Il messianismo di Sap. 2.12–20." Pages 205–217 in *Il Messianismo. Atti della XVIII settimana biblica*. Brescia: Paideia.

Albright, W. F.
1919–20 "The Goddess of Life and Wisdom," *AJSL* 36:258–294.
1946 *From the Stone Age to Christianity*. Baltimore.
1960 "Some Canaanite-Phoenician Sources of Hebrew Wisdom." Pages 1–15 of *Wisdom in Israel and in the Ancient Near East*, presented to H. H. Rowley, eds. M. Noth and D. W. Thomas. Leiden.

Allan, D. J.
1955 "The Practical Syllogism." Pages 325–340 in *Autour d'Aristote: receuil d' études . . . offert à Monseigneur A. Mansion*. Louvain.

Allevi, L.
1943 "L'ellenismo nel libro della Sapienza," *Scuola cattolica* 71: 337–348.

Alt, A.
1951 "Die Weisheit Salomos," *TLZ* 76: 139–143.

Amir, Y.
1977 "The Wisdom of Solomon and the literature of Qumran." Pages 329–335 in Proceedings of the Sixth World Congress of Jewish Studies, vol. 3. Jerusalem. (Hebrew section).

Antoine, P.
1930 "Sagesse palestinienne et sagesse alexandrine," *Revue apologétique* 50: 531–548.

Armstrong, A. H., ed.
1967 *Cambridge History of Later Greek and Early Medieval Philosophy*. Cambridge.

Attridge, H. W.
1976 *First-Century Cynicism in the Epistles of Heraclitus*. Missoula: Scholars Press.

Baars, W.
1970 "A Little-Known Latin Fragment of the Wisd. of Sol." *VT* 20: 230–233.

Bailey, C.
1928 *The Greek Atomists and Epicurus*. Oxford.

Baldry, H. C.
1965 *The Unity of Mankind in Greek Thought*. Cambridge.

Baumgartner, W.
1933 *Israelitische und altorientalische Weisheit*. Tübingen.

Beaucamp, E.
1968   *Les Sages d'Israel ou le fruit d'une Fidélité*. Québec.
1970   *Man's Destiny in the Books of Wisdom*. Translated by J. Clarke. New York.

Beauchamp, P.
1964   "Le Salut corporel des justes et la conclusion du livre de la Sagesse," *Biblica* 45: 491–526.
1967   "La Cosmologie religieuse de Philon et la lecture de l'Exode par le livre de la Sagesse: le thème de la manne." Pages 207–219 in *Philon d'Alexandrie: Colloques nationaux du Centre National de la Recherche Scientifique*. Paris.

Beel, A.
1931a   "Auctor libri Sapientiae," *Collationes Brugenses* 31: 134–142.
1931b   "Analysis libri Sapientiae," *Collationes Brugenses* 31: 196–202.

Bell, H. I.
1948   "Philanthropia in the Papyri of the Roman Period." Pages 31–37 in *Hommages à J. Bidez et à F. Cumont*. Brussels.
1957   *Cults and Creeds in Graeco-Roman Egypt*. Chicago.

Berwick, W. P.
1957   "The Way of Salvation in the Wisdom of Solomon." Dissertation, Boston University.

Bevan, E.
1927   *Later Greek Religion*. London and Toronto.
1940   *Holy Images*. London.

Bickerman, E.
1976   *Studies in Jewish and Christian History*, Arbeiten zur Geschichte des antiken Judentums und des Urchristantums, IX, Part I. Leiden.

Bidez, J., and F. Cumont.
1938   *Les Mages Hellénisés*, 2 vols. Paris.

Bigot, L.
1899–1950   "Sagesse (Livre de)," *Dictionnaire de Théologie catholique*, 14, 703–744. Paris.

Billings, T.
1919   *The Platonism of Philo Judaeus*. Chicago.

Blakeney, E. H.
1937a   *The Axiochus on Death an Immortality*, ed. with translation and notes. London.
1937b   *The Praises of Wisdom*. Oxford.

Blank, S. H.
1962   "Wisdom," *IDB* 4. 852–861. New York.

Blumenthal, F.
1913   "Der ägyptische Kaiserkult," *Archiv für Papyrusforschung* 5: 317–345.

den Boeft, J.
1970   *Calcidius on Fate*. Leiden.

Bois, H.
1890   *Essai sur les origines de la philosophie Judéo-Alexandrine*. Toulouse.

La Bonnardière, A. M.
    1970   *Biblia Augustiniana A. T. Le Livre de la Sagesse.* Études Augus-
           tiniennes. Paris.
Botte, P.
    1930   "La Sagesse dans les livres Sapientiaux," *RSPT* 19: 83–94.
    1932   "La Sagesse et les origines de la christologie," *RSPT* 21: 54–67.
Bourke, M. W.
    1963   "The Eucharist and Wisdom in I Corinth." Pages 367–381 in
           Studiorum Paulinorum. Congressus internationalis catholicus, 1961,
           I. Rome.
Bousset, W. [ed. H. Gressmann.]
    1966   *Die Religion des Judentums.* Reprint, Tübingen.
Boyce, M.
    1975   *A History of Zoroastrianism,* Handbuch der Orientalistik achter
           Band, erster Abschnitt, Lieferung 2, Heft 2A. Leiden.
Braun, F.-M.
    1962   "Saint Jean, la Sagesse, et l'histoire." Pages 123–147 in *Festschrift
           O. Cullmann,* Novum Testamentum Supplement 6. Paris.
Bréhier, E.
    1950   *Les Idées philosophiques et religieuses de Philon d'Alexandrie.*
           Paris.
Bretschneider, C. G.
    1804   "De Libri Sapientiae Parte Priore Cap. I–XI Duobus Libellis
           Diversis Conflata." Dissertation, Wittenberg.
Bruns, J. E.
    1973   "Philo Christianus: The Debris of a Legend," *HTR:* 141–145.
de Bruyne, D.
    1929   "Étude sur le texte latin de la Sagesse," *RBén* 41: 101–133.
Buber, M.
    1958   *Hasidism and Modern Man.* New York.
Bückers, H.
    1938   *Die Unsterblichkeitslehre des Weisheitsbuches,* ATA 13.4. Münster.
Bultmann, R.
    1910   *Der Stil der paulinischen Predigt und die kynisch-stoische Diatribe.*
           Göttingen.
Burgess, T. G.
    1902   "Epideictic Literature," *Studies in Classical Philology* 3: 89–261.
Burmester, O. H. E.
    1934   "The Bohairic Pericopae of Wisdom and Sirah," *Biblica* 15:
           451–462;
    1935   16: 25–32, 141–152.
Burrows, E.
    1939   "Wisd. 10.10," *Biblica* 20: 405–407.
Bussmann, C.
    1971   *Themen der paulinischen Missionspredigt auf dem Hintergrund der
           spätjüdisch-hellenistischen Missionsliteratur.* Frankfurt/Main.
Cabaniss, A.
    1956   "Wisd. 18.14: An Early Christmas Text," *VC* 10: 97–102.

Camps, G. M.
    1953   "Midras sobre la historia de las plaguas." Pages 97–113 in *Miscellanea Biblica B. Ubach*. Montserrat.

Cantore, E.
    1960   "La Sapienza biblica-ideale religioso del credente," *TivB* 8: 1–9, 129–143, 193–205.

Castellino, G.
    1961   "Il paganesimo di Romani 1. Sapienza 13–14 e la storia delle religioni." Pages 255–263 in *Studiorum Paulinorum Congressus Internationalis Catholicus II*. Rome.

Causse, A.
    1936   "L'humanisme juif et le conflit du judaïsme et de l'hellénisme." Pages 525–537 in *Mélanges Franz Cumont* 2. Brussels.

Cerfaux, L.
    1928   "Influences des mystères sur le judaisme Alexandrien avant Philon," *Le Muséon* 37: 29–88.

Ceuppens, F.
    1935   "De conceptu sapientiae divinae in libris didacticis A.T." *Angelicum* 12: 333–345.

Childs, B. S.
    1974   *The Book of Exodus, A Critical, Theological Commentary*. Philadelphia.

Cohn, J.
    1915   "Die Weltschöpfung in der Sapienz." Pages 22*ff* in *Festschrift zum Siebzigsten Geburtstag Jakob Guttmanns*. Berlin.

Collins, J. J.
    1972   *The Sibylline Oracles of Egyptian Judaism*. Missoula.
    1977a *The Apocalyptic Vision of the Book of Daniel*. Missoula.
    1977b "Cosmos and Salvation: Jewish Wisdom and Apocalyptic in the Hellenistic Age," *HR* 17.2: 121–142.

Colombo, D.
    1950–51 "Πνεῦμα Σοφίας eiusque actio in mundo in libro Sapientiae," *Schola Biblica Franciscana* 1: 107–160.
    1951   "Quid de vita sentiat Liber Sapientiac," *Schola Biblica Franciscana* (Liber Annuus) 2: 87–118.
    1953   *Doctrina de providentia divina in libro Sapientiae*. Rome.

Conze, E.
    1968   *Thirty Years of Buddhist Studies*. Columbia, S.C.

Conzelmann, H.
    1964   "Die Mutter Der Weisheit." Pages 225–234 in *Zeit und Geschichte. Dankesgabe an Rudolf Bultmann*. Tübingen.

Cumont, F.
    1942   *Recherches sur le symbolisme funéraire des Romains*. Paris.
    1949   *Lux Perpetua*. Paris.

Dähne, A. F.
    1834   *Geschichtliche Darstellung der jüdisch-alexandrinischen Religions-Philosophie* 2. 152–180. Halle.

Dalbert, P.
  1954 *Die Theologie der hellenistisch-jüdischen Missions-Literatur unter Ausschluss von Philo und Josephus.* Hamburg.
Delcor, M.
  1955 "L'immortalité de l'âme dans le Livre de la Sagesse et dans les documents de Qumran," *NRT* 77: 614–630.
Denniston, J. D.
  1952 *Greek Prose Style.* Oxford.
Didymos der Blinde
  1968 *Kommentar zu Hiob* I, ed. A. Henrichs, *Papyrologische Texte und Abhandlungen* 1. Bonn.
Diels, H.
  1958 *Doxographi Graeci.* Berlin.
Dillistone, F. W.
  1948 "Wisdom, Word and Spirit. Revelation in the Wisdom Literature," *Interpretation* 2: 275–287.
Dillon, J.
  1977 *The Middle Platonists.* London.
Dillon, R.
  1962 "Wisdom Tradition and Sacramental Retrospect in the Cana Account (Jn 2, 1–11)," *CBQ* 24: 268–296.
Dodds, E. R.
  1959 *The Greeks and the Irrational.* Berkeley.
——, ed.
  1963 Proclus, *The Elements of Theology.* Oxford.
Doignon, J.
  1956 "Sacrum, sacramentum, sacrificium dans le texte latin du Livre de la Sagesse," *REL* 34: 240–253.
Dörrie, H.
  1957 "Kontroversen um die Seelenwanderung im kaiserzeitlichen Platonismus," *Hermes* 85: 414–435.
Drouet, J.
  1966 *Le Livre de la Sagesse.* Paris.
Drubbel, A.
  1936 "Le Conflit entre la Sagesse profane et la Sagesse religieuse," *Biblica* 17: 45–70, 407–428.
Drummond, J.
  1969 *Philo Judaeus or the Jewish-Alexandrian Philosophy* 1. 177–229. Reprint, 2 vols. in one, Amsterdam.
Dubarle, A. M.
  1946 *Les Sages d'Israel.* Paris.
  1953 "Une Source du livre de la Sagesse?" *RSPT* 37: 425–443.
  1956 "Le Péché original dans les Livres sapientiaux," *RevThom* 56: 597–619.
  1964 "La tentation diabolique ($\pi\epsilon\iota\rho\acute{a}\zeta\omega$) dans le livre de la Sagesse (2,24)," in *Mélanges Eugène Tisserant* I. Rome.

Duesberg, H.
1939   *Les scribes inspirés* 2. 441–592. Paris.
————, and I. Fransen
1966   "Les mystères sauveurs de la Sagesse." Pages 753–865 in *Les scribes inspirés*, rev. ed. Tournai: Éditions de Maredsous.

Dulière, W. L.
1960   "Antinoüs et le livre de la Sagesse," *Cahiers Renan* 6: 1–24.

Dummer, J.
1965   "Epiphanius, Ancoratus 102, 7 und die Sap. Sal." *Klio* 43/5: 344–350.

Dupont-Sommer, A.
1935   "Les Impies du Livre de la Sagesse sont-ils des Épicuriens?" *RHR* 111: 90–112.
1939   "'Adam, Père du Monde' dans la Sagesse de Salomon," *RHR* 119: 182–203.
1949   "De l'immortalité astrale dans la Sagesse de Salomon," *REG* 62: 80–87.

Düring, I.
1961   *Aristotle's Protrepticus*. Studia Graeca et Latina Gothoburgensia 12. Göteborg.

Dürr, L.
1932   *Das Erziehungswesen im AT und im AO*, MVAG 36.2. Leipzig.
1938   *Die Wertung des göttlichen Wortes im AT und im Antiken Orient*, MVAG 42.1. Leipzig.

Eising, H.
1951   "Die theologische Geschichtsbetrachtung im Weisheitsbuch." Pages 28–40 in *Festschrift für M. Meinertz*. Münster.
1959   "Der Weisheitslehrer und die Götterbilder," *Biblica* 40: 393–408.

Eissfeldt, O.
1965   *The Old Testament: An Introduction*. Translated by P. Ackroyd. New York and Evanston.

Emerton, J. A.
1965   "Commentaries on the Wisdom of Solomon," *Theology* 68: 376–379.

Emmanuele da S. Marco
1963   "'L'ira di Dio si manifesta in ogni genere di empietà e di ingiustizia' (Rom. 1.18), confronti con Sap. cc. 13–15." Pages 259–269 in *Studiorum Paulinorum Congressus Internationalis Catholicas* 1. Rome.

Fakhry, M.
1970   *A History of Islamic Philosophy*. New York

Feldmann, F.
1902   *Textkritische Materialien zum Buche der Weisheit gesammelt aus der sahidischen, syrohexaplarischen und armenischen Übersetzungen*. Freiburg i.Br.

1909a "Zur Einheit des Buches des Weisheit," *BZ* 7: 140–150.
1909b "Die literarische Art von Weisheit Kap. 10–19," *TGl* 1: 178–184.

Festarozzi, F.
1967 "La Sapienza e la storia della Salvezza," *RivB* 16: 151–162.

Festugière, A. J.
1950 *La Révélation d'Hermès Trismégiste.* 4 vols. Paris.
1973 *Les trois "protreptiques" de Platon.* Paris.

Feuillet, A.
1955 "Jésus et la Sagesse divine d'après les Évangiles Synoptiques," *RB* 62: 161–196.
1966 *Le Christ Sagesse et Dieu d'après les Épitres pauliniennes.* Études Bibliques. Paris.
1966 "Mystique et Eschatalogie dans quelques écrits bibliques tardifs," *Revue du clergé africain* 21: 19–32. Mayidi (Kongo).
1970 "Les attaches bibliques des antithèses pauliniennes dans la première partie de l'Épitre aux Romains (1–8)." Pages 323–349 in *Festschrift Rigaux.*

Fichtner, J.
1933 *Die altorientalische Weisheit in ihrer israelitisch-jüdischen Ausprägung.* BZAW 62. Giessen.
1937 "Die Stellung der Sapientia Salomonis in der Literatur- und Geistesgeschichte ihrer Zeit," *ZNW* 36: 113–132.
1939 "Der AT-Text der Sap. Sal." *ZAW* 57: 155–192.

Finan, T.
1960 "Hellenistic Humanism in the Book of Wisdom," *ITQ:* 30–48.

Finkel, J.
1962 "The Alexandrian Tradition and the Midrash Ha-Neʻelam." Pages 77–103 in the *Leo Jung Jubilee Volume.* New York.

Fiorenza, Elisabeth S.
1975 "Wisdom Mythology and the Christological Hymns of the New Testament." Pages 17–41 in *AWJEC.*

Focke, F.
1913 *Die Entstehung der Weisheit Salomos.* FRLANT, n.s. 5. Göttingen.
1923 "Synkrisis," *Hermes* 58: 327–368.

Fransen, I.
1961 "Cahier de Bible: le livre de la Sagesse," *BVC* 38: 25–34.

Fraser, P. M.
1972 *Ptolemaic Alexandria.* 3 vols. Oxford:

Freudenthal, J.
1875–79 *Hellenistische Studien.* 3 vols. Breslau and Berlin.
1890 "Are There Traces of Greek Philosophy in the Septuagint?" *JQR* 2: 205–222.
1891 "What is the Original Language of the Wisd. of Sol.?" *JQR* 3: 722–746.

Friedländer, M.
1903 *Geschichte der jüdischen Apologetik.* Zürich.
1904 "Pseudo-Solomon." Chapter 6 in *Griechische Philosophie im Alten*

Testament: Ein Einleitung in die Psalmen und Weisheitsliteratur. Berlin.

Früchtel, U.
 1968 *Die kosmologischen Vorstellungen bei Philo von Alexandrien.* Leiden.

Furley, D. J.
 1967 *Two Studies in the Greek Atomists.* Princeton.

Gaiser, K.
 1959 *Protreptik und Paränese bei Platon.* Stuttgart.

Gallucci, D.
 1930 Filosofia greca e Sapienza ebraica. *Scuola cattolica* 58: 197–230; 336–361.

Gärtner, E.
 1912 *Komposition und Wortwahl des Buches der Weisheit.* Berlin.

Geffcken, J.
 1907 *Zwei griechische Apologeten.* Leipzig and Berlin.

Gemoll, W.
 1933 "Zur Sap. Sal." *Philologische Wochenschrift* 53: 108–110.

Genzmer, E.
 1952 "Pondere, numero, mensura." Pages 468–494 in *Archives d'histoire du droit oriental et Revue internationale des droits de l'antiquité* 1. Bruxelles.

George, S.
 1965 "Der Begriff Analogos im Buch der Weisheit." Pages 189–197 in *Parousia. Festgabe für Johannes Herschberger,* ed. K. Flasch. Frankfurt.
 1970 "Philanthropie im Buche der Weisheit," *BibLeb* 11: 189–198.

Georgi, D.
 1964 "Der Vorpaulinische Hymnus Phil. 2.6–11." Pages 263–293 in *Zeit und Geschichte. Dankesgabe am R. Bultmann,* ed. E. Dinkler. Tübingen.

Gfrörer, A.
 1895 *Philo und die jüdisch-alexandrinische Theosophie.* 2 vols. Stuttgart.

Gilbert, M.
 1970 "La Structure de la prière de Salomon," *Biblica* 51: 301–331.
 1971 "Volonté de Dieu et don de la Sagesse," *NRT* 93: 145–166.
 1973 *La Critique des dieux dans le livre de la Sagesse,* AnBib 53. Rome.

Gill, D.
 1965 "The Greek Sources of Wisdom XII 3–7," *VT* 15: 383–386.

Ginzberg, L.
 1954 *The Legends of the Jews.* 7 vols. Philadelphia.

Giussani, C.
 1896 *Studi Lucreziani.* Turin.

Goldin, J.
 1971 *The Song at the Sea.* New Haven and London.

Goldstain, J.
 1967 *Les Sentiers de la Sagesse.* Paris.

Goodenough, E. R.
  1928 "The Political Philosophy of Hellenistic Kingship," *Yale Classical Studies* 1: 55–101.
  1967 *The Politics of Philo Judaeus.* Reprint. Hildesheim.
  1969 *By Light Light.* Reprint. Amsterdam.
Göttsberger, J.
  1919 *Die göttliche Weisheit als Persönlichkeit im A.T.* Münster i.W.
Graetz, H.
  1888 *Geschichte der Juden,* 4th ed. Vol. 3.2, pp. 382–385, 611–613. Leipzig.
Grafe, E.
  1892 "Das Verhältniss der paulinischen Schriften zur Sapientia Salomonis." Pages 253–286 in *Theologische Abhandlungen C. v. Weizsäcker gewidmet.* Freiburg i.Br.
Grant, R. M.
  1967 *After the New Testament.* Philadelphia.
Gray, J.
  1965 *The Legacy of Canaan,* 2d rev. ed. Leiden.
Grelot, P.
  1958 "La Légende d'Hénoch dans les Apocryphes et dans la Bible," *RSR* 46: 5–26; 181–210.
  1961a "L'eschatologie de la Sagesse et les apocalypses juives." Pages 165–178 in *Mémorial A. Gelin.* Le Puy.
  1961b "Sagesse 10.21 et le Targum de l'Exode," *Biblica* 42: 49–60.
Gutman, Y.
  1958–63 *The Beginnings of Jewish-Hellenistic Literature.* 2 vols. Jerusalem. (Hebrew)
Hadas, M.
  1962 "Wisdom of Solomon." *IDB* 4. 861–863. New York.
Hadot, J.
  1970 *Penchant mauvais et volonté libre dans la Sagesse de Ben Sira.* Brussels.
Harris, J. R.
  1921–22 "Stoic Origins of the Prologue to St. John's Gospel," *BJRL* 6: 439–451.
  1922–23 "Athena, Sophia, and the Logos," *BJRL* 7: 56–72.
Hartlich, P.
  1889 *De exhortationum a Graecis Romanisque scriptarum historia et indole.* Leipziger Studien 11.
Headlam, W.
  1903 "Version. From the Wisd of Sol 18:5." *Classical Review* 17: 229–231.
Heinemann, I.
  1941 "Die Kontroverse über das Wunder im Judentum der hellenist. Zeit." Pages 170–191 in *Jubilee Volume in Honor of Professor Bernhard Keller.* Budapest.

1948 "Synkrisis oder aüssere Analogie in der Weisheit Salomos," *TZ* 4: 242–251.
1968 "Die griechische Quelle der Weisheit Salomos." Pages 136–153 in *Poseidonios' Metaphysische Schriften* 1. Reprint. Hildesheim.

Heinisch, P.
1908 *Die griechische Philosophie im Buche der Weisheit*, ATA 1. Münster i.W.
1910 "Das jüngste Gericht im Buche der Weisheit," *TGl* 2: 89–106.
1923 *Die persönliche Weisheit des A.T. in religionsgeschichtlicher Beleuchtung. Biblische Zeitfragen gemeinverständlich erörtert* 11, 1/2. Münster.

Heinze, M.
1872 *Die Lehre vom Logos.* Oldenburg.

Hengel, M.
1974 *Judaism and Hellenism.* 2 vols. Philadelphia.

Henrichs, A.
1975 "Two doxographical notes. Democritus and Prodicus on religion," *HSCP* 79: 92–123.

Hesselgrave, C. E.
1910 *The Hebrew Personification of Wisdom.* New York.

Hirzel, R.
1912 *Plutarch.* Leipzig.

Holtzmann, J.
1903 *Die Peschitta zum Buche der Weisheit: Eine kritisch-exegetische Studie.* Freiburg i.Br.

Huby, P.
1967 "The First Discovery of the Free Will Problem," *Philosophy* 42: 353–362.

Hulsbosch, A.
1952 "Die Eschatologie van het boek der Wijsheid," *Studia Catholica* 27: 113–123.
1963 *Sagesse créatrice et éducatrice.* Rome.

Imschoot, P. von
1934 "La Sagesse dans l'Ancien Testament est-elle une hypostase?" *Collationes Gandavenses* 21: 3–10, 85–94.
1938 "Sagesse et esprit dans l'Ancien Testament," *RB* 47: 23–49.

Jacobson, H.
1976 "Wisdom XVIII 9," *JSJ* 7.2: 204.

Jadrijevic, A.
1942 "Notae ad Textum Sap. 12.3–7," *VD* 22: 117–121.

Jaeger, H.
1961 "The Patristic Conception of Wisdom in the Light of Biblical and Rabbinic Research," *Studia Patristica et Neotestamentica* 4 (TV 79): 90–106.

Jaeger, W.
1948 *Aristotle.* Oxford.

Jaubert, A.
    1963   *La Notion d'alliance dans le Judaïsme*. Paris.
    1972   "Écho du livre de la Sagesse en Barnabé 7.9." Pages 193–198 in *Judeo-Christianisme. Recherches historiques et théologiques offerts en hommage Jean Daniélou. RSR Tome* 60. Paris.

Johannes, A.
    1909   "Der Begriff Weisheit im Buche der Weisheit," *Theologisch-praktische Monatsschrift* 18: 449–455.

Kaibel, G.
    1878   *Epigrammata Graeca*. Berlin.

Kasher, M.
    1955   "A Hellenistic Midrash on the Exodus from Egypt." Pages 145–160 in his *Haggadah Shelemah*. Jerusalem. (Hebrew)

Katz, P.
    1957   "The Johanine Epistles in the Muratorian Canon," *JTS* 8: 273–274.

Kaufmann, Y.
    1937–56   *History of the Israelite Religion*. 8 vols. Tel Aviv. (Hebrew)

Kayatz, C.
    1966   *Studien zu Proverbien 1–9*. Neukirchen-Vluyn.

Keel, O.
    1974   *Die Weisheit spielt vor Gott*. Fribourg.

Keller, C. A.
    1970   "Glaube in der Weisheit Salomos." Pages 11–20 in *Festschrift Eichrodt*. Zürich.

Keyser, P. G.
    1971   "Sapientia Salomonis und Paulus." Dissertation, Halle.

Klasen, F.
    1878   *Die alttestamentliche Weisheit und der Logos der jüdisch-alexandrinischen Philosophie*. Freiburg i.B.

Klausner, J.
    1951   *History of the Second Commonwealth* 5. 54–65. Jerusalem. (Hebrew)

Kleucker, J. F.
    1795   *Solomonische Denkwürdigkeiten*. Riga.

Knox, W. L.
    1937   "The Divine Wisdom," *JTS* 38: 230–237.
    1939   *St. Paul and the Church of the Gentiles*. Cambridge.

Köberlein, E.
    1962   *Caligula und die ägyptischen Kulte*. Meisenheim am Glan, Germany.

Kohler, K.
    1906   "Wisdom of Solomon." In *JE* 12. 538–540.

Kroon, J.
    1922a   "Sanabiles fecit nationes (Sap. 1.14)," *VD* 2: 238–240.
    1922b   "Esse continens," *VD* 2: 264–269.

Kübel, F. E.
    1865   "Die ethischen Grundanschaungen der Weisheit Salomos," *TSK* 38: 690–722.

Kuhn, G.
  1929 "Beiträge zur Erklärung des Buches der Weisheit," *ZNW* 28: 334–341.
  1931 "Exegetische und testkirtische Anmerkungen zum Buch der Weisheit," *TSK* 103: 445–452.
Kustas, G. Z.
  1976 Diatribe in Ancient Rhetorical Theory. Twenty-second Colloquy of the Center for Hermeneutical Studies. The Graduate Theological Union and The University of California. Berkeley.
Lacon, F. M., and J. G. Gourbillon
  1966 "La Sagesse, une source d'immortalité," *Évangile* 61: 22–32.
Lagrange, M. J.
  1907 "Le Livre de la Sagesse, sa doctrine des fins dernières," *RB* 4: 85–104.
  1930 "Les cultes hellénistiques en Égypte et le Judaisme," *RevThom* 309–328.
Lambert, W. G.
  1960 *Babylonian Wisdom Literature.* Oxford.
———, and A. R. Millard
  1969 *Atra-Ḫasīs, The Babylonian Story of the Flood.* Oxford.
Lampe, G. W. H.
  1961 *A Patristic Greek Lexicon.* Oxford.
Lang, B.
  1972 "Das jüdische und das cristliche Ghetto." Pages 69–74, 88 in *Am Tisch des Wortes,* eds. K. Jockwig and W. Massa, Neue Reihe 123. Stuttgart.
  1975 *Frau Weisheit.* Düsseldorf.
Lange, S.
  1936 "The Wisdom of Solomon and Plato." *JBL* 55: 293–306.
Langen, J.
  1875 "Die Anthropologie des Buches der Weisheit," *Katholik* 2: 225–250.
Laporte, J.
  1975 "Philo in the Tradition of Biblical Wisdom Literature." Pages 103–141 in *AWJEC.*
Larcher, C.
  1954a "La connaissance naturelle de Dieu d'après le livre de la Sagesse," *Lumière et Vie* 14: 53–62. Lyon.
  1954b "De la nature à son auteur d'après le livre de la Sagesse 13.1–9," *Lumière et Vie* 41: 197–206.
  1960 "L'Origine du pouvoir d'après le livre de la Sagesse," *Lumière et Vie* 18: 84–98.
  1969 *Études sur le Livre de la Sagesse.* Paris.
Lattimore, R.
  1962 *Themes in Greek and Latin Epitaphs.* Urbana.
Learoyd, W. H. A.
  1939–40 "The Envy of the Devil in Wisd. 2.24," *ExpT* 51: 395–396.

Leisegang, H.
    1927   "Sophia." In PW 3. 1019–1039.
di Lella, A. A.
    1966   "Conservative and Progressive Theology: Sirach and Wisdom."
           CBQ 28: 139–154.
Licht, J.
    1957   "The Concept of Nedabah in the Dead Sea Scrolls." Pages 77–84 in
           Studies in the Dead Sea Scrolls, ed. J. Liver. Jerusalem. (Hebrew)
Lieberman, S.
    1942   Greek in Jewish Palestine. New York.
    1950   Hellenism in Jewish Palestine. New York.
    1968   Siphre Zutta (The Midrash of Lydda). New York. (Hebrew)
    1974   Texts and Studies. New York.
Lincke, L.
    1903   Samaria und seine Propheten. Tübingen.
Lloyd, G. E. R.
    1966   Polarity and Analogy. Cambridge.
    1968   Aristotle. Cambridge.
Loening, R.
    1903   Geschichte der strafrechtlichen Zurechnungslehre 1. Die
           Zurechnungslehre des Aristoteles. Jena.
Long, A. A.
    1970   "Stoic Determinism and Alexander of Aphrodisias' De Fato,"
           Archiv für Geschichte der Philosophie 52: 247–268.
Long, A. A., ed.
    1971   Problems in Stoicism. London.
Luck, U.
    1967   "Weisheit und Leiden. Zum problem Paulus und Jakobus," TLZ
           92: 253–258.
Lütgert, W.
    1906   Das Problem der Willensfreiheit in der vorchristlichen Synagoge.
           Beiträge zur Förderung christlicher Theologie 10. 2. Gütersloh.
Lyonnet, S.
    1958   "Le sens de πειράζειν en Sap. 2.24 et la doctrine du péché original,"
           Biblica 39:27–33.
MacDonald, D. B.
    1965   The Hebrew Philosophical Genius. Reprint. New York.
Maclachlan, H.
    1920   St. Luke, the Man and his Work. Manchester. Pp. 244–256 (on
           Luke and Wisd).
Mack, B. L.
    1973   Logos und Sophia. Studien zur Umwelt des N.T. Bd. 10. Göttingen.
Maier, G.
    1971   Mensch und freier Wille. Tübingen.
Maly, E. H.
    1962   The Book of Wisdom. New York.
Marböck, J.
    1971   Weisheit im Wandel. Bonn.

Marchel, W.

1963 *Abba, Père! La Prière du Christ et des Chrétiens, AnBib.* Rome. (Pages 73–81 on Wisdom of Solomon.)

Marcus, R.

1950 "On Biblical Hypostases of Wisdom," *HUCA* 23: 157–171.

Margoliouth, D. S.

1890 "Was the Book of Wisdom Written in Hebrew?" *JRAS* 6: 263–297.

1900 "The Wisdom of Ben Sira and the Wisdom of Solomon," *Expositor* 1: 141–160, 186–193.

Mariès, L.

1908 "Remarques sur la forme poétique du livre de la Sagesse," *RB* 5: 251–257.

1935 "Rhythmes quantitatifs dans le livre de la Sagesse," *CRAI:* 104–117.

Marmorstein, A.

1950 *Studies in Jewish Theology,* eds. J. Rabbinowitz and M. Lowe. London.

Marx, A.

1921 "An Aramaic Fragment of the Wisdom of Solomon," *JBL* 40: 57–69.

Menzel, P.

1889 *Der griechische Einfluss auf Prediger und Weisheit Salomos.* Halle.

Merrill, E. H.

1975 *Qumran and Predestination.* Leiden.

Metzger, B. M.

1957 *An Introduction to the Apocrypha.* New York.

Middendorp, T.

1973 *Die Stellung Jesu Ben Siras zwischen Judentum und Hellenismus.* Leiden.

Milik, J. T.

1976 *The Book of Enoch.* Oxford.

Mohrmann, C.

1952 "A propos de Sap. 15.18," *VC* 6: 28–36.

Moore, G. F.

1950 *Judaism in the First Centuries of the Christian Era.* 3 vols. Cambridge, Mass.

Motzo, B.

1924 *Saggi di storia e letteratura giudeo-ellenistica.* Firenze.

1926 "L'età e l'autore della Sapienza," *Ricerche religiose* 2: 39–44.

Moulton, R. G.

1903 *Ecclesiastes and the Wisdom of Solomon.* New York.

Murphy, R. E.

1968 "To Know your Might is the Root of Immortality," *CBQ* 25: 88–93.

Nachtigal, J. C. C.
   1799   *Die Versammlungen der Weisen.* 2 Teil: *Das Buch der Weisheit.* Halle.
Newman, H. L.
   1931   "The Influence of the Book of Wisdom on Early Christian Writings," *Crozer Quarterly* 8: 361–372.
Nicholson, R. A.
   1950   *Rumi Poet and Mystic.* London.
   1963   *The Mystics of Islam.* London.
Nickelsburg, G. W. E., Jr.
   1972   *Resurrection, Immortality, and Eternal Life in Intertestamental Judaism.* Cambridge.
Ninot, S. P. Y.
   1972   *La Palabra de Dios en los libros Sapienciales.* Barcelona.
Nock, A. D.
   1966   *Sallustius.* Reprint, Hildesheim.
   1972   *Essays on Religion and the Ancient World,* ed. Z. Stewart. 2 vols. Oxford.
Norden, E.
   1913   *Agnostos Theos.* Leipzig und Berlin.
Nucho, F.
   1966   *Berdyaev's Philosophy.* New York.
Oesterly, W. O. E., and G. H. Box
   1911   *The Religion and Worship of the Synagogue.* London.
Pack, R. A.
   1937   "A Passage in Alexander of Aphrodisias Relating to the Theory of Tragedy," *AJP* 58: 418–436.
Palm, J.
   1955   *Über Sprache und Stil des Diodorus von Sizilien.* Lund.
Pautrel, R.
   1963   "Ben Sira et le Stoicisme," *RSR* 51: 535–549.
Peek, W.
   1960   *Griechische Grabgedichte.* Darmstadt.
Pelletier, A.
   1962   *Flavius Josèphe, adaptateus de la Lettre d'Aristée.* Paris.
Pépin, J.
   1976   *Mythe et Allégorie.* Paris. Nouvelle édition, revue et augmentée.
Perdue, L. J.
   1977   *Wisdom and Cult.* Missoula: Scholars Press.
Perez, F.
   1871   *La Sapienza di Salomone, saggio storico-critico.* Firenze.
   1883   *Sopra Filone Alessandrino e il suo libro detto la sapienza di Salomone.* Palermo.
Peters, N.
   1916   "Ein hebräischer, alphabetischer Psalm in der Weisheit Salomos c. 9," *BZ* 14: 1–14.

Peterson, E.
    1923 "Der Gottesfreund. Beiträge zu Gesch. eines religösen Terminus," *ZKG*, n.f. 5, 42: 161–202.

Pfeiffer, R. H.
    1949 *History of New Testament Times with an Introduction to the Apocrypha*. New York.

Pfitzner, V. C.
    1967 *Paul and the Agon Motif*. Leiden.

Pflaum, H. G.
    1962 "Les Sodales Antoniniani." *CRAI:* 118–121.

Pfleiderer, E.
    1886 *Die Philosophie des Heraklit vom Ephesus im Lichte der Mysterienidee*. Berlin.

Philonenko, M.
    1958 "Le Maître de justice et la Sagesse de Salomon," *TZ* 14: 81–88.

des Places, E.
    1959 "Un Emprunte de la Sagesse (11.20–21) aux Lois de Platon," *Biblica* 40: 1016–1017.
    1965 *De Libro Sapientiae* (13–15). Rome: Pontificio Instituto Biblico. (Private printing)
    1969 "Le Livre de la Sagesse et les influences grecques," *Biblica* 50: 536–542.

Planas, F.
    1948 "Como la sombra (Sap. 5.8–14)," *CB* 5: 248–252.

Pohlenz, M.
    1940 *Grundfragen der stoischen Philosophie*. Göttingen.
    1955 *Die Stoa*. 2 vols. Göttingen.
    1966 *Freedom in Greek Life and Thought*. Dordrecht.

Porter, F. C.
    1908 "The Preexistence of the Soul in the Book of Wisdom and in the Rabbinical Writings," *AJT* 12: 53–118.

Preuss, H. D.
    1971 *Verspottung fremder Religionen im Alten Testament*. Stuttgart, Berlin, Köln, Mainz.

Prigent, P.
    1961 *Les Testimonia dans le christianisme primitif: L'Épitre de Barnabé I–XVI et ses sources*. Paris.

Purinton, C. E.
    1928 "Translation Greek in the Wisdom of Solomon," *JBL* 47: 276–304.

Quasten, J.
    1950 *Patrology*. 3 vols. Utrecht-Antwerp.

von Rad, G.
    1972 *Wisdom in Israel*. Nashville and New York.

Rankin, O. S.
    1954 *Israel's Wisdom Literature*. Reprint, Edinburgh.

Reese, J. M.
  1965 "Plan and Structure in the Book of Wisdom," *CBQ* 27: 391–399.
  1970 *Hellenistic Influence on the Book of Wisdom and Its Consequences.*
        Rome.
Reesor, M.
  1965 "Fate and Possibility in Early Stoic Philosophy." *Phoenix* 19:
        288–297.
Reusch, F. H.
  1861 *Observationes criticae in librum Sapientae.* Bonn.
Ricken, F.
  1968 "Gab es eine hellenistische Vorlage für Weisheit 13–15?" *Biblica*
        49: 54–86.
Rieth, O.
  1933 *Grundbegriffe der stoischen Ethik.* Berlin.
Ringgren, H.
  1947 *Word and Wisdom.* Lund.
  1963 *The Faith of Qumran.* Philadelphia.
Risberg, B.
  1913 "Textkritische und exegetische Anmerkungen zur Weisheit
        Salomos," *ZAW* 33: 206–221.
Robinson, J.
  1975 "Jesus as Sophos and Sophia: Wisdom Tradition and the Gospels."
        Pages 1–16 in *AWJEC.*
Robinson, J. M., ed.
  1977 *The Nag Hammadi Library.* New York.
Robinson, T. M.
  1970 *Plato's Psychology.* Toronto.
Romaniuk, C.
  1967a "Le Traducteur grec du livre de Jésus Ben Sira n'est-il pas l'auteur
         du livre de la Sagesse?" *RivB* 15: 163–170.
  1967b "More about the Author of the Book of Wisdom. An Answer to
         Prof. G. Scarpat," *RivB* 15: 543–545.
  1967–68 *Le Livre de la Sagesse dans le Nouveau Testament. NTS* 14:
           498–514.
  1968a Liber Sapientiae qua lingua ubi scriptus sit. *VD* 46: 175–180.
  1968b *Eschatologia Ksiegi Madrosci.* Collectanea Theologica (Wars-
         zawa) 38: 89–102.
  1969 "Die Eschatologie des Buches Weisheit." *BibLeb* 10: 198–211.
Rosik, S.
  1971 "Death and Survival after Death in Wisdom of Solomon 1–5."
        Master's Thesis, Hebrew University, Jerusalem. (Hebrew)
Ruppert, L.
  1972 *Der leidende Gerechte. Forschung zur Bibel* 5. Würzburg.
Rylaarsdam, J. C.
  1946 *Revelation in Jewish Wisdom Literature.* Chicago.
Sambursky, S.
  1959 *Physics of the Stoics.* London.
Scarpat, G.
  1967 "Ancora sull' autore del Libro della Sapienza," *RivB* 15: 171–189.

Scazzocchio, L.
1962 "Tobia, Sapienza di Salomone alla luce dei Testi di Qumran," *RSO* 37: 199–209.
Schechter, S.
1936 *Some Aspects of Rabbinic Theology.* New York.
Schencke, W.
1913 *Die Chokma in der jüdischen Hypostasenspekulation.* Kristiania (Oslo).
Schmieder, H. E.
1853 "Über das Buch der Weisheit." In *Vorträge auf Veranstaltung des Evangelischen Vereins für kirchliche Zwecke zu Berlin.* Berlin.
Schmitt, A.
1976 *Entrückung, Aufnahme, Himmelfahrt. Forschungen zum Bibel,* 2d ed. Stuttgart: Verlag Katholisches Bibelwerk.
1977 "Struktur, Herkunft und Bedentung der Beispielreihe in Weish 10," *BZ* 21: 1–22.
Schoedel, W. R.
1975 "Jewish Wisdom and the Formation of the Christian Ascetic." Pages 169–199 in *AWJEC.*
Scholem, G. G.
1960 *Jewish Gnosticism, Merkabah Mysticism, and Talmudic Tradition.* New York.
Schürer, E.
1891 *A History of the Jewish People* II, III. 230–237. New York.
Schütz, R.
1935 *Les idées eschatologiques du livre de la Sagesse.* Strasbourg.
Scroggs, R.
1967–68 "Paul: Σοφός and πνευματικός," *NTSt* 14: 33–35.
Seeligmann, I. L.
1958 "Deiksai autō phōs," *Tarbiz* 327: 127–141.
Shestov, L.
1932 *In Job's Balance.* London.
Siebeneck, R. T.
1960 "The Midrash of Wisd. 10–19," *CBQ* 22: 176–182.
Siegfried, C.
1970 *Philo von Alexandria als Ausleger des A.T.* Reprint, Amsterdam.
Skehan, P. W.
1938 "The Literary Relationship between the Book of Wisdom and the Protocanonical Wisdom Books of the Old Testament." S.T.D. Thesis Catholic University, Washington, D.C.
1945 "The Text and Structure of the Book of Wisdom," *Traditio* 3: 1–12.
1971 *Studies in Israelite Poetry and Wisdom,* CBQ Monograph Series 1. Washington, D.C.
Smallwood, E. M.
1976 *The Jews under Roman Rule.* Leiden.
Smith, J.
1949 "De Interpretatione Sap. 13.9," *VD* 27: 287–290.

Smith, M.
1972   "Pseudepigraphy in the Israelite Literary Tradition." Pages 191–227
in *Pseudepigrapha* I, ed. K. von Fritz. Geneva.

Sparks, I. A.
1972   "A Fragment of Sapientia Salomonis from Oxyrhyncus." *JSJ* 3.2:
149–152.

Speiser, E. A.
1923–24   "The Hebrew Origin of the First Part of the Book of Wisdom,"
JQR 14: 455–487.

Spicq, C.
1958   "La Philanthropie hellénistique, vertu divine et royale," *ST* 12:
169–191.

Stein, E.
1934   "Ein jüdisch-hellenistischer Midrasch über den Auszug aus Aegyp-
ten," *MGWJ* 78: 558–575.

Stern, M.
1976   *Greek and Latin Authors on Jews and Judaism.* Jerusalem.

Strobel, A.
1967   *Die Weisheit Israel.* München.

Suggs, M. J.
1957   "Wisdom of Solomon 2.10 – 5.1: A Homily Based on the Fourth
Servant Song," *JBL* 76: 26–33.
1970   *Wisdom, Christology, and Law in Matthew's Gospel.* Cambridge.

Sweet, J. P. M.
1965   "The Theory of Miracles in the Wisdom of Solomon." Pages
113–126 in *Miracles,* ed. C. F. D. Moule. London.

Tarán, L.
1975   *Academica: Plato, Philip of Opus and the Pseudo-Platonic Epinomis.* Philadelphia.

Ta-Shema, I.
1968   "Mamzer Eino Hai." Pages 33–36 in *Beth Mikra.* (Hebrew)

Taylor, L. R.
1931   *The Divinity of the Roman Emperor.* Middletown, Conn.

Taylor, R.
1966   "The Eschatological Meaning of Life and Death in the Book of
Wisdom 1–5," *ETL* 42: 72–137.

Tcherikover, A.
1945   "III Macc as an Historical Source of Augustus' Age," *Zion* 10:
1–20. (Hebrew)

Tcherikover, V. A., and A. Fuks, eds.
1957   *Corpus Papyrorum Judaicarum,* 3 vols. Cambridge, Mass.

Techert, M.
1930   "La Notion de la Sagesse dans les trois premiers siècles de notre
ère," *Archiv für Geschichte der Philosophie* 39: 9ff.

Tennant, F. R.
1901   "The Teaching of Ecclesiasticus and Wisdom on the Introduction of
Sin and Death," *JTS* 2: 207–223.

Thackeray, H. St. J.
1900   *The Relation of St. Paul to Contemporary Jewish Thought.* London.
1904–05   "Rhythm in the Book of Wisdom." *JTS* 6: 232–237.
Theiler, W.
1966   *Forschungen zum Neuplatonismus.* Berlin.
Thesleff, H.
1965   *The Pythagorean Texts of the Hellenistic Period.* Abo (Turku),
        Finland.
Thielmann, P.
1893   "Die lateinische Übersetzung des Buches der Weisheit," *Archiv für
        lateinische Lexikographie und Grammatik* 8: 235–277.
Thils, G.
1947   "De libro Sapientiae," *Collectanea Mechliniensia* 32, n.s. 17:
        270–274.
Till, W. C.
1955   "Die koptischen Versionen der Sap. Sal." *Biblica* 36: 51–70.
Tobac, E.
1926   *Les cinqs livres de Salomon.* Bruxelles.
Tregelles, S. P.
1867   *Canon Muratorianus.* Oxford. (Pages 51–55 on Wisd.)
Treves, M.
1962   "Il Libro della Sapienza," *Parola del Passato* 17: 192–201.
van Unnik, W. C.
1971   'Αφθόνως μεταδίδωμι. Verhandelingen der Koninklijke Vlaamse
        Akademie van Wetenschappen, Letteren en Schone Kunsten, Klasse
        der Letteren. Brussels.
1972   "Der Neid in der Paradiesgeschichte nach einigen gnostischen
        Texten." Pages 120–132 in *Essays on the Nag Hammadi Texts in
        Honour of Alexander Böhlig,* ed. M. Krause. Leiden.
1973   *De ἀφθονία van God in de oudchristelijke literatuur.* Amsterdam,
        London.
Urbach, E. A.
1969   *Ḥazal.* Jerusalem. (Hebrew)
Usener, H.
1966   *Epicurea.* Reprint of 1887 ed. Stuttgart.
Vacherot, E.
1965   *Histoire critique de l'École d'Alexandrie.* Reprint, Amsterdam.
Vanhoye, A.
1962   "Mesure ou démesure en Sap. 12.22," *RSR* 50: 530–537.
de Vaux, R.
1939   Review of J. Fichtner, *Weisheit Salomos. RB* 48: 444–447.
Vellas, B.
1961   *The Influence of Greek Philosophy on the Book of Wisdom.* Athens.
        (Greek: Ἡ ἐπίδρασις τῆς Ἑλληνικῆς φιλοσοφίας ἐπὶ τοῦ βιβλίου τῆς
        Σοφίας Σολομῶντος.)

Verbeke, G.
1945 *L'évolution de la doctrine du Pneuma du Stoicisme à St. Augustin.* Paris-Louvain.
1968 Aristotelisme et Stoicisme dans le De Fato d'Alexandre d'Aphrodisias. *Archiv für Geschichte der Philosophie und Soziologie* 50: 73–100.

Vigoroux, F.
"Sagesse (Livre de la)." In *Dictionnaire de la Bible* 5. 1351–1360.

Volz, P.
1934 *Die Eschatologie der jüdischen Gemeinde im neutestamentlichen Zeitalter.* Tübingen. (Second ed. of *Jüdische Eschatologie von Daniel bis Akiba.* 1903.)

Vosté, J. M.
1949 "La Version syro-hexaplaire de la Sagesse," *Biblica* 30: 213–217.

Wallach, B. P.
1976 *Lucretius and the Diatribe Against the Fear of Death.* Leiden.

Walter, N.
1964 *Der Thoraausleger Aristobulos,* TU 86. Berlin.

Walzer, R.
1962 *Greek Into Arabic.* Oxford.

Watt, W. M.
1948 *Free Will and Predestination in Early Islam.* London.

Weber, J.
1951 *Le Livre de la Sagesse.* Paris.

Weber, W.
1904 "Die Komposition der Weisheit Salomos," *ZWT* 48: 145–169.
1905 "Die Unsterblichkeit der Weisheit Salomos," *ZWT* 48: 409–444.
1908–09 "Die Seelenlehre der Weisheit Salomos," *ZWT* 51: 314–332.
1911–12 "Heimat und Zeitalter des eschatologischen Buches der Weisheit," *ZWT* 53: 322–345.
1912–13 "Die Auferstehungsglaube des eschatologischen Buches der Weisheit," *ZWT* 54: 205–239.

Wendland, P.
1912 *Die hellenistisch-römische Kultur in ihren Beziehungen zu Judentum und Christentum.* Tübingen.

Weinfeld, M.
1972 *Deuteronomy and the Deuteronomic School.* Oxford.

Weisengoff, J. P.
1941 "Death and Immortality in the Book of Wisdom," *CBQ* 3: 104–133.
1949 "The Impious in Wisd. 2," *CBQ* 11: 40–65.

Westcott, B. F.
1888 "Wisdom of Solomon." In Smith's *Dictionary of the Bible* 4. 3545–3551. Boston.

Whybray, R. N.
1974 *The Intellectual Tradition in the Old Testament.* Berlin and New York: Walter de Gruyter.

Wiesmann, H.
1911 "Der zweite Teil des Buches der Weisheit," *ZKT* 35: 21–29, 449–465, 665–673.
Wilckens, U.
1959 *Weisheit und Torheit,* BHT 26. Tübingen.
"Sophia." In *TDNT* 7. 465*ff*.
Williams, C. S. C.
1956 "Armenian Variants in the Book of Wisdom," *JTS,* n.s. 7: 243–246.
Windisch, H.
1914 "Die göttliche Weisheit der Juden und die paulinische Christologie." Pages 222–223 in *Neutestamentliche Studien G. Heinrici.* Leipzig.
Winston, D.
1966 "The Iranian Component in the Bible, Apocrypha, and Qumran," *HR* 5.2: 183–216.
1971 "The Book of Wisdom's Theory of Cosmogony," *HR* 11.2: 185–202.
1973 "Freedom and Determinism in Greek Philosophy and Jewish Hellenistic Literature," *Studia Philonica* 2:40–50.
1974–75 "Freedom and Determinism in Philo of Alexandria," *Studia Philonica* 3: 47–70.
1976 Published with critiques and further discussion in the *Protocol of the Twentieth Colloquy of the Center for Hermeneutical Studies in Hellenistic and Modern Culture,* ed. W. Wuellner, Berkeley.
1975 "Philo's Theory of Cosmogony." Chapter 8 in *Religious Syncretism in Antiquity,* ed. B. A. Pearson. Missoula: Scholars Press.
197? "Philo's Ethical Theory." To be published in *ANRW.*
Wolfson, H. A.
1948 *Philo.* 2 vols. Cambridge, Mass.
1951 *Religious Philosophy.* Cambridge, Mass.
Wood, J.
1967 *Wisdom Literature: An Introduction.* London.
Worrell, J. E.
1968 "Concepts of Wisdom in the Dead Sea Scrolls." Dissertation, Claremont.
Wright, A. G.
1965 "The Structure of Wisd. 11–19," *CBQ* 27: 28–34.
1967a *The Literary Genre Midrash.* Staten Island, New York: Alba House.
1967b "Numerical Patterns in the Book of Wisdom," *CBQ* 29: 218–232.
1967c "The Structure of the Book of Wisdom," *Biblica* 48: 165–184.
Wust, E.
1958 "Von den Anfängen des Problems der Willensfreiheit," *Rheinisches Museum* 101: 95.
Yetter, F. J.
1947–48 "The Wisdom of Solomon," *RL* 17: 70–81.
Zaehner, R. G.
1961 *The Dawn and Twilight of Zoroastrianism.* New York.
1972 *Zurvan, A Zoroastrian Dilemma.* Reprint, New York.

Zeller, E.
　1963　*Die Philosophie der Griechen.* Reprint, Hildesheim.
Zenner, J. K.
　1898　"Der erste Theil des Buches der Weisheit," *ZKT* 22: 417–431.
Ziegler, J.
　1961a　*Chokma, Sophia, Sapientia,* Würzburger Universitätsreden 32. Würzburg.
　1961b　"Zur griechischen Vorlage der Vetus Latina in der Sap. Salomonis." Pages 275–291 in *Lex Tua Veritas.* Festschrift für H. Junker. Trier.
Ziener, G.
　1956　*Die Theologische Begriffssprache im Buche der Weisheit,* BBB 11.
　1957　"Die Werwendung der Schrift im Buch der Weisheit," *TTZ* 66: 138–152.
　1957　"Weisheitsbuch und Johannesevangelium," *Biblica* 38: 396–418; 39: 37–60.
Zimmermann, F.
　1966　"The Book of Wisdom: Its Language and Character," *JQR* 57: 1–27, 101–135.
Zorell, F.
　1922　"Salomonis pro imploranda Sapientia ad digne gubernandum populum Dei oratio," *VD* 2: 264–269.
　1927　"Principes invitantur ad quaerendam sapientiam. Sap. ex graeco," *VD* 7: 28–32.

COMMENTARIES

I. *Pre-Nineteenth Century*

Rabanus Maurus
　856　*Commentariorum in Sapientiam libri tres, PL* 109.671–763. Paris, 1852.
Hugo a s. Caro
　1260　*Postilla in librum Sapientiae,* Opera omnia, T. 3. Lyon, 1669.
S. Bonaventura
　1274　*Commentarius in librum Sapientiae,* Opera omnia 6. 105–235. Quarachi (Italy), 1893.
Nicolaus Liranus
　1341　*Postilla,* Opera omnia T. 3. Venice, 1588.
Robertus Holkot
　1349　*In Librum Sapientiae praelectiones CCXXIII.* Venice, 1509. Basileae, 1587, 180*ff.*
M. Cantacuzenus
　1370　'Η σοφία τοῦ Σολομῶντος ἐξηγηθεῖσα, Vat. Graec. 1233. Latin

translation between 1586–1594 by G. Brunelli, *Sapientia Salomonis explicata a religiosissimo rege domino Matheo Cantacuzeno*. Rome: P.U.G. Archivio II. 1345: 131*ff.*

Dionysius Carthusianus
  1471 *Ennarationes in Sapientiam et Ecclesiasticum*. Paris, 1548.

Petrus Nannius
  1557 *Scholia et commentaria in Librum Sapientiae*. Basileae, 1551.

C. Jansenius, Episcopus Gondavensis
  1569 *Annotationes in librum Sapientiae Salomonis*, 247–279. Antwerp, 1614.

J. Lorin
  1607 *In Librum Sapientiae commentarius*. Lyon, 1619.

Christophorus de Castro
  1613 *In Sapientiam brevis ac dilucidus Commentarius*. Lyon.

Cornelius à Lapide
  1627 *Commentarius in librum Sapientiae*, Opera omnia. Paris.

C. Jansenius, Episcopus Iprensis
  1644 *Analecta in Proverbia, Ecclesiasten, Sapientiam*. Louvain.

Le Maistre de Sacy
  1673 *Le Livre de la Sagesse*. Traduit en français avec une explication tirée des saints Pères. Brussels, 1713.

Badvellus, Castellio, Clarius, Lucas Brugensis, and Grotius
  1698 *Annotata ad Sapientiam Solomonis: Critici Sacri* 6. Amsterdam.

A. Calmet
  1713 *Commentaire littéral sur le livre de la Sagesse*. Paris.
  1792 *Commentarius in omnes libros sacros*. Wirceburgi (Würzburg).

Hugo Grotius
  1732 *Opera Omnia theologica in quatuor tomos divisa*, Tom. 1: Annotationes ad VT: In librum Sapientiae Salomonis, 588–610. Basileae.

Gulielmus Smits
  1749 *Sapientia vulgatae editionis dilucidata*. Antwerp.

Lucas Brugensis, Estius, Mariana, Malvenda, Ménochius, Tirin, Gordon, and Bossnet
  1751 *Liber Sapientiae: Biblia Sacra Vulgata editionis . . . cum selectissimis Litteralibus Commentariis* 14, 200–478. Venice.

J. J. Duguet and J. V. D'Asfeld
  1755 *Explication du livre de la Sagesse*. Paris.

Naphtali Hirtz Wessely
  1780 *Sefer Hokmath Shelomo* (with commentary *Ru'aḥ Ḥen*) Berlin. (Hebrew)

C. F. Houbigant
  1797 *Notae criticae in universos V.T. libros* 1. 465–480. Frankfurt/M.

II. *Nineteenth Century*

Bauermeister, J.
  1828 *Commentarius in Sapientiam Salomonis*. Göttingen.

Grimm, C. L. W.
  1837 *Kommentar über das Buch der Weisheit.* Leipzig.
  1860 *Das Buch der Weisheit,* Kurzgefasstes exegetisches Handbuch zu
    den Apokryphen des A.T. g. Leipzig. (All Grimm references are to this
    volume.)
Gutmann, M.
  1841 *Die Apokryphen des Alten Testament.* Altona.
Schmid, J. A.
  1865 *Das Buch der Weisheit.* Vienna. First ed. Eichstätt, 1856.
Corluy, J.
  1874 *Commentarius in Librum Sapientiae.* Louvain.
Gutberlet, C.
  1874 *Das Buch der Weisheit.* Münster.
Reuss, E.
  1878 *La Sapience.* Paris.
Bissell, E. C., ed.
  1880 *The Apocrypha of the Old Testament.* Edinburgh.
Lesêtre, H.
  1880 *Le Livre de la Sagesse.* Paris. Second ed. 1896.
Deane, W. J.
  1881 *The Book of Wisdom.* Oxford.
Farrar, F. W.
  1888 *The Wisdom of Solomon, Apocrypha* 1, ed. H. Wace. London.
Zöckler, O.
  1891 *Die Weisheit Salomos.* Kurzgefasster Kommentar zu den heiligen
    Schriften A. und N.T. A 9. München.
Fillion, L.-Cl.
  1894 *Le Livre de la Sagesse,* La Sainte Bible commentée 5. Paris.

III. *Twentieth Century*

Siegfried, K.
  1900 *Die Weisheit Salomos,* Die Apokryphen und Pseudepigraphen des
    A.T. 1, ed. E. Kautzch. Tübingen.
Gregg, J. A. F.
  1909 *The Wisdom of Solomon,* Cambridge Bible for Schools. Cambridge.
Cornely, R.
  1910 *Commentarius in librum Sapientiae.* Opus postumum, ed. F. Zorell.
    Cursus Scripturae Sacrae 2.18, vol. 5. Paris.
Heinisch, P.
  1912 *Das Buch der Weisheit,* Exegetisches Handbuch zum A.T. 24.
    Münster i.W.
Goodrick, A. T. S.
  1913 *The Book of Wisdom.* London.
Holmes, S.
  1913 *The Wisdom of Solomon, APOT,* ed. R. H. Charles, 1. Oxford.

Oesterley, W. O. E.
1918 *The Wisdom of Solomon*. London, New York.
Kalt, E.
1925 *Das Buch der Weisheit, übersetzt und erklärt*. Missions-druckerei Steyl (Netherlands).
Feldmann, F.
1926 *Das Buch der Weisheit*. Bonn.
Stein, M.
1936 *Sefer Hokmath Shelomo*, in *Ha-Sefarim Ha-Hitzonim*, ed. A. Kahana. Tel-Aviv. (Hebrew)
Henne, E.
1937 *Das Buch der Weisheit*. Paderborn.
Fichtner, J.
1938 *Weisheit Salomos*. Tübingen.
Gerotti, P. G., ed.
1938 *Il Vecchio Testamento 6: I Sapienziali*. Turin.
Weber, J.
1939 *Le Livre de la Sagesse*. Paris.
Fischer, J.
1950 *Das Buch der Weisheit*. Echter Bibel, Das A.T. 10. Würzburg.
Osty, E.
1950 *Le Livre de la Sagesse*. Paris. (E. Osty and J. Trinquet, *La Bible* [Lausanne, 1971], 241–365 [reviewed by M. Gilbert in *NRT* 93 (1971) 1092–1095].
Lattey, C.
1953 *The Book of Wisdom: A Catholic Commentary on Holy Scripture*, eds. B. Orchard, E. F. Sutcliffe, R. C. Fuller, R. Russel. London.
Drubbel, A.
1957 *Wijsheid*, De Boeken van het Oude Text. 8. Roermond-Maaseik.
Reider, J.
1957 *The Book of Wisdom*. New York.
Guillaumont, A.
1959 *La Sagesse de Salomon*, Bible de la Pléiade. Paris.
Geyer, J.
1963 *The Wisdom of Solomon*, Torch Bible Commentaries. London.
des Places, E.
1965 *De libro Sapientiae* (cap. 13–15). Rome.
Drouet, A.
1966 *Le Livre de la Sagesse*, Paroles de vie 5. Paris.
Wright, A. G.
1968 "Wisdom" in *The Jerome Biblical Commentary* 1, eds. R. E. Brown, J. A. Fitzmeyer, R. E. Murphy. Englewood Cliffs, N.J. Pages 556–558.
Watson, W.
1969 *Wisdom: A New Catholic Commentary on Holy Scripture*, eds. R. C. Fuller, L. Johnston, C. Kearnes. London.

Vílchez, J.
  1969 *Sabiduría,* La Sagrada Escritura, Texto y commentario, A.T. 4.
    Madrid.
Romaniuk, K.
  1969 *Pismo Święte Starego Testamentu,* Tom VIII. 3: *Księga Mądrości.*
    Katolicki Uniwersytet Lubelski. Poznan-Warszawa: Pallottinum.
Clarke, E. G.
  1973 *The Wisdom of Solomon.* The Cambridge Bible Commentary. New
    English Bible.

WISDOM OF SOLOMON
Translation and Notes

A. WISDOM'S GIFT OF IMMORTALITY (1–6:21)

I. Exhortation to Justice which brings immortality (1:1–15)
II. Speech of the wicked who have covenanted with Death (1:16–2:24)

Problems of Reward and Retribution (III–V)

III. Sufferings of the immortal just only a trial (3:1–12)
IV. Sterility of the virtuous will ultimately be converted to fruitfulness (3:13–4:6)
V. Early death a token of God's solicitous care (4:7–20)

VI. Vindication of the just and Final Judgment (5:1–23)
VII. Exhortation to Wisdom which is easily found and brings immortality and sovereignty (6:1–21)

I. EXHORTATION TO JUSTICE WHICH
BRINGS IMMORTALITY
(1:1–15)

1   1 Love justice, you who rule the earth;
     be mindful of the Lord in goodness,
     and seek him in singleness of heart.
2 For he is found by those who do not test him,
     and reveals himself to those who have full trust in him.
3 Devious thoughts cut men off from God,
     and the divine power, when made trial of,
     exposes the foolish.
4 For Wisdom will not enter a fraudulent mind,
     nor make her home in a body mortgaged to sin.
5 The holy spirit, that divine tutor, will fly from cunning
           stratagem;
     she will withdraw from unintelligent thoughts
     and will take umbrage at the approach of injustice.
6 Wisdom is a benevolent spirit
     and she will not hold a blasphemer immune from his own
           utterances;
     because God is a witness of his thoughts,
     the real guardian of his mind,
     who hears his every word.
7 For the spirit of the Lord fills the world,
     and that which holds all things together has knowledge of all
           articulate sound.
8 No one, therefore, who celebrates injustice will escape
           notice,
     nor will justice the accuser pass him by.
9 The schemings of the godless man will be scrutinized,
     and a report of his words will come before the Lord
     for the conviction of his lawless acts.
10 For an impassioned ear overhears all,
     and the murmur of his muttering does not go undetected.

11 Beware, then, of futile grumbling
   and refrain from slanderous speech;
   for no secret utterance will go unheeded,
   and lying speech spells self-destruction.
12 Do not court death through a deviant way of life,
   nor draw down destruction by your own actions.
13 For God did not make death,
   nor does he take delight in the destruction of the living;
14 he created all things that they might endure.
   All that has come into existence preserves its being,
   and there is no deadly poison in it.
   Death's rulership is not on earth,
15 for justice is immortal.

NOTES

1:1–15. The author begins with an exhortation to the pagan rulers of the earth to love justice and seek God with single-minded devotion and trust. The terms 'justice,' 'goodness,' 'wisdom,' 'spirit of the Lord,' 'holy spirit,' and 'power,' are here employed synonymously (cf. 9:17), personified as a divine entity which cannot abide fraudulence and injustice and swiftly withdraws from their presence. Like the Stoic *pneuma,* an intelligent 'gas' composed of fire and air, the divine spirit is described as pervading all things and thus holding the world together. (The materialistic Stoic terminology was undoubtedly understood figuratively by the author, as it had been by Philo.) Inasmuch as it also constitutes the reasoning element in man, no human thought or sentiment, however fleeting or unarticulated, may escape its scrutiny, and the godless should therefore be forewarned. Cf. *Test.Naphtali* 2:4: "For there is no inclination of thought which the Lord knoweth not, for He created every man after His own image."

1:1. *Love justice.* Cf. Ps 45:7–8.

who rule the earth. For 'judge' in the sense of 'ruler,' see Amos 2:3; Micah 4:14; Ps 2:10; Wisd 6:1. Similarly, in the Ugaritic Baal cycle, 'judge' (ṭpṭ) seems to be synonymous with 'prince': "Strike the back of Prince Yamm, / Between the arms of Judge Nahar" (*ANET*:131 lines 14–15). So distinctive of the royal office was the function of justice, that in the *Aqht* text Dn'el's resumption of his normal routine after his ceremonial seclusion is described as follows: "He rises to take his seat at the opening of the gate. . . . He decides the case of the widow, he judges the suit of the orphan." (Gray 1965:221; *ANET*:151.) The author is clearly addressing the pagan world-rulers. The fiction of Solomonic authorship requires that that renowned monarch address his pagan colleagues; cf. I Kings 5:14, 10:23–24. Reese would take the royal address figuratively. Such an address was characteristic of the Hellenistic tracts on Kingship (e.g. Dio of Prusa's four orations on Kingship which appear to have been delivered in the presence of the Emperor Trajan; Plutarch's *To an Uneducated Ruler*). "The author was showing that true kingly dignity is a life of justice and wisdom, for God fashioned men to rule his creation 'in piety and justice' (9:3) and destined them to share in his eternal kingship (5:16; 6:21)" (1970:149–150).

goodness. Cf. Philo *LA* 1.59: "Now the tree of life is virtue in the most comprehensive sense, which some term goodness. From it the particular virtues derive their existence."

singleness of heart. Cf. I Chron 29:17, LXX; I Macc 2:37; *Test. Reuben* 4:1; *Test.Levi* 13:1; Eph 6:5. The opposite is "with a double heart," i.e. with duplicity: Ps 12:3 (*bĕlēb walēb*); cf. I Chron 12:33; Sir 1:28; I Enoch 91:4; James 1:8; Euripides *Hippolytus* 612: "My tongue has sworn, but my heart is unsworn"; Aristophanes *Thesmophoriazusae* 275; *Ranae* 101, 1471; *SVF* 2.132; 3.554; *BT Meg.* 14a; *Tanḥ*. Buber, *Ki Tavo* 3. See Lieberman 1942:142–143. The fundamental virtue in *Test. XII* is *haplotēs* (see R. Eppel. *Le piétisme juif dans les Testaments des douze Patriarches* [Paris, 1930]:148ff; Jaubert 1963:274ff). "In the same way, says Otzen, the parallel concepts to this wholeheartedness *tom* and *yošer* are central in the Dead Sea Scrolls" (Ringgren 1963:136); cf., however, H. C. Kee, "The Ethical Dimensions of the Testament of the XII as a Clue to Provenance," *NTS* 24:2 (1978):259–270. See also J. Amstutz, *Haplotēs: Eine begriffsgeschichtliche Studie zum jüdisch-christlichen Griechisch* (Bonn, 1968). Among the Stoics, Marcus Aurelius is apparently the only one to refer to *haplotēs* as an ethical ideal. Cf. 6.30; 4.26 (*haplōson seauton*, "study to be simple"); 4.37: 'A moment and thou wilt be dead; and not even yet are thou simple (*haplous*), nor unperturbed"; 9.37; 7.31. Cf. also Philo *Op.* 156: "prompted by a mind devoid of steadfastness and firm foundation, Eve gave her consent and ate of the fruit, and gave some of it to her husband; this instantly brought them out of a state of simplicity and innocence into one of wickedness"; *Op.* 170; *LA* 3.44; Plotinus 6.9.11.23.

Love . . . be mindful . . . seek. The Aorist imperatives here are ingressive, expressing "the coming about of conduct which contrasts with prior conduct" (BDF 337.1).

2. *test him*. Cf. Deut 6:16; Mal 3:15; Pss 78:18; 95:8–9; Isa 7:12 (see

also Lieberman 1950:177; F. Rosenzweig, *The Star of Redemption* [New York, 1970–71], 265–267).

3. *Devious thoughts.* Cf. Theognis 1.1147: *adikōn andrōn skolion logon. full trust.* Cf. 6:12; Jer 29:13–14, Isa 55:6; Prov 8:17.

cut men off. Cf. Isa 59:2; *Test.Reuben* 4:6 (*chōrizousa theou*); *Test.Simeon* 5:3; Philo *Mut.* 265: "God is the season which departs far away from all the impious."

4. *fraudulent. kakotechnos,* a poetic word. Cf. *ILIAD* 15.14; *AP* 5.129 (where it refers to lascivious postures); IV Macc 6:25. Philo refers to the intellectually uprooted apostates as *kakotechnountes* or malicious critics of the law (*Agr.* 157; cf. *Sacr.* 32; III Macc 7:9).

nor make her home. We have here a favorite conception of the Late Stoa, which was frequently used by Philo: "Be zealous therefore, O soul, to become a house of God (*theou oikos*), a holy temple, a most beauteous abiding-place, for perchance, perchance the Master of the whole world's household shall be thine too and keep thee under his care as his special house, to preserve thee evermore strongly guarded and unharmed" (*Somn.* 1.149); cf. *QE* 2.51; *Virt.* 188; *Sob.* 62; *Somn.* 2.251; *Fug.* 117; *Praem.* 123; Plato *Tim.* 90C; Epictetus *Discourses* 2.8.14: "It is within yourself that you bear Him, and do not perceive that you are defiling Him with impure thoughts and filthy actions. Yet in the presence of even an image of God you would not dare do anything of the things you are now doing. But when God Himself is present within you, seeing and hearing everything, are you not ashamed to be thinking and doing such things as these, O insensible of your own nature, and object of God's wrath!" id.1.14.13; Seneca *Ep.* 83: "Nothing is shut off from the sight of God. He is witness of our souls, and he comes into the very midst of our thoughts— comes into them, I say, as one who may at any time depart"; *Ep.* 87.21; Porphyry *Ad Marcellam* 11 and 19; I Cor 3:16; Theophilus *Ad Autolycum* 1.2: "As a burnished mirror, so ought man to have his soul pure. When there is rust on the mirror, it is not possible that a man's face be seen in the mirror, so also when there is sin in a man, such a man cannot behold God." For the non-Platonic body-soul distinction, cf. II Macc 7:37; 15:30; 14:38; Ps 84:3.

mortgaged. katachreos is first attested in Polybius 13.1.1, and used metaphorically only here. Cf. II Kings 17:17; Jub 7:23; I Macc 1:15; Rom 7:14.

5. *The holy spirit.* The LXX uses the same expression (*to pneuma to hagion*) at Isa 63:10 and Ps 51:13. For the association of Wisdom and Spirit, cf. Isa 11:2, "where every attribute assigned to the Spirit of the Lord is connected with wisdom," and I Enoch 49:3, where the spirit which dwells in the Elect One is the "spirit of wisdom, insight, understanding, and might" (Suggs 1970:54).

will take umbrage. The word *elengchthēsetai* has baffled all the commentators. Grimm translates: 'frightened or driven off' (citing late Greek usage, especially Chrysostom); Fichtner (1938): 'insulted'; *RV:* 'will be put to confusion'; *JB:* 'is taken aback'; *NEB:* 'will throw up her case.' The idea is clearly that the holy spirit is unable to abide the presence of evil, and is virtually driven away by it. Cf. *BT Kid.* 31a: "R. Isaac said: He who transgresses in secret is as though he pressed the feet of the *Shekhinah,* for it is written, 'Thus saith the Lord, the heaven is my throne, and the earth is my footstool' (Isa 66:1)"; *BR* 19.7: "The main dwelling of the *Shekhinah* was originally below, but after the sin of Adam, she took off to the first heaven"; I Enoch 42:2: "Wisdom went forth to make her dwelling among the children of men, and found no dwelling-place. Wisdom returned to her place, and took her seat among the angels"; 44:5; IV Ezra 5:10: "Then shall intelligence hide herself and wisdom withdraw to its chamber"; II Bar 48:36; *CH, Asclepius* 24: "Godhead will go back from earth to heaven"; Philo *QG* 1.40: "For wisdom is most common, most equal and most helpful. But when it sees them perversely increase in the opposite direction and being altogether uncontrolled and willful, it returns to its own place." (For wisdom's dwelling in heaven, see I Bar 3:29; Sir 24:4–5.) We find the same notion in Greek literature: Theognis 1.1135: "Hope is the one good God yet left among mankind; the rest have forsaken us and gone to Olympus. Gone ere this was the great Goddess Honesty (*Pistis*), gone from the world was Self-Control (*Sōphrosynē*)"; Hesiod *Op.* 197: "And then *Aidōs* and *Nemesis,* with their sweet forms wrapped in white robes, will go from the wide-pathed earth and forsake mankind to join the company of the deathless gods"; Aratus *Phaenomena* 96–136; Virgil *Ecl.* 4.6. Similarly, in Egyptian literature, we find that in the era of the primordial gods "Maat came down from heaven and joined those who lived on earth. At that time there was no injustice, no pain, no hunger" (Theban Temple, 95K, from the Greek and Roman period. This text clearly implies the return of Maat to heaven. See K. Sethe, *Amun und die acht Urgötter von Hermopolis* [Berlin, 1929]:125). It was on the basis of some of this data that Bultmann had suggested that Matt 23:34–39 (Luke 11:49–51; 13:34–35) was based on a speech by Sophia cited from some lost wisdom document which recounted the myth of a searching and disappointed Wisdom, whose conclusion "you will not see me again until . . ." was explained in terms of "the myth of the divine wisdom who, after tarrying in vain on earth, and calling men to herself takes departure from earth, so that one now seeks her in vain (cf. Prov 1:28; *Gospel of Thomas,* Saying 38; I Clement 57.3*ff*)." (R. Bultmann, "Der religionsgeschichtliche Hintergrund des Prologs Johannesevangelium," in *Eucharisterion, Festschrift H. Gunkel* [Göttingen, 1923]:II. 1–26; *Die Geschichte der synoptischen Tradition* [Göttingen,

1964]:120–121); J. M. Robinson and H. Koester, *Trajectories Through Early Christianity* (Philadelphia, 1971):103–104. A critique of Bultmann's theory may be found in E. S. Fiorenza 1975:17–41.

6. *benevolent.* For *philanthrōpon* cf. Philo *Op.* 81 and see NOTE on 7:23.

from his own utterances. Cf. Sir 1:29: "keep guard over your lips."

thoughts. Literally, reins. Cf. Greek *phrenes* (R. B. Onians, *The Origins of European Thought* [rep. New York, 1973] 23*ff*, identifies the *phrenes* with the lungs); Pss 16:7; 73:21; Prov 23:16; Jer 11:20; 17:11; 12:2; Rev 2:23; *BT Ber.* 61a: "Our Rabbis taught: Man has two kidneys, one of which prompts him to good, the other to evil" *BR* 61.1, Th-Alb:657: "The Holy One blessed be He made his [Abraham's] two kidneys serve like two teachers, and these welled forth truth and taught him wisdom."

witness . . . guardian. For the collocution *martys kai episkopos,* cf. *Iliad* 22.254; *Sib Or* Frag. 1.3–4; Philo *LA* 3.43; Herodian *Historiae* 7.10.3. See also Job 20:29, LXX; Ps 94:9; Philo *Virt.* 219; *Deus* 9; *Jos.* 265; *Mig.* 135, 115, 81; *Somn.* 1.91; *Mut.* 216, 39; Sir 17:19–20; 23:18–20; 42:18–20; Ps-Aristeas 133: "He showed that even if a man but think of compassing evil, and not alone if he actually do it, he could not escape notice"; *Test.Judah* 20:5: "And the spirit of truth testifieth all things, and accuseth all, and the sinner is burnt up by his own heart and cannot raise his face to the judge." Cf. also Xenophanes of Colophon: "God is all eye, all mind, all ear" (DK, B.24).

hears his every word. Cf. Ps 139:4.

7. *fills the world.* Cf. Jer 23:24; Isa 6:3; Ps 139:7*ff;* Philo *Her.* 188.

that which holds all things together. The phrase is Stoic. Cf. *SVF* 2.439 (*to synechon,* i.e. pneumatic being, contrasted with *to synechomenon,* i.e. hylic being); 2.448 (*hen ti synechei ton te synolon kosmon*); D.L. 7.148. Although not found in the extant works of Plato, the formula is already employed by Xenophon *Mem.* 4.3.13 (*ho ton holon kosmon synechōn*); *Cyropaedia* 8.7.22. It is also found in Philo *Conf.* 136 (*hypo de tou theou peplērōtai ta panta, periechontos, ou periechomenou*); *Somn.* 1.63–64 (for *periechō* cf. Anaximines, DK, B.2; Anaximander, DK, A.11; Epiphanius *Haereses* 31.5); *LA* 3.6; *Mos.* 2.133; Ps-Aristotle *De Mundo* 398b 20–25; *CH* 11.5.13; Col 1:17.

8. *escape notice.* Cf. Job 34:21–3; Sir 16:17; 17:19; Ps-Aristeas 210: *outhen an lathoi adikon poiēsas.* In a fragment from a Greek satyr-play variously ascribed to Euripides or Critias, Sisyphus gives an atheistic account of the origins of 'The Divine.' The gods, he says, are the invention of a wise and clever man who introduced them as the official watchdogs of public morality: "Hence he introduced the Divine, saying that there is a God flourishing with immortal life, hearing and seeing with his mind, and thinking of everything and caring about these things, and having divine na-

ture, who will hear everything said among mortals, and will be able to see all that is done. And even if you plan anything evil in secret, you will not escape the gods in this (*tout' ouchi lēsei tous theous*), for they have surpassing intelligence" (Critias, *TrGF* 43F 19.16*ff*).

justice the accuser. elengchō occurs sixty-four times in the LXX, and *elengchos* is used thirty-one times for Hebrew *tokaḥat*. (See *TDNT* 7. 913.) *Dikē* was personified in Greek literature. One of the Horae (Hesiod *Theogonia* 902), she reports to Zeus the wrongdoings of men: "And there is a virgin Justice, the daughter of Zeus . . . and whenever anyone hurts her with lying slander (*skoliōs onotazōn*), she sits beside her father Zeus, the son of Kronos, and tells him of men's wicked heart . . ." (Hesiod *Op.* 256–264). In Aratus (*Phaenomena* 96*ff*), she is the constellation Virgo, who finally left the earth when the Bronze Age began (Cf. NOTE on v. 5 above); some (as Ovid *Met.* 1.149–150) call her Astraea in this connection. For justice as avenger, see Plato *Laws* 715E (where he is following Orphic tradition); 872E; *Epinomis* 988E; Sophocles *Electra* 475, 528; Aeschylus *Agamemnon* 1432; Ps-Demosthenes (-Kern, *Orphicorum Fragmenta* 23) 25.11: "each juryman must reflect that he is being watched by hallowed and inexorable Justice, who, as Orpheus, that prophet of our most sacred mysteries, tells us, sits beside the throne of Zeus and oversees all the works of men"; *SIG* 1176; Jos. *J.W.* 1.3.6; Wisd 11:20; IV Macc 4:13,21; 9:9. Philo adapts the old tradition of Dikē as "assessor" of Zeus (*Dios paredros:* Pindar *Olympia* 8.22); *Mut.* 194; Jos. 48,170; *Conf.* 118; *Decal.* 95. See *TDNT* 2. 178*ff;* E. Goodenough 1969:59*ff;* E. Bréhier, *Les Idées philosophiques et religieuses de Philon d'Alexandrie* (Paris, 1950):149*ff:* R. Hirzel, *Themis, Dike und Verwandtes* (Leipzig, 1907):138*ff*, 412*ff*.

pass him by. parodeuein is used five times by our author (here, and in 2:7; 5:14; 6:22; 10:8), and in its transitive sense is found only in late Greek prose. Cf. Diodorus Siculus 32.27; Plutarch *Moralia* 973D; Lucian *Nigrinus* 36.

9. *schemings.* For *diaboulion* cf. Ps 10:2, LXX (Hebrew *mĕzimôt*); Sir 15:14; 44:4; Ezek 11:5, LXX; Hosea 4:9, LXX.

10. *an impassioned ear. ous zelōseōs,* an imitation of Hebrew adjectival genitive. Cf. Num 5:14, LXX; Xenophon *Cyropaedia* 8.2.10; Philo *Somn.* 1.140 (the 'ears' and 'eyes' of the great king).

murmur of his muttering. Cf. Eccles 5:1; II Enoch 61:5: "And if his words made it [the gift for God], but his heart murmur . he has not any advantage"; 63:2: "But if his heart murmur, he commits a double evil, ruin of himself and of that which he gives"; III Bar 8:5; 13.4. Tempting God (above, v. 2) and murmuring are connected by Paul (I Cor 10:9–10), working backwards through Numbers 21 and 14. For the murmuring motif, see G. W. Coats, *Rebellion in the Wilderness* (Nashville,

1968); B. S. Childs, *The Book of Exodus* (Philadelphia, 1974): 256–264.

muttering. For *gongusmos*. Cf. Exod 16:8; Num 17:5–10, LXX.

ous . . . throus. Play on words. Grimm reproduces it in German: Lauschen und Rauschen.

11. *grumbling*. *katalalia* is first attested here and *Test.Gad* 3:3; cf. II Enoch 52:2; III Bar 8:5; 13:4; II Cor 12:30; I Peter 2:1. The corresponding verb, however, is frequent in the LXX (in Num 21:5, 12:8; Pss 77:19; 49:20; Hosea 7:13, it is used in the sense of speaking evil of God).

spells self-destruction. Through sin the soul forfeits its 'true' life. "The writer is thinking of that soulless existence of the wicked which, metaphorically speaking, is death" (Gregg). Cf. *BT Ber*. 18b: "The wicked even when alive are called dead"; Philo *Det*. 49; *Fug*. 55; *Spec*. 1.345: "For in very truth the godless are dead in soul."

12. The sentiment expressed here is already found in the beautiful poem in Proverbs 8. In vv. 32–36 we have in effect "a summons in the form of an ultimatum, to listen to wisdom, for on this depends life or death" (von Rad); in vv. 35–36: "For he who finds me finds life . . . all who hate me love death." Cf. *CH* 1.28: "Why, earth-born men, have you surrendered yourselves unto death, since you have the power to partake of immortality? Repent, you who travel in the company of error and who have fellowship with ignorance." In the Gnostic cosmogonies Sophia is intimately linked with Zoe the celestial counterpart of Eve. In the *Hypostasis of the Archons* and *On the Origin of the World*, Zoe is usually the daughter of Sophia, but in some passages of the latter we find Sophia called Sophia Zoe. (Robinson 1977:158, 172). See G .W. MacRae, "The Jewish Background of the Gnostic Sophia Myth," in *Essays on the Coptic Gnostic Library* (Leiden, 1970):93.

draw down destruction. Cf. Isa 5:18, LXX.

by your own actions. The notion that man is responsible for his evil actions in spite of the fact that everything takes place in accordance with Divine Providence was widespread in ancient literature. Thus Ben Sira emphatically states: "Say not: 'From God is my transgression,' for that which He hateth made He not (15:11)." We find virtually the same words in an Egyptian text: "Beware lest thou say: Every man is according to his own character; ignorant and learned are all alike; Fate and upbringing are graven on the character in the writing of God himself." (A. Gardiner, *Hieratic Papyri in the British Musem*, 3d ser. [London, 1935]:43). Similarly, we read in the *Egyptian Coffin Texts*: "I did not command [men] that they do evil, (but) it was their hearts which violated what I had said." (*ANET*:8). J. Crenshaw has pointed out that the simple prohibition formula *'al-tōm'ar* can be traced back as far as the Egyptian *In-*

struction of Ani and continues in use as late as the *Instructions of Onchsheshonqy* ("The Problem of Theodicy in Sirach: On Human Bondage," *JBL* 94:1 [1975]:48–49). The negative formula 'Do not' is already found in the Sumerian *Instructions of Šuruppak*. Cf. I Enoch 103:9; 104:7; II Macc 7:16,19. For a detailed discussion of the problem of freedom and determinism, see Introduction VII.8, and also NOTE on 1:16 below. Cf. I Enoch 98:4: "Sin has not been sent upon the earth, / But man of himself has created it"; Ps Sol 3:5: "The righteous stumbleth and holdeth the Lord righteous"; Philo *Det.* 122: "For Moses does not say, as some impious people do, that God is the author of ills. Nay, he says that 'our own hands' cause them, figuratively describing in this way our own undertakings, and the voluntary movement of our minds to what is wrong."

13. *God did not make death.* A bold statement which, without further interpretation, sounds like an echo of Zoroastrian teaching, although the author certainly did not mean to go that far. (For other Zoroastrian echoes in the book, see NOTES on 2:24; 7:22; 15:19.) Cf. Ezek 33:11: "As I live, saith the Lord God, I have no pleasure in the death of the wicked, but that the wicked turn from his way and live"; I Enoch 69:11: "Man was created exactly like the angels to the intent that he should continue righteous and pure, and death which destroys everything could not have taken hold of him"; II Bar 17:3; 19:8; 23:4; IV Ezra 8:60: "For the Most High willed not that men should come to destruction; but they have themselves defiled the name of him who made them, and have proved themselves ungrateful to him who prepared life for them." In the light of the author of Wisd's Platonist view of the relationship of body and soul revealed in 9:15, it is likely that he is here referring to spiritual rather than to physical death. The rabbis, too, refer to God's original intention that man should not be subject to death, but, unlike our author, it is physical death which they have in mind. See *Pes.R.,* Piska 48 (*Shor o Keseb*) Braude: 813: "The words 'that which hath been is now' (Ecc 3:15) allude to the fact that when the Holy One, blessed be He, created Adam, He created him with the intention of having him live and endure for ever like the ministering angels, for 'the Lord God said: Behold, the man is become as one of us' (Gen 3:22). . . . Indeed, R. Judah, the son of R. Simon, carried the explication of this verse still further to an idea difficult to grasp, for he takes the verse to be saying, 'The man is become as the One of us'—that is, become like the Unique One of the world, who lives and endures for ever and ever. . . . But God's intentions for Adam came to nought when Adam did not abide by the command given him, and forthwith mortality was decreed for him." Cf. also *The Teaching of Silvanus* 91: "For death did not exist, nor will it exist at the end" (Robinson 1977:350; *ShR* 32.1: "Said the Holy One blessed be He: 'I had taken

you for divine beings' (Ps 82:6), but you followed in Adam's footsteps, 'indeed you shall die as men do'"; *Wayyik.R.* 18.3; 27.4; *BR* 9.5, Th-Alb:70. See Urbach 1969:371–380. That God is altogether good and cannot be the direct cause of evil was a cardinal doctrine of Plato (*Rep.* 379B; *Tim.* 69C), the Stoics (*SVF* 2.1168–1186), and Philo (*Mut.* 30; *Conf.* 179). The rabbis held a similar view. Cf. *Sifra, Beḥukkōtai* 4: "'It has been of your own doing' (Mal 1:9); evil never proceeds from me, and so it is written, 'It is not at the word of the Most High, that weal and woe befall' [following the reading of the Gaon] (Lament 3:38)"; *Lament.R.* on 3:38: "R. Eleazar expounded the verse 'It is not at the word of the Most High that weal and woe befall' thus: From the moment that the Holy One, blessed be He, said: 'See, I set before you this day life and prosperity, death and adversity' (Deut 30:15), good has not gone forth to him who does evil nor evil to him who does good, but only good to the doer of good and evil to the doer of evil, as it is written, 'the Lord reward the evil-doer according to his wickedness' (I Sam 3:79)"; *Test. Orpheus* (Aristobulus' version), line 9: "He from His store of goods never prescribes evil for men" (*FPG* 1:65).

destruction. "*Apōleia* is common in the LXX sense of 'perishing,' 'destruction.' The concepts *thanatos, hadēs,* and *apōleia* are all used together for it, being often personified as man's worst enemy (Job 26:6; 28:22; Prov 15:11). In the Synoptics, and especially in Paul and John, *apōleia* is used for eternal destruction (Matt 7:13; Rom 9:22; Philip 1:28; I Tim 6:9; John 17:12. It is also a favorite word in II Peter (2:1, 3, 3:7, 16). What is meant here is not a simple extinction of existence, but an ever-lasting state of torment and death" (*TDNT* 1. 396–397). R. J. Taylor thinks that *apōleia* here bears its technical New Testament meaning, and S. Rosik suggests that its usage here marks the beginning of a process of development from the meaning of earthly destruction to that beyond physical death.

14. *All that has come into existence. geneseis* refers to all things created or generated; cf. Plato *Phaedrus* 245E: "Thus that which moves itself must be the beginning of motion. And this can be neither destroyed nor generated, otherwise all the heavens and all creation (*pāsan te genesin*) must fall in ruin and stop."

preserves its being. For *sōtērioi,* cf. Ps-Aristotle *De Mundo:* "For God is indeed the preserver (*sōtēr*) of all things" (397b 20); Philo *Mos.* 1.96: "the same elements which He shaped for their preservation (*sōteriōs*) to create the universe (*epi genesei tōn holōn*) He turned into instruments for the perdition (*apōleian*) of the impious whenever He would"; *Prov.* 2.63 (106): *sōtērias de pothos.* The principle of self-preservation was a cardinal doctrine of Stoicism; cf. D.L. 7.85: "The prime impulse of an animal is towards self-preservation, because Nature makes it well-disposed to itself (*oikeiousēs hautō*) from the outset, as Chrysippus says in the first book of his work *On Ends*. . . . And Nature, they say, made no difference originally between plants and animals, for she regulates the life of plants too, in their case without impulse and sensation, just as also certain processes go on of a vegetative kind in us." Cf. Philo *Aet.* 35*ff*: "Nature in each case strives to maintain and conserve (*diatērein kai diasōzein*) the thing of which it is the nature and if it were possible to render it immortal. Tree nature acts so in trees, animal nature in each kind of animal, but the nature of any particular part if necessarily too feeble to carry it into a perpetual existence. For privation or scorching or chilling or the vast multitude of other circumstances which ordinarily affect it descend to shake it violently and loosen and finally break the bond which holds it together, though if no such external force were lying ready to attack it, so far as itself was concerned, it would preserve all things small or great proof against age. The nature of the world then must necessarily desire the conservation of the All. For it is not inferior to the nature of particular parts that it should take to its heels and leave its post and try to manufacture sickness rather than health, destruction rather than complete preservation (*sōtērias pantelous*). . . . But if this is true the world will not be susceptible to destruction. Why so? Because the nature which holds it together (*hē synechousa physis*) fortified by its great fund of strength is invincible and prevails over everything which could injure it." Elsewhere (*Op.* 44), Philo argues that nothing in the world is really perishable, inasmuch as the species to which every individual thing belongs is eternal: "For God willed that nature should run a course that brings it back to its starting-point, endowing the species with immortality, and making them sharers of eternal existence (*aidiotētos*)." In explaining the perpetuity of the species Philo employs the Stoic term 'seminal essences': *spermatikai ousiai*. Cf. *QG* 2.12: "in order that the divine purpose which was formed at the creation of the world might forever remain inextinguishable by that saving of the genus.") (The precise meaning of this phrase seems to have eluded most previous translators. *RSV:* "and the generative forces of the world are wholesome"; *NEB:* "The creative forces of the world make for life"; *JB:* "the world's created things have health in them.")

no deadly poison. This almost sounds like an anti-Gnostic polemic. We read, for example, in a Nag Hammadi tractate on the Soul (the so-called *Authoritative Teaching*): "The adversary who spies on us lies in wait for us like a fisherman. . . . For he casts many foods before our eyes, which are the things of this world. He wishes to make us desire one of them and to taste only a small thing, so that he may seize us with his hidden poison and bring us out of freedom and take us into glory." (See G. W. MacRae, "A Nag Hammadi Tractate on the Soul," in *Ex Orbe Religionum* [Leiden,

1972]: 1. 471–479. MacRae is uncertain, however, whether this tractate should properly be called Gnostic.) Similarly, in his attack on the material creation, Ahriman fills it with deadly poison: "And upon the earth he let loose reptiles in corporeal form . . . reptiles biting and poisonous—serpent and scorpion, venomous lizard, tortoise and frog, so that not so much as a needle's point on [the whole] earth remained free from creeping things. . . . And upon the plants he brought so much poison that in a moment they dried up." (*Greater Bundahishn* 42.14 – 43.8; see Zaehner 1961:262.)

Death's rulership. This phrase is laden with mythical connotations. The Ugaritic Baal texts provide a graphic description of the underground realm of Death: "Descend to the House of the Corruption of the earth, And be numbered with those who go down into the earth. Then, indeed, shall ye set face towards his city Ruin. Dilapidation is the throne on which he sits, most ruthless of the gods; Come not near to Mot the son of El, Lest he make you like a sheep in his mouth, And ye be carried off in his jaws" (Gray 1965:55–56). Cf. the destruction of Death as an eschatological enemy in Isa 25:7 and Rev 30:14. (For a similar notion in Zoroastrianism and in Qumran, see Winston 1966:206–207.) See also N. J. Tromp, *Primitive Conceptions of Death and the Nether World* (Rome, 1969):125. For *basileion* in the sense of 'kingdom,' cf. I Kings 14:8, LXX, A. In Polybius 3.15.3 it means 'seat of empire,' 'capital.'

15. Goodrick writes: "The A.V. [*KJV*] places this sentence in a parenthesis, and indeed it seems to break the thread of the argument. If, however, we accept the supplementary line given in the Sixtine Vulgate and the Complutensian—'But injustice is the very attainment of death'—we have a connection with what follows and what precedes. Against the genuineness of this addition, which is accepted by Fritzche and Grimm [Reuss, Zenner, Siegfried, and Cornely], it may be urged that it occurs in no Greek MSS. at all, and according to Deane is found in very few Latin ones of weight." (It is rejected by Bauermeister, Reusch, Gutberlet, Deane, Feldmann, Gregg, Heinisch, and Fichtner.) Cf. Ps-Aristeas 212: "Injustice is the deprivation of life."

II. SPEECH OF THE WICKED WHO HAVE COVENANTED WITH DEATH
(1:16–2:24)

1   16 But godless men have summoned Death through word and
            deed;
        thinking him a friend they pined for him,
        and made a pact with him,
        for they are worthy to be members of his party.

3   1 But the souls of the just are in God's hand,
        our life is short and full of trouble;
        there is no remedy at man's end,
        and no one has been known to have returned from the grave.

     2 By mere chance did we come to be,
        and thereafter we shall be as though we had never been,
        for the breath in our nostrils is but a puff of smoke;
        our reason is a mere spark within our throbbing heart,

     3 and when that is extinguished, our body will turn to ashes,
        and our life breath will be scattered like thin air.

     4 Our name will be forgotten with the passage of time,
        and none will recall our deeds;
        our life will be gone like the traces of a cloud
        and dispersed as mist,
        pursued by the sun's rays
        and overborne by its heat.

     5 For our time is the passing of a shadow,
        and there is no reversal of our end;
        it has been sealed, and none overturns it.

     6 Come then, let us enjoy the good things at hand,
        and make use of creation with youthful zest.

     7 Let us take our fill of costly wine and perfumes,
        and let no spring blossom pass us by.

     8 Let us crown ourselves with rosebuds before they wither.

9 Let no meadow fail to share in our revelry,
   let us everywhere leave tokens of our merriment,
   for this is our portion and our birthright.

10 Let us tyrannize the poor honest man,
   let us not spare the widow,
   nor reverence the elder's hair long grey.

11 Let brute force be the standard of our right,
   for weakness is proved ineffectual.

12 Let us entrap the just man, for his presence is inconvenient
         to us,
   and he opposes our actions;
   he reproaches us for our lawlessness,
   and charges us with falseness to our training.

13 He professes a knowledge of God, and styles himself child of
         the Lord.

14 He is a living refutation of our designs.
   His very sight is oppressive to us,

15 for his life-style is odd,
   and his ways are weird.

16 He regarded us as counterfeits,
   and avoids us like filth;
   he pronounces the final lot of the just happy,
   and boasts that God is his father.

17 Let us see if his statements are true,
   and make trial of what will happen to him in the end;

18 for if the just man is God's son, he will assist him
   and rescue him from the clutches of his opponents.

19 Let us afflict him with outrage and torment him,
   so that we may gauge the measure of his reasonableness
   and assay his forbearance of evil.

20 Let us condemn him to a shameful death,
   for on his own showing he will receive deliverance.

21 So they argued and were misled;
   blinded by their malice

22 they were ignorant of God's mysteries;
   they entertained no hope that holiness would have its reward,
   and passed up the prize of unblemished souls.

23 But God created man for immortality,
   and made him an image of his own proper being;

24 it was through the devil's envy that Death entered into the
  cosmic order,
and they who are his own experience him.

NOTES

1:16. *summoned . . . pined . . . made. prosekalesanto . . . etakēsan
. . . ethento.* Gnomic Aorists. *tēkōmai* in its metaphorical sense of waste
or pine away is a poetic word (cf. Homer *Odyssey* 5.396; Euripides
Medea 159; Theocritus 1.66, 82, 88, 91). For the notion of pining for
Death, cf. *Apoc. Abraham* 23: "They who will to do evil . . . over them I
gave him [Azazel] power, and to be beloved of them"; 13: "Those who
follow thee [Azazel] and love what thou willest." For the personification
of Hades, cf. IV Ezra 8:53; Rev 6:8; 20:14. The rabbis saw Satan, man's
evil inclination, and the angel of death as identical (*BT Baba Batra* 162).

made a pact. Cf. Isa 28:15: "We have made a covenant with Death,
concluded a pact with Sheol"; Philo *Her.* 45: "The life that looks to creation has never risen at all nor sought to rise, but makes its lair in the
recesses of Hades and rejoices in a form of living, which is not worth the
pains"; *Somn.* 1.151: "the depths of Hades are the abode allotted to the
bad, who from first to last have made dying their occupation . . ."; *Deus*
56: "But those who have made a compact and a truce with the body
. . ."; *LA* 2.18: "So from the vices is he called unjust and foolish and un-
manly, whensoever he has invited (*proskalesētai*) to himself and given a
hearty welcome to the corresponding dispositions"; *Mig.* 16: "But some
make a truce with the body and maintain it till their death, and are buried
in it as in a coffin or shell or whatever else you like to call it."

worthy to be members of his party. For *meris* in sense of 'party,' 'faction,' cf. Plato *Laws* 692B; Demosthenes 18.64; Plutarch *Moralia* 203B.
The idea of being worthy either of wisdom or of death recurs in our book
more than once. Wisdom goes about seeking them that are worthy of her
(6:16). Grace and mercy are to God's chosen (*eklektois,* 3:9; cf. I Enoch
5:7). In contrast to the wicked, the righteous were found by God to be
worthy of himself (3:5); cf. 11:25: "or how could that which was undesignated by you have been preserved?"; Eccles 6:10 "Whatever happens
it was designated (*niqrā'*) long ago and it was known that it would happen"; IV Ezra 10:57: "Thou art blessed above many, and art named before the Most High as but few"; *Mek. Pisḥa,* on Exod 13:2: "There were
three whose names were given to them (*niqrī'û*) by The Holy One,
blessed be He. . . . We find that the names of the righteous and their
deeds are revealed before God even before they are born . . ."; Rom

8:28–30: "And those whom He predestined he also called"; *CD* 2.11: "And in all of them He raised for Himself 'men called by name' "; *BR* 3.8. For the problem of freedom and determinism, see Introduction, VII.8, where it is shown that a concept of relative freedom does not necessarily contradict the notion of predestinarianism. For *meris,* cf. 2:24; II Macc 1:26; Ps Sol 5:6: "For man and his portion (*meris*) lie before thee in the balance; he cannot add to, so as to enlarge, what has been prescribed by thee"; *Apoc. Abraham* 22, where the wicked are Azazel's portion assigned to him from the beginning; II Bar 42:7: "For corruption shall take those that belong to it, and life those that belong to it." The word *goral* plays a similar role in the Qumran scrolls; cf., for example, 1QS 4.24; 11.7–8; 3.24; IQH 3.22–23; 11.11–12; 1QM 1.1; 13.12.

2:1–20. The arguments of the wicked may be briefly summarized. Death, they claim, is final and our destiny unalterable. Life is a mere chance event; it is short and troublesome and will soon be forgotten. The unavoidable conclusion is self-evident: Let us enjoy while we can, for this is clearly our allotted portion. Moreover, since experience shows that might is right, it would be inexpedient to avoid the exploitation of helpless weaklings. Indeed, we must further take the initiative and exterminate men of integrity who espouse ideal principles of justice. It is only proper that these blind fanatics be put to the final test along with their fatuous philosophy of life. It should be clear at once that the wicked described here do not represent any particular philosophical group or political faction. The wicked of all ages have cynically culled whatever has suited them from the philosophical and scientific literature of their respective periods to bolster their frankly aggressive and opportunistic designs. Although the Epicurean emphasis on the finality of death, the denial of Divine Providence, and the legitimacy of pleasure have to some extent been harnessed by the godless crew described in this chapter to further their own ends, only a grossly distorted understanding of Epicureanism could conceivably reconcile that philosophy with the latter's crude and unprincipled brand of hedonism. (Completely unconvincing is Dupont-Sommer's attempt to identify the wicked of this chapter with the Epicureans [1935:90–109]; cf. Weisengoff 1949:40–65.) The Cyrenaic philosophy would undoubtedly come much closer to the views of the wicked, but that school of thought (which flourished in the second half of the fourth and the first quarter of the third centuries BCE) had already disintegrated before the advance of the more successful Epicureans and could hardly have been the model used by them. The commentary will attempt to distinguish the various components utilized in the speech of the wicked and the popular origin of much of it.

2:1. The author prefers to let the unjust aggressors speak for themselves in the manner of the Hellenistic diatribe, which often makes use of an imaginary adversary. (See Bultmann 1910 and 1976 and the literature there cited.) The speech of the sinners in I Enoch 102:6–11 is somewhat similar to that of the wicked in our passage. See Larcher 1969:106–112; Nickelsburg, Jr. 1972: 128–129; Motzo 1924:53–55. The pessimism expressed in the speech of the wicked is a feature frequently apparent in the popular thought and poetry of Hellenistic and Imperial times (see Nock 1966:xxxiii; Cumont 1949:131).

to themselves. This must be the meaning of *en heautois* in view of 2:6, 9 (Fichtner).

short and full of trouble. Cf. Gen 47:7; Job 14:1–2: "Man that is born of woman is of few days, and full of trouble. He comes forth like a flower, and withers; he flees also as a shadow, and continues not"; Job 10:20; Eccles 2:22–23; Lucretius 3.914–915: "Brief is this enjoyment for us puny men: soon it will be past, nor ever thereafter will it be ours to call it back"; Catullus 5.4–6: "for us, when the short light has once set, remains to be slept the sleep of one unbroken night"; Syrian inscription: "nothing remains any longer; the sum of things is life, death, and toil." "There is the mosaic representing a skeleton, with the motto *Gnōthi Sauton,* in the Museo dei Termi in Rome. Cf. [Menander] Frag. 538: 'When thou wouldst know thyself and who thou art, look on the gravestones as thou journeyest by. There are the bones and unsubstantial dust of men who once were kings . . . Hades is the common lot of mortals all. Look thou on these and know thyself the man thou art.' Other commonplaces are the Syrian favourite *oudeis athanatos,* which means, 'no one is not subject to death,' and is not a denial of life hereafter, as also, *hosa gennatai teleitai,* 'All things that are born die,' and *eis auto egennēthēs,* 'Thou wast born to have this end'" (Nock 1966:xxxii–xxxiv). There is also the famous maxim repeated so often on epitaphs that it is sometimes expressed only by initials: "I was not; I was; I am not; I do not care" (H. Dessau, *Inscriptiones Selectae Latinae* [1892–1916], 8162). Cf. also Amphis (fourth century BCE, in his comedy *Government by Women*): "Drink! Play! Life is mortal, short (*oligos*) is our time on earth. Death is deathless once one is dead" (Athenaeus 336C); M. Aurel. 4.2: "Fail not to note how short-lived are all mortal things, and how paltry—yesterday a little mucus, tomorrow a mummy or burnt ash [*tephra.* Cf. Wisd 2:3]." There is a long poem in a Roman inscription directed against the old-style eschatology of the underworld: "There is no boat in Hades, no ferry man Charon, no Aeacus keeper of the keys, nor any dog called Cerberus. All of us who have died and gone below are bones and ashes (*ostea, tephra gegonamen*): There is nothing else." See R. Lattimore, *Themes in Greek and Latin Epitaphs* (reprint Urbana, 1962):75.

returned. Cf. Job 7:9–10. For *analyein* in this sense, cf. 5:12; I Esd 3:3; Tobit 2:9 (B); III Macc 5:21; II Macc 15:28; Luke 12:36. It could also mean 'redeem.' Cf. the Egyptian *Song of the Harper:* "There is none who comes back from (over) there, / That he may tell their state, / That he may tell their needs, / That he may still our hearts, / Until we (too) may travel to the place where they have gone" (*ANET*:467).

2. *By mere chance.* The adverb *autoschediōs* ('offhand,' 'rough and ready') is first attested here. Cf. Philo *Somn.* 2.50; Pausanius 6.24.3. Chance played a crucial role in the Epicurean cosmology. Cf. Lucretius 2.1–58: "And the seeds of things themselves of their own accord, jostling from time to time by chance, were driven together in many ways, rashly, idly, and in vain, at last those united, which, suddenly cast together, might become ever and anon the beginnings of great things, of earth and sea and sky, and the race of living creatures"; Plutarch *Moralia* 964C: "an atom swerves to the very smallest extent in order that the heavenly bodies, living things, and chance may come into existence and that what is in our power may not perish." (See C. Bailey's commentary [1947] on Lucretius, vol. 2, pp. 964–965.) Moreover, the formation of the Whirl or Vortex, the second stage in the process of world production according to the Atomic theory of Leucippus and Democritus, could be described in Aristotelian terms as taking place by chance (*apo tautomatou:* Artistotle *Physica* B4, 196a24). Democritus would have said that it took place by necessity (*kat' anangkēn:* D.L. 9.45). Chance as a cause of physical events in Atomism is mentioned only by commentators and critics. Cf. Cicero *Tusc.* 1.22: "[Democritus] makes the soul consist of minute smooth round bodies brought together in some sort of accidental collision." See W. K. C. Guthrie, *A History of Greek Philosophy* (Cambridge, 1965): 2. 414–419. In Ecclesiastes, the term *miqreh,* 'chance,' is used seven times, and refers to the fixed and unalterable 'destiny of death' which hangs over every man and meets him at the appointed time without reference to his conduct (2:14,15; 3:19; 9:2*f*) (Hengel 1.119).

as though we had never been. Cf. Obad 16, LXX: *kai esontai kathōs ouch hyparchontes;* Job 10:19; Sir 44:9 (*kai egenonto hōs ou gegonotes*); I Enoch 102:11: "Nevertheless they perished and became as though they had not been (*egenonto hōs ouk ontes*)."

2–3. *smoke . . . scattered like thin air.* Cf. *Iliad* 23.100: "but the spirit like a vapor (*kapnos*) was gone beneath the earth, gibbering faintly"; Plato *Phaedo* 70A: "and when the soul leaves the body and departs from it, straightway it flies away and is no longer anywhere, scattering like a breath or smoke (*kapnos*)"; Lucretius 3.233: "for it is a certain thin breath that deserts the dying"; 3.455: "And so it is natural that all the nature of the mind should also be dissolved, even as is smoke, into the high breezes of the air"; Seneca *Troades* 393*ff;* Sext. *Math.* 9.72: "and are not, as Epicurus said, 'dispersed like smoke (*kapnou dikēn*) when released from their bodies'"; Cicero *Tusc.* 1.11.24: "if the soul is breath it will perhaps be dispersed in space; if fire it will be quenched."

2. *a mere spark.* The Stoics conceived of the *hēgemonikon* or ruling part of the soul as a fiery intelligent breath (*pneuma noeron enthermon: SVF* 2.779, 773; 1.135–136; 3.49) that has its seat in the heart. Cf. Philo *Cher.* 30: "reason with its fierce and burning heat (*enthermon kai pyrōaē*)." For the view of the soul as consisting of the purest type of fire which rises until it finds its natural place in the sphere of the fixed stars, see Cicero *Tusc.* 1.43 (also attested for Heraclides of Pontus by Tertullian *De Anima* 9). Cf. Seneca *De Otio* 5.5: "or whether that theory is true which strives especially to prove that man is part of the divine spirit, that some part, sparks, as it were, of the stars fell down to earth and lingered here in a place that is not their own." Macrobius says that Heraclitus described the soul as a "spark of the substance of the stars" (DK, A.15. Macrobius' report, however, is unreliable). In the *Chaldean Oracles* (Frag. 44, Des Places), the human soul is composed of a spark of the cosmic soul (*psychaion spinthēra*), mingled with portions of the 'Paternal Intellect,' and of 'Will.' The spark gives it immortal life. The Gnostics liked to speak of the divine sparks of light in favored men: Irenaeus 1.24.1; Epiphanius *Haereses* 23.2.2; 23.1.9; 37.4; 39.2; *Excerpta ex Theodoto* 1:3; 3:1; Hippolytus *Refutatio omnium Haeresium* 6.17.7; *Paraphrase of Shem:* 46.12*ff.* See W. Bousset, *Kyrios Christos* (trans. J. B. Steely, New York, 1970):259, n.53.

heart. In the ancient world the party favoring the brain as the organ of ultimate control was a minority. It included Alcmaeon, the author of *The Sacred Disease*, Plato, and Straton. Empedocles, Democritus, Aristotle, Diocles, Praxagoras, most of the Stoics [some Stoics located the *hēgemonikon* in the brain: *SVF* 2.910; 3.33], and the Epicureans, all hold that 'thought,' or 'mind' has its seat in the heart (or in the chest). The matter should have been settled by the dissections of Herophilus (third century BCE) which clearly showed that the nerves originated in the brain. But though his discovery was confirmed by Erasistratus (who lived in Alexandria together with and after Herophilus), Chrysippus would not give up the heart as the central organ and fell back on the authority of Praxagoras (second half of the fourth century BCE). See F. Solmsen, "Greek Philosophy and the Discovery of the Nerves," *Kleine Schriften* (Hildesheim, 1968) 1. 536–582, esp. 577 and 580.

3. *extinguished.* Cf. Philo *Somn.* 1.31: "When we die is it [the *hēgemōn nous*] quenched (*sbennytai*) and does it share the decay of our bodies?"; Plutarch *Moralia* 987D: "until it [the spirit of many beasts] is quenched (*engkatasbesthē*) altogether like a fire and perishes"; M. Aurel. 7.32: "Of Death: Either dispersion (*skedasmos*) of atoms; or, if a single whole, either extinction (*sbesis*) or a change of state (*metastasis*)"; 12.5 (*to panteles apesbēkenai*); 8.25 (*ē sbesthēnai to pneumation*); 11.3; Philo *Abr.* 258; *Her.* 276.

4. *forgotten.* Cf. Eccles 2:16; 9:5; M. Aurel. 4.6: "Within a very short time both thou and he will be dead, and a little later not even your names will be left behind you"; 2.17: "All the life of man's body is a stream that flows, all the life of his mind, dream, and delirium; his existence a warfare and a sojourn in a strange land; his after-fame, oblivion."

traces of a cloud. Cf. Hosea 13:3; Job 7:9.

dispersed. Cf. Plato *Phaedo* 77D: "You have the childish fear that when the soul goes out from the body, the wind will really blow it away and scatter it (*diaskedannysin*); M. Aurel. 6.4, 24; 10.7.

5. *reversal.* The noun *anapodismos* is first attested here. Cf. Vettius Valens 226.1.

6. *let us enjoy.* We have here an ancient and very popular motif. Cf. Isa 22:13: "Eat and drink, for tomorrow we die"; cf. I Cor 15:32; Eccles 9:7; 11:9. Our theme appears on what may well be the earliest known Greek inscription in Jerusalem, the graffito from the tomb of Jason dating from the time of Alexander Janneus: *euphrainesthe hoi zōntes to de loipon . . . pein homa phagein* (P. Benoit, '*Atiqot* [1964]:39; *IEJ* 17 [1967]:112–113; B. Lifshitz, *RB* 73 [1966]:248–255); Hengel 1974: 1. 60. Euripides *Alcestis* 782ff: "All men have to pay the debt of death, and there is not a mortal who knows whether he is going to be alive on the morrow . . . cheer up, drink, reckon the days yours as you live them; the rest belongs to fortune"; "Remembering that the same end awaits all mortals, enjoy life as long as you live. This teaching I give, Euodus, to all mortals: do not grudge yourself any good thing. Why do you struggle? Enjoy yourself and so delight in life. For know this well: once you have descended to the drink of Lethe, you will see no more of those things that are above, once this soul has flown out of this body" (Peek 1960: nos. 371 and 465). Horace *Odes* 1.11.8: *carpe diem;* 1.9.13–16: "Cease to ask what the morrow will bring forth, and set down as gain each day that fortune grants! Nor in thy youth neglect sweet love nor dances, whilst life is still in its bloom and crabbed age is far away!"; Petronius *Satryicon* 34: [after a slave brought in a silver skeleton and put it on the table, Trimalchio said] "Alas for us poor mortals, all that poor man is is nothing. So we shall all be, after the world below takes us away. Let us live then while it goes well with us" (cf. Herodotus 2.78, where this custom is attributed to the Egyptians): Philo *Det.* 33ff; Seneca *Ep.* 123.10; Egyptian *Song of the Harper:* "Follow thy desire, as long as thou shalt live. Put myrrh upon thy head and clothing of fine linen upon thee, . . . Fulfill thy needs upon earth, after the command of thy heart, Until there come for thee that day of mourning. . . . [Refrain:] Make holiday, and weary not therein! Behold, it is not given to a man to take his property with him. Behold, there is not one who departs who comes back again!" (*ANET*:467).

the good things at hand. "*tōn ontōn agathōn* may denote either those ready to hand or 'that really exist,' are not clouds or shadows or imaginary delights like those of virtue, but tangible sources of enjoyment" (Goodrick following Grimm). Cf. Philo *Conf.* 182; Xenophon *Mem.* 2.1.28.

with youthful zest. Cf. Eccles 11:9. Grimm, with the support of some manuscripts, would read *hōs en neotēti.*

7. *costly wine and perfumes.* Cf. Aelianus *Varia Historia* 12.31 (where we are told that the ancients were wild about a mixture of wine and perfume called *myrrinē*).

8. *crown ourselves with rosebuds.* A Greek touch. Cf. Judith 15:13; Lucretius 3.912–915: "This, too, men often do, when they are lying at the board, and hold their cups in their hands, and shade their brows with garlands: they say from the heart, 'Brief is this enjoyment for us puny men: soon it will be past, nor ever thereafter will it be ours to call it back"; Horace *Odes* 1.36.15; 2.3.13: "Hither bid slaves bring wines and perfumes and the too brief blossoms of the lovely rose, while fortune and youth allow, and the dark threads of the Sisters Three"; *Anacreontea* 32: "Why at my grave your unguents pour? Why vain anoilment give? While yet I live, embalm my forehead o'er. Bring roses, and some maiden fair; for ere to join I go, the rout below, I fain would banish care"; Robert Herrick: "Gather ye rosebuds while ye may, / Old Time is still a-flying, / And this same flower that smiles today, / Tomorrow will be dying."

9. *revelry.* Cf. II Macc 9:7; III Macc 2:3.

portion. Cf. Isa 57:6: *ekeinē sou hē meris, houtos sou ho klēros* ("that is thy portion, this is thy lot"); Jer 13:25, LXX; Eccles 2:10; 3:22; 9:9.

10. *tyrannize.* For *katadynasteuō,* cf. 15:14; 17:2; Ezek 18:12, LXX; Sir 48:12; Ps-Aristeas 24, 146–148; Acts 10:38. The verb is practically a *koinē* word, first appearing in Xenophon *Symposium* 5.8; cf. Strabo 270.

grey. Cf. II Macc 6:23

11. *brute force.* Cf. Plato *Gorgias* 483D*ff.*

12. *entrap the just man, for his presence is inconvenient.* Virtually a quotation from the LXX version of Isa 3:10, where the Hebrew is quite different. It is quoted by many of the Church Fathers, following its citation in Barnabas 6:7, as referring to Christ; cf. Justin Martyr *Dial.* 17; Eusebius *PE* 13.13; Clem. Alex. *Strom.* 5.14 (where Plato *Rep.* 361E is also quoted: "the just man will have to endure the lash, the rock, chains, the branding-iron in his eyes, and finally, after every extremity of suffering, he will be crucified"); Augustine *Civ.Dei* 17.20.1: "In one of these books that is called the Wisdom of Solomon Christ's passion is most clearly prophesied. For surely it is his wicked slayers who are recorded as saying: 'Let us set an ambush for the righteous man. . . .'" The seventeenth-century commentator C. à Lapide saw in the "shameful death" of v. 20 a direct allusion to the cross, and in the word *achrēstos* ('ineffectual') of v. 11 an insulting play on the name *Christos.*

13. *child of the Lord.* The author's treatment of the suffering and vindi-

cation of the child of God is a homily based chiefly on the fourth Servant Song in Isa 52:12 with some help from earlier and later passages in that book. Although the meaning 'child' for *pais* is here fixed by v. 16d and 18a, this may be due to our author's misunderstanding of the LXX's oscillation between *pais* and *doulos*. In Isa 49:1–6, *doulos* is used twice and *pais* only once, while in Isa 52:13; 53:1, *pais* only is used. See Suggs 1957:26–33; cf. J. Jeremias, "Amnos tou Theou/pais Theou," *ZNW* 34 (1935): 188*f;* id. in *TDNT* 5. 684; Philonenko 1958:81–88. Philonenko's arguments that our author is referring to the Teacher of Righteousness from Qumran are inconclusive. In *Joseph and Asen,* Joseph is designated "son of God" (6:6; 13:10, Philonenko). Cf. Philo *Conf.* 145–148; *Sobr.* 56; *QG* 1.92; *Somn.* 1.173. See L. K. K. Dey, *The Intermediary World and Patterns of Perfection in Philo and Hebrews* (Missoula: Scholars Press 1975):40–42.

14. *oppressive to us.* Cf. Isa 53:2; Philo *Prob.* 28: "It is this which Antisthenes had in view when he said that a virtuous man is heavy to carry"; John 3:20: "For every one who does evil hates the light."

15. *is odd* (*anomoios tois allois*). By the rhetorical figure *comparatio compendiaria* ('short comparison') *for anomois tō tōn allōn*='unlike other men's'; cf. 7:3; *Iliad* 17.51; Rev 13:11 (Grimm).

16. *avoids us.* Cf. Philo *Mut.* 38: "though actually existing he [Enoch] was hidden from us and shunned our company."

final lot. Cf. Sir 1:13; 7:36; 51:14.

father. Cf. Isa 63:16; 64:7; Sir 23:1,4.

17. *in the end* (*en ekbasei autou*). *ekbasis* in the sense of 'end of a person's life' is first found here. Cf. *P. Fay.* 91.21 (first century CE); Heb 13:7. Similarly, when Joseph's brothers plot his death, they say, "let us kill him, and we shall see what will become of his dreams' (Gen 37:20) (Nickelsburg 1972:49).

18. *he will assist him.* Cf. Isa 42:1: *antilēmpsomai autou;* Matt 27:43. Both Matthew and our own text are reminiscent of Ps 22:9. For further discussion, see K. Stendahl, *The School of St. Matthew* (Philadelphia, 1968):140–141. For *antilēmpsetai,* ('assist') cf. Isa 59:16, LXX.

19. *afflict.* For *etazō* in this sense, cf. Gen 12:17, LXX.

forbearance of evil (*aneksikakia*). First attested in Wisd; cf. Plutarch *Moralia* 90E; Lucian *De Parasito* 53; Heliodorus 10.12; Epictetus *Enchiridion* 10. For the just man's reasonableness and forbearance, cf. Isa 53.7

20. *a shameful death.* The dative *aschēmoni thanatō* is late Greek (classical form could be either *katadikazein tina thanatou* or *k. thanaton tinos*). Diodorus 1.77; 13.101; Aelianus *Varia Historia* 12.49; Matt 20:18 (Grimm).

22. *God's mysteries.* Doctrine concerning the afterlife is referred to as a mystery in I Enoch 103:2: "I know a mystery and have read the heavenly

tablets, and have seen the holy books, and have found written therein and inscribed regarding them: That all goodness and joy and glory are prepared for them, and written down for the spirits who have died in righteousness"; 104:12; 61:5. See R. Brown, "The Semitic Background of the New Testament Mysterion," *Biblica* 39 (1958) 426–448; 40 (1959) 70–87; cf. I Cor 15:51: "Listen, I will unfold a mystery: we shall not all die"; 4:1–5.

23. *immortality. aphtharsia* is an Epicurean term. Cf. Epicurus *Epistulae* 1.77; 3.123; Philodemus *Peri Theōn* 3.8. It is quite frequent in Philo: *Op.* 153; *Sacr.* 5; *Agr.* 100; *Ebr.* 140; *Abr.* 55: *epei syngenes men aidiotētos aphtharsia* ("since imperishableness is akin to eternality"); *QG* 3.11. See also IV Macc 9:22; II Cor 15:53.

his own proper being. Some codices read *aidiotētos,* which would make the two lines parallel. Cf. Philo *Op.* 44.

24. *devil's envy.* "In Ps 108:6, LXX, *diabolos* is the 'accuser'; in Esther 7:4; 8:1, LXX, Haman is called *diabolos* in the sense of 'opponent' or 'enemy.' In I Macc 1:36, the *akra* is called a *diabolos* in the sense of 'obstacle.' The LXX also used diabolos for Hebrew satan, in the sense of 'the one who separates,' 'the enemy,' 'the calumniator,' 'the seducer.' Since this is an innovation in the LXX, we can only deduce the meaning from the rendering and from the context. The latter seldom suggests 'calumniator,' but rather 'accuser,' or 'adversary.' This is so in I Chron 21:1 and Job 1 and 2, unless we prefer 'seducer'" (Foerster, in *TDNT* 2. 72). For the devil's envy, see II Enoch 31:3–6; *Vita Adae* 12–17 (12:1:"With a heavy sigh, the devil spoke: 'O Adam! all my hostility, envy, and sorrow is for thee, since it is for thee that I have been expelled from my glory"); III Baruch 4:8; *Tosef. Sotah* 4:17; *BT Sotah* 9b; *BR* 18.6; *BT Sanh.* 59b; *ARN* 1; Jos. *Ant.* 1.1.4. (For envy attributed to God, see *Apoc. Moses* 18:4; *Hypostasis of the Archons* 138, 6–10; *On the Origin of the World* 119 and *Testimony of Truth,* [Robinson 1977:174 and 412]: *PRE* 13. For the counterargument that God was not jealous, see Theophilus *Ad. Autolycum* 2.25; Irenaeus *Adv. Haer.* 5.24.20; Ps-Clement 17.16). Bois (1890) and Gregg (1909) thought this verse referred to Cain. "The murder of Abel by Cain," wrote Gregg, "was unquestionably prompted by jealousy. . . . Moreover, in 10:1–4, the author makes the sin of Adam of small importance, while Cain is the first 'unrighteous man,' the ancestor and symbol of all who afterwards deserted wisdom." If the allusion of our verse is to Genesis 3[4E], as is most likely, it is one of the earliest extant Jewish texts to equate the serpent with the devil.

A closely analogous attempt to attribute death to the devil's envy is to be found in Theophilus *Ad Autolycum* 2.29: "When Satan saw that Adam and his wife not only were alive but had produced offspring, he was overcome by envy (*phhonō pheromenos*) because he was not strong enough to put them to death; and because he saw Abel pleasing God, he worked upon his brother called Cain and made him kill his brother Abel. And so the beginning of death came into this world, to reach the whole race of men to this very day." Similarly, according to the *Hypostasis of the Archons,* Ialdabaoth envies the high station of his son Sabaoth, who had been endowed with a psychic nature capable of elevation. His envy takes on an existence of its own, and in its turn gives rise to Death (144, 3–14 [Ballard:39 and 112]. (In Irenaeus *Adv. Haer.* 1.30.9, envy and death are linked together as the legacy of Cain's murder of Abel). See W. C. van Unnik 1972:120–32; *De aphthonia van God in de oudchristelijke literatur* (Amsterdam, London, 1973).

Death entered into the cosmic order. Except for Wisd and II and IV Maccabees, *kosmos* is used in the LXX only in the original meaning of 'ornament,' 'arrangement,' or 'drawing up of an army.' See Freudenthal 1890:217. The notion that death came into the world through the devil's envy seems to be an echo of Zoroastrian teaching, although, as noted above (on 1:13), the author of Wisd, unlike the Iranian sources, is undoubtedly referring to spiritual rather than physical death. According to Zarathustra, the original static world was perfect, and alteration came into it only through the malicious assault of the Hostile Spirit. "Once death and destruction had been brought into the world, immortality ceased for *gētig* [i.e. material] creatures, and was replaced by the inevitable processes of birth and death. In this state of things devout sacrifice has a *spenta* ('bounteous,' 'beneficent') function, furthering the struggle of the good creation—a function which will continue till the last sacrifice takes place at the end of limited time, and immortality becomes again the lot of all God's creatures" (Boyce:231). Moreover, the attack of Ahriman is motivated by envy: "The Destructive Spirit, ever slow to know, was unaware of the existence of Ohrmazd. Then he rose up from the depths and went to the border from whence the lights are seen. When he saw the light of Ohrmazd intangible, he rushed forward. Because his will is to smite and his substance is envy (*arišk-gōhrīh*), he made haste to destroy it" (*Greater Bundahishn* 1.7, translation in Zaehner 1972:313). Cf. *Yasna* 9.5: "Under the rule of brave Yima, there was neither heat nor cold, neither old age nor death, nor envy created by the daevas"; *Yašt* 15.16; translation in F. Wolff, *Avesta* (Strassburg, 1910):31, 269). Nor was it difficult for the author of Wisd to identify the serpent of Genesis with Ahriman, since in his attack on the material world we are informed that "he rushed upon it in envious desire. . . . Like a serpent he darted forward, trampled on as much of the sky as was beneath [*sic*] the earth, and rended it" (*GB* 41.10 – 42.6. See Zaehner 1961:262). For the knowledge of Zoroastrianism in Alexandria, see Pliny the Elder *NH* 30.2.4; D.L. 1.8; Bidez-Cumont 1938: 1. 85–88; Hengel 1974: 1. 230. It may also be noted that in the *Apoc. Abraham* 23, the serpent is identified as the instrument of

Azazel. In *Apoc. Moses* 16, he is the devil's vessel and in III Bar 9:7 Sammael took the serpent as a garment. (According to *Vita Adae* 33 and II Enoch 31, it was the devil who led Eve astray.)

experience him. A. M. Dubarle proposed the following translation: "and they who belong to his [the devil's] party put the world to the test." The notion of perverse spirits who seek to mislead man was current in books like I Enoch, Jubilees, *Test.XII,* and the writings of Qumran. See Dubarle 1964:187–195; cf. S. Lyonnet 1958:27–36.

III. SUFFERINGS OF THE IMMORTAL JUST
ONLY A TRIAL
(3:1–12)

3 1 But the souls of the just are in God's hand,
and torment shall in no way touch them.
2 In the eyes of the foolish they seemed to be dead;
their end was reckoned as suffering
3 and their journey hence utter ruin.
But they are at peace.
4 For even if in the sight of men they shall have been punished,
their hope is full of immortality;
5 and after a brief chastisement, they will be treated with great
kindness,
for God has tried them
and found them worthy to be his.
6 As gold in a blast furnace he tested them,
and as a whole burnt offering he accepted them.
7 In the moment of God's gracious dispensation they will blaze
forth,
and like sparks in the stubble they will fly in all directions.
8 They will judge nations and hold sway over peoples,
and the Lord shall be their sovereign for all eternity.
9 Those who have put their trust in him shall attain true
understanding,
and the faithful shall abide with him in love;
for grace and compassion are for his holy ones,
and a gracious visitation for his chosen.
10 But the godless will receive punishment tailored to their
scheming,
they who were careless of justice and rebelled against
the Lord.

11 Wretched indeed is he who sets at naught the discipline of
        wisdom;
   empty are such men's hopes, their efforts unavailing,
   their deeds futile;
12 their wives are frantic,
   their children worthless,
   their lineage under a curse.

NOTES

3:1–12. The author assures his readers that the physical death of the just is in reality only the beginning of a better existence, inasmuch as their souls would enjoy a blissful immortality after a brief period of chastisement during which they were tested and their sacrificial death accepted. Screened by the divine power, they will subsequently exercise judgment and sovereign rule over the nations. The author is deliberately vague, however, as to the precise timing and location of these post-mortem events. Some have suggested that, with the author of I Enoch (22), he envisaged the temporary abode of all souls in Sheol until the Final Judgment (cf. IV Ezra 7), but others consider it more likely that the judgment takes place immediately after death. See Grelot 1961:165–178; Delcor 1955:614–630; Larcher 1969:301–327; Nickelsburg 1972:88–89, 144–180; J. J. Collins, "Apocalyptic Eschatology as the Transcendence of Death," *CBQ* 36 (1974):21–43. See Introduction, VII.2.

3:1. *in God's hand.* Cf. I Enoch 102–105 (103:4: "And the spirit of you who have died in righteousness shall live and rejoice, and their spirits shall not perish"); *Sifre Num.* 139: "When a man dies, his soul is placed in the treasury, for it is written, 'yet the soul of my lord shall be bound in the bundle of life' (I Sam 25:29). I might conclude that this includes both the righteous and the wicked; the text reads: 'and the souls of thine enemies, them shall he sling out, as from the hollow of a sling.'" (Cf. *Koheleth R.* on Eccles 3:21; *BT Shab.* 152b: "The souls of the righteous are preserved under the throne of glory"; Philo *Abr.* 258: "[wisdom taught Abraham] that death is not the extinction of the soul but its separation and detachment from the body and its return to the place whence it came; and it came, as was shown in the story of creation, from God"; *QG* 1.86: "the end of worthy and holy men is not death but translation. . . . [Enoch] is said to have moved from a sensible and visible place to an incorporeal and intelligible form"; *Jos.* 264; *Det.* 49; *Spec.* 1.345. Josephus presents us with a radically dualistic anthropology very similar to that of Philo: "All of us, it is true, have mortal bodies, composed of perishable matter, but the soul lives forever, immortal; it is a portion of the Deity housed in our bodies" (*J.W.* 3.8.5); cf. the words placed by Josephus in the mouth of the Zealot leader Eleazar at Masada: "Life, not death, is man's misfortune. For it is death which gives liberty to the soul and permits it to depart to its own pure abode, there to be free from all calamity, but so long as it is imprisoned in a mortal body and tainted with all its miseries, it is, in sober truth, dead, for association with what is mortal ill befits that which is divine" (*J.W.* 7.8.7). In the extrabiblical apocalyptic literature, the dead are no longer described as 'shades' but as 'souls' or 'spirits' and survive as individual conscious beings who may either enjoy a blissful existence as a reward for their righteousness or receive punishment for their wickedness. We find a similar distinction in Homer's view of the soul of the dead as a mere shadow or 'idol' (*eidōlon*) without conscious life, and the Orphic-Pythagorean view of the soul as something separable from the body, which must be kept pure and immaculate to enable it to return to its divine home after death. Pindar, however, still employs the term *eidōlon* for the new Orphic view of the soul as an entity of divine origin, which has the power of foreseeing the future (*Frag.* 131). The Orphic reversal of the order of existence is perhaps best expressed in the Euripidean fragment quoted by Plato: "Who knoweth if to live is to be dead, and to be dead, to live?" (*Gorgias* 492E). See W. Jaeger, "The Greek Ideas of Immortality," *HTR* 52 (1959):135–147.

2. *In the eyes of the foolish.* The author of I Enoch puts these words into the mouth of the sinners: "As we die, so die the righteous, and what benefit do they reap for their deeds? Behold, even as we, so do they die in grief and darkness, and what have they more than we?" (102:6–7).

3. *journey.* For *poreia*, cf. Eccles 12:5, LXX; Luke 22:22; Plato *Phaedo* 107D; 115A: *tēn eis Hadou poreian.*

utter ruin. For *syntrimma*, cf. Isa 22:4; 59:7, LXX; Sir 40:9; I Macc 2:7.

at peace. Cf. Isa 57:2; 32:17, LXX; *Par.Jer.* 5:32: "I bless you, God of heaven and earth, the Rest (*hē anapausis;* cf. Wisd 4:7) of the souls of the righteous in every place"; *BR* 9.5, Th-Alb:7: "Why was death decreed for the righteous? Since as long as they are alive, they are at war with their evil impulse, but when they die, they are given respite, and this is the meaning of the verse, 'and there the weary are at rest' (Job 3:19)." "The usual custom in Palestine when mentioning a departed righteous person was to say (*PT Erubin* 3, end, 21C; *Pesaḥim* 4.1, 30d) *noaḥ nefesh,* 'whose soul is at rest,' as is clearly stated by Resh Lakish: 'Some are mentioned and blessed (with the word *noaḥ*), others are mentioned and cursed' (*Wayyik.R.* 32.6). . . . The expression *noaḥ nefesh* is indeed found on the Palestine tombstones of the first centuries c.e." (Lieberman 1942:70). See also A. Parrot, *Le 'Refrigerium' dans l'au delà* (Paris, 1937); Lieberman 1974:32–33.

4. *immortality*. Although the rabbis never speak of the 'immortality' of the soul, they quote Aquila's translation to Ps 48:15 *"Al mut-athanasia,"* which they refer, however, to the future world 'in which there is no death' (*PT Meg.* 3.4, 73b; *Wayyik.R.* 11.9; cf. *BT Avoda Zara* 35b). (See Urbach 1969:208); cf. IV Macc 18:23 (*psychas hagnas kai athanatous apeilēphotes para tou theou*); 16:13.

5. *after a brief chastisement*. Cf. Isa 54:7–8: "For a little while I forsook you, but with vast love I will bring you back. In slight anger, for a moment, I hid my face from you; but with kindness everlasting I will take you back in love—said the Lord your Redeemer"; 57:17, LXX: *brachy ti elypēsa auton; Test.Joseph* 2:6 (*en brachei aphistamenos*). Under the impact of the Antiochean persecution, the author of II Maccabees provides his readers with a more elaborate explanation in order to justify the great calamities which had come upon them: "Now, I appeal to those who happen upon this book, not to be cast down by these misfortunes, but rather to consider that these were retributions not intended to destroy, but rather only to discipline our people. As a matter of fact, it is a mark of favor not to leave impious ones alone for any length of time, but to inflict immediate punishment on them. When it comes to other nations the Lord shows his forbearance, and delays punishing them until they have reached the fullness of their iniquity, but for us he had determined differently, in order that he may not be compelled to punish us later when our sins have reached finality. For this reason he never withdraws his mercy from us" (6:12); cf. 7:33: *bracheōs epōrgistai;* 7:36; *Test.Benjamin* 5:5; I Peter 1:6; 5:10. Our author similarly writes at 12:22 below: "We, then, are thus chastened, but our enemies you scourge ten thousandfold"; cf. 16:3,5,11. Cf. also Philo *LA* 2.33–34: "But God will not let the offspring of 'the seeing' Israel be in such wise changed as to receive his death blow by the change, but will force him to rise and emerge as though from deep water and recover"; *Assumption of Moses* 12:11–12: "but those who sin . . . shall be punished with many torments by the nations. But wholly to root out and destroy them is not permitted." Jos. *Ant.* 4.6.6: "Yet misfortunes may well befall them of little moment and for a little while, whereby they will appear to be abased, though only thereafter to flourish once more to the terror of those who inflicted these injuries upon them"; *Ant.* 3.15.1; Ps Sol 13:4–10.

has tried them. Cf. Exod 16:4; Deut 8:16; Ps 26:2; Prov 3:11; Sir 2:1–5; I Enoch 108:9: "And the Lord tried them and their spirits were found pure"; Ps Sol 10:1–2; II Enoch 49:2. For suffering as discipline, see the Elihu speeches in Job 32–37.

6. *As gold in a blast furnace.* Cf. Zech 13:9; Mal 3:3; Ps 66:10; Prov 17:3; Sir 2:5; 1QH 5.15–15; Dan 11:35; 12:10; Philo *Sacr.* 80: "Again, let the fresh ripeness of the soul be 'roasted,' that is tested by the might of reason, as gold is tested by the furnace"; Seneca *De Providentia* 5:10: "Fire tests gold, misfortune brave men"; 16.1.6: "God does not make a spoiled pet of a good man; he tests him, hardens him, and fits him for his own service"; 4.7: "God hardens, reviews, and disciplines those whom he approves, whom he loves. Those, however, whom he seems to favor . . . he is really keeping soft against ills to come"; 3.3; Menander Frag. 691, Kock. *chōneutērion* ("smelting furnace") is found only in the LXX (I Kings 8:51 and elsewhere) and Patristic literature. (For *edokimasen,* cf. Ps 65:10, LXX; Sir 2:5; and for *prosedeksato,* cf. Amos 5:22, LXX.)

7. *God's gracious dispensation. episkopēs. episkopē,* 'visitation,' translates Hebrew *pekudah,* which can be used both in a bad sense and in a good sense, i.e. a visitation bringing either punishment or pardon. Cf. Jer 10:15, LXX; Isa 10:3; 29:6, LXX; Isa 23:17, LXX; Zech 10:3, LXX; 1QS 3.18; 4.18,26; *CD* 7.21. See Beyer, *TDNT* 2. 602; Volz:164–165.

blaze forth . . . like sparks in the stubble. For the imagery, cf. Zech 12:6; Exod 9:23, LXX; Isa 1:3; Joel 2:5; Obad 18; Nahum 2:4: *hōs astrapai diatrechousai;* Mal 4:1; I Enoch 48:9 Philo *Mig.* 123: "For a smoldering spark (*spinthēr*), even the very smallest, when it is blown up and made to blaze, lights a great pile; and so the least particle of virtue, when, warmed into life by bright hopes, it has shone out (*analampsē*). . . ." The notion of the future star-like brilliance of the righteous was quite common in Jewish apocalyptic. See Dan 12:3; I Enoch 104:2: "but now ye shall shine as the lights of heaven, ye shall shine and ye shall be seen"; 38:4; 39:76; IV Ezra 7:97: "how their force is destined to shine as the sun, and how they are destined to be made like the light of the stars, henceforth incorruptible"; II Bar 51:10; IV Macc 17:5: "not so majestic stands the moon in heaven, with its stars, as you stand; lighting the way to piety for your seven star-like sons; honored by God, and with them fixed in heaven"; II Enoch 66:7; cf. Matt 13:43; *Sifre Deut.* 10, Finkelstein:18 (the faces of the righteous in the future will be like the sun, moon, and stars). For astral immortality, see Hengel 1974: 1. 197. (Dupont-Sommer [1949] has sought to correct *kalamē* to *galaksiē,* but on insufficient grounds; cf. Larcher 1969:319, n.2.)

8. *will judge nations.* We similarly read in Dan 7:22: "and judgment was given for the saints of the Most High; and the time came, and the saints possessed the kingdom." Cf. 1 QpHab 5.4: "God will execute the judgment of the nations by the hand of his elect"; Matt 19:28; I Cor 6:2; Rev 20:4. We find a similar tableau in a late midrash: "In the future age, the Holy One, blessed be He, will be seated, while the angels will place crowns upon the exalted ones of Israel, and they will be seated, and the

Holy One, blessed be He, will sit among them as Court President and they will judge the nations of the world . . ." (*Tanḥ.* Buber, *Kedoshim* 1; cf. *ShR* 5.12).

sovereign for all eternity. Cf. Ps 10:16.

9. *shall attain true understanding.* Cf. Dan 11:33, LXX; *synēsousin;* 12:3: *hoi synientes;* 12:10: "but they that are wise shall understand."

for grace and compassion are for his holy ones. Cf. I Enoch 5:7: *kai tois eklektois phōs kai charis kai eirēnē.*

10. *punishment. epitimia* in the sense of punishment is first found here. Cf. *OGIS* 669.43 (Egypt, first century CE): *P. Lond.* 77.53; Jos. *Ag.Ap.* 2.199; II Cor 2:6 (also found in Patristic literature).

tailored to their scheming. Foreshadowing of the principle of talion which assumes such a dominant role in part C of the book.

11. Alternation of singular and plural is not uncommon in wisdom literature; 11a should be read as a parenthesis (Fichtner 1938).

sets at naught. Cf. Prov 1:7, LXX.

empty . . . hopes. Cf. Job 7:6, LXX; Sir 31.1.

12. *their children worthless.* Cf. Ezek 16:44: "As the mother, so her daughter"; Sir 41:5: "What a loathsome brood are the children of sinners; IV Ezra 9:17: "As is the ground so the sowings."

IV. STERILITY OF THE VIRTUOUS WILL ULTIMATELY BE CONVERTED TO FRUITFULNESS
(3:13 – 4:6)

3   13 Blessed indeed is the barren woman who is unstained,
    who has not gone to bed in sin,
    she shall be fruitful at the great assize of souls.
    14 And the eunuch who has not acted unlawfully
    or meditated wickedness against the Lord
    will receive the exquisite gift of grace in return for his
          steadfastness
    and a portion in the temple of the Lord to delight his heart
          the more.
    15 For the fruit of honest toil is glorious,
    and the root of wisdom is unfailing.
    16 But the children of adulterers will not reach maturity,
    and the seed of unlawful union will be destroyed.
    17 For even if they attain length of life, they will be of no
          account,
    and in the end their old age will be without honor.
    18 And if their end come swiftly, they will be without hope
    or consolation on the day of decision.
    19 For hard is the end of an unjust generation.

4   1 It is better to be childless, provided one is virtuous,
    for in virtue's remembrance there is immortality,
    since it wins recognition both from God and from men.
    2 Men imitate it when it is present,
    and when it is gone they yearn for it;
    and through all time, crowned with the victory wreath, it
          proceeds triumphally,
    a winner in the contest for prizes undefiled.
    3 But the swarming multitude of the wicked will be of no
          profit;

sprung from bastard shoots they will not strike deep root
nor secure a firm footing.
4 For even if their branches blossom for a season,
standing unstably they shall reel in the wind
5 and be uprooted by powerful gusts. Their shoots will be
snapped off before reaching full growth,
and their fruit will be useless, unripe for eating,
and fit for nothing.
6 For children who are products of illicit sex
are witnesses against their parents' vice on their day of
scrutiny.

NOTES

3:13 – 4:6. A person's status and stature in the Middle East were deeply
affected by the number of his progeny. Sexual sin, whether intentioned or
inadvertent, was believed to result in sterility. When Rachel finally gave
birth, she greatly rejoiced because "God has taken away my disgrace"
(Gen 30:23; cf. Luke 1:25). The author of I Enoch is quite explicit on
this point: "And barrenness has not been given to the woman, but on account of the deeds of her own hands she dies without children" (98:5).
Similarly, according to the midrash, during the period of Sarah's sterility,
Hagar told visiting women that Sarah was only seemingly righteous, for
otherwise she would not have been barren all those years (*BR* 45.4, Th-
Alb:451; cf. *BR* 54.22, Th-Alb:577). Our author, however, emphatically
denies any necessary connection between sin and sterility.

3:13. *barren. steira* is the recurring LXX rendering of Hebrew *'akarah*.
bed. koitē, used of sexual connection, is frequent in the LXX, where it
renders Hebrew *miškav*. Cf. Heb 13:4 (*hē koitē amiantos*).
fruitful. "The gist of the passage is that sterility, if pure, is redeemed by
a spiritual fertility" (Gregg). Cf. Philo *Deus* 13–15: "We might well expect, then, that the barren woman, not meaning the childless, but the firm
or solid [a play on words: *steiran-sterran*], who still abounds in power,
who with endurance and courage perseveres to the finish in the contest,
where the prize is the acquisition of the Best, should bring forth the
Monad which is of equal value with the Seven; for her nature is that of a
happy and goodly motherhood. And when she says that she who has had
many children languishes, her words are as clear as they are true. For
when the soul that is one departs from the one and is in travail with many

. . . she is pregnant with the lusts of the belly and those which have their seat below it."

14. *the eunuch.* The reference is clearly to Isa 56:3–5, where the prophet refers to those Jewish youth who were castrated at the hands of the Babylonian tyranny, and had consequently despaired of any share in Israel's future redemption (Deut 23:1–2). Isaiah encouraged them with the divine assurance: "I will give them in My House and within My walls, a monument and a name better than sons or daughters." According to *BT Sanh.* 93b, the captivity of Daniel, Hananiah, Mishael, and Azariah is the fulfillment of Isa 39:7 [=II Kings 20:18], and Rab takes the word 'eunuchs' in that verse literally. (The Talmud also identifies the "eunuchs who observe my Sabbaths" in Isa 56:4 with Daniel and his three associates.) Cf. Jerome's *Commentary on Daniel* 1:3 [*PL* 25:496]; Origen's *Commentary on Matthew* 15:5 [*PG* 13:1263–1265]; *PT Shab.* 6.9, 8d (where we are told that Daniel and his associates were eunuchs but were healed by passage through the fiery furnace). It should be noted that whereas Isa 56:3 refers to the Eunuch's observance of the Sabbath, our verse speaks only vaguely about his refraining from *anomēma.*

in the temple of the Lord. Probably, in heaven, though it may refer to the future temple; cf. Pss 11:4; 18:7; I Bar 2:16; Rev 7:15. Excluded from the earthly sanctuary, he shall have a place in the heavenly one.

to delight . . . the more. thumarēs is a Homeric word (*Iliad* 9.336; *Odyssey* 23.232); also in later prose (Lucian *Amores* 43). Cf. Philo *Abr.* 245; *Cont.* 66.

15. A man's true glory and fame consists not so much in his numerous physical offspring as in the fruit of his virtue and wisdom. Cf. *BR* 30.6, Th-Alb:271: " 'This is the line of Noah, Noah was a righteous man' (Gen 6:9), it is this which Scripture says, 'The fruit of the righteous is a tree of life' (Prov 11:30). What are the fruits of the righteous? Life, commandments, and good deeds." (Margoliouth quotes the more elaborate version of *Tanḥ.* Buber, on Gen 6:9): "At the time a man departs childless from this world he is grieved and cries. God says to him: Why are you crying that you haven't raised fruit in the world, when you have fruit more beautiful than children? . . .") Cf. Philo *Abr.* 31: "a sage has no house or kinsfolk or country save virtues and virtuous actions; 'for these,' he says, 'are the generations of Noah' "; *Deus* 117–18.

root of wisdom. I.e. the root which consists in wisdom. For the appositive genitive, see *BDF* 167.

16. *will not reach maturity.* Cf. Sir 23:25: "Her children shall not spread out their roots, and her branches shall bear no fruit"; I Enoch 10:9: "Proceed against the bastards . . . and against the children of fornication . . . for length of days shall they not have"; *BT Yeb.* 78b: "So also did R. Huna state: A bastard's stock does not survive. . . . Those who

are known survive; those who are not known [sc. as bastards] do not survive; and those who are partly known and partly unknown survive for three generations but no longer. A certain man once lived in the neighborhood of R. Ami, and the latter made a public announcement that he was a bastard. As the other was bewailing the action, the Master said to him: I have given you life." See Ta-Shema.

17. *of no account*. Cf. Sir 16:1–3: "Desire not a multitude of unprofitable sons, and delight not in corrupt children. . . . Trust not those in their life, nor rely on their end; for better is one than a thousand, and to die childless than to have a presumptuous posterity."

in the end. For *ep eschatōn*, cf. Prov 25:8, LXX.

18. *decision*. For *diagnōsis* in this sense, cf. Demosthenes 18.7; Jos. *J.W.* 2.2.2; Acts 25:21; *IG* 14. 1072: *epi diagnōseōn tou Sebastou*.

4:1. This verse takes up again the theme of 3:13.

better to be childless, provided one is virtuous. A characteristically Platonic note is sounded here. It is the life of the soul that is paramount, so that physical childlessness is of little moment, provided the soul is productive. Cf. *Symp*. 208E: "'They are in love with what is immortal. Now those who are teeming in body betake them rather to women, and are amorous on this wise: by getting children they acquire an immortality, a memorial (*athanasian kai mnēmēn*), and a state of bliss, which in their imagining they "for all succeeding time procure." But pregnancy of soul—for there are persons,' she declared, 'who in their souls still more than in their bodies conceive those things which are proper for soul to conceive and bring forth; and what are those things? Wisdom and virtue in general. . . . Every one would choose to have got children such as these rather than the human sort.'" See S. Lange:293–306.

in virtue's remembrance there is immortality. Cf. Ps 112:6; Prov 10:7; Sir 44:8–15; Xenophon *Mem*. 2.1.33: "When comes the appointed end, [the virtuous] lie not forgotten and dishonored, but live on, sung and remembered for all time"; Diodorus 1.2.4. Except for Wisd and II, III, and IV Maccabees, *aretē* is never found in the LXX in its ethical meaning. See Freudenthal 1890:215–216.

both from God and from men. Cf. Xenophon *Mem*. 2.1.32: "I [Virtue] am first in honor among the gods and among men that are akin to me."

2. *through all time*. Cf. IV Macc 17:18. "Whereas Greek in general distinguishes between *chronos* and *aiōn*, using the former for time in itself, and the latter for the relative time allotted to a being, Plato distinguishes between *aiōn* as timeless, ideal eternity, and *chronos* as the time which is created with the world as a moving image of eternity (*Tim*. 37D)." (*TDNT* 1. 187ff; and cf. NOTE on 13:9 below.)

crowned with the victory wreath. Cf. 5:16 below; Prov 4:9; Ps-Aristeas

280; *Test.Levi* 8:2,10; *Test.Benj* 4:1; II Macc 6:7; IV Macc 17:15; Sir 1:11; 6:31; 15:6; Judith 15:13; Philo *Abr.* 35; *Praem.* 13; *BT Ber.* 17a; 1QS 4.7–8; 1QH 9.24; I Cor 9:25. For *stephanēphoreō,* cf. Philo *Jos.* 18, 138.

for prizes undefiled. "*amiantōn athlōn* may either mean 'of unstained prizes,' or 'of unstained struggles.' With the first translation the meaning is 'perfect rewards, unstained by unfairness of winning or savage passions on the part of the competitors,' as in earthly contests. The second, which Grimm adopts, is explained as 'the struggles of the virtuous life, unstained by selfishness or sin.' The latter is more in accordance with the philosophic idea of life as a warfare, which is found in Plato *Phaedo* 114C; *Rep.* 621C; and often in Epictetus (*Enchiridion* 29.2; *Discourses* 1.18.21; 3.10.8; cf. Philo *Mig.* 26; *LA* 3.14), and is elaborated in IV Macc 17:16" (Goodrick [1913]; cf. Heinisch). "The Hellenistic origin of the picture of Virtue's Agon and victory is not only supported by the similar image in IV Macc 17:11–16, but also by the phrase *tōn amiantōn athlōn.* It would seem highly probable that one should see in this phrase the traditional contrast between the sage's contest for virtue and the 'unholy' athletic contests as we have observed it in the diatribe and in Philo (*Agr.* 113, 119; *Mut.* 106; *Abr.* 48), a contrast which is then transferred to the prizes in both contests" Pfitzner:55; cf. 33–37 and 38–48). On athletic imagery in Christian texts, see also R. Merkelbach, *ZPE* 18 (1975):108–131.

4. *standing unstably.* For *episphalōs bebēkota,* cf. Archilochus frag. 114.4, West.

5. *unripe. aōros* may be an intentional play on the well-known designation for those who die prematurely (the *aōroi*). Cf. NOTE on 14:15.

6. *witnesses.* We find a similar notion in *Wayyik.R.* 23.12, Margaliot:545: " 'The eye also of the adulterer waiteth for the twilight,' R. Shimeon b. Lakish said: so that you may not say that whoever commits adultery with his body is called an adulterer, but he who commits adultery with his eyes is [also] called an adulterer, for it is written 'the eye also of the adulterer waiteth for the twilight,' and this adulterer sits in wait watching for the twilight or evening to come, 'in the twilight, in the evening of the day' (Prov 7:9), but he is unaware that He who dwells in the secret place of the universe, the Holy One blessed be He, moulds his [the foetus'] facial lineaments (*charaktērion*) in his image in order to publicize him." Cf. *Tanḥ.* Buber, *Naso* 6; Sir 23:18; *Gospel of Philip* 78: "The children a woman bears resemble the man who loves her. If her husband loves her, then they resemble her husband. If it is an adulterer, then they resemble the adulterer. Frequently, if a woman sleeps with her husband out of necessity, while her heart is with the adulterer with whom she usually has intercourse, the child she will bear is born resembling the adul-

terer. Now you who live together with the Son of God, love not the world, but love the Lord, in order that those you will bring forth may not resemble the world, but may resemble the Lord" (Robinson 1977:147). The same idea appears in Greek and Latin literature: Hesiod *Op.* 182, 235; Ps-Phocylides 178 (*FPG*:154); Aeschines *Against Ctesiphon* 3.111; *AP* 6.353; Menander Rhet., pp. 404, 407, Spengel; Chariton 2.11.2; Theocritus 17.44; Horace *Carmina* 4.5.23; Terence *Hautontimorumenos* 1018; Catullus 61.221; Martial 6.27.39; cf. Diels, *Dox.* 423, 17–21.

V. EARLY DEATH A TOKEN OF GOD'S SOLICITOUS CARE
(4:7–20)

4   7 But the righteous man, though he die an untimely death, will
      be at rest.
  8 For it is not length of life that makes for an honorable old
     age,
    nor is it measured by numbers of years;
  9 but rather is it wisdom which constitutes a man's silvery
     brow,
    and a spotless life the true ripeness of age.
10 Being well-pleasing to God he was dearly loved,
    and while yet living among sinful men he was translated.
11 He was snatched away lest evil alter his intelligence,
    or wile deceive his mind.
12 For the witchery of evil dims excellence,
    and the giddy distraction of desire perverts the guileless
     mind.
13 Perfected in a short span, he completed a full measure of
     time.
14 For his soul was pleasing to the Lord,
    therefore he urged it forth out of the midst of wickedness.
    The masses see this and do not understand
    nor do they take such a happening to heart;
15 [that grace and compassion are for his chosen,
    and a gracious visitation for his holy ones]
16 —but the just man dead shall condemn the godless who are
     alive,
    and swiftly perfected youth the old age of the unrighteous
     rich in years—
17 for they will see the wise man's end
    and will not understand what the Lord purposed for him
    and to what end he took him into safe keeping.

18 They will see and account it as nought,
  but it is they whom the Lord will laugh to scorn.
19 They shall thereafter become an ignominious carcass,
  an object of outrage among the dead forever;
  for he will smash them speechless headlong,
  rocking them out of their foundations,
  and they shall be made an utter desert,
  and shall be in anguish
  and their memory shall perish.
20 In the reckoning of their sins they will come cringing,
  and their lawless acts will convict them to their face.

NOTES

4:7–20. The problem of premature death was a disturbing one for any theodicy, and our author takes great pains to account for it. He employs a popular philosophical conceit that a man's true age is not measured chronologically but by maturity of intellect and character, and he further resorts to a Jewish exegetical tradition that Enoch had been removed by God early to forestall the imminent perversion of his moral character, in order to extract from it a general principle of Divine Providence (paralleled in Hellenistic literature) which would justify the early death of the righteous.

4:7. *an untimely death. phthanein* with the infinitive instead of the participle is rare in Classical Greek, but more frequent in later writers (Kühner-Gerth 484.32).

will be at rest. The wicked, on the other hand, "shall have no rest" (*ouk estin hymin anapausai:* I Enoch 99:14); cf. *Test. Abraham* B 9:8; Philo *Fug.* 174; NOTES on 3:3 and 8:16.

8. *not length of life.* We have here a very widespread literary theme. Cf. Menander *Frag.* 553, Körte: "Not from white heads has wisdom always sprung; Nature gives it to some men while they're young" (J. M. Edmonds, *The Fragments of Attic Comedy,* 3 vols. [Leiden, 1957], III. B:810); Cicero *Tusc.* 5.5; 1.45: "No one has lived too short a life who has discharged the perfect work of perfect virtue" (see A. Michel, *Rhétorique et Philosophie chez Cicéron* [Paris, 1960]:671); Seneca *Ep.* 78.28 (quoting Posidonius) 93.2: "We should strive, not to live long, but to live rightly. . . . A life is really long if it is a full life, but fullness is not at-

tained until the soul has rendered to itself its proper Good"; Plutarch *Moralia* 111D; Virgil *Aen.* 9.311. Philo is especially fond of this notion. In his description of the Therapeutae he writes: "After the prayers the seniors recline according to the order of their admission, since by senior they do not understand the aged and grey headed who are regarded as still mere children if they have only in late years come to love this rule of life, but those who from their earliest years have grown to manhood and spent their prime in pursuing the contemplative branch of life" (*Cont.* 67); "for the true elder is shown as such not by his length of days but by a laudable and perfect life. Those who have passed a long span of years in the exist- ence of the body without goodness or beauty of life must be called long- lived children who have never been schooled in the learning worthy of grey hairs" (*Abr.* 271); *Fug.* 146; *Her.* 49, 290; *Deus* 120; *Sobr.* 7ff; *Legat.* 1.142; *Plant.* 168; *Praem.* 112; *QE* 2.20. "In the first century CE" writes Curtius, "we find the frequent rhetorical exaggeration—the boy to be praised had the maturity of an old man (Silius Italicus *Punica* 8.64; Pliny the Younger *Epistulae* 5.16.2; Apuleius *Florida* 9.38; *AP* 7.603). Gregory the Great began his life of St. Benedict with the words: 'He was a man of venerable life . . . even from his boyhood he had the under- standing of an old man.' This becomes a hagiographic cliché, whose influence continues into the thirteenth century. The reverse formula also appears. The desert father Macarius (d. 391) was called 'child-old man' (*paidariogerōn*) even as a youth (*PG,* LXVIII, 1069A). There is also an ancient Indian parallel. According to Manu (2.150ff) the young Brahmin Kawi instructed his paternal uncles in sacred learning, addressing them as 'sons.' Angered, they complained to the gods, who gave the following an- swer: 'The lad addressed you rightly, for the unknowing is a child . . . not because he is white-headed is a man old; he who has read the scripture, even though he be young, him the gods account old.' We further find that in various religions saviors are characterized by the combination of child- hood and age. The name Lao-tzu can be translated as 'old child.' Among the Etruscan gods we find Tages, 'the miraculous boy with grey hair and the intelligence of old age, who was ploughed up out of the ground by a plowman at Tarquinii [Cicero *De Diviniatione* 2.50; Ovid *Metamorphoses* 15.553]. From the nature worship of the pre-Islamic Arabs the fabulous Chydhyr passed into Islam. 'Chydhyr is represented as a youth of bloom- ing and imperishable beauty who combines the ornament of old age, a white beard, with his other charms'" (E. R. Curtius, *European Literature and the Latin Middle Ages* [New York, 1953]:98–101). We similarly find in *BT Kid.* 32b: "R. Jose the Galilean said, *zaken* or elder means only he who has acquired wisdom." See also II Bar 17:1.

9. *spotless. akēlidōtos* is first attested here and 7:26 below (Prov 25:18, LXX should read *akidōtos*). Cf. Philo *Virt.* 222 (*akēlidōton diaphylaks-*

asa ton heautēs bion), 205; *Spec.* 1.150,167; *Cher.* 95; *Sacr.* 139; *Det.* 171; Ecphantus, Thesleff:80, line 17; *Apoc.Abraham* 17 (where 'spotless' is one of God's attributes).

10. *Being well-pleasing to God.* The reference is clearly to Enoch (Gregg and Heinisch say it refers to the just man of v. 7, though using language reminiscent of Enoch). Cf. Gen 5:24, LXX: *euērestēsen Enōch tō theō kai ouk heurisketo, hoti metethēken auton ho theos.* These words are virtually repeated in the Greek version of Sir 44:16 (*euērestēsen Kyriō kai metetethē*). Cf. Heb 11:5. "We have here the first example of the curious avoidance of proper names which marks the author of Wisdom. According to one view it was unnecessary to name them because the book was addressed to Jewish apostates or waverers. A precisely opposite explanation, that the heathen princes to whom the book is addressed would not care to know the names of Hebrew saints, is suggested by Grimm. Margoliouth's idea that the writer avoided proper names because he did not wish to spoil the appearance of his Greek, is peculiar" (Goodrick). Yet another explanation is that Wisdom's omission of the proper names of Israel's heroes is in keeping with the style of the protreptic discourse, which deals with persons as types (Reese 1970:119; cf. Bois 1890:215). For the author of Wisdom, however, the biblical personalities are historical figures and not mere types as they are for Philo. Riddling speech (*griphōdes*), however, was a characteristic of some of the more erudite literary productions of Hellenistic Alexandria, and this may well account for what seems to a modern reader as an exceedingly bizarre idiosyncrasy on the part of our author. A good example of this style of writing is Lycophron's *Alexandra* (a collateral name for Cassandra), "which must be classified as a tragedy because of its iambic meter but is, in fact, a single messenger's speech reporting to Priam Cassandra's predictions on the day that Paris set out for the rape of Helen. Every line of the poem is an enigma. Persons, gods, places, are almost never called by their names but referred to by the most remote and abstruse allusions; if the allusion strikes the reader as recognizable he is surely wrong, for some more remote and more paradoxical reference is intended. To modern readers the work, happily unique in its kind, appears to be the chef d'oeuvre of an erudite madman; but . . . such madness may have had an appreciative audience in Alexandria" (M. Hadas, *A History of Greek Literature* [New York, 1950]:192–193). But while Lycophron's *Alexandra* represents an extreme case of the riddling style, the author of Wisd did not intend his allusions to cause any serious puzzlement but rather to provide the reader familiar with the Bible the enjoyment of virtually immediate recognition of the biblical figures described but unnamed. Georgi has suggested that the author's object in omitting proper names is to emphasize that concrete historical reality is only an appearance and that true existence is

on a higher level (1964:272). Along similar lines, J. Collins has observed that "Wisd is not interested in the historical differences between these figures but only in the repeated manifestations of a universal type, 'the righteous man'" (*JAAR,* 1 Supp. [March 1977]: B:14). It may also be noted that in the so-called *Testament of Orpheus* both Abraham and Moses are alluded to without their names being mentioned (27–32, 41–42 [*FPG* 166]).

11. *He was snatched away.* The verb *harpzaein* served, on the one hand, as one of the oldest Greek terms for 'translation,' and, on the other hand, was frequently used in epitaphs for being snatched away by an early death (Peek 1960 nos. 149,3; 157,2; 268,1; 269,1; 276,8; etc.; see Schmitt 1976:188). Philo understood Gen 5:24 to mean that Enoch "journeyed as an emigrant from the mortal life to the immortal" (*Mut.* 38; *QG* 1.85).

lest evil alter his intelligence. Cf. Isa 57:1–2. The motive here given for the removal of Enoch is different from that assumed either in the Greek ("an example of repentence to all generations") or in the Hebrew version ("a sign of instruction to future generations") of Sir 44:16, but agrees with that given in *BR* 25.1, Th-Alb. 238: "R. Aibo said, Enoch was a hypocrite, at times he was righteous, at other times wicked; said the Holy One blessed be He, while he is yet righteous, I shall remove him." (Cf. *Kohel.R.* 7.32; *Wayyik.R.* 32.4. The rabbis applied a similar mode of reasoning to the law of the rebellious son and that concerning a thief who is caught in the act of breaking in. "Should he [the rebellious son] die because he consumed his father's money? Rather is he condemned because of what his end will be; it is better that he die innocent and not guilty." *Sifre Deut.* 218, Finkelstein: 251. Cf. *M. Sanh.* 8.5; *BT Sanh.* 72a.) See also Philo *Mig.* 26: "Even him [Jacob] he forbids to keep up his wrestlings to the end, lest one day by perpetually meeting them, he should contract from them a pernicious taint." Seneca the Younger similarly writes: "Do you complain, Marcia, that your son did not live as long as he might have lived? For how do you know whether it was advisable for him to live longer? . . . Human affairs are unstable and fleeting, and no part of our life is so frail and perishable as that which gives most pleasure, and therefore at the height of good fortune we ought to pray for death. . . . And your son who was so handsome. . . . What assurance have you that he could have escaped the many diseases there are, and so have preserved the unimpaired beauty of his person down to old age? And think of the thousand taints of the soul! For even noble natures do not support continuously into old age the expectations they had stirred in their youth, but are often turned aside; they either fall into dissipation, which coming late is for that reason the more disgraceful, and begins to tarnish the brilliance of their first years. . . . If you will consider all these possibilities, you will learn that those who are treated most kindly by Nature are those whom

she removes early to a place of safety [cf. v. 17 below: *ēsphalisato*], because life had in store some such penalty as this" (*De Consolatione ad
Marciam* 22). So, too, Plutarch *Consolatio ad Apollonium* 117D: "For
who knows but that God, having a fatherly care for the human race, and
foreseeing future events, early removes some persons from life untimely
(*aōrous*)?" (cf. Peek 1960, no. 314,9*f;* and Ps-Plato, *Axiochus* 367C).
See also Grelot 1958:5–26, 181–210.

12. *giddy distraction*. *rhembasmos* is found only here, but appears again
in Patristic Greek (*rhembazō,* intensive of *rhembō,* occurs only in Patristic
Greek). It may have been a Stoic coinage, although it is not attested in
any of our fragments. Zeno, for example, had defined *pathos* as a *ptoia* or
violent fluttering of the mind (*SVF* 1.206), and Marcus Aurelius writes:
kai pausai rhembomenos (*Meditations* 2.7: "cease being carried aside
hither and thither.") Cf. 4.22: *mē aporrembesthai.*) The same expression
is found in *Sib Or* Frags. 1:26: *pausasthe mataioi rhembomenoi skotiē:*
"cease vain mortals roaming in darkness"). Cf. Seneca *De Vita Beata* 28:
"Are not your minds even now whirled and spun about as if some hur-
ricane had seized them?"; *De Tranquillitate Animi* 2.8: "and then creeps
in the agitation of a mind (*animi iactatio*) which can find no issue."
Spinoza had adopted the term *animi fluctuatio,* after the Latin translation
of Descartes's *Les Passions de l'Âme* 2.59; 3.170.

perverts. In his characteristic manner, Goodrick comments as follows:
"*metalleuei* is an obvious blunder for *metallassei*. It means 'digs for
metals' and is repeated in its false sense in 16:25. . . . The rendering of
metalleuein:metapherein, in Suidas, seems to be taken from these two
passages of Wisdom. The anxiety of commentators to defend the qualifica-
tions of Pseudo-Solomon as a Greek scholar is proved by Gregg's suggestion [so, too, Heinisch] that 'papyri yet to be discovered may prove this to
have been a popular Alexandrian use.'" Reese, however, has pointed out
that "by the time Wisdom was composed, the papyri show that the classical verb *metallassō* had become the technical term in Egypt for 'die.' Another word for 'change,' *metalloioō,* appears in the lexica, but it is late and
rare [though it occurs in Ps-Aristeas 17; Philo *Post.* 83,98. Skehan
(1971:251) believes that *metalleuō* in Wisd is due to a scribal error which
confused this verb with *metalloioō.* Fichtner (1938) assumed that the author of Wisd confused the two verbs]. The plausible explanation for the
Sage's choice of the word *metalleuō* . . . is that it was then in current use
in the general sense of undergoing a change, the conception that he wishes
to convey in both passages. A confirmation of the extension of meaning is
that the verb means 'undermine' in Josephus, *AJ* [*Ant.*] 17.10.3"
(1970:29). More important, however, in my opinion is the fact that in
Philo *Gig.* 65 most of the manuscripts read either *metalleusantes* or *met-
alleuontes* (Wendland's emendation is: *metalloiōsantes*), which would in-

dicate that *metalleuō* did come to have the meaning of 'change' and was either so used by Philo himself, or was readily substituted for an original *metalloiōsantes* by scribes who were familiar with such a usage. In Patristic Greek we again find *metalleuō* in the sense of *metallassō* (Lampe:853).

13. *Perfected in a short span.* Seneca writes in a similar vein: "Whatever has reached perfection, is near its end. Ideal Virtue hurries away and is snatched from our eyes, and the fruits that ripen in their first days do not wait long for their last. The brighter a fire glows, the more quickly it dies. . . . So with men—the brighter their spirits, the briefer their day" (*De Consolatione ad Marciam* 23.3–5).

he completed a full measure of time. For *eplērōsen,* cf. Plato *Laws* 866A; Sir 26:2; IV Macc 12:14; Jos. *Ant.* 4.4.6. Precisely the same idea is found in Philo, who undoubtedly got it from the Middle Stoa, since it also occurs in the writings of Seneca. Commenting on Exod 23:26 (*ton arithmon tōn hēmerōn sou anaplērōsō:* "The number of thy days I will fill"), Philo writes: "That it is most excellent and fine that the lives of his worshippers should be reckoned not by months nor by numbers but by days. For they are really of equal value with eternity when taken into account and number." Cf. *Praem.* 112: "Therefore he held that the wise man's single day rightly spent is worth a whole lifetime"; Seneca *Ep.* 78.28: "One day in the life of the educated lasts longer than the longest lifetime of the uneducated"; 92.25: "in the slightest possible moment of time virtue completes an eternity of good"; 93.7; Cicero *Tusc.* 1.109: "No one has lived too short a life who has discharged the perfect work of perfect virtue." On the qualitative sense of time, cf. Ps 84:11: "Better one day in your courts than a thousand [anywhere else]" (quoted by Philo *Her.* 290).

14. *he urged it forth.* "Grimm adopts the translation 'his soul hastened away' [so, too, Fichtner], which he endeavors to bring in harmony with line one thus, 'his early removal was in accordance with the wish of his soul, which joyfully hastened to obey God's call'—an obviously tame explanation. There is no difficulty in using *speudō* transitively of things, but no example of its use with a person as object seems to exist elsewhere. Nonnius, quoted by Grimm, would read *espasen,* 'snatched away.' Siegfried thinks the construction imitated from that of the Hebrew *maher* with the accusative as in Gen 18:6, I Kings 22:9" (Goodrick). In support of Grimm's translation, we may quote from the following epitaph of the third century CE: "for it [the immortal soul of young Calocaerous] hastened along the divine way [*speuden hodon theiēn*], left the cares of bitter life to go aloft in purity" (Peek 1960: no. 296, line 3; cited by Schmitt 1976:190). See also Lattimore 36, 50 (*speusas es athanatous*).

take . . . to heart. The Greek corresponds to Hebrew *śîm 'al lēb.* Cf. Isa 57:1.

15. This verse is bracketed by Ziegler; it is virtually identical with 3:9b.

16. "The anacoluthon is obvious. The best explanation would be to regard v. 16 as an interpolation (possibly of the author's own), and *gar* at the beginning of v. 17 as added by the interpolator or an editor. This view is adopted by Gutberlet and practically by Deane" (Goodrick).

18. *will laugh to scorn.* Cf. Prov 1:26; Ps 2:4; I Enoch 94:10: "and your Creator will rejoice at your destruction"; *Sifre, Koraḥ* 117: "there is joy before God when those who anger him are rooted out of the earth"; *Mid.Teh.* 2.6; *Tanḥ.* Buber, *Noah* 28; *Naso* 9; *BT Aboda Zara* 3b. (See Marmorstein 1950:29.)

19. *ignominious carcass.* Cf. Isa 14:19; 66:24; Job 18.

20. *will convict them to their face.* The words are reminiscent of the Zoroastrian notion that after death the wicked will meet his own evil thoughts and deeds in the form of a hideous wench who will rebuke him and detail his hideous deeds to his face (*Mēnōk i Khrat* 2.73–122; Zaehner 1961:304). Cf. Jer 2:19: "Thy own wickedness shall correct thee, and thy backslidings shall reprove thee."

VI. VINDICATION OF THE JUST AND FINAL JUDGMENT
(5:1–23)

5   1 Then the just man will take his stand with poised
                confidence
      to outface his oppressors
      and those who made light of his sufferings.
   2 At the sight of him they will be shaken with fearful terror,
      and will be astounded at the unexpectedness of his
          deliverance.
   3 Remorseful, each will say to the other
      groaning and gasping for breath:
   4 "This was the man whom we once held in derision
      and for a byword of reproach, fools that we were;
      his life we accounted madness,
      and his end without honor.
   5 How was he reckoned among the sons of God,
      and how is his portion among the holy ones?
   6 We strayed, it seems, from the path of truth,
      and were not illumined by the light of justice,
      and the sun never rose for us.
   7 We were entangled in the prickles of lawlessness and
                destruction,
      and made our way through trackless wastes,
      but the Lord's highway we ignored.
   8 What good was our arrogance,
      and what did wealth and false posturing bring us?
   9 All those things have gone by like a shadow,
      like a messenger flitting past.
  10 Like a ship cutting through the swelling surge,
      of whose passage not a trace is to be found,
      nor the track of her keel among the waves;
  11 or as when a bird flies through the air,

there is no token of her flight,
but the insubstantial breeze, lashed by the stroke of her
     pinions
and cleft by the force of her onrush,
was traversed by the whirring of her wings,
and thereafter no sign was found of her assault;

12 or as when an arrow is shot at a mark,
the air is parted and instantly closes up again,
so that none discerns its passage.

13 So we too were dead as we were born,
and had no token of virtue to show,
but in our wickedness were utterly consumed."

14 For the hope of the godless is like down flying on the wind,
and like thin frost swept before a howling gale,
and like smoke which the wind scattered,
and like the memory of a guest for a day it passed through.

15 But the just live forever; their reward is in the Lord,
and the Most High has them in his care.

16 Therefore they will obtain majestic royalty
and a resplendent diadem from the hand of the Lord,
for he will shelter them with his right hand
and with his arm he will shield them.

17 He will take his indignation as full armor
and make creation a weapon for the repulse of his foes.

18 He will don justice as his coat of mail,
and put on undissembled judgment as his helmet;

19 he will take holiness for his indomitable shield

20 and sharpen his relentless anger into a sword,
and the cosmos will join him in all-out war against the
     madmen.

21 Shafts of lightning will proceed on target;
as if from a well-rounded bow, from the clouds, they shall
     leap upon the mark,

22 and from a catapult a fury of hail will cut loose.
The waters of the sea shall rage against them,
and torrential streams wash over them relentlessly;

23 a powerful blast will rise against them,
and scatter them like chaff before a whirlwind.
So lawlessness will lay waste the entire earth,
and criminal action will overturn the thrones of dynasts.

NOTES

5:1–23. The whole chapter is colored by Isaianic language and imagery (Isa 52:13*ff;* 59:16–17). The wicked will be astounded at the unexpected deliverance of the just man. In the agony of their remorse they will vividly perceive the fundamental error of their way of life, and the utter transiency of all that they had once prized. (The speech of the wicked in vv. 4–13 is the counterpart to their former speech in 2:1–20). Finally, in an apocalyptic vision the author envisages the future royal spendor of the just and the simultaneous annihilation of the wicked through the smashing attack of the cosmic elements led by the Divine Warrior (cf. 16:17). For a form-critical analysis of the author's use of the "story of the Righteous Man" and the "Isaianic Exaltation Tradition," see Nickelsburg 1972:48–66.

5:1. *the just man will take his stand.* Cf. Isa 52:13*ff.*

with poised confidence. For *parrēsia,* cf. Prov 13:5, LXX; *Test.Reuben* 4:2; Jos. *Ant.* 9.10.4; II Cor 7:4. *Parrēsia,* 'outspokenness,' and *anaideia,* 'shamelessness,' were the twin qualities which made Cynicism famous (D.L. 6.69; Lucian *Demonax* 3; Philo *Her.* 27).

made light of. *atheteō* is very frequent in the LXX for a variety of Hebrew words. For the meaning "set at nought," cf. Polybius 8.36.5; I Kings 2:17, LXX. Here it refers to the habitual contempt of the wicked for the painful life of the righteous.

2. *At the sight of him.* Cf. Isa 49:7: "Kings shall see and stand up." The author of I Enoch made a similar use of Isaiah's "servant" passages in describing the Son of Man: "And there shall stand up in that day all the kings and the mighty, and the exalted and those who hold the earth, and they shall see and recognize how he sits on the throne of his glory . . . and they shall be terrified . . . and pain shall seize them" (62:3); cf. 27:3: "In the last days there shall be upon them the spectacle of righteous judgment in the presence of the righteous forever"; 97:3–6; 108:15; IV Ezra 7:36; II Bar 30:4–5; 51:5; *PRK* 28; *Datastan i Denik* 19.4 (where the sinner in hell can see the heavenly throne of Ahura Mazda and the bliss of the righteous).

astounded. For *ekstēsontai,* cf. Judith 11:16; Ruth 3:8, LXX; Isa 13:8, LXX.

unexpectedness of his deliverance. Cf. III Macc 6:33.

3. *Remorseful.* Cf. IV Ezra 7:81–87; I Enoch 63:1–11.

gasping for breath. *stenochōria* is fairly frequent in the LXX, and for the verb *stenochōreō,* cf. Isa 28:20; IV Macc 11:11: *to pneuma stenoch-ōroumenos.*

4. *for a byword of reproach.* Cf. Jer 24:9, LXX; Tobit 3.4. With vv. 4–5, cf. Barnabas 7:9; Mark 15:39; Matt 27:54. See A. Jaubert, "Écho du Livre de la Sagesse en Barnabé 7,9," *RSR* 60 (1972) 193–198.

5. *among the sons of God . . . among the holy ones?* We have here a conception similar to that found in Daniel, I Enoch, and the Qumran scrolls. The just, it is believed, can be elevated to the heavenly sphere to join the angelic host (Dan 12:2–3; I Enoch 104:2, 6; Similitudes of Enoch 39:5; 1QH 3:19–23; II Bar 51:5–13). See Larcher 1969:320–321; H.-W. Kuhn, *Enderwartung und gegenwärtiges Heil* (Göttingen, 1966): 44–78; Nickelsburg 1972:152–156; Collins 1977a:210–211, 177.

6. *We strayed.* Cf. Isa 53:6, LXX; Plato *Politicus* 263A.

it seems. The particle *ara* expresses the surprise attendant upon disillusionment. See J. D. Denniston, *The Greek Particles* (Oxford, 1954): 35.

the light of justice. Cf. Mal 4:2, LXX: *hēlios dikaiosynēs;* Aristobulus: "And He gave us for rest the seventh day, which in reality (*physikōs*) could be called the prime source of light, in which all things are comprehended. The latter could also be transferred metaphorically to wisdom, for all light comes from her" (*FPG:*224).

7. *entangled in the prickles of lawlessness.* For a discussion of the reading *eneplechthēmen tribolois* which is adopted by Ziegler (and was already suggested by Bretschneider), see Ziegler's edition of the text, p. 32. Cf. *skoliais hodois poreuomenos emplakēsetai;* II Tim 2:4; *Sib Or* Frag. 1:24; Philo *LA* 3.253; *Somn.* 2.161.

trackless wastes. Cf. Jer 12:10, LXX; Ps 63:1, LXX; Aeschylus *Prometheus Bound* 2 (*abaton eis erēmian*); Philo *Mos.* 1.172.

9. *flitting past.* For *paratrechousa.* Cf. Philo *Deus* 177: *alla skiā tis ē aura prin hypostēnai paratrechousa.*

10. *Like a ship.* Cf. Prov 30:18–19.

the track of her keel. atrapon tropios. Play on words. In the *Hymn to Isis* from Andros, we read of Isis keeping the swift keel straight (153: *thoan tropin ithyneskon*).

11. *through the air.* Cf. Virgil *Georgics* 1.406–409: "Wherever she flees, cleaving the light air with her wings, lo! savage and ruthless, with loud whirr Nisus follows through the sky."

assault. epibasis in sense of "attack" first attested here. Cf. Lucian *Quomodo Historia Conscribenda sit* 49; Philo *Mos.* 1.202; *Aet.* 147. In Herodotus 6.61, it means "a handle against," "a means of attacking one."

12. *closes up again. anelythē* means literally "dissolved" or "resolved." Bissell translates: "is at once resolved into itself again." Deane takes it in the sense of "returns."

13. *were dead as we were born.* Cf. Sir 44:9.

14. The author employs in what follows four similes to illustrate his point. Cf. 7:25, where he employs five metaphors in his description of the origin of wisdom.

like down. Cf. Pss 1:4; 35:5, LXX: Isa 17:13, LXX; Hosea 13:3.

thin frost. Cf. 16:29. Other manuscripts have *achnē,* "foam," or *arachnē,* "spider's web" (Gregg cites in connection with the latter Job 8:13–14, LXX).

a guest for a day. Cf. Jer 14.8. For *monoēmeros,* cf. *Batrachomy-omachia* 303 (where it means "finished in a day"); Paris Magical Codex 1. 2442 (where it means "on the selfsame day"). For the comparison of life with the stay at a hospice, cf. Cicero *De Senectute* 84; Seneca *Ep.* 102.24; 120.14; *Wayyik.R.* 34.3, Margaliot: 777 (where Hillel compares the soul to a humiliated guest [*ksenos*] in the house or body); Gnostic *Hymn of the Pearl* 23 in *Acta Thomae* 109, p. 220, 19f, Bonnet: "Since I was one and all alone, I was a stranger to my fellow-dwellers in the inn." This recalls the following passage from Mani's Gospel: "The truth I have shown to my fellow-travelers" (*Mani Codex* 67.2). See A. Henrichs, *HSCP* 77 (1973) 38.

15. *the just live forever.* Cf. Philo *Jos.* 264: "In my judgment, no good man is dead, but will live forever (*ton aei chronon*), proof against old age, with a soul immortal in its nature no longer fettered by the restraints of the body."

16. *majestic royalty.* For *basileion* in the sense of "tiara," "diadem," cf. II Kings 1:10, LXX; II Chron 23:11, LXX. *basileion tēs euprepeias* and *diadēma tou kallous* are probably parallel and modeled on Isa 62:3: "You shall be a glorious crown (*'ăteret tip'eret*) in the hands of the Lord, and a royal diadem (*ṣenîp* [following the Qere] *mĕlûkâ*) in the palm of your God."

diadem. *diadēma* is a band or fillet, especially the band round the tiara worn by the Persian king (Xenophon *Cyropaedia* 8.3.13; Plutarch *Moralia* 488D; Esther 8:15, LXX; I Macc 13:32; Jos. *J.W.* 1.33.9). It was taken over from Persia by Alexander and his successors as a symbol of royalty. See Hans-Werner Ritter, *Diadem u. Königsherrschaft* (Munich and Berlin, 1965). Cf. 1QS 4.7–8: "and eternal joy in life within and a crown of glory and a garment of majesty in unending light"; 1QH 9.24; *BT Ber.* 17a; see S. Kraus, "The Jewish Rite of Covering the Head," *HUCA* 19 (1945–46) 126.

he will shelter them with his right hand. Cf. 19:8; Isa 51:16, LXX; IV Macc 17:19 (quoting Deut 33:3, LXX).

will shield them. *hyperaspizō* is very frequent in the LXX.

17. The following verses are modeled on Isa 59:17, where God is represented as a warrior arming himself with his own attributes (right-

eousness, salvation, vengeance, and zeal) for the chastisement of the wicked and the deliverance of the godly. (For the theme of the Divine Warrior, see Frank M. Cross, *Canaanite Myth and Hebrew Epic* [Cambridge, Mass., 1973]:91–194; P. Miller, *The Divine Warrior in Early Israel* (Cambridge, 1973). Cf. Eph 6:14–17; I Thess 5:8; Rom 13:12; II Cor 6:7. We find similar imagery in *Test.Levi* 8:2, where Levi is told in a vision to "put on the robe of the priesthood, and the crown of righteousness, and the garment of truth, and the breastplate of understanding, and the plate of faith, and the turban of the head, and the ephod of prophecy." The same type of imagery appears again even more elaborately in the Pahlavi work *Menok i Xrat,* 43: "To confound Ahriman . . . is possible if they make the spirit of wisdom a shield for the back, and wear on the body the spirit of contentment like a coat of mail and valor, and the spirit of thankfulness like a club, and the spirit of devotedness like a bow, and the spirit of liberality like an arrow, and the spirit of moderation like a javelin, and the spirit of perseverance as a gauntlet." Cf. Philo *Abr.* 243: "When reason puts on its panoply (*panteuchian*) of the virtues."

make creation a weapon. Cf. Judg 5:20 (the fighting of the stars here rests on the mythological identification of the stars with divine beings, the heavenly host); Sir 39:28–31; I Enoch 41:8; 100:10–13 ("And He will summon to testify against you every cloud and mist and dew and rain; for they shall all be withheld because of you from descending upon you, and they shall be mindful of your sins"); Philo *Mos.* 1.96: "The chastisement was different from the usual kind, for the elements of the universe—earth, fire, air, water—carried out the assault. God's judgment was that the materials which had served to produce the world should serve also to destroy the land of the impious; and to show the mightiness of the sovereignty which He holds, what He shaped in his saving goodness to create the universe He turned into instruments for the perdition of the impious wherever He would"; *Mos.* 2.53*ff;* Jos. *Ant.* 2.13.4: "for to them that rouse the divine ire dread calamities arise from all around them: to them neither earth nor air is friendly, to them no progeny is born after nature's laws, but all things are hostile and at enmity"; *Clementine Homilies* 11.10: "Against you who dishonor the Maker of all, the whole creation is hostile"; *Recognitions of Clement* 5.27: "for the creature hastens to take vengeance on the wicked." Cf. Empedocles DK, B.115: "For the mighty air chases them [divine spirits who sinfully stained themselves with bloodshed] into the Sea, and the Sea spews them forth on to the dry land; and the Earth drives them towards the rays of the blazing Sun; and the Sun hurls them into the eddies of the Aether"; Virgil *Aeneid* 6.740; Cicero *Tusc.* 1.42; Seneca *Consolatio ad Helviam* 20.2; Plutarch *De Facie in Orbe Lunae* 943C; *CH Asclepius* 28. See Cumont 1949:208*ff*—*hoplopoieō* ("make or use as a weapon") is found only here. (The substantive *hoplopoiētikē* occurs in Patristic Greek.)

18. *will don . . . put on. endysetai . . . perithēsetai.* Cf. Sir 6:31; Herodotus 3.98.

undissembled judgment. "*Krisin anypokriton* presents the same kind of verbal oxymoron as II Cor 7:10: *metanoia ametamelētos*" (Gregg). *anypokritos* is first found here (and in 18:15). It occurs only once in Philo *QG* 3.29: *to tou ēthous anypokriton,* "a sincere nature" (Greek fragment from Procopius); cf. Rom 12:9; I Cor 6:6; James 3:17; Iamblichus *De Vita Pythagorica* 69.

19. *indomitable. akatamachēton* is first attested in Wisd. Cf. LXX, Symmachus, Song of Songs 8:6; Ezek 28:7; 30:11; M. Aurel. 8.48; Ps-Callisthenes 2.11.

20. *relentless. apotomos* in its metaphorical meaning only poetical in Classical period (Euripides *Alcestis* 118, 981; Sophocles *Oedipus the King* 877). Used five times by our author (here; 6:5; 11:10; 12:9; 18:15). Cf. Diodorus 2.57.5; Longinus 27; Philo *Sacr.* 32.

sword. rhomphaia is very frequent in the LXX.

madmen. paraphronas is a poetic word (Sophocles *Electra* 473; Bacchylides 10.103) used by Plato (*Laws* 649D), and later by Plutarch (*De Pompeio* 72). It is also found in LXX, Symmachus, I Samuel 21:15 for Hebrew *mištage'a.*

21. *Shafts of lightning.* For *bolides astrapōn,* cf. Zech 9:14, LXX. For the figure, see II Sam 22:15; Hab 3:11; II Esd 16:13.

from the clouds. The preposition *apo* is omitted before *nephōn.* This is a well-known Greek idiom. See L. Edmonds, *HSCP* 80 (1976) 42–43, with examples and bibliography (cf. Smyth:1673).

leap. For *halountai,* cf. *Iliad* 4.125.

22. *catapult. petrobolos* is distinguished from *katapeltēs* in Polybius 8.7.2, but in Diodorus 18.51 we find catapults both for bolts and for stones.

torrential streams . . . relentlessly. potamoi . . . apotomōs. Play on words.

wash over them. For *synklysousin,* cf. Isa 43:2, LXX; Song of Songs 8:7, LXX.

23. *scatter them like chaff.* Cf. Isa 41:16.

criminal action. kakopragia in this sense is first attested here. Cf. Jos. *Ant.* 2.4.4. For the plural, "misdeeds," see Isocrates 15.300. The word is very frequent in Philo in the sense of "misfortune," but never in the sense of "ill-doing."

VII. EXHORTATION TO WISDOM WHICH IS EASILY FOUND AND BRINGS IMMORTALITY AND SOVEREIGNTY
(6:1–21)

6 1 Hear then, you kings, and understand;
   take note, lords of the far corners of the earth.
2 Give ear, you who hold sway over peoples,
   whose pride is in nation masses.
3 It was the Lord who gave you dominion;
   your sovereignty is from the Most High.
   He will scrutinize your actions and search out your plans.
4 Though vicars of his kingdom, your judgment was not
         straight;
   you did not maintain the law
   nor live according to God's will.
5 Horribly and swiftly will he descend upon you,
   for relentless judgment overtakes the high and the mighty.
6 The small man may be mercifully pardoned,
   but the mighty will be mightily tried.
7 For the master of all will not shrink from a countenance
   or have regard for greatness.
   Small and great he himself made,
   and all alike are under his providence,
8 but over the powerful a vigorous inquiry impends.
9 To you, then, O despots, are my words directed,
   that you may learn wisdom and not go astray.
10 Those who have kept the holy ordinances in holiness, shall
         be made holy,
   and those that have been taught them will find their defense.
11 Set your heart, then, upon my words,
   long for them and you will be instructed.
12 Bright and unfading is Wisdom,
   easily beheld by those who love her,
   and found by those who seek her.

13 She is first to make herself known to those who desire her;
14 he who anticipates the dawn on her behalf will not grow
weary,
for he will find her seated before his door.
15 To set one's mind on her is perfect wisdom,
and he that is vigilant for her sake will soon be free of care.
16 For she herself seeks out those who are worthy of her;
with gracious good will she appears to them on their path,
and in every thought comes to meet them.
17 The true beginning of Wisdom is the desire to learn,
and a concern for learning is love for her;
18 love for her means the keeping of her laws;
attention to the law is a surety of immortality;
19 and immortality makes one near to God.
20 Thus the desire for Wisdom leads to sovereignty.
21 If, then, you take delight in your thrones and scepters, you
rulers of nations,
honor Wisdom so that you may reign forever.

NOTES

6:1. *Hear . . . take note. . . . Give ear.* Cf. *ANET*:414; 421; Isa 1:10;
Ps 49:2; Prov 5:1; 22:17.
far corners of the earth. The reference is very likely to the spreading
power of Rome. For *perata gēs,* cf. *Iliad* 8.478; *Odyssey* 4.563; Thucydides 1.69; I Sam 2:10; Pss 2:8; 22:28 (Hebrew: *'afse 'eretz*); cf. Philo
Legat. 144: "The great regions which divide the habitable world, Europe
and Asia, were contending with each other for sovereign power, with the
nations of both brought up from the uttermost parts of the earth waging
grievous war all over sea and land."
2. *Give ear.* enōtizesthai is very frequent in the LXX. Cf. Ps 2:10.
3. *who gave you dominion.* That kings rule and are deposed at God's
pleasure was accepted biblical doctrine. See I Chron 29:11–12; Dan 2:21;
John 19:11; Rom 13:1; I Cor 61:1; Sir 10:4,8; Ps-Aristeas 219, 224:
"It is God who apportions fame and great wealth to all kings, and no one
is king by his own power . . . it is a gift of God"; IV Macc 12:11. In Prov
8:15, Wisdom claims this power for herself. Cf. Jos. *J.W.* 2.8.7 (where it
is given as an Essene belief; also in *Ant.* 15.10.5). The word *kratēsis* is

found in *M. A.Z.* 1.3 (*Tosef.* 1.4). "The Talmuds explain the word to mean: 'The day on which Rome seized an empire,' or more explicitly, 'in the days of Queen Cleopatra,' namely the day on which the Romans conquered Egypt in the time of Cleopatra. Now, the papyri frequently record the dating *tēs kaisaros kratēseōs.* Wilcken proved that *kratēsis* here refers to the date of the capture of Alexandria by Augustus. He quoted the decree of the Roman Senate establishing this day (the first of August, 30 BCE) as a festival and as the beginning of an era (Dio Cassius 51.99.6)" (Lieberman 1942:9–10). Very likely the reference here is to this event. See also Scarpat 1967:174–175.

4. *the law.* Grimm correctly noted that *nomos* here refers not to the Mosaic Law, but to natural principles of justice, a knowledge of which could be expected even of pagan rulers. On the other hand, a number of Jewish Hellenistic writers viewed the Torah itself as an expression of natural law (Ps-Aristeas 161; IV Macc 1:16–17 and 5:25; Philo *Op.* 3, 143; *Mos.* 2.52; *Abr.* 16, 60, etc.). See my article, "Philo's Ethical Theory" in *ANRW*.

5. *Horribly.* The adverb *phriktōs* is found only here. Cf. Philodemus *On the Gods* 1.17, where the gods are described as *phreiktous.*

the high and the mighty. For *en tois hyperechousin,* cf. Herodotus 7.10; Horace *Odes* 2.10.9; Luke 12:48; *BR* 32.3 (God only tests the righteous).

6. *mercifully pardoned.* It is difficult to construe the genitive *eleous,* since the genitive with *syngnōstos* is usually that of the thing in respect of which pardon is given. Cf. Philo *Jos.* 53; Philostratus *Vita Sophistarum* 1.8.490.

7. *the master of all.* Cf. 8:3; Job 5:8, LXX; Sir 3:1.

Small and great. Cf. Job 34:19; 31:13–15; Deut 1:17, LXX; Prov 14:31; 17:5; *Instruction of Amen-em-Opet,* chap. 25 (*ANET*:424); I Sam 2:7; Ps 75:8.

10. *in holiness, shall be made holy.* Cf. Philo *Mut.* 208: *hosiōs hermēneuein ta hosia.*

12. *Bright.* Cf. Ps 19:9. *lampros* is an adjective frequently used by Philo to characterize wisdom or virtue. Cf. *LA* 3.171 (of the Divine Logos): *Op.* 30 (of the intelligible); *LA* 3.35 (of the *nous* in us); *LA* 1.18 (of virtue); *Plant.* 40 (of wisdom).

unfading. amarantos is first attested in inscriptions and papyri of the second century BCE in connection with immortality (*CIG* 2942C, 4 [Tralles]; *IPE* 2.286). Here it points to the immortality of Wisdom. Cf. I Peter 1:4; 5:4.

13. *first to make herself known.* For *phthanein* with infinitive, see NOTE on 4:7. Cf. Sir 15:2; 51:26; Philo *Congr.* 123: "Often knowledge rids herself of grudging pride, runs out to meet the gifted disciples, and draws

them into her company"; *Fug.* 141: "but the seeking of God . . . gladdens us the moment we begin our search, and never turns out fruitless, since by reason of His gracious nature He comes to meet us with His pure and virgin graces, and shows himself to those who yearn to see Him"; *Ebr.* 145.

14. *anticipates the dawn. orthrizō* found only in LXX (where it is very frequent) and *NT* (Attic uses *orthreuō*). Cf. *Test.Joseph* 3:6.

will not grow weary. Cf. 16:20; Ps-Aristotle *De Mundo* 391a13: "So the soul, by means of philosophy, taking the mind as its guide, has crossed the frontier, and made the journey [to the heavenly region] out of its own land by a path that does not tire the traveler (*akopiaton tina hodon*)." Similarly, according to Philo, the Royal Road of Wisdom leading to God causes no flagging or fainting (*Deus* 160; cf. *Post.* 31), and Leah [in Philonic allegory, Leah represents Virtue] means rejected and weary (*kopiōsa*), because we all turn away from virtue and think her wearisome (*Mut.* 254; *Mig.* 145; *Cher.* 41).

before his door. Cf. Prov 8:34.

15. *perfect wisdom.* For Plato *phronēsis* was both a theoretical (*Phaedo* 79D 6–7) and a practical virtue (*Symp.* 209A 5–7), whereas Aristotle, who allotted theoretical knowledge to *sophia*, eventually confined *phronēsis* to the practical sphere (*EN* 1140b20). Our author clearly follows the Platonic tradition. Cf. 8:21; 7:7; 8:7.

vigilant. For this figurative use of *agrupneō*, cf. Prov 8:34, LXX; II Esd 8:59; Ps 101:7, LXX; Sir 36:16a. Aratus' *Phaenomena* are described as *Arētou symbolon agrypniēs* in Callimachus *Epigrammata* 27.4, Pfeiffer.

free of care. Cf. Aristobulus: "Those who follow wisdom will be continuously undisturbed (*atarachoi*) throughout their lives" (*FPG:* 224, line 17).

16. *worthy of her.* See NOTE on 1:16.

17. The author here (vv. 17–20) employs a six-part chain syllogism, a well-known rhetorical device known as *sorites* (alternatively: *klimaks* or *epoikodomēsis;* see Longinus 39.3; 23.1). The latter was "a set of statements which proceed, step by step, through the force of logic or reliance upon a succession of indisputable facts, to a climactic conclusion, each statement picking up the last key word (or key phrase) of the preceding one" (H. A. Fischel, "The Uses of Sorites in the Tannaitic Period," *HUCA* 44 [1973] 119–151). Fischel distinguishes the following types: the Transmissional Sorite (*Iliad* 2.102ff; *M. Aboth* 1.1; Sextus Pomponius, in *Digesta* 1.2.35–53; D.L. 9.116; Joel 1:3); the Catastrophic Sorite (Virgil *Ecl.* 2.63; Athenaeus 2.36c–d; *Aphorisms of Hippocrates* 7.87; *BT Baba Batra* 10a; *Kohel. R.* 7.2; Hosea 2:23); the Ethical and Ethico-Metaphysical Sorite (Seneca *Ep.* 85.2; 11; Cicero *Legibus* 1.7.23; M. Aurel. 12.30; Epictetus *Meditations* 1.14.10; Xenophon *Mem.* 4.3; *M. Sotah* 9.15; *Midrash Tannaim* on Deut 23:15; *ŠHŠR* 1.1.9; *BT A.Z.*

20b; *ARN*, B, chap. 33: Schechter 1936:72; Rom 5:3; Wisd 6:17; Confucius, *The Great Learning* (a second century BCE compilation) (James Legge, *The Chinese Classics* [Shanghai, 1935³]:355–59); *Works of Mencius,* chap. 12; *Analects of Confucius, Lun Yü* (Legge, 13.5–7, pp. 263*f*); the Circular Sorite (Augustine *Confessiones* 7.10; *Auctor ad Herennium* 4.25.34; D.L. 1.27–33; *M. Aboth* 3.21 [in manuscript version of Genizah fragments of the Antonia collection in Leningrad]); the Defensive Sorite (Demosthenes 18.179; Rom 10:14; 8:29); the Numerical Sorite (*BR* 8.2; *Rutilius Namatianus* 1.13). One of the sources of the Greco-Roman sorite were the famous logical fallacies of some of the philosophical schools expressed in soritic form (Cicero *Fin.* 4.50; *Academicae Quaestiones* 2.49; *ND* 3.43–52; *De Divinatione* 2.11; Seneca *Ep.* 83.9; 49.8; *Beneficiis* 5.9; Gellius 1.3–5; 18.9; D.L. 1.108; 7.187). Further examples of sorites not mentioned by Fischel are the following: M. Aurel. 4.4. (cf. Cicero *Legibus* 1.23); Philo *Prob.* 59: "He who always acts sensibly, always acts well: he who always acts well, always acts rightly: he who always acts rightly, also acts impeccably, blamelessly, faultlessly, irreproachably, harmlessly, and, therefore, will have the power to do anything, and to live as he wishes, and he who has this power must be free. But the good man always acts sensibly, and, therefore, he alone is free." In Indian literature we may refer to the *Saṁyutta-nekāya* (in *A Source Book in Indian Philosophy,* eds. S. Rhadakrishnan and C. A. Moore [Princeton, 1957]:278), and the Maitri Upanishad (in *Hindu Scriptures,* ed. R. C. Zaehner [London, 1966]:225: "By ascetic practice Goodness, By Goodness mind is won, By mind the Self, which gotten, no more return [to earth]"). A good Chinese analogue is chap. 16 of *Tao Tê Ching:* "Reality is all-embracing. To be all-embracing is to be selfless. To be selfless is to be all-pervading. To be all-prevading is to be transcendent. To be transcendent is to attain Tao. To attain Tao is to be everlasting" (Chang Chung-Yuan, *Tao* [Harper paperback, 1975]:47). There is a somewhat similar passage in the Egyptian *Instructions* of *Onchsheshonqy:* "Do not insult a nobleman, for when insult occurs fighting follows. When fighting occurs killing follows, and killing does not happen without God knowing, for nothing happens except what God ordains" (22.21–25; in S. R. K. Glanville, *Catalogue of Demotic Papyri in the British Museum,* vol. 2 [London, 1955]).

18. *keeping of her laws.* For *tērēsis nomōn,* cf. Sir 35(32):23; 2:15; John 14:15.

surety. The term *bebaiōsis* is very frequent in Philo in the sense of "confirmation" or "firm foundation," but can also mean more specifically "legal warranty" (Aeschines *Against Ctesiphon* 3.249; *P.Tebt.* 311.27 [second century CE]).

19. *makes one near to God.* The same idea is expressed by Philo *Fug.*

58: "This is a most noble definition of deathless life, to be possessed by a love of God and a friendship for God with which flesh and body have no concern."

20. *leads to sovereignty*. This marks the conclusion of the sorites. The desire for wisdom has been shown to make one near to God, and it is this divine intimacy which is the true source of all sovereignty, both spiritual and earthly. (For the well-known Stoic paradox that the wise are the only real kings, see *SVF* 3.617ff; Philo *Agr.* 41; *Sobr.* 57; *Post.* 138; *Prob. passim.*) Cf. *Test.Levi* 13:9. The author thus turns in the next verse to his royal audience and draws the obvious conclusion that if they wish to retain their earthly sovereignty, they had better pursue wisdom. It should further be noted that the author has carefully contrived not to repeat any of the key words in his soritic succession of clauses, but to employ synonymy instead. Thus *epithymia* is replaced by *phrontis, tērēsis* by *prosochē, bebaiōsis aptharsias* by the simple *aptharsia,* and *engus einai theou* by *basileia.* Moreover, the six-part sorites constitutes seven concepts, a number undoubtedly deliberate (Grimm). (Cf. 17:17–18, where the author employs a succession of seven figures.)

21. Gregg writes: "Solomon argues: you love your external kingship with its symbols of authority: honor wisdom, then, and you shall enter upon a higher kingship." (So, too, Heinisch and Fichtner.)

reign forever. "Either the ordinary Oriental exaggeration as seen in the salutation, 'O king, live forever!' I Kings 1:31; Neh 2:3; Dan 2:4; or it may allude to the immortality supposed to attend on just deeds and merciful actions" (Goodrick).

B. THE NATURE AND POWER OF WISDOM AND SOLOMON'S QUEST FOR HER (6:22 – 10:21)

VIII. THE NATURE OF WISDOM AND HER MYSTERIES WILL BE REVEALED
(6:22–25)

6 22 What Wisdom is, and how she came into being, I will relate;
    I will conceal no mysteries from you,
    but will track her from her first beginnings
    and bring the knowledge of her into the open;
    in no way will I bypass the truth.
  23 Nor will I have fellowship with pining envy,
    for the latter has nothing in common with Wisdom.
  24 A multitude of wise men is the salvation of the world,
    and a wise king is the stability of his people.
  25 Be instructed then by my words, and you will be profited.

NOTES

6:22. *What Wisdom is.* A description of Wisdom is given in 7:22–27.

I will conceal no mysteries. Cf. 7:21; Sir 4:18; 14:20; I Enoch 37:3–4: "It were better to declare (them only) to the men of old time, but even from those that come after we will not withhold the beginning of wisdom. Till the present day such wisdom has never been given by the Lord of Spirits . . . by whom the lot of eternal life has been given to me" (cf. 103:2; 104:12; 51:3: "And the Elect One shall in those days sit on My throne, and his mouth shall pour forth all the secrets of wisdom and counsel"). Ben Sira (44:16, in manuscript B of the Cairo Genizah) designated Enoch as "sign of knowledge for all generations" (cf. Jub 4:24; 4:17). A favorite Qumran expression is "to give knowledge in the marvelous mysteries of God" (1QH 4:27; 7:27; 11:9). Cf. also the Isis Aretalogy from Kyme 38: "No one is glorified without knowledge (*gnōmēs*) of Isis." Contrast Job 28:12–14,21–23, and the common apocalyptic command to seal the book (e.g. Dan 12:4).

the knowledge of her. For *gnōsis,* cf. 1:7; 2:13; 7:17; 10:10; 14:22.

23. *pining envy.* Plato had already banished envy from the region above the heaven where souls behold the absolute "Forms" (*Phaedrus* 247A: "for jealousy [*phthonos*] is excluded from the celestial band"; *Tim.* 29E: "The [Demiurge] was good, and in him that is good no envy ariseth ever concerning anything; and being devoid of envy He desired that all should be, so far as possible, like unto Himself"). Cf. Aristotle *Metaphysica* 1.983a: "But it is impossible for the Deity to be jealous (*phthoneron*)"; Philo *Congr.* 13.122–123; *Spec.* 1.320–321 (where Philo attacks the pagan mysteries for their secretiveness); 2.249; 4.75; *Post.* 150–151; *Prob.* 13–14: "But since we have it on the sacred authority of Plato that envy has no place in the divine choir, and wisdom is most divine and most free-handed, she never closes her school of thought but always opens her doors to those who thirst for the sweet water of discourse, and pouring on them an unstinted stream of undiluted doctrine, persuades them to be drunken with the drunkenness which is soberness itself. Then when like initiates in the mysteries they have taken their fill of the revelations, they reproach themselves greatly for their former neglect." (In this passage we have the two chief motifs of vv. 22–23: the designation of wisdom's teaching as mysteries, and the banishment of envy; *QG* 4.103; 107: "the good is far removed from envy and grudgingness, for without storing up and keeping them for itself, it gives up the various kinds of knowledge and hides nothing as some Sophists do"; *CH* 4.3. For the personification of envy, see Ovid *Metamorphoses,* 2.770–780 [*intabescitque videndo:* "and with the sight she pines away."])

24. *stability.* For *eustatheia,* cf. II Macc 14:6; III Macc 3:26; 6:28; *OGIS* 669,4 (edict of Tiberius Julius Alexander, 68 CE: *tēn Aigypton en eustatheia diagousan*). The ideal of *eustatheia* or inner calm and stability is a central theme running through Philo's writings (*Post.* 23, 27; *Cher.* 19; *Somn.* 1.158; 2.219; *Virt.* 32; *Legat.* 113; *Conf.* 130–132; *Fug.* 174; *Abr.* 27; *Ebr.* 100, 76; *Sacr.* 8; *Flac.* 135). Cf. NOTE on 8:16. For the earliest application of the term *eustathēs* to the human soul, see Democritus DK, B.191; cf. Epicurus Frag. 11, Bailey; Epictetus *Discourses* 1.29; *SVF* 3.280, 264; Musonius Rufus Frag. 38; Ps-Aristeas 261.

salvation of the world. The notion of the wise man as the foundation (Prov 10:25) and salvation of the world is a widespread motif both in Philo and in rabbinic literature. Philo *Mig.* 121: "For in truth the righteous man is the foundation on which mankind rests" (at 124, he is described as "a central pillar [*stylon*] in a house"; cf. *BT Ber.* 28b; Gal 2:9); *Sacr.* 121: "Every wise man is a ransom for the fool, whose existence could not endure for an hour, did not the wise provide for his preservation by compassion and forethought"; *QG* 2.11: "In the first place, it is clear evidence that because of one righteous and worthy man, many men are saved (*sōzontai*) through their relation to him"; *QE* 1.21; *Spec.*

2.47. For the rabbinic sources, see *Tosef. Sotah* 10.1 ("When the right-eous come into the world, good comes into the world, and trouble is re-moved from the world . . ."); *BT Sanh.* 113b; *Suk.* 45b ("Hezekiah fur-ther stated in the name of R. Jeremiah who said it in the name of R. Simeon b. Yoḥai, I am able to exempt the whole world from judgment from the day that I was born until now, and were Eliezer, my son, to be with me [we could exempt it] from the day of the creation of the world to the present time, and were Jotham the son of Uzziah with us [we could ex-empt it] from the creation of the world to its final end"), *Sanh.* 97b; *Ḥulin* 92a; *BR* 49.18; *BT Ber.* 17b; *Ta'an.* 24b; 14a.

IX. SOLOMON IS ONLY A MORTAL
(7:1–6)

7 1 I too, indeed, am a mortal like all the rest,
descended from the first-molded man, earthborn,
and in my mother's womb I was sculpted into flesh
2 during a ten-month's space, curdled in blood
by virile seed and the pleasure that is joined with sleep.
3 When I was born I breathed the common air
and fell upon the earth that suffers the same from all,
howling out my first cry the same as all;
4 I was swaddled and reared with care.
5 No king has begun life otherwise;
6 for all have one entry into life and a like departure.

NOTES

7:1. *a mortal like all the rest.* The human side of royalty was often emphasized in kingship tracts, sometimes in close relationship with its divine aspect. Cf. Ps-Aristeas 262–263: "How may one avoid yielding to arrogance? . . . By preserving equality and reminding himself at each turn that he is a man as well as a leader of men"; 282: "What man is worthy of admiration? . . . He that is furnished with renown and wealth and power, and yet is in spirit on an equality with all men (*ison pasin onta*)"; 257. According to Ecphantus, in the terrestrial part of the universe, "man is the best endowed by nature, but among men the king is the most divine, having more of the better elements in our common nature; for while in body he is like the rest of us, being made of the same substance, he has none the less been created by the best of Artificers, who shaped him with Himself as the model" (On Kingship, in E. Barker, *From Alexander to Constantine*

[Oxford, 1959]:367). Philo had similarly written: "In his material substance (*ousia*), the king is just the same as any man, but in the authority of his rank he is like the God of all. For there is nothing upon earth more exalted than he. Since he is a mortal, he must not vaunt himself; since he is a god he must not give way to anger. For if he is honored as being an image of God, yet he is at the same time fashioned from the dust of the earth, from which he should learn simplicity to all" (Frags., Mangey, 2:673; translation in Goodenough, 1967:99). When Hispania ulterior (Further Spain, i.e. the part beyond the Ebro) made an offer of a temple to Tiberius, he declined it, and, according to Tacitus (*Annales* 4.38), asserted: "I call you to witness, conscript fathers, and I desire posterity to remember that I am but a mortal, discharging the duties of a man. . . ." cf. Introduction IX.

first-molded. *prōtoplastos* is first attested here (and 10:1). Cf. Philo *QE* 2.46: "differing from the earthborn first moulded man (*prōtoplastou*)"; *Test. Abraham* A, 11: *ho prōtoplastos Adam; Sib Or* 3:25: *ton prōton plasthenta*: 1:285; III Bar 4:9; *Test. Solomon* D 1:2.

earthborn. *gēgenous* refers to Adam as "formed from the earth" (Gen 2:7; cf. Sir 17:1; I Cor 15:47), and is found frequently in Philo (*Op*. 82, 136; *LA* 1.79; *Abr*. 12, 56; *Virt*. 199, 203). Cf. Plato *Politicus* 269B.

womb. *koilia* is frequent in the LXX for Hebrew *reḥem*.

2. *during a ten-month's space*. The compound *dekamēniaios* is first attested here, and is also found in the Isis Aretalogy (the only full version of which was discovered in Kyme in 1925 and is dated to the first or second century CE): "I have ordained for woman to bring forth the ten-month foetus into the light (*dekamēniaion brephos eis phōs eksenengkein*) (M18[K]. The Ios inscription reads: *dekamēnon*. See A. Deissmann, *Light from the Ancient East* [New York and London, n.d.]:140; D. Müller, *Ägypten und die griechischen Isis-Aretalogien* [Berlin, 1961]:45–46). Cf. Plutarch *Numa* 12.2. Grimm suggested that lunar months of twenty-eight days are meant. According to Roman law (*XII Tables* 4.4), ten lunar months made up the full period of gestation. We read in *Atra-Ḥasīs* 1.280ff: "[At the] destined [moment] the tenth month was summoned. / The tenth month arrived / And the elapse of the period opened the womb" (Lambert and Millard: 63). The Hittite code (1.17) also contemplates a pregnancy of ten months (*ANET*:190. Cf. E. Neufeld, *The Hitite Laws* [London, 1951]:137–138). Cf. Aristotle *Historia Animalium* 7.4; Pliny the Elder *NH* 7.5; Herodotus 6.63–69; Machon, in Athenaeus 8.349E; Menander Frag. 343, Körte; Plautus *Cistellaria* 163; Terence *Adelphoe* 475; Virgil *Ecl*. 4.61; Ovid *Fasti* 1.33; Seneca *Ep*. 102.23; Aulus Gellius *Noctes Atticae* 3.16; D.L. 8.29; Hippolytus *De Septimestri* 4 and 7; IV Macc 16:7; Tertullian *De Anima* 37. In text no. 300Z.2 from the Esna Temple, the Egyptian god Chnum declares: "For

a period of ten months, I have prepared nourishment for you; thereafter you joyfully come to earth." See S. Sauneron, "Les dix mois précédant la naissance," *BIFAO* 58 (1959) 33*ff;* J. Bergman, "Decem Illis Diebus," in *Ex Orbe Religionum, Studia Geo Widengren Oblata* (Leiden, 1972) 1. 340. The rabbis considered the ordinary duration of pregnancy to consist of nine solar months, i.e. 271–273 (*BT Nid.* 38a) or 274 days (*PT Nid.* 1.3, 49b), although an exceptional twelve-month pregnancy is also recognized (*BT Yeb.* 80b).

curdled in blood. Cf. I Enoch 15:4: "You have defiled yourselves with the blood of women, and have begotten (children) with the blood of flesh." We have here a commonplace of Greek science. Aristotle concludes in chapters 19 and 20 of the first book of his *Generation of Animals* that the female does not produce any semen, as earlier philosophers had held, but that the menstrual blood is the material from which the seminal fluid, in giving to it a form, will cause the complete embryo to be produced. This was not a new idea, but had already been suggested by the author of the Hippocratic *Peri Gonēs,* where in section 14 it is stated that the embryo is nourished by maternal blood, which flows to the foetus and there coagulates (*pēgnymenou*), forming the embryonic flesh. (What was quite new here was the idea that the semen supplied or determined nothing but the form; cf. Philo *Op.* 132.) Aristotle further notes that "The action of the semen of the male in 'setting' the female's secretion in the uterus is similar to that of rennet upon milk" (*Gen. An.*739b21). In India, too, the *Suśruta-Saṃhita* (dating from the first two or three centuries CE) says that the embryo is formed of a mixture of semen and blood. The blood in question is specifically referred to as menstrual (*ārtava*), both by Suśruta and Caraka. Moreover, the Aristotelian comparison of the formation of the embryo with the clotting of milk into cheese also occurs in Indian embryology. The *Suśruta-Saṃhita* says that as the semen and blood undergo chemical changes through heat, seven different layers of skin (*kalā*) are formed, like the creamy layers formed in milk. Cf. Job 10:10: "Hast thou not poured me out as milk, and curdled me like cheese?" *BT Nid.* 31a. See Joseph Needham, *A History of Embryology* (2d ed., New York, 1959):25–69; E. Lesky, "Die Zeugungs- und Vererbungslehre der Antike und ihr Nachwirken," *Abhandl. Mainz, Geistes- und sozialwiss. Klasse* 19 (1950) 1361*f.* There is an echo of the cheese analogy in the recently discovered *Mani Codex,* where Mani speaks of the human body as originally created in loathsomeness and procreated in a process comparable to cheese-making (*etyrōthē*) (*Cologne Mani Codex* 85, 6–12. See A. Henrichs, "Mani and the Babylonian Baptists," *HSCP* 77 [1973] 58). For *pageis,* cf. Job 10:10, LXX, A (*epēksas*); D.L. 8.29: *prōton pagen en hēmerais tessarakonta;* Philo *Op.* 124.

pleasure. The mention of pleasure, according to Fichtner, simply constitutes part of the author's scientific description. Cf. Artistotle *Generation of Animals* 728a10: "The pleasure which accompanies copulation is due to the fact that not only semen but also pneuma is emitted"; Philo *LA* 2.17: "apart from pleasure nothing in mortal kind comes into existence"; *Abr.* 100: "Now in a marriage where the union is brought about by pleasure, the partnership is between body and body, but in the marriage made by wisdom it is between thoughts which seek purification and perfect virtues"; *Op.* 161. In the Hermetic writings, on the other hand, sexual pleasure appears to have a deeper mystical significance: "Take it then to heart as a truth more sure and evident than any other, that God, the master of all of nature, has devised and bestowed upon all beings this mystery of eternal reproduction, with all the affection, all the joy and gladness, all the yearning and the heavenly love inherent in it" (*CH, Asclepius* 21, 10–14). The secret of embryogony is awesomely wondrous for the Psalmist (139:13–16), and the author of II Maccabees is similarly impressed (7:22–23; cf. *BT Nid.* 31a). Though no less awed by the divine creativity, our own author is characteristically unable to resist the urge to supply some of the physiological details of the formation of the embryo in accord with the latest findings of the science of his day. This is especially understandable when we recall that "the medical achievement of Alexandria, especially in the third century BCE, reached a level never achieved before, or indeed again until the seventeenth century" (Fraser 1972] 1. 341).

3. *I breathed the common air.* Cf. Menander Frag. 740, Körte (*espasas ton aera ton koinon*); Philemon Frag. 119 (Edmonds III A.69); *Egyptian Coffin Texts,* B3C, 570 (dating to Middle Kingdom, 2000 BCE): "I [the creator-God] made the four winds that every man might breathe thereof *like his fellow* in his time" (*ANET:*7); Antiphon, DK, B.44, Frag. B, col. 2, line 27: "We all breathe into the air through mouth and nostrils"; Eccles 3:19. Cf. R. Kassel, *Untersuchungen zur griechischen u. römischen Konsolationsliteratur, Zetemata* 18 (1958):64.

that suffers the same from all. I.e. mother earth which all both use and misuse. Cf. M. Aurel. 5.4: "and falling upon that earth from which my father drew his vital seed, my mother her blood, my nurse her milk; from which for so many years I am fed and watered day by day; which bears my footsteps and my misusing it for so many purposes"; II Bar 13:11: "But now, ye peoples and nations, ye are guilty because ye have always trodden down the earth (*katapatēsantes tēn gēn*) and used the creation unrighteously" (*FPG* 119); *Atra-Ḫasīs,* Tablet II, col. 1: "Twelve hundred years had not yet passed / When the land extended and the peoples multiplied. / The land was bellowing like a bull" (Lambert and Millard: 73); Yasht 13.9: "the broad, Ahura-created Earth . . . which carries all material being" (see H. Lommel, *Die Religion Zarathustras* [rep. Hildesheim, New York, 1971] 259–260); Stasinos *Cypria,* Frag. 3: "There was a time when the countless tribes of men, though wide-dispersed, oppressed the surface of the deep-bosomed earth" (trans. in LCL *Hesiod, Homeric*

Hymns and Homerica); Virgil *Ecl.* 4.40–41: [in the new Golden Age] "the earth shall not feel (*patietur*) the harrow, nor the vine the pruning-hook; the sturdy plowman, too, shall now loose his oxen from the yoke." (Heinisch: "that suffers the same from all," i.e. earth upon which all fall at birth. Cf. *Iliad* 19.110. Grimm: the earth that all men tread.)

my first cry. A literary commonplace. Cf. Empedocles DK, B.118: "I wept and wailed when I saw the unfamiliar land [at birth]"; Ps-Plato *Axiochus* 366D; Lucretius 5.222–227: "Then again, the child, like a sailor tossed ashore from the cruel wars, lies naked on the ground, dumb, lacking all help for life, when first nature has cast him forth by travail from his mother's womb into the coasts of light, and he fills the place with woeful wailing, as is but right for one for whom it remains in life to pass through so much trouble." Seneca *De Consolatione ad Polybium* 4.3: "Do you not see what sort of life Nature has promised us—she who decreed that the first act of man at birth should be to weep?" For the Epicurean explanation, see Sext.*Math.* 11.96: "When it is born and is not as yet a slave to opinions, it cries and screams as soon as it is smitten by the air's unwonted chill"; Philo *Op.* 161. Shakespeare *King Lear* IV vi 187–188: "When we are born, we cry that we are come / To this great stage of fools."

5. *begun life.* For *geneseōs archēn,* cf. Philo *Op.* 67: *to sperma tōn zōōn geneseōs archēn einai symbebēke.*

6. *one entry . . . and a like departure.* Cf. Sir 40:1: "A heavy yoke is upon the sons of man, from the day that they go out of their mother's womb, till the day that they return to the mother of all things . . . from him that sitteth on a throne of glory, unto him that is humbled in earth and ashes"; Horace *Odes* 1.4.13: "Pale Death with foot impartial knocks at the poor man's cottage and at princes' palaces"; Theodoret *Oratio* 9: *ou monon de tēn eis ton bion eisodon mian, alla kai tēn eksodon isēn echomen* (undoubtedly quoting from this verse).

X. SOLOMON PREFERS WISDOM ABOVE ALL ELSE
(7:7–14)

7   7 Therefore I prayed, and understanding was granted me;
         I called for help, and a spirit of wisdom came to me.
      8 I preferred her above scepter and throne,
         and held riches as nought by comparison.
      9 I reckoned no priceless gem her equal,
         since all gold in her sight is but a pinch of sand,
         and before her silver is accounted as clay.
     10 I loved her above health and shapeliness,
         and preferred her to the light of day;
         for her radiance never sets.
     11 But all good things came to me with her together,
         and wealth past counting in her hands;
     12 and I rejoiced in all since Wisdom leads them forth,
         yet I was unaware that it was she who bore these things.
     13 Guilelessly did I learn, and unstintingly do I share;
         I do not hide her riches.
     14 She is an inexhaustible treasure for mankind,
         and those who acquire it attain friendship with God,
         commended by the gift derived from her instruction.

NOTES

7:7–14. Solomon preferred Wisdom above all external goods, but subsequently discovered that the latter were ultimately attained along with
her. There appears to be a faint echo here of the well-known philosophical
debate between the Peripatetics and the Stoics as to the relative importance of external goods (such as health, beauty, honor, and wealth, all of
which are explicitly mentioned by our author in vv. 8 and 10) for the

happy life. The Stoics had placed special stress on the notion that virtue is self-sufficient for happiness (*autarkēs pros eudaimonian*) and the only good properly speaking (*monon to kalon agathon*) (*SVF* 1.187; 3.29–45, 49–67; D.L. 7.101). The Peripatetic view of the triple good (Aristotle *EN* 1098b) is explicitly attacked by Philo. Joseph's coat of many colors, he says, indicates this tangled position. Joseph is "one who moulds his theories with an eye to statecraft rather than to truth. This appears in his treatment of the three kinds of good things, those pertaining to the outside world, to the body, and to the soul. . . . He argues that each of the three classes mentioned has the character of a part or element and that it is only when they are all taken together in the aggregate that they produce happiness. In order, then, that he may be taught better ideas than these, he is sent to men who hold that nothing is a good thing but what has true beauty, and that this is a property belonging to the soul as soul" (*Det.* 6–9; cf. *Post.* 95, 133; *Spec.* 2.48, 73; *Deus* 150–151; *Ebr.* 75; *Virt.* 5–6; *Sobr.* 67–68; *QG* 4.167). In *Her.* 285–286, however, Philo seems to follow the compromise adopted by Antiochus of Ascalon, who distinguished the *vita beata,* which depends only on virtue, from the *vita beatissima,* which requires also the possibility of using external goods (Cicero *Academica Posteriora* 1.22; 2.22; 1.134). When will a man, asks Philo, have attained to a life of true bliss and happiness? "When there is welfare outside us, welfare in the body, welfare in the soul, the first bringing ease of circumstance and good repute, the second health and strength, the third delight in virtues." (See my "Philo's Ethical Theory" in *ANRW,* and Dillon 1977:146–148.) The author of Wisdom seems to reflect to some extent Philo's position in its more moderate mood. One should seek Wisdom for her own sake, but all other goods, we are assured, will later follow in any case. (Cf. Philo *Praem.* 104: "For those who possess stored up in Heaven the true wealth whose adornment is wisdom and godliness have also wealth of earthly riches in abundance. For under the providence and good care of God their storehouses are ever filled, because the impulses of their minds and the undertakings of their hands are never hindered in carrying out successfully the purposes which they ever zealously pursue." Similarly, at 119 it is said that God promises that those who cultivate virtue will receive as well the gift of complete freedom from disease.)

7:7. *Therefore I prayed.* The author is undoubtedly referring to Solomon's vision (I Kings 3:6–15) and prayer (I Kings 8:12–53). For *phronēsis* and *sophia,* see NOTE on 6:15. Cf. Sir 51:13–14.

I called for help. epikaleō (both active and middle) means to summon or invoke a god; in the middle it often means to call in as helper or ally. For the verb without object expressed, see Acts 7:59.

8. *riches.* Cf. I Kings 3:11; Job 28:15*ff;* Prov 3:14*ff;* 8:10*ff;* 16:16; Ps 119:72; 1QH 15.22.

by comparison. en synkrisei used in this way is first attested here. Cf. Philo *Aet.* 46; *Flac.* 187, 162; *Spec.* 2.42; *Mos.* 2.198; Babrius 101.8. *pros synkrisin* in *IG* 5.268.53 (Mantinaea, first century BCE); frequent in late prose.

9. *priceless. atimēton* in this sense is first attested here. Cf. III Macc 3:23; *PT Peah* 1.1,15d: "Artaban sent to R. Judah the Holy a priceless (*atimēton*) precious stone and requested that he send him something correspondingly precious in return. He sent him a *mezuzah*. He said to him: I sent you something priceless and you sent me something worth one coin (*pholleron*. Latin *follis*). He answered: Both your possessions and mine cannot equal it. Moreover, you sent me something which I must guard, whereas I have sent you something which when you die will guard you, as it is written, 'when thou walkest, it shall lead thee'" (Prov 6:22); *Test. Levi* 13:7; *BR* 35, end. (Shakespeare, *Richard III* I iv 27: "inestimable stones, unvalued jewels.") Cf. Isis Aretalogy from Kyme, 26: "I make the just man stronger than gold and silver."

10. *never sets. akoimētos* is literally 'unsleeping,' and Philo frequently speaks of the unsleeping eyes (*akoimētois ommasi*) of the mind; *Mut.* 5, 40; *Spec.* 1.49; 4.201 ("the unsleeping eyes of justice, the assessor of God" [cf. Wisd 9:4; 6:14]); *Jos.* 146–147: "Heaven is an eternal day," for it is "kept in unsleeping (*akoimētō*) wakefulness by active forces which do not err or stumble"; *Mos.* 1.185, 289. Cf. Epictetus 1.14.12: "He [Zeus] has stationed by each man's side as guardian his particular genius (*daimona*) . . . and that too a guardian who never sleeps (*akoimēton*) and is not to be beguiled."

11. *came to me.* Though willing to forgo external goods, they came to me unasked along with wisdom. Cf. I Kings 3:13: "I give you also what you have not asked, both riches and honor"; II Chron 1:12; Prov 3:16: "Length of days is in her right hand; in her left hand riches and honor"; 8:18; Matt 6:33. According to the rabbis, Solomon chose wisdom, knowing that wisdom once in his possession, all else would come of itself. R. Simeon b. Ḥalafta utilizes the following parable. The matter is similar, he says, to the king's counsellor, who when asked to request what he desired most, reflected as follows: "If I request silver and gold, he will bestow them; precious stones and diamonds, he will bestow them; I will ask for his daughter's hand and all will be included" (*ŠHŠR* 1.1.9; *Pes. R.* 14,59a).

12. *I was unaware.* The imperfect *ēgnooun* indicates that it was his continuing belief that external goods were simply unnecessary for the happy life, until he learned to his delight that Wisdom ultimately brings them along in her wake.

who bore. genetin, feminine of *genetēs*, is first attested here. Cf. Aglaïas 10. The author is fond of describing Wisdom by means of female substantives (7:21: *technitis;* 8:4: *mystis, hairetis*). The method of forming feminine substantives from their masculine counterpart was a practice popular with late Hellenistic writers (e.g. *ekdotis* from *ekdotēs; kynēgetis* from *kynēgetēs; syngenis* from *syngenēs;* etc.). See L. R. Palmer, *A Grammar of the Post-Ptolemaic Papyri* (London, 1946) 1. 92. (Reese 1970:7.) Cf. Philo *Ebr.* 30: "The architect who made this universe was at the same time the father of what was thus born, whilst its mother was the knowledge possessed by its Maker." Wolfson suggests that the term 'leads them' (*hēgeitai*) and 'mother of them' (*genetin*) "undoubtedly reflects the double meaning of the three Hebrew consonants *aleph, mem, nun* which in Philo are given the meaning of nurse ('*ômên*) and 'mother' ('*îman* (1948: 1. 269). Cf., however, V. Nikiprowetzky, *Le Commentaire de l'Écriture chez Philon d'Alexandrie* (Leiden, 1977) 72–73.

13. *Guilelessly.* For *adolōs,* cf. Philo *Ebr.* 49: "For these [the whole range of the school culture] ever secure the favors of wisdom to those who woo her in guilelessness (*adolōs*) and sincerity"; *Virt.* 62: "and those who love her [Wisdom] with a love that is guileless and pure and genuine."

unstintingly. See NOTE on 6:23. For *aphthonōs metadidōmi,* cf. the stele from about 200 BCE recording the decree conferring citizenship of Samia upon an otherwise unknown philosopher, Epicrates of Heraclea, because he "communicated without stint" (*metadidous aphthonōs*) M. N. Tod, "Sidelights on Greek Philosophers," *JHS* 77 [1957] 135; Reese 1970:18); Ps-Aristotle *De Mundo* 391a17: *pasin aphthonōs metadounai boulētheisa* (the divine soul wished to impart to all unsparingly); Philemon *Frag.* 154, Edmonds IIIA; Plato *Symp.* 210A: " 'However I will speak of them.' [the rites and revelations], she said, 'and will not stint my best endeavors' (*prothumias ouden apoleipsō*)"; Sir 20:30–31: "Hidden wisdom and concealed treasure, what profit is there in either? Better is the man that hideth his folly than a man that hideth his wisdom" (cf. T. H. Gaster, "Samaritan Proverbs," in *Studies . . . A. A. Neuman* [Leiden, 1962]:235, proverb 49). Philo *Her.* 213; *LA* 3.164; *Somn.* 2.282. Reese has pointed out that adverbs of manner are a characteristic feature of late Hellenistic prose, replacing the adjectival construction of earlier Greek. Wisd has twenty-one of these adverbs of manner, extending throughout the work, from *autoschediōs* in 2:2 to *apechthōs* in 19:5 (1970:18).

14. *inexhaustible. anēklipēs* is found only here, although it occurs again in Patristic Greek (Clement *Strom.* 5.4). The more usual form is *anellipēs,* which is found fairly often in Philo, or *anekleiptos* (Luke 12:33). Cf. *Post.* 136: "from the wisdom of God, that never failing spring (*tēs anellipous pēgēs*)"; *Congr.* 4; *Spec.* 1.285; *Plant.* 91; *Praem.* 102; *Mos.* 1.189; *Spec.* 4.144; *Aet.* 75; Plutarch *Moralia* 495C; *SIG* 799.17; Sext. *Math.* 8.439.

acquire it. Many commentators prefer the well-attested reading *chrēsa-menoi,* reasoning that since *chrēsthai* with the accusative is rare (found only in later Greek), it was readily changed by some scribes into *ktēsamenoi* (Grimm, Heinisch, Fichtner). In Greek philosophy, *ktēsis* and *chrēsis aretēs* are sometimes contrasted. Cf. Aristotle *EN* 1098b32. According to Eudorus of Alexandria, the aim of life is "to live in accordance with Virtue, and that in turn means both the acquiring (*ktēsis*) and the exercising (*chrēsis*) of perfect virtue" (see Dillon:123).

XI. GOD IS SOLE SOURCE OF ALL-ENCOMPASSING WISDOM
(7:15–22a)

7   15   God grant that I speak in accord with his wish,
      and conceive thoughts worthy of his gifts,
      for he himself is both the guide of Wisdom
      and corrector of the wise.
    16   Both we and our words are in his hands,
      as well as all understanding and craftsmanship.
    17   For it was he who gave me unerring knowledge of existent
        being,
      to know the structure of the universe and the operation of
        the elements;
    18   the beginning, and end, and middle of times,
      the changes of the solstices and the vicissitudes of the
        seasons;
    19   the cycles of years and the positions of the stars;
    20   the natures of living creatures and the tempers of beasts;
      the violent force of spirits and the reasonings of men;
      the species of plants, and the virtues of roots.
    21   I learned both what is hidden and what is manifest,
   22a   for Wisdom, the artificer of all, taught me.

NOTES

7:15–22a. Divine Wisdom is identified in this passage in the most explicit terms with the full range of human science and philosophy (i.e. ontology, cosmology, physics, astronomy, biology, botany, esoteric knowledge). Cf. Aeschylus *Prometheus Bound* 436–506, on which see M. Griffith, *The Authenticity of the Prometheus Bound* (Cambridge, 1977):

217–220. Our passage is largely inspired by the teleological argument *apo tōn ergōn* (God's *opera* as a manifestation of his existence and wise regime) as we find it in Plato, Aristotle, the Stoa, Philo, and Christian writers. See A. Henrichs, *HSCP* 79 (1975):105–106. For the debate over the relative value of the "encyclical" studies, see T. Conley, *General Education in Philo of Alexandria,* Colloquy 15 of the *Center for Hermeneutical Studies,* ed. W. Wuellner, Berkeley, 1975; Duesberg and Fransen:781*ff.*

7:15. *in accord with his wish. kata gnōmēn,* sc. *autou.*

guide. Isis is similarly praised as *hodēgos* (*P. Oxy.* XI 1380, 122).

corrector. For *diorthōtēs,* cf. Diodorus 15.6.1 (*tōn poiēmatōn . . . diorthotas*); Plutarch *Solon* 16.3 (*tēs politeias diorthōtēn*); Epictetus 3.7.1.

16. *in his hands.* The same sentiment is expressed in the Qumran scrolls: "It is thou who hast created breath for the tongue and thou knowest its words; Thou didst establish the fruit of the lips before ever they were. Thou dost set words to measure and the flow of breath from the lips to meter. Thou bringest forth sounds according to their mysteries . . ." (1QH 1.28). Philo similarly writes: "All are God's possessions and not yours, your reflections, your knowledge of every kind, your arts, your conclusions, your reasonings on particular questions, your sense-perceptions, in fact the activities of your soul, whether carried on through the senses or without them" (*Cher.* 71).

craftsmanship. ergateia is a rare word found only here and in *BGU* 1159.9 (1 BCE), but occurs later in Patristic Greek.

17. *structure of the universe.* For the expression *systasin kosmou* see Plato *Timaeus* 32C; Ps-Aristotle *De Mundo* 396b23; Philo *Aet.* 25; *CH* 23.52.

the operation of the elements. The words *energeia* and *stoicheia* are part of the Greek philosophical vocabulary. *Dynamis* and *energeia* are Aristotelian technical terms (*Metaphysica* 1046a26; *Physica* 206a24; etc.), used also by Philo (*Her.* 110: *energeias te kai dynameis autōn; LA* 2.24, 36–7, 40; *Cher.* 62, 70; etc.); *energeia* occurs eight times in Ps-Aristeas (at 266 in reference to God). Cf. 13:4 below; II Macc 3:29; III Macc 4:21; 5:12; Eph 1:19. *Stoicheia* was first used by Plato to designate the elements (still called by Empedocles, DK, B.6, *rhidzōmata* or 'roots'): *Theaetetus* 201E; *Politicus* 278D; *Tim.* 48B. Cf. 19:18 below; IV Macc 12:13; Philo *Cher.* 127; *Cont.* 3–4; *Aet.* 29; II Peter 3:10.

18. *the beginning, and end, and middle of times.* A common collocution in Classical and Hellenistic literature. According to the Orphic theogony, Zeus, having created all things anew, becomes "beginning, middle, and end of all" (O. Kern, *Orphicorum Fragmenta* [Berlin, 1922] 21, 168). The same Orphic verse is quoted in the fourth century BCE Derveni papy-

rus, which proves that it is pre-Hellenistic. See R. Merkelbach, *ZPE* 1 (1967) 23; W. Burkert, *Antike und Abendland* 14 (1968) 93–114, esp. p. 96, n.6. We find the same expression in the Jewish-Orphic poem (*FPG* 166); Plato *Parmenides* 145A; *Philebus* 31A; *Laws* 715E (probably quoting an Orphic poem); Aristotle *De Caelo* 268a,11 (according to the Pythagoreans the world is summed up in the number three, "for end, middle, and beginning give the number of the whole, and their number is the triad"); Cicero *Tusc.* 1.64; Philo *Her.* 126; *QG* 4.8; 3.3; 1.91; Jos. *Ag.Ap.* 2.190; Ps-Aristotle *De Mundo* 401b25; Plutarch *Moralia* 5C; Sallustius 6 (a triad of gods is necessary for the four cosmic operations, since each has a beginning, a middle, and an end). On the base of a statue of *Aiōn* erected during the time of Augustus at Eleusis, the inscription describes him as having neither beginning, middle, nor end (Dittenberger, *SIG*, 1125). According to Ezekiel the Tragedian, Moses' father-in-law interprets Moses' view in his dream of the entire earth, what was below it, and what was above the heavens, as signifying that he would know the present, the past, and the future (*FPG*: 210, 24–26) (cf. *Iliad* 1.70). Similarly, in the Pahlavi writings it is often said of Ohrmazd that he "is, was, and will be," *ke hast, būt ut bavēt*. A similar formula is employed in the Atharvashira Upanishad. See G. Widengren, *Die Religionen Irans* (Stuttgart, 1965):287–288, 306. According to Berrosus, Uta-napištim was instructed to write "beginnings, middles, and ends" on tablets and to bury them in Sippar, where they were found after the flood. (See Lambert 1960:93.) In the *Palestinian Talmud* (*Sanh.* 1.1) it is reported in the name of R. Reuben that the seal of the Holy One, blessed be He, is *Emet* (truth), which is then explained by R. Bon as a *notarikon* (acrostic) for *Elohîm melek tāmîd,* i.e. that he is the living God and eternal King. Resh Lakish, however, interprets it as follows: *Alef* is at the head of the alphabet, *mem* in the middle [not precisely so], and *taw* at its end, i.e. "I the Lord am the first" (Isa 41:4), since I have not received sovereignty from another, "and beside me there is no God" (44:6), since I have no partner, "and with the last I am the same" (41:4), since I shall not bestow it on another. Reinach made the interesting suggestion that the three letters of *Emet* are really a transcription of the initials of the Greek words *archē, meson, telos* (in his notes to Jos. *Ag.Ap.* 2.190) (cited by Thackeray in his LCL translation, p. 369, note c).

the changes of the solstices, and the vicissitudes of the seasons. For *tropōn allagas,* cf. Job 38:33, LXX. Philo makes frequent use of the collocation *tropai kai metabolai* for the changes and variations that take place in heaven and earth, *tropai* being especially common in connection with atmospheric changes and the seasons. The terms *kairos* and *eniautos* are also included in a number of these passages. (Cf. Gen 1:14, LXX; Philo *LA* 1.8; *Cher.* 88; *Det.* 87; *Ebr.* 91; *Her.* 149, 247; *Congr.* 104;

Mos. 1.200; 2.18, 124–125; *Spec.* 4.235: "The fourfold partition of the year into what we call the annual seasons involves changes and alternations in the air and in these changes and alternations [*tropais kai metabolais*] it shows a marvelous order in disorder. For as it is divided by an equal number of months into winter, spring, summer and autumn, three for each season, it carries the year to its fulfillment and the year, as the name *eniautos* indicates [cf. Plato *Cratylus* 410D], contains as it runs to its completion everything in itself, which it would not have been able to do if it had not accepted the law of the annual seasons"; 1QS 10.6–7.)

19. *the cycles of years.* Cf. Philo *Somn.* 1.20: "that it [the air] undergoes all kinds of change (*tropas kai metabolas pantoias*); that it is the source of winter and summer, and of the autumn and spring seasons, that is, of the constituent parts that fix the limits of the year's cycle (*eniautou kyklos*)."

the positions of the stars. Cf. Jub 2:8: *kai tas tōn astrōn theseis kai ta stoicheia* (*FPG:* 71); I Enoch 2 and 72–82; *LAB* 18.5: "God raised Abraham above the firmament and showed him all the orderings of the stars (*omnium astrorum dispositiones*)"; Cicero *ND* 2.153: "We alone of living creatures know the risings and settings, and the courses of the stars, the human race has set limits to the day, the month, and the year, and has learnt the eclipses of the sun and moon, and foretold for all future time their occurrence, their extent, and their dates. And contemplating the heavenly bodies the mind arrives at a knowledge of the gods" [cf. 13:5 below and NOTE]: Philo *Congr.* 133: "the host of the stars, performing their courses in ranks of ordered harmony"; 1QH 1.12: "the stars to their paths."

20. *the natures of living creatures.* Cf. I Kings 4:33: "[Solomon] spoke also of beasts, and of birds, and of reptiles, and of fish."

the violent force of spirits. pneumatōn bias may mean either the violent force of winds or of spirits. For the former translation, cf. Philo *Op.* 58 (*nēnemias kai bias pneumatōn*); Quran 21:81: "and to Solomon we subjected the wind, strongly blowing." The structure of the verse, however, would seem to require the latter translation (*zōa-thēria; phyta-rhizai; pneumata-anthrōpoi:* first the general, then the particular) (Grimm). A passage in 1QH, 1.9–11, may help to bridge the two translations: "Thou hast created all the spirits [and hast established a statute] and law for all their works . . . the mighty winds (*rûḥôt'ōz*) according to their laws before they became angels [of holiness] and eternal spirits in their dominions." Cf. Jub 2:2: "the angels of the spirit of the winds" (*angeloi pneumatōn pneontōn, FPG:* 71); "[and the angels] of all the spirits of his creatures (*pantōn tōn pneumatōn tōn ktismatōn autou*) which are in the heavens and on the earth" (*FPG:* 72); I Enoch 60:12–22; 41:3*ff;* 18:1–5; 76:1–14; 15:4: *kai pneumata zōnta aiōnia*

(*FPG:* 29); Ps 104:4; Sir 39:28: "There are spirits (*pneumata*) that are created for vengeance. . . . Fire and hail, and famine, and death . . .";
1Qap Gen 20:20: "for a spirit (*ruḥā'*) smote all of them."

the species of plants. For *diaphoras phytōn,* cf. Philo *Somn.* 1.203: *kai phytōn diaphoras.*

the virtues of roots. Cf. I Kings 4:33. Contrast I Enoch 8:3 where such knowledge is part of the forbidden information revealed to man by rebel angels. See Hengel 1. 243. According to Josephus (*J.W.* 2.8.6), the Essenes "made investigations into medicinal roots and the properties of stones." Josephus also provides us with a detailed account of Solomon's magical knowledge: "There was no form of nature with which he was not acquainted or which he passed over without examining, but he studied them all philosophically and revealed the most complete knowledge of the art used against demons for the benefit and healing of men. He also composed incantations by which illnesses are relieved, and left behind forms of exorcisms with which those possessed by demons drive them out, never to return." He goes on to say that this kind of cure is still a living tradition and he describes how one Eleazer exorcised a demon by putting "to the nose of the possessed man a ring which had under its seal one of the roots prescribed by Solomon, and then, as the man smelled it, drew out the demon through his nostrils" (*Ant.* 8.2.5). Verses 17–20 may perhaps imply the notion of universal sympathy, a concept which was very potent in the Hellenistic age. "The one who through his insight and divinely granted revelation," writes J. M. Hull, "perceives the nature of the mystic bonds which tie everything from the lofty stars down to the earthbound roots in one throbbing unity, he is at once saint, seer, philosopher and magus" (*Hellenistic Magic and the Synoptic Tradition* [Naperville, Ill., 1974] 34). (See D.L. 7.140; see also S. Giverson, "Solomon und die Dämonen," *Essays on the Nag Hammadi Texts in honor of A. Böhlig,* ed. M. Krause [Leiden, 1972] 16–25; D. Duling, "Solomon, Exorcism, and the son of David," *HTR* 68 [1975].)

22a. *The artificer.* For the feminine form *technitis,* cf. NOTE on v. 12 above. *technitis* appears first in inscriptions from Delphi dating from the second century BCE (Delphi 3.230; 3.54). Cf. Prov 8:30, LXX: *ēmēn par autō harmozousa,* which Wolfson (1948:1.267) translates "I was with Him as one working as a joiner," and which, according to him, shows that the underlying Hebrew reading for the LXX was *'aman* ("artisan") (cf. *BR* 1.1). We may also compare, in this connection, the Stoic definition of Nature as "an artistically working fire (*pyr technikon*) going on its way to create" (D.L. 7.156); cf. Cicero *ND* 2.58: "The nature of the world itself . . . is styled by Zeno not merely 'craftsmanlike' but actually 'a craftsman' (*artifex*)" (see A. S. Pease's commentary [1955] ad loc.); *CH* 23.64: *tōn sympantōn kosmopoietēs kai technitēs.* Commenting on Prov 8:22, Philo (using the terminology of Plato's *Timaeus* 49A–50D) describes Wisdom as mother and nurse (*tithēnē*) of the All (*Ebr.* 31). At 9:1–2 we are told more explicitly that it was by means of *sophia* that God created all things. For Wisdom as tutor, cf. 1QH 1:22: "These things I know by the wisdom which comes from thee, for now thou hast unstopped my ears to marvelous mysteries"; Isis Aretalogy, Cyrene 12: *ha kai brotois edeiksa.* A striking parallel to vv. 17–21 may be found in Ps-Plato *Axiochus* 370B: "Surely mortal nature would never rise to such a height of noble daring as to scorn the violence of wild beasts (*thēriōn bias*) far surpassing man in strength, to traverse oceans, to build cities, to found commonwealths, to gaze up to heaven and discern the revolutions of the stars (*periphoras astrōn*), the course of the sun and moon, their risings and settings, their eclipses and their swift [periodic] return, the equinoxes and the two sol- stices (*tropas dittas*), the wintry skies of the Pleiades (*Pleiadōn chei- mōnas*), the summer winds and rainy downpours, and violent onrush of hurricanes, to chart for eternity the vicissitudes of the cosmos—were there not really some divine breath (*theion pneuma*) in man's soul, whereby it obtained knowledge and intelligence of matters so great? Hence, my dear Axiochus, you will suffer a change not into death but immortality (*athanasian*)" (tr. by E. H. Blakeney [London, 1937]). Cf. also Philo *Det.* 87–88; Seneca *Consolat. ad Helviam* 20.2.

XII. NATURE OF WISDOM: HER TWENTY-ONE
ATTRIBUTES
(7:22b–24)

7   **22b** For in her is a spirit intelligent and holy,
           unique of its kind yet manifold, subtle,
           agile, lucid, unsullied,
           clear, inviolable, loving goodness, keen,
    23 unhindered, beneficent, humane,
           steadfast, unfailing, untouched by care,
           all-powerful, all-surveying,
           and pervading all spirits,
           intelligent, pure, and most subtle.
    24 For Wisdom is more mobile than any motion,
           she pervades and permeates all things by reason of her
                      pureness.

NOTES

7:22b–24. Wisdom is here described in a series of twenty-one (7×3) epithets, borrowed largely from Greek philosophy. In the representation of the initiation into immortality delivered in the so-called *Mithras Liturgy,* part of the great Paris Magical Codex (presumably compiled in the early fourth century CE), *Aiōn* is similarly invoked with twenty-one epithets, which consistently refer to him as god of light and fire (see A. Dieterich, *Eine Mithrasliturgie* [Leipzig and Berlin, 1923] 8–10). Similarly, the *Ahuna Vairya* (known in later times simply as the *Ahunvar*), "the most sacred and probably the most ancient of the Zoroastrian formulas of devotion," in its twenty-one words, contained in germ the whole revelation of the Good Religion and the twenty-one Nasks of which it was made up (*Greater Bundahishn* 1.15; *'Ulema i Islam* 46 [21 Nasks divided into 3 groups of 7 each]). See Zaehner 1961:261; 1972:314, 415; E. Beneveniste, "La prière Ahuna Vairya," *IIJ* 1 (1957) 77–85; W. Hinz, "Zum Ahuna-

Vairya Gebet," *IIJ* 4 (1960) 154–159; Boyce:260–261. "Held to have existed before the Creation, this prayer is conceived as a hypostasis, a veritable Logos-Sophia" (H. Corbin, "Cyclical Time in Mazdaism and Ismailism," *Man and Time* [Bollingen Series XXX.3, New York, 1957] 122, n.16. Ohrmazd is manifested through the act of creation, and his Wisdom through the *dēn* [Religion] and the Ahunvar prayer which is its quintessence [*Denkart,* ed. Madon, 133.3. See Zaehner 1972:107, 133. The Stoic philosopher Cleanthes heaps up twenty-six divine attributes (*SVF* 1.557), and in the *Apocalypse of Abraham* (17) we find in the celestial song of Abraham a rather long series of attributes attached to the deity. Philo similarly assigns 147 epithets to the pleasure-lover (*Sacr.* 32). Moreover, in Indian literature, 'Perfect Wisdom' (*Prajnaparamita*) is praised by a litany enumerating her thirty-two attributes. (See Conze 1968:208.) We find a somewhat similar motif in rabbinic literature, where we read in *Sifre Deut.* 306, Finkelstein: 341: " 'For the name of the Lord I proclaim' (Deut 32:3). We find that Moses mentioned the name of the Holy One blessed be He only after twenty-one words [counting from the beginning of Moses' song which starts at Deut 32:1]. From whom did he learn? from the ministering angels; for the latter mention the Holy Name only after a threefold *kadosh,* as it is written, 'And one would call to the other, "Holy, holy, holy! The Lord of Hosts!"' (Isa 6:3). [Israel, on the other hand, mentions the name after two words. See *BT Ḥulin* 91b.] Said Moses: 'It is enough for me to be less than in a one to seven relationship with the ministering angels.'" [D. Hoffmann, quoted by Finkelstein in his edition of the *Sifre,* explained: In regard to the words, Moses was in a one to seven relationship with the angels, since they mention the name after three words, and he after twenty-one words; whereas in regard to the letters, he was in less than a one to seven relationship, since they mention the name after twelve letters and he after eighty-five letters] (Stein). Finally, in the highly syncretistic Isis cult, we find this goddess bearing so many cult names that she is often called *myriōnymos* (Plutarch *Is. et Os.* 372E; *OGIS* 695; *PGM* 57, 13). An Oxyrhynchus papyrus (no. 1380: early second century CE) gives us a long invocation of her, and it is interesting to note that no distinction is made there between genuine epithets (of which there are well over twenty, e.g. holy, mightiest, undefiled, trusty, bountiful, savior, initiate, intelligence, wisdom) and the names of other deities identified with her. (See A. D. Nock, *Conversion* [Oxford 1933] 150–151; Apuleius *Metamorphoses* 11.5.) Comparable is the epithet *polyōnymos* used of Isis in the post-Augustan *Anubis-hymn* from Cius in Bithynia and *P. Oxy.* xi 1380, 97 and 101. This epithet is used also of Demeter, with whom Isis was identified as early as the fifth century BCE (Herodotus 2.59) and of Hades (*Homerici Hymni* 2.18; Ps-Aristotle *De Mundo* 401a, 13). Cf. also *myriomorphos* (*The Greek*

Anthology, trans. W. R. Paton, 5 vols. [LCL] 16.264) and *dea multi-nominis* (Apuleius *Metamorphoses* 11.22). The Egyptian (*š*) *rnw,* "with many names," is used of a number of gods—Amon, Rē, Horus, Osiris, and Hathor. Isis could well have borrowed the designation from Hathor, but an instance applying it to Isis does not seem to occur. Similarly, the epithet *myriomorphos* is paralleled by (*š*) *ḫh prw,* "with many forms." A Nineteenth Dynasty tomb describes the sun-god as "with many forms and with many names." Isis, again, is not the recipient of the designation. The Greek epithet represents, then, a process assigned to the goddess by the Greek interpretation and involving a detailed assimilation of the functions of numerous other goddesses (J. W. Griffiths, *Plutarch De Iside et Osiride* [Cardiff, 1970] 502–503). Another close parallel for the litany-like use of divine epithets is the collection of Orphic Hymns, generally dated in the second century CE. See W. Quandt, *Orphic Hymns* (Berlin, 1955). Shorter but similar examples can be found among the oracles of Clarian Apollo. See L. Robert, *Comptes rendus de l'Académie des Inscriptions* (Paris, 1971; published January 1972) 597ff, esp. pp. 602 and 611. Philo applied the epithet *polyōnymos* to wisdom: "By using many words for it Moses has already made it manifest that the sublime and heavenly wisdom is of many names; for he calls it 'beginning,' and 'image,' and 'vision of God.'" (*LA* 1.43; cf. *Somn.* 2.254 [*polyōnymōn tou ontos dynameōn*]; cf. *Conf.* 146.) It was also employed by the Stoic Cleanthes for Logos-Zeus in the opening line of his famous hymn. Cf. also Ps-Aristotle *De Mundo* 401a12; D.L. 7.135, 147: "[The Deity] is called many names according to its various powers"; *CH* 5.10; Irenaeus *Adv. Haer.* 1.23.1; *Acta Petri et Pauli* 35. See Festugière 1953: 3. 161; G. Lüdemann, *Untersuchungen zur Simonianischen Gnosis* (Göttingen, 1968) 51; Mack (1973) 111, n.2. Grimm (citing Lipsius) notes that it may be this passage in Wisdom that won for the book the title *Panaretos Sophia,* "the Wisdom which comprises all virtues," given to it by Epiphanius (*De Mensuris et Ponderibus* 4) and John of Damascus (*De Fide Orthodoxa* 4.17).

7:22b. *a spirit intelligent.* Posidonius called God *pneuma noeron diēkon di' hapasēs ousias* (Frags. 100–101, Kidd). Cf. *CH* 3.1.

holy. Isis is called holy (*hageian*) in *P. Oxy.* XI 1380, 36.

unique of its kind. Demeter, Persephone, and Athene are each given the epithet *mounogenēs* in the *Orphic Hymns* (40; 29; 32). Cf. Parmenides, DK, B.8.4; Plato *Tim.* 31B3: *heis hode monogenēs ouranos;* John 1:14: *doksan hōs monogenous para patros.*

manifold. polymerēs is first attested in Aristotle *De Anima* 411b11. The noun *polymereia* is found in Philo *Her.* 236.

subtle. Anaxagoras (DK, B.12) and Diogenes of Apollonia (DK, A.20) describe *nous* as *leptotaton.* The Stoics defined the soul as a *sōma lep-*

tomeres eks heautou kinoumenon ("a subtle self-moving body": *SVF* 2. 780, 785; 1.484). Cf. Timaeus Locrus *De Natura mundi et animae* 98d: *eidos pyros eukinatotaton kai leptomerestaton;* Philo *Cher.* 115; *LA* 3.170 (*Logos* described as *leptos*); Philodemus *On Death* 8.13, Kuiper: *leptomerēs gar ousa kai teleōs eukinētos hē psychē*.

agile. Democritus considered *nous* and fire as *eukinētotaton,* DK, A.101. Cf. Plato *Tim.* 58E; 56A (the most mobile figure is assigned to fire); Aristotle *Categoriae* 13a27; *Magna Moralia* 1199b32 (soul more easily moved than body). Philodemus also applies *eukinētos* to the soul (*On Death* 8.14). Cicero *ND* 2.11.30: "That glowing heat of the world is far purer and more brilliant and far more mobile."

lucid. tranon is very frequently used in Philo of clear impressions (*Op.* 71, etc.). Isis has allotted to men "to know these things clearly" (*tranōs*) (Isis Aretalogy, Cyrene 14) (Roussell:150).

unsullied. amolyntos is first found here (frequent in Patristic Greek). Cf. Musonius Rufus Frag. 18B; Epictetus 4.11.8 (of the soul).

loving goodness. Cf. Aristotle *Magna Moralia* 1212b19; Philo *Mos.* 2.9. It is also used as an honorary epithet in inscriptions of religious associations: *IG* 2². 1326.8.

keen. Cf. Philo *Her.* 140: "Thus God sharpened the edge of his all-incising Logos and divided universal being"; 130. Cf. NOTE on 18:15.

23. *unhindered.* Cf. Philo *Praem.* 119. Very frequent in Epictetus (1.4.18; 2.19.32; 4.1.69, 73, 100). The adverb *akōlytōs* appears in Plato *Cratylus* 415D (of the unimpeded flow of the good soul); in Philo (*Deus* 160; *Sobr.* 40; *Fug.* 191; *Spec.* 1.113); Ps-Aristotle *De Mundo* 401b10 (cf. *Heimarmenē* moving without hindrance); and in Chrysippus *SVF* 2. 937.

beneficent, humane. Cf. 1.6; 12:19. Chrysippus refers to the gods as benefactors (*euergetikoi*) and lovers of the human race (*philanthrōpoi:* *SVF* 2. 1115). In Ps-Aristeas, the king is described as benefactor of his subjects (190, 205, 249). He feels affection (*philanthrōpia*) for his people (257, 208, 290). Cf. Plato *Laws* 713D; *Symp.* 189D; Aristotle *Rhetorica* 1388b12; *EN* 1171b16; Ps-Plato *Definitions* 412E; Diodorus 19.86; Epictetus 4.8.32; 4.10.12; *SVF* 3. 292; Plutarch *Moralia* 824D; III Macc 3.15; II Macc 4:11; *Joseph and Asenath* 12:16, Battifol. Philo encapsuled the Stoic concept of active beneficence developed by Panaetius (Cicero *Off.* 1.20) in the word *philanthrōpia* (*Virt.* 51–174). For Plutarch's elaborate ues of the concept of *philanthrōpia,* see Hirzel 1912:23–32. See also Festugière 1950:2. 301–309; S. Tromp de Ruiter, "De Vocis quae est Philanthrōpia Significatione atque Usu," *Mnemosyne* 59 (1931) 271–305; Spicq 1958:169–191; R. Le Déaut, "Philanthropia dans la littérature grecque jusqu'au Nouveau Testament," in *Mélanges Eugène Tisserant* 1 (1964) 255–294; B. Snell, *The Discovery of the Mind* (Cambridge, Mass., 1953)

246–263; H. Martin, "The Concept of Philanthropia in Plutarch's Lives," *AJP* 82 (1961) 164–175; Bell 1948:31–37; A. Nissen, *Gott und der Nächste im antiken Judentum* (Tübingen, 1974) 466–470, 485–502; and Introduction.

steadfast. Cf. Ps-Aristotle *De Mundo* 400b30: "God is a stronger and more stable (*bebaioteros*) law than those inscribed on tablets"; Philo *Somn.* 2.223: "But indeed so vast in its excess is the stability (*tou bebaiou*) of the Deity that He imparts to chosen natures a share of his steadfastness to be their richest possession."

unfailing. Philo is fond of joining the words *bebaios* and *asphalēs* or *asphaleia.* Cf. *Conf.* 106; *Cher.* 103; *Spec.* 3.130; *Somn.* 1.158: "the sure God (*asphalēs theos*) is the support and stay, the firmness and stability (*bebaiotēs*) of all things."

all-powerful. pantodynamos is found only here (and in 11:17; 18:5), but is frequent in Patristic Greek. Cf. Plotinus 5.9.9.11 (*pandynamou*); II Macc 11:13 (*tou dynamenou theou*); Elias [sixth-century CE Neoplatonist philosopher] *In Porphyrii Isagogen commentaria* 17.18. Cf. Aelius Aristides, *Orationes* 2: "From what has been said, one would not go wrong in calling her [Athena] the Power of God" (Bevan:160).

all-surveying. panepiskopos is first attested here. Cf. *AP* 7.245; *MAMA* 1. 171 (Laodicea Combusta); *Sib Or* 1:152; 2:177 (found in Patristic Greek).

intelligent, pure, and most subtle. I.e. it pervades even the subtlest spirits.

24. *more mobile.* For the neuter *kinētikōteron,* cf. 17:10; Artistotle *EN* 1099a24: *ariston ara . . . hē eudaimonia;* Plato *Protagoras* 328C; *Rep.* 366A; *Meno* 70A. For the swiftness of mind, see D.L. 1.35: *tachiston nous;* Plato *Cratylus* 412B–D; Cicero *ND* 2.42: "But the stars occupy the region of aether, and as this has a very rarefied substance and is always in lively motion, it follows that the animal born in this region has the keenest senses and the swiftest power of movement"; Philo *Cher.* 28: "For exceeding swift (*oksykinētotaton*) and of burning heat is Logos and chiefly so the Logos of the [Great] Cause, for it alone preceded and outran all things . . .": *Mut.* 179: "He [Homer *Odyssey* 7.36] is showing the swiftness of the mind's intensity. . . . For the mind moves at the same moment to many things material and immaterial with indescribable rapidity."

she pervades and permeates all things. The phraseology is Stoic. Cf. *SVF* 2. 416: *to diēkon dia pantōn pneuma;* 2. 1021; 2. 1033: *to di' holon kechōrēkos pneuma; Dox.* 306.8; D.L. 7.139. For the principle of "body going through body" (*sōma dia sōmatos chōrein*), see Sambursky 1959:1–48; R. B. Todd, *Alexander of Aphrodisias on Stoic Physics* (Leiden, 1976) 29–88.

pureness. Cf. D.L. 7.139: "According to Chrysippus, the *hegēmonikon* is the purer part of the aether." In *Strom.* 5.89.2–4, Clement asserts that the Stoic doctrine of *pneuma* was based on a misunderstanding of this passage in Wisdom. Cf. Isis Aretalogy, *P. Oxy.* XI 1380, 175: *kai hapanta diakathaireis.*

XIII. FIVEFOLD METAPHOR DESCRIBING WISDOM'S ESSENCE AND HER UNIQUE EFFICACY (7:25 – 8:1)

7   25 She is an exhalation from the power of God,
a pure effluence from the glory of the Almighty;
therefore nothing tainted insinuates itself into her.

26 She is an effulgence of everlasting light,
an unblemished mirror of the active power of God,
and an image of his goodness.

27 Though but one she can do everything,
and abiding in herself she renews all things;
generation by generation she enters into holy souls
and renders them friends of God and prophets,

28 for nothing is pleasing to God but the man who lives with
Wisdom.

29 She is fairer than the sun
and surpasses every constellation;
compared to the light of day she is found more radiant;

30 for day is superseded by night,
but over Wisdom no evil can prevail.

8   1 She stretches in might from pole to pole
and effectively orders all things.

NOTES

7:25 – 8:1. Employing a fivefold succession of metaphors [exhalation, effluence, effulgence, mirror, image], the author states quite emphatically that Wisdom is an emanation from God's power, glory, light, or goodness. This is very bold language indeed for someone who is writing within the biblical tradition. Even the more philosophically ambitious Philo backs off from such explicit terms as *aporroia, aporroē,* or *apaugasma* for his description of the origin of the Divine Logos. He readily applies such terms to the effluences of the Logos, but when it comes to the Logos itself, he prefers to employ verbs which clearly imply that it is a divine emanation without actually so designating it. (See NOTE on "effluence" below.) Furthermore, in describing Wisdom's unique capacity for a cosmic efficacy which is self-abiding, our author foreshadows the Neoplatonic doctrine that within the so-called process of emanation, in giving rise to the effect, the cause remains undiminished and unaltered (Plotinus 3.8.10; 4.8.6; 5.1.3 and 6; 5.2.1; Proclus *Elements* 26–27; *CH* 12.1). The Platonic text on which Plotinus (5.4.2) and Proclus (*Platonic Theology* 5.18.283) base this is *Tim.* 42E, but, as Dodds (1963:214) has pointed out, "it seems to be a product of the Middle Stoa, and to have originated in the attempt to give God a real place in the Stoic system over against the cosmos" (cf. Philo, *Det.* 90; *Gig.* 27; *Conf.* 136; Ps-Aristotle *De Mundo* 397b20–25; 398b14–25; M. Aurel. 8.57; Numenius, ap. Eusebius *Praeparatio Evangelica* 11.18; *ŠHŠR* on Song of Songs 3:10; Augustine *Confessions* 9.5.1; *BT Sanh.* 39a; *BR* 68.9; *Tanḥ. Buber, Behaʻalot.* 29a).

7:25. *exhalation. atmis* is properly "moist vapor," "steam." The author may have had in mind Exod 19:18 as quoted by Philo (*Her.* 251: *hōsei atmis kaminou*) and Lev 16:13, LXX. Cf. also Sir 24:3. (Goodrick notes that the Armenian version, as quoted by Margoliouth, and the Ethiopic must have read *aktis*.) For *tēs tou theou dynameōs,* cf. Philo *LA* 2.86.

effluence. The term *aporroia* was already employed by Empedocles (DK, B.89). Cf. Aristotle *De Sensu* 438a4; Epicurus *Epistulae* 1.46; Philo *Spec.* 1.27, 40. Our passage, however, is the earliest attestation of its explicit application to the Logos or Sophia as an emanation from God. Even in Plotinus, *aporroia* is used only for the effluences from *Nous* or the stars upon man and what is below him (2.3.11.9; 3.4.3.26). He does, however, use the term *aporroē* for the effluences from the One (6.7.22.8); cf. Plato *Phaedrus* 251B. The earliest attested use of *aporroia* for effluences from God (apart from our text) is in Marcus Aurelius (2.4; cf. 12.2, 26). It is very likely, however, that the notion of an outflow from God was already used by adherents of the Middle Stoa (perhaps by Posidonius), since Cicero writes: "And if mankind possesses intelligence, faith, virtue and concord, whence can these things have flowed down (*defluere*) upon the earth if not from the powers above?" (*ND* 2.79). It also appeared in Neopythagorean writings. See Sext. *Adversus Physicos* 2.281: "But some assert that the body is constructed from one point; for this point when it has flowed (*rhyen*) produces the line, and the line when it has flowed makes the plane, and this when it has moved towards depth generates the body which has three dimensions." Cf. Hermippus 1.18.135, Kroll-Viereck: *ho theos, aph hou kathaper ek pēgēs erryē ta panta;* Hippolytus 4.43.4; *CH* 4.10. There is also a dim suggestion in Nicomachus of

Gerasa of the process of Procession from and Return to the One which is characteristic of Plotinus' philosophy. See Dillon 1977:355–356. Although Philo does not employ the term *aporroia* for the divine effluence he does use the verbs *ombreō* and *plēmmyrō* (*Somn.* 2.221: "Whence showers forth [*ōmbrēse*] the birth of all that is, whence streams [*eplēmmyre*] the tide of Wisdom"); cf. *Fug.* 198. Moreover, Philo employs the verbs *aporreō* and *rheō* for the effluences of the Logos. *Det.* 83: "To the faculty which streams forth (*aporryeisa*) from the fountain of reason breath has been assigned" [The fountain here is apparently the Archetypal Logos, of which, Philo has just informed us (*Det.* 82), God is the fountain]; *Fug.* 137; *Deus* 176; *Sacr.* 82; *Op.* 144; *Det.* 117. In *LA* 1.63, Philo implies that generic virtue flows (he actually says: *lambanei tas archas,* 'takes its start') from the wisdom of God [Eden], and refers to the four particular virtues as *aporroiai* from the largest river, generic virtue. At *Spec.* 1.40, the simile employed would seem to imply that the Logos is an emanation from God: "For the very seeking, even without finding, is felicity in itself, just as no one blames the eyes of the body because when unable to see the sun itself they see the emanation (*aporroia*) of its rays as it reaches the earth." (*aporroia* is also found in Ezek 1:14, LXX, Aquila; I Kings 14:27, LXX, Symmachus.) For the image of overflow, cf. Zech 12:10; Isa 11:9; Joel 3:1; Sir 1:9; I Enoch 49:1. For the use of this image in Egyptian literature, see Plutarch *Is. et Os.* 366a; *Songs of Isis and Nephthys* 9.26 (*JEA* 22 [1936] 127): "The Nile is the efflux of Osiris' body"; *CH* 23 (*Korē Kosmou*), 62; *Odes Solomon* 6.7. (See R. Reitzenstein, *Poimandres* [Leipzig, 1904] 16, n.4, and Mack 1973:70.)

pure. For *eilikrinēs*. Cf. Plato *Symp.* 211E; *Phaedo* 81BC; Posidonius F 17, Kidd; Philo *Op.* 8 (the active Cause is the perfectly pure [*heilikrinestatos*] and unsullied Mind of the universe); *Op.* 31 (no object of sense is *heilikrines*).

glory. Cf. Philo *Spec.* 1.45: "but I [Moses] beseech thee that I may at least see the glory that surrounds thee, and by thy glory I understand the powers that keep guard around thee" [powers here refer to the ideal 'Forms' within the Divine Logos].

the Almighty. pantokratōr is very frequent in the LXX for Hebrew ṣebā'ôt and šadday.

nothing tainted. For *memiammenon,* cf. Plato *Phaedo* 81B: "if when it departs from the body the soul is defiled (*memiasmenē*) and impure"; Philo, *Fug.* 50: "wisdom has obtained a nature free from every defiling touch (*apsaustou kai amiantou physeōs*)." Isis is *amiantos* (*P. Oxy.* XI 1380, 109).

insinuates itself. For *parempiptei,* cf. Plutarch *Is. et Os.* 59 (Mack).

26. *effulgence. apaugasma* is first attested here. Cf. Heliodorus 5.27;

Philo *Op.* 146: "Every man, in respect of his mind, is allied to the divine Reason, having come into being as a copy or fragment or ray (*apaugasma*) of that blessed nature"; *Plant.* 50; *Spec.* 4.123; *Test. Abraham* A 16. (Again, it should be noted that Philo applies the term *apaugasma* only to the human mind, never to the Logos.) In the Isis Aretalogy from Kyme we read: "I am in the rays (*augais*) of the sun." Heb 1:3 refers to Christ as the *apaugasma* of God's glory. Cf. *apaugasmos* in Plutarch *Moralia* 83D; 934D; and *kataugasma* in *PGM* 4.1130.

everlasting light. Fragment 3 (34) of the *Sibylline Oracles* speaks of God as "deathless endless light (*aphthiton aenaon phōs*)." Light for Plotinus is the incorporeal *energeia* of the luminous body [the sun], closely parallel to life, the *energeia* of the soul (2.1.7.26; 4.5.6 and 7, 1.6.3.18). Plato had already suggested that the heavenly fire was of special purity (*Philebus* 19B*ff*). Philo, too, sometimes speaks of an incorporeal light (*Praem.* 37; *Somn.* 1.113).

umblemished mirror. The mirror metaphor also occurs in Philo *QG* 1.57 (though in a slightly altered context): "For in a certain sense the wisdom of the world was a mirror of the powers of God, in accordance with which it became perfect and this universe is governed and managed"; cf. *Decal.* 105: "for in it [the Seven], as in a mirror, the mind has a vision of God as acting and creating the world and controlling all that is"; *Mig.* 190 (for *esoptron,* cf. Sir 12:11; Philo, *Mig.* 98; and for *akēlidōton,* cf. Cicero *ND* 2.31, and see NOTE on 4:9). Cf. also I Cor 13:12. Mani's celestial Twin (also an emanation) is termed *ekeino to eueidestaton kai megiston katoptron* in the *Mani Codex* (17.13*ff*). See *ZPE* 19 (1975) 18–19, and 79.

image. A Platonic metaphor. Cf. *Tim.* 29B: "it is wholly necessary that this Cosmos should be a Copy (*eikona*) of something"; Philo *Op.* 25: "Now if the part is an image of an image (*eikōn eikonos*), it is manifest that the whole is so too"; *Fug.* 101 (the Divine Logos is himself the Image of God); *Conf.* 146.

27. *Though but one.* Cf. Isis Aretalogy, Cyrene 6.

she can do everything. Cf. Isis Aretalogy, Cyrene 15: "nothing happens without me."

abiding in herself. Anaxagoras' *Nous* similarly remains unmixed and motionless while moving all things (Aristotle *Physica* 256b25; DK, B.12: *monos autos ep' eōytou estin*). So, too, Xenophanes (DK, B 26: "And he [God] always remains in the same place [*en tautō mimnei*], not moving at all, nor is it fitting for him to change his position at different times." Cf. Plato *Tim.* 42E: "So He, then, having given all these commands, was abiding in His own proper and wonted state (*emenen en tō heautou kata tropon ēthei*)"; Plotinus 3.2.1.45; cf. Philo *Her.* 156; the Eleusis inscription under the statue of *Aiōn: Aiōn ho autos en tois autois aiei physei theia menōn; CH* 11.4: *diamenousa tē tautotēti;* Proclus *Elements* 26: *menon auto eph' heautou.*

she enters into. metabainein is the technical Pythagorean expression for the process of transmigration (*Dox.* 590, 12). A similar notion is found in the Ps-Clementine *Homilies* 3.20, where Christ is depicted as having changed his forms and his names from the beginning of the world, thus reappearing again and again until coming upon his own times (cf. *Recognitions* 2.22). The same conception may be seen in the Manichaean doctrine of the cyclic incarnation of the True Prophet. "The Apostle of Light, the god-sent messenger to the world and the herald of the redemption of mankind, made his appearance in the Patriarchs of the Hebrew Bible, in the religious leaders of the East, in Jesus and Paul, in Marcion and Bardaisan, and finally in Mani" (*Keph.* 12.9*ff*; *Hom.* 68, 15*ff*); see A. Henrichs, "Mani and the Babylonian Baptists," *HSCP* 77 (1973) 25. (It should be noted that the recently discovered *Mani Codex* published by Henrichs and Koenen names the founder of the sect against which Mani rebelled as Alchasaios, and we are informed by Hippolytus *Refutatio omnium Haeresium* 10.25, that the Elchasaites affirmed that "Jesus was continually being transfused into bodies and was manifested in many different bodies at different times.") Cf. H. J. Schoeps, *Theologie und Geschichte des Judenchristentums* (Tübingen, 1949) 102–10. So, too, the Sufi mystic Jili (second half of fourteenth century) holds that in every age the Perfect Men are an outward manifestation of the essence of Muhammad, which has the power of assuming whatever form it will. In the sixtieth chapter of the *Insánu'l-kámil* he depicts Muhammad as the absolutely perfect man, the first-created of God and the archetype of all other created beings. (See R. A. Nicholson, *Studies in Islamic Mysticism* [Cambridge, 1921] 87.) For Hallevi's similar concept of the *amr ilāhī*, divine thing, see the excellent analysis by H. Davidson, "The Active Intellect in the *Cuzari* and Hallevi's Theory of Causality," *REJ* 131 (1972): 381–396. (The *amr ilāhī* is "on the lookout for those who are worthy" of it.)

friends of God. The notion of friendship with God is an ancient and widespread motif. Cf. Isa 41:8; II Chron 20:7; 22:7, Vulgate; Exod 32:11, LXX; Jub 30:20–21; *Apoc. Abraham* 9 and 10; *Test. Abraham* A 15, 16; James 2:23; *Sib Or* 2:245; Philo *Sobr.* 56 (quotes Gen 18:17 with the addition of the words "my friend"; LXX has "my servant"; *Mos.* 1.156 ["the prophet is called the friend of God"]; *Her.* 21; *Prob.* 44; *Abr.* 129; *LA* 3.204; *Cont.* 90; cf. John 15:14); Qur'an 4.124; *Historia Augusta, Claudius* 2.4–5: "Moses, the friend of God (*familiarem dei*), as he is called in the books of the Jews"; *BT Menahot* 53b; *Tosef. Ber.* 7.13 (the *geonim,* citing Mal 1:2, say the reference here is to Jacob); *Sifre Num.* 115 and *Deut.* 352, Finkelstein: 409; *Mek.* on Exod 12:11 and 15:17; *Lament R., Petih.* 24; IV Ezra 3:14; Prayer of Azariah 12; Jub

19:9; *Targ.Yerush.* on Gen 18:17; *ARN* (Version B) 43. In the Ethiopic *Mota Muse,* Moses bears the title of friend of God; *Gedulat Mosheh* 3b. That the wise were friends of God was a commonplace of Greek literature. Cf. Plato *Laws* 716C–D; *Tim.* 53D; *Symp.* 193B; *Rep.* 621C; Maximus of Tyre 20.6; 14.6; Epictetus 2.17.29; 4.3.9; 3.22.95; 3.24.60; D.L. 6.37.72; Polybius 10.2.7; 21.23.9; Ps-Plutarch *De Vita et Poesi Homeri* 143; Philodemus *On the Gods* 3, Diels, 16,17; Macrobius *Saturnalia* 1.11.45; H. Usener (1887), *Epicurea* 386; Plotinus 2.9.9.73. Caracalla was known as *philosarapis* (E. Breccia, *Iscrizioni greche e latine* (Cairo, 1911), no. 83). See Peterson 1923:161–202.

28. *lives with.* In view of chap. 8, the metaphor is probably that of marriage. Cf. Herodotus 1.91 and 93; Euripides *Medea* 242.

29. *fairer than the sun.* According to Philo, the sun is only a copy or image of Wisdom (*Mig.* 40). Similarly, in *Rep.* 7.517B Plato tells us that the 'Form' of the Good is "the cause for all things of all that is right and beautiful, giving birth in the visible world to light." According to Aristobulus, too, "all light comes from wisdom" (*FPG:* 224, 10–11). In *LAB* 12.1–3, we read that when Moses came down from the mountain, he was covered with invisible light, and "the light of his face overcame the brightness of the sun and moon."

more radiant. Cf. 6:12. Most manuscripts, however, read *protera,* 'foremost,' which Grimm preferred to what Thilo called the 'elegant' reading.

30. *prevail.* For *katischyei* with genitive, cf. Jer 15:18, LXX; Matt 16:18; Aelianus *De natura animalium* 5.19. The same notion is found in John 1:5. Philo points out that the divisions of time only exist from the point of view of man on earth, whereas in the heavens there is one continuous 'Today' (*Fug.* 57; cf. *LA* 1.46; Seneca *Ep.* 102.28; Origen *In Johannem Commentarius* 1.32 [*PG* 14.77]), where "all moves in most radiant light" (*Jos.* 146). Cf. *Evangelium Veritatis* 32,26: "that you may speak of the Day that is above, which has no night, and of the Light which is not wont to set [cf. Wisd 7:10], for it is perfect." For a Hindu parallel, cf. *The Principal Upaniṣads,* trans. S. Rhadakhrishnan (London, 1953) 386: "Verily for him who knows this, this mystic doctrine of Brahma, the sun neither rises nor sets. For him it is day forever." See J. Whittaker, *God Time Being* (Oslo, 1971). Cf. I Enoch 65:9: "And they will live eternally, and then too there will be amongst them neither labor, nor sickness . . . nor night, nor darkness, but great light"; *Sib Or* 3:787. The notion goes back to Isa 60:19–21.

8:1. Most commentators join this verse to chap. 7.

stretches . . . from pole to pole. According to the Stoic doctrine of *tonikē kinēsis,* which is reproduced by Philo, there is a continuous outward-inward pneumatic motion, either from the center of the cosmos to its extreme boundaries, or from the center of any given entity to its surface (*Conf.* 136; *Plant.* 9; *Mig.* 181; *Deus* 35–36; *Mut.* 28; *Det.* 90). *SVF* 2. 451–452, 551. The exact nature of this motion is by no means clear. David E. Hahm believes that "the image of compressed air gives, on the whole, the most satisfactory explanation of the pneumatic motion and its effects. Such pressure has a local motion and the fact that it acts simultaneously in opposite directions could have given rise to the notion that it comprises a simultaneous motion toward the center and toward the periphery" (*The Origins of Stoic Cosmology* [Columbus, Ohio, 1977] 167. The Stoic concept of *tonos* is first met with in the fragments of Cleanthes, who said that it was a "stroke of fire" [*plēgē pyros*]: *SVF* 1. 563. For the origin of the concept of *tonos,* see Hahm:155) Philo consistently uses the verb *teinō* in this connection to indicate the tensional character of pneumatic motion. The pneuma must be everywhere continuously since nothing can hold together without it. Cf. Plato *Tim.* 34B: "and in the midst thereof [of the Cosmos] He set Soul, which He stretched (*eteine*) throughout the whole of it." For the phrase *apo peratos epi peras,* cf. Philo *Mos.* 1.112: *apo peratōn epi perata; Mut.* 22; *Plant.* 9; *Mig.* 181; *Conf.* 136. That Wisdom penetrates the cosmos is already expressed in Sir 24:5–6; cf. John 1:10.

orders. dioikei is also found in 12:18, 15:1, and is a Platonic and Stoic term. Cf. Plato *Phaedrus* 246C; *Laws* 896D; 905E; D.L. 7.133; *SVF* 1.87, 98; 2. 528, 416, 912–913, 1063 (Posidonius says that Zeus is so-called, as being the All-Regulator [*ton panta dioikounta*], but Crates says he is the all-pervading one [*ton eis panta diēkonta*]); Diodorus 1.11.5 (Osiris and Isis regulate [*dioikein*] the entire universe); Philo *Op.* 3; *Conf.* 170; *Mos.* 2.133.

XIV. SOLOMON SOUGHT TO MAKE WISDOM HIS BRIDE
(8:2–16)

8   2 Her I loved and sought out from my youth,
     and longed to make her my bride,
     and I became a lover of her beauty.
   3 She magnifies her noble birth by enjoying intimacy with God,
     and the Master of All loved her.
   4 For she is initiate in the knowledge of God,
     and chooser of his works.
   5 If riches be a possession to be desired in life,
     what is richer than Wisdom, maker of all things?
   6 If understanding is productive,
     who more than she is the artificer of all that is?
   7 And if one prizes justice,
     the fruits of Wisdom's labor are virtues;
     self-control and understanding are her teaching,
     justice and courage,
     and in the life of man nothing is more useful than these.
   8 But if one also longs for wide experience,
     she knows the past and infers the future;
     she understands the intricacies of argument and the
          resolutions of riddles,
     she foreknows signs and wonders
     and the outcome of critical seasons and times.
   9 I determined, then, to take her to live with me,
     knowing that she would be my counselor in prosperity,
     and my comfort in anxiety and grief.
   10 Through her I shall have repute among the masses
     and honor among the elders, young though I am.
   11 In judgment I shall be found acute,
     and in the presence of rulers I will win admiration.
   12 When I am silent they shall wait for me,

when I speak they will attend,
and when I hold forth at length
they will lay a hand upon their mouth.

13 Through her I shall have immortality,
and shall leave an enduring memorial to those who come
after me.

14 I shall govern peoples, and nations will be subject to me.

15 Dread despots will take fright when they hear of me,
in popular assembly I shall show myself noble, and in war
courageous.

16 When I come home I shall find rest in her;
for intercourse with her has no bitterness,
nor living with her pain,
but only cheer and joy.

NOTES

8:2. *loved.* Cf. Prov 7:4; Sir 15:2: "and as a youthful wife will she receive him"; *Kohel.R.* 9.9; *Mid.Mishle* on Prov 5:18. *The Dead Sea Psalms Scroll* has provided us with a portion of the original poem at the end of Sir (51:13*ff*) in which form it constitutes a series of artful double entendres each of which possesses an erotic as well as a moralistic sense. Its erotic overtones are reminiscent of the imagery employed by our author:

> I was a young man before I had erred
> when I looked for her.
> *She came to me in her beauty*
> when finally I sought her out.
>
> . . . .
>
> And she became for me *a nurse;*
> to *my teacher* I give my *ardor.*
> I purposed *to make sport:*
> I was zealous for pleasure,
> without *pause.*
> *I kindled* my desire for her
> *without distraction*
> I bestirred my desire for her,
> *and on her heights I do not waver.*

> I spread my hand(s) . . .
> and perceive her *unseen parts.*
> (Translation, verbatim, by J. A.
> Sanders, *The Dead Sea Psalms Scroll*
> [Ithaca, 1967] 115.)

In the famous 'Choice of Heracles,' the Sophist Prodicus of Ceos personifies virtue as a fair maiden of high bearing who invites him to choose her (Xenophon *Mem.* 2.1.21–33; cf. Philo *Sacr.* 21*ff*). See Heinisch 1908:32–35.

to make her my bride. The sexual imagery here is paralleled in a famed allegory of Philo's that goes back to a Greek source. In *On Mating with the Preliminary Studies,* Philo develops an allegory in which Abraham, the soul, is married to Sarah, who stands for Wisdom. The union, however, is unproductive, because the soul is not at first ripe for it, and Sarah is barren. She therefore sends the soul to mate with Hagar the Egyptian, who stands for the preliminary training of the Encyclical or School studies. In time, however, Sarah can bear a child to Abraham, and then Hagar and Ishmael must be cast out. The allegory goes back to Bion of Borysthenes (ca. 325–255 BCE), who is quoted by Plutarch (*Moralia* 7D) as saying that those who, unable to win philosophy, wear themselves out in preliminary learning are like the suitors of Penelope, who when they could not win the mistress contented themselves with the maids. (The same allegory is also ascribed to Ariston of Chios [*SVF* 1. 350] and to others; cf. A. Henrichs, "Philosophy, the Handmaiden of Theology," *GRBS* 9 [1968] 437–450.) At *Congr.* 74, Philo speaks autobiographically in terms very reminiscent of our author: "When first I was incited by the goads of philosophy to desire her I consorted (*hōmilēsa*) in early youth with one of her handmaids, Grammar, and all that I begat by her, writing, reading, and study of the writings of the poets, I dedicated to her mistress. And again I kept company with another, namely Geometry, and was charmed with her beauty. . . . Again my ardor moved me to keep company (*synelthein*) with a third." Cf. *QG* 3.21; *Ebr.* 49 (where philosophy is called the elder sister); *Cher.* 49; *Cont.* 12; *Abr.* 100 ("in the marriage made by wisdom, the partnership is between thoughts which seek purification and perfect virtues"); *Post.* 79 (those held worthy of wisdom that needs no other teaching, accept from God's hands Reason as their plighted spouse); Plato *Symp.* 206CE; *Theaetetus* 151AB; *Rep.* 490AB; cf. G. Scholem, *Elements of the Kabbalah and Its Symbolism* (Jerusalem, 1976):261 (Hebrew); Isis Aretalogy, *P. Oxy.* XI 1380, 30.

lover. For *erastēs,* cf. Plato *Meno* 70B: *erastas epi sophia; Phaedo* 66E; *Phaedrus* 228C; *Rep.* 490B.

3. *noble birth.* Cf. Prov 8:22; Philo *Fug.* 50: "and it is wisdom's name

that holy oracles proclaim by 'Bethuel,' a name meaning in our speech 'Daughter of God.' "

intimacy. Cf. Prov 8:30. For *symbiōsin,* cf. Philo *Cont.* 68: eager to have wisdom for their life mate (*symbioun spoudasasai*); *Congr.* 5; cf. *Ebr.* 30: "With His knowledge God had union, not as men have it, and begat created being." The multiplication of symbolic images which we find here (Wisdom as Bride of Solomon, Daughter of God, Bride of God) is also characteristic of Philo. Aelius Aristides, in his second oration addressed to Athena (his name for personified Sophia), speaks of her as begotten of God the Father in the beginning, "the Only One of the Only One," and as "always cleaving to his side and sharing his life" (Bevan 1927:157).

4. Our author is saying in effect that Wisdom is essentially synonymous with the Divine Mind, and thus represents the creative agent of the Deity. The similarity of this conception with Philo's Logos doctrine is unmistakable.

initiate. Cf. *P. Oxy.* XI 1380, 111, where *mystis* is given as an epithet of Isis; *AP* 9.229. The word occurs only once in Philo (*Sacr.* 60).

5. The four successive clauses beginning with *ei* are another example of the author's striving for rhetorical effect.

6. *artificer.* See NOTE on 7:21. Cf. Cicero *Fin.* 1.42: "Wisdom is desired [according to the Epicureans] because it is the artificer (*artifex*) that procures and produces pleasure."

7. *self-control and understanding . . . justice and courage.* The division of virtue into four classes goes back to Plato (*Phaedo* 69C; *Rep.* 427E*ff; Laws* 631C; cf. Aeschylus *Seven Against Thebes* 610; Xen. *Mem.* 3.9.1–5; 4.6.1–12; Isocrates *De Pace* 63; Demosthenes 18.215). Two of the cardinal virtues are dealt with by Aristotle in *EN* 3, and the other two in *EN* 5 and 6, but he has no fourfold scheme as such. The Epicureans similarly rejected the cardinal division, though they were at pains to show how all four virtues minister to pleasure (Cicero *Fin.* 1.42–54). The Stoics, however, accepted it together with the Platonic notion that they implied one another (*antakolouthia*) and Zeno expressed three of the cardinal virtues in terms of the fourth, wisdom (*SVF* 3.255; 256–61). Philo, too, repeats the fourfold division (*LA* 1.71–72), though he sometimes substitutes *eusebeia* for *phronēsis* (*Spec.* 4.147; *Decal.* 119). Like our author, he derives them from the Wisdom or Logos of God (*LA* 1.63–65). (The actual phrase "the cardinal virtues" seems to derive from St. Ambrose *In Lucam* 5.) Cf. also IV Macc 1:18; 5:23.

8. *intricacies of argument.* For *strophas logōn* cf. Prov 1:3, LXX; Sir 39:2–3.

signs and wonders. Cf. Deut 29:3, LXX; Dan 6:27.

critical seasons and times. Cf. Dan 2:21, LXX.

9. *to live with me.* For *symbiosin,* cf. Philo *QG* 3:29: "For there are some who flee from virtue not because of hate, but because of reverential awe, for they believe themselves to be unworthy to live with (*symbioun*) their mistress."

comfort. The context requires that *parainesis* mean 'comfort,' but this meaning is unattested elsewhere. It has been suggested that perhaps the original reading was *parainetis* (cf. *hairetis, genetis, technitis:* see NOTE on 7:12), parallel to *symboulos* in the first half of the verse (Bauermeister and Fichtner).

10. *repute.* Similarly, in the Isis Aretalogy from Kyme, 40, no one is glorified without knowledge of Isis (*outhēs doksazetai aneu tēs emēs gnōmēs*).

12. *when I speak they will attend.* Cf. Sir 15:5.

will lay a hand upon their mouth. Cf. Job 21:5; 29:7–11; 40:4; Sir 5:12; Prov 30:32. Cf. Aelius Aristides in his second oration: "And grant me to be consummate in thought and speech. May whoever speaks in opposition to me have reason to be sorry!" (Bevan 1927:161).

13. *immortality.* Cf. Philo *Fug.* 97: "The man who is capable of running swiftly it bids stay not to draw breath but pass forward to the supreme Divine Logos, who is the fountain of Wisdom, in order that he may draw from the stream, and released from death, gain life eternal as his prize." According to the Isis Aretalogy, *P. Oxy.* XI 1380, Isis was especially the goddess of immortality (13), which she conferred upon her husband and brother Osiris (242–243), and her son Horus (246–247).

an enduring memorial. Cf. Ps 112:6, LXX.

16. *I shall find rest in her.* The same idea is found in Sir 6:28: "In the end you will find the rest (*anapausin*) she offers." Similarly, according to Aristobulus, if we unremittingly follow Wisdom, we shall remain undisturbed (*atarachoi*) all through life (*FPG:* 224, line 15). The ideal of inner calm is a central Philonic theme (cf. 6:24 above and NOTE). Cf. *Abr.* 27: "That rest [*anapausis:* translation of Hebrew name Noah] is appropriate also, since its opposite, unnatural movement [*tēn para physin kinēsin:* the Stoic definition of *pathos,* SVF 3.462, 476], proves to be the cause of turmoil and confusion and factions and wars. Such movement is sought by the worthless, while a life which is calm, serene, tranquil and peaceful to boot is the object of those who have valued nobility of conduct"; *LA* 3.77; *Post.* 23: "Proximity to a stable object produces a desire to be like it and a longing for quiescence. Now that which is unwaveringly stable is God, and that which is subject to movement is creation. He therefore that draws nigh to God longs for stability"; Plotinus 6.9.11; 6.9.8; 4.8.1; 4.8.5; Plato *Rep.* 532E; 490B: "but [the true lover of knowledge] holds on his way with a passion that will not faint or fail until he has laid hold upon the essential nature of each thing with that part of his soul

which can apprehend reality because of its affinity therewith; and when he has by that means approached real being and entered into union with it, the offspring of this marriage is intelligence and truth; so that at last, having found knowledge and true life and nourishment, he is at rest from his travail" (trans. by F. M. Cornford, New York, 1945). The Gnostics used the term *anapausis* to designate the initial condition of the *pleroma,* and also as an attribute of the *Propator* (in the *Acts of Thomas* it is also applied to Christ). It is seen as the fruit and goal of gnosis, and is only fully attained after death. For full discussion with many examples, see P. Vielhauer, *Aufsätze zum Neuen Testament* (München, 1965) 215–234; O. Hofius, *Katapausis* (Tübingen, 1970) 75–90.

bitterness. For *pikria,* cf. *SVF* 3.394 (*pikriai* as species of orgē); 3.395.

intercourse. For *synanastrophē,* cf. III Macc 2:31,33; 3:5; Ps-Aristeas 169; Epicurus *Sententiae Vaticanae* 18; Philodemus *On the Gods* 3, Frag. 87,13; Jos. *Ant.* 18.6.9.

cheer and joy. For the Stoics, *chara* was one of the three *eupatheiai* or rational emotions, and *euphrosynē* was one of the forms of *chara* and was defined as "the joy which follows the actions of one who is self-controlled" (*SVF* 3.431–432). Cf. Philo *Her.* 315: "It ends in the attainment of the wisdom of God, that truly great river, brimming over with joy and gladness (*charās kai euphrosynēs*) and all other blessings"; *Abr.* 201–207; I Macc 5:54; Sir 6:28. In the Isis Aretalogy, *P. Oxy.* xi 1380, 19 and 31, *euphrosynē* is a title of Isis.

XV. WISDOM A SHEER GIFT OF GOD'S GRACE
(8:17–21)

8   17 After thinking this over in my mind,
        and pondering in my heart
        that there is immortality in kinship with Wisdom,
     18 and in her friendship sheer delight,
        and in the labors of her hands unfailing wealth,
        and in training in her society understanding,
        and great renown in the sharing of her words,
        I went about in search of how I might make her my own.
     19 I was, indeed, a child well-endowed,
        having had a noble soul fall to my lot;
     20 or rather being noble I entered an undefiled body.
     21 But knowing that I could not otherwise gain possession of
                her, except God give her—
        and to know the source of this grace was a mark of
                understanding—
        I petitioned the Lord and supplicated him,
        and with all my heart I said:

NOTES

8:17. *kinship.* The theme of man's kinship (*syngeneia*) with God occurs in Plato and is a characteristic teaching of the Stoa. Plato writes in *Tim.* 90A: "We declare that God has given to each of us, as his daemon, that kind of soul which is housed in the top of our body and which raises us— seeing that we are not an earthly but a heavenly plant—up from earth towards our kindred (*ksynegeneian*) in the heaven." Cf. *Tim.* 90C; Posidonius F 187, 6, Kidd: "[The cause of *pathē* is] not following the daimon within us which is akin (*syngenei*) and of like nature with the one that orders the whole universe"; Sext. *Math.* 7.93. Philo takes up the theme with equal vigor: "But it is the lot of man, as we see, to occupy the place of highest excellence among living creatures because his stock is near akin to God, sprung from the same source in virtue of his participation in reason which gives him immortality, mortal though he seems to be" (*Spec.* 4.14); *Op.* 145–146: "Now what is this kinship (*syngeneia*)? Every man, in respect of his mind, is allied to the Divine Reason, having come into being as a copy or fragment or ray of that blessed nature"; *QG* 2.60; *Decal.* 41 (cf. Wisd 2:23). Diogenes of Apollonia had already taught that "the air within us has perception because it is a small part (*morion*) of the God" (DK, A.19). Cf. Plotinus 6.9.8.29; cf. E. des Places, *Syngeneia* (Paris, 1964).

18. *training. syngymnasia* is a rare word. The passive form of the verb *syngymnazō* (*syngegymnasmenos*) was frequently used by the Stoics in their definitions of *technē* (*SVF* 1.73; 2.93*ff;* Philo *Congr.* 141; cf. *Dox.* 387; *SVF* 3.214; 1.129; D.L. 7.169). For the *Agōn* motif in Wisdom, see NOTES on 4:1 and 10:12. The Cynics argued for the priority of *askēsis psychikē* over *askēsis sōmatikē,* claiming that they were the true athletes in their struggles for virtue (D.L. 6.70; Dio Chrysostom *Orationes* 28.535; Lucian *Anacharsis* 21; Demetrius *De Elocutione* 260). Cf. Antisthenes, Frag. 64, Caizzi (text preserved on an ostracon in Cologne and edited by A. Henrichs in *ZPE* 1 [1967] 45–53).

19. This verse is as clear a statement of the concept of preexistent souls as one could wish, and there is no need to explain it away as many commentators have done. (For a good summary of their views, see Larcher 1969:270–279). Cf. II Enoch 23:4–5: "for all souls are prepared to eternity, before the formation of the world"; II Bar 23:5. On the other hand, the more elaborate Greek doctrine of metempsychosis does not appear to be a part of our author's thinking (nor was it a part of rabbinic thinking). For Philo's doctrine of preexistence, cf. *Somn.* 1.135*ff; Plant.* 12; *Gig.* 6; *Her.* 240. For the Essene belief in the preexistence of the soul, see Jos. *J.W.* 2.8.11 (Josephus' account, however, is suspected of adaptation to Greek ideas), and for a similar rabbinic view, which appears, however, only in the Amoraic period, cf. *BT Hag.* 12b; *A.Z.* 5a; *Yeb.* 62a; *Nid.* 13b; *BR* 8.7, Th-Alb:61; *Tanḥ. Niṣavim* 3; *Pekude* 3. See Freudenthal 1975–79: 1. 72; Lieberman 1974:241, n.41; Urbach 1969:209 (but his arguments with regard to Wisd are unconvincing). For a full discussion, see Introduction, VII.1.

well-endowed. For *eyphyeis,* cf. Plato *Rep.* 409E: *eyphyeis ta sōmata kai tas psychas.* The noun *eyphyia,* however, is an Aristotelian term (*EN* 1114b12). Both forms are very frequent in Philo: "God drops from above the ethereal wisdom upon minds which are by nature apt (*eyphyesi*)" (*Fug.* 138); *LA* 3.96; *Sacr.* 7; *Congr.* 71, 122; *Mut.* 212; *Gig.* 2; *Cher.*

101 (*eyphyia* brings quickness of apprehension, perseverance, and memory. Without *eyphyia* and *didaskalia* as foundations, the mind cannot be brought to its fullness): *Her.* 212 (*eyphyia* and *aphyia* contrasted). Moses, too, according to Philo, had a *euphyēs psychē,* and from birth "an appearance of more than ordinary goodliness" (*Mos.* 1.9,15,18). In apocryphal and Gnostic literature, the heavenly redeemer (Christ; the immortal parts of one's soul; invariably some sort of preexistent divine hypostasis) is often described as a handsome boy: (1) In the *Mani Codex,* the celestial Twin is called "that most beautiful and great mirror" (17.13; cf. NOTE on 7:26); (2) *Acta Pauli,* ed. C. Schmidt, p. 3: *eueidēs pais;* (3) *Acta Andreae et Matthiae* 18, p. 87.11, Bonnet: *paidion hōraiotaton eueides;* (4) The epiphany of Christ as *puerulus speciosus* (Evodius *De Fide* 38). See E. Peterson, *Frühkirchen, Judentum und Gnosis* (1959) 191*ff.*

20. *or rather.* The expression *mallon de* is often used, as here, to correct and state with greater precision what was first stated more loosely. Cf. Philo *Jos.* 119: "or rather (*mallon d'*), if the truth be said . . ."; *Legat.* 22; Gal 4:9.

being noble I entered an undefiled body. For *sōma amianton,* cf. Philo *Spec.* 1.250: "He [one who has taken the Nazirite Vow] must keep his body pure and undefiled (*amianton*)"; Hermas *Similitudes* 5.7.1. *amiantos* is a title of Isis, *P. Oxy.* XI 1380, 109. Gregg (1909) correctly remarks: "He finds himself unable to apply to the body a more generous epithet than undefiled, owing to his tendency as an Alexandrian towards dualism." Cf. 9:15. The notion of God's adapting the body to the soul is found in *Test.Naphtali* 2:2: "For as the potter knoweth the vessel how much it is to contain, and bringeth clay accordingly, so also doth the Lord make the body after the likeness of the spirit (*pros homoiōsin tou pneumatos*), and according to the capacity of the body doth he implant the spirit. And the one does not fall short of the other by a third part of a hair; for by weight and measure and rule was all the creation made."

21. *gain possession of.* "The omission of a genitive after *engkratēs* is unusual, but is perfectly paralleled by Sir 6:27" (Goodrick [1913]). *engkratēs* was taken by Augustine (as also by Grimm) to mean 'continent' or 'self-controlled,' but the context clearly precludes such an interpretation. (For St. Augustine's mistranslation, cf. H. Wolfson 1951:167.)

XVI. WITHOUT WISDOM NO HUMAN ENTERPRISE
CAN SUCCEED
(9:1–6)

9   1 God of my fathers and Lord of mercy,
       who by your Word made all things,
     2 and through your Wisdom framed man
       to be master of the creatures who have their being through
             you,
     3 and to administer the world in holiness and righteousness
       and pass judgment with an upright heart,
     4 give me Wisdom, your throne-companion,
       and do not reject me from among your children.
     5 For I am your servant, the son of your maidservant,
       a feeble and ephemeral man,
       short of understanding justice and law;
     6 for let a man be ever so perfect in the eyes of man,
       he will be of no account in the absence of your Wisdom.

NOTES

9:1–18. The chapter consists of three strophes (9:1–6, 7–12, 13–18) chiastically arranged. The author presents his own version of Solomon's prayer. Cf. I Kings 3:6–9; II Chron 1:8–10. Verses 4, 10, and 17 contain the central theme, the petition for Divine Wisdom, which is thus found both at the center of the chapter and toward either end. A similar pattern may be seen in chap. 1, where we find *dikaiosynē* in vv. 1 and 15, and *adika/dikē* in v. 8. There are parallelisms between the first strophe (9:1–6) and the second strophe (9:7–12) which are chiastically arranged. (The creative work of God and Wisdom—man's vocation : : the king's vocation—creative work of God and Wisdom. The parallelisms are also verbal: *poiēsas-epoiēs—euthytēs-euthes*.) Moreover, the last verse of the second strophe (9:12) speaks of the future realization of the king's vocation, whereas the last verse of the third strophe (9:18) speaks of the past realization of man's vocation. Both verses contain three stichs beginning with *kai*. There are also major and minor 'inclusions.' The major one is: *tē sophia . . . anthrōpon* (9:2) and *anthrōpoi . . . tē sophia* (9:18). The minor ones are: *sophia . . . anthrōpon* (9:2) and *anthrōpōn sophias* (9:6); *laou* (9:7) and *laon* (9:12); *anthrōpos* (9:13) and *anthrōpoi* (9:18). For a detailed structural analysis which demonstrates the great skill with which the author has composed Solomon's prayer, see Gilbert 1970:301–331.

9:1. *God of my fathers.* Cf. I Chron 28:9, 29:18.

by your Word. Cf. Ps 33:6; *Sib Or* 3:20: "Who by his word (*logō*) created all"; Jub 12:4; II Bar 21:4; 14:17; II Enoch 25:3: "all creation which I had thought to create"; 30:8: "On the sixth day I commanded my Wisdom to create man"; *Test. Abraham* A 9:6: "all the creations which you established through one word" (cf. *M. Aboth* 5.1); IV Ezra 6:38; Heb 11:3.

2. *through your Wisdom.* God's creative wisdom is an emphatic theme in the Qumran scrolls. Cf. 1QH 1.14: "Thou hast fashioned [all] their [inhabi]tants according to thy wisdom"; 1.20: "In the wisdom of thy knowledge thou didst establish their destiny before ever they were"; II Enoch (A)30:8: "On the sixth day I commanded my wisdom to create man from seven consistencies"; *On the Origin of the World* (*CG* II), 113:12 – 114:15.

framed. For *kataskeuasas,* cf. IV Macc 2:21.

to be master. Cf. 10:2; Gen 1:26,28; Sir 17:2–4; Ps 8:6–8; 1QS 3.18: "He has created man to govern the world"; II Bar 14:18: "And thou didst say that thou wouldst make for thy world man as the administrator of thy works, that it might be known that he was by no means made on account of the world, but the world on account of him"; *Sib Or* Frag. 3:13: "He has constituted man as the divinely appointed ruler of all"; II Enoch (A) 58:3: "And the Lord appointed him ruler over all, and subjected to him all things under his hands, and made them dumb and made them dull (lit. deaf) that they be commanded of man, and be in subjection and obedience to him"; A30:12: "and I appointed him as ruler to rule on earth and to have my wisdom, and there was none like him of earth of all my existing creatures"; IV Ezra 8:44: "But the son of man who has been fashioned with thine own hands, and is made like thine own image, for whose sake thou hast fashioned all things"; IV Ezra 6:54; Philo *QG* 1.94; *Mos.* 2.65; *Op.* 88, 84 (where heavenly beings are exempted from man's dominion as "having obtained a portion more divine"). See David Jobling, " 'And Have Dominion . . .'," *JSJ* 8:1 (1977) 50–82.

3. *administer.* *diepō* is "to manage or conduct, especially as deputy or substitute": *P. Tebt.* 522 and *P. Lond.* 3.908.19 (both papyri second century CE). Cf. Philo *Mos.* 2.187; *Flac.* 105.

pass judgment. For *krisin krinē,* cf. Demosthenes 21.64: *hot' ekrineto . . . krisin thanatou.*

4. *throne-companion.* Cf. I Enoch 84:3; *On the Origin of the World (CG* II), 106:11–18; Pindar *Olympia* 8.22, where Themis is designated as the *paredros* of Zeus; Euripides *Medea* 843; Sophocles *Oedipus Coloneus* 1382; 1267; Aelius Aristides *Orationes* 2: "Since Zeus could not have distributed all the things of the world, had he not caused Athena to sit beside him, his assessor and counsellor" (Bevan 1927:158); *Orphic Hymns* 62. Although in reality only an aspect of the Logos, there are passages in Philo (an author who loves to multiply images) where justice as assessor (*paredros*), surveyor, and ruler of all things, seems to acquire an independent existence (*Mut.* 194; *Jos.* 48; *Mos.* 2.53; *Decal.* 177; *Spec.* 4.201. Cf. also the Isis Aretalogy from Kyme, 43: "I attend [*paredreuō*] the Sun in his course"; Andros, 139; Prov 8:30). (Kyme, the port. Andros, the island in the Aegean.) *thronōn* is the plural of majesty. (See also NOTE on 1:8.)

5. *servant.* Borrowed from Ps 116:16; 86:16.

a feeble and ephemeral man. Cf. I Chron 29:15. Philo similarly writes: "Yet this our piece of moulded clay, tempered with blood for water, has imperative need of God's help . . . since our race cannot of itself stand firmly established for a single day" (*Her.* 58).

6. *in the absence of your Wisdom.* Philo never tires of insisting that without God's bounteous help, man could accomplish nothing, and that he who ascribes anything to his own powers is a godless villain. Cf. *Post.* 136: "For whence is it likely that a mind thirsty for sound sense should be filled save from the wisdom of God. . . . For the teaching of virtue awaits those who come down from empty self-conceit."

9   7 You chose me above all as king of your people
       and judge of your sons and daughters;
     8 you commanded me to build a temple on your holy
            mountain,
       and an altar in the city of your abode,
       a copy of the sacred tabernacle which you prepared from the
            very first.
     9 And with you is Wisdom who knows your works
       and was present when you created the world,
       and knows what is pleasing in your eyes
       and what is right according to your ordinances.
   10 Send her forth from the holy heavens
       and dispatch her from your majestic throne,
       so that she may labor at my side
       and I may learn your pleasure.
   11 For she knows and understands all things,
       and will guide me prudently in my actions,
       and guard me in her magnificence.
   12 So shall my works be acceptable,
       and I shall judge your people justly,
       and be worthy of my father's throne.

NOTES

9:7. *your sons and daughters.* Cf. Isa 43:6.

8. *your holy mountain.* I.e. Mount Moriah, which according to rabbinic tradition (accepted by the Church) is identical with the place where Abraham was commanded to sacrifice Isaac (II Chron 3:1; I Chron 21:15; *BR* 55.7; *PT Ber.* 4.5; *BT Ber.* 62b. Cf. Jos. *Ant.* 1.3.2).

a copy of the sacred tabernacle. mimēma is a *vox Platonica* and is meant to emphasize by contrast the greater reality of the archetype. See, for example, *Politicus* 300E; *Tim.* 48E; 50C; *Laws* 668B: cf. Heb 8:2:

"The true tent which is set up not by man but by the Lord." According to the rabbis there was both a heavenly and an earthly Holy of Holies (*PT Ber.* 4.5; *BT Hag.* 12b; cf. *BR* 1.4; 69.7, Th-Alb:6, 796–797; *Num.R.* 12.12 [cf. I Chron 28:12]; *Mek. Shirta* on Exod 15:17: " 'The Exact Location of Thy Abode,' (that is,) directly facing Thine abode. This is one of the scriptural statements to the effect that the terrestrial Throne [apparently, the ark] faces over against the celestial Throne [by reading the consonants *mkwn* (vocalized *makon*) as *mekuwwan*]." See Goldin 1971:234–235; cf. also Prov 8:27, LXX; II Enoch 25:4; *Sifre Deut.* 37, Finkelstein: 70 [the sanctuary is one of several things created before the world came into existence]; *Mid.Teh.* 30.1). In *Tanḥ.* Buber, *Naso* 19, we are told that God indicated to Moses that it was not for want of a dwelling place that he commanded the building of a temple, since even before the creation of the world there already existed a supernal temple, as it is written: "Thou throne of glory, on high from the beginning, place of our sanctuary (Jer 17:12)." "But on account of my love for you," God continues, "I shall abandon the heavenly temple and shall descend to dwell among you." See also *BT Menaḥot* 29a, where R. Jose says that an ark, table, and candelabrum of fire came down from heaven to serve as a model for Moses, and *Sanh.* 94b, where Sennacherib is said to have threatened first to destroy God's earthly abode, then his heavenly one. (Cf. *Pesaḥim* 54a; *Nedarim* 39b; *Pesik.R.* 98ab.) See A. Aptowitzer, "The Heavenly Temple According to the Aggada" (Hebrew), *Tarbiz* 2 (1931) 137–153, 257–287; I. Seeligman, "Jerusalem in Jewish-Hellenistic Thought" (Hebrew), in *Yehuda we-Yerushalayim* (Jerusalem, 1957) 198–208. The same notion is found in the Dead Sea scrolls (J. Strugnell, "The Angelic Liturgy at Qumran," *VT* Suppl. 7 (1960) 318–345), and is also widespread in the pseudepigrapha: I Enoch 14:16–20; 26; 90:28–29; *Test. Levi* 3:4–6; 5:1–2; II Bar 4:2–6; cf. also Heb 8:5. Philo naturally interpreted the tradition in the light of his own Platonic theory of 'Forms': "He [Moses] saw with the soul's eye the immaterial forms of the material objects about to be made . . . so the shape of the model was stamped upon the mind of the prophet, a secretly painted or moulded prototype, produced by immaterial and invisible forms" (*Mos.* 2.74–76; cf. *QE* 2.90). Elsewhere he tells us that the tabernacle is a copy of wisdom or divine virtue: "When God willed to send down the image of divine excellence from heaven to earth in pity for our race, that it should not lose its share in the better lot, he constructs as a symbol of the truth the holy tabernacle and its contents to be a representation and copy (*apeikonisma kai mimēma*: a frequent collocution in Philo) of wisdom" (*Her.* 112; cf. *Det.* 160–161; *Congr.* 116. There may already be a reference to the heavenly temple in Sir 24:8–10: [Wisdom says] "The Creator caused my tabernacle to rest. . . . He created me from the beginning before the world . . . in the holy tabernacle I served before him and so I was established in Zion"). On the other hand, Philo also made a distinction between the temple made by hands, and the highest temple, namely, the whole universe, having the heaven for its sanctuary, and the angels or pure intelligences for its priests (*Spec.* 1.66–67; cf. Ps-Plato *Epinomis* 983E–984B, the earliest instance in Greek literature of the notion of the cosmos as a temple, Heb 8:2; 9:11). (See also NOTE on 18:24 below.) Finally, it ought to be noted that the notion of heavenly archetypes of earthly things was well known in ancient Babylonia. The earliest document concerned with the divine plan for a temple is the inscription of Gudea, ensi ('governor') of the Sumerian city of Lagash. (See *CAH* 1, part 2, p. 103.) In Gudea's dream there appeared a hero who "held a slab of lapis lazuli in his hands, and set down thereon the ground-plan of the House (to be built)." When Sennacherib was founding Nineveh as the center of his kingdom, he spoke of it as "planned from far away time in the writing of heaven." (See E. Burrows, "Some Cosmological Patterns in Babylonian Religion," in *The Labyrinth,* ed. S. H. Hooke [London, 1935] 45–70; M. Eliade, *Cosmos and History* (New York, 1959) 6*ff;* H. W. F. Saggs, *The Greatness that was Babylon* [London, 1962] 364*ff;* R. J. McKelvey, *The New Temple* [Oxford, 1969] 25–41.) A companion concept to the notion of the heavenly temple was that of the heavenly Jerusalem. See McKelvey, and E. A. Urbach, "Lower Jerusalem and Upper Jerusalem," in *Jerusalem Throughout Its Generations* (Jerusalem, 1969) (Hebrew).

9. *present when you created the world.* Aristobulus writes: "One of our forefathers, Solomon, said more clearly and aptly that wisdom existed before heaven and earth" (*FPG:* 224, line 19). Similarly, Philo writes: "Thus in the pages of one of the inspired company, wisdom is represented as speaking of herself after this manner: 'God obtained me first of all his works and founded me before the ages' (Prov 8:22)" (*Ebr.* 31; cf. *Virt.* 62).

in your eyes. A Hebraism corresponding to *enōpion sou* in Isa 38:3; Deut 12:8; 12:28, LXX.

right. euthes only in later LXX translators for *euthy.*

10. *Send her forth.* Cf. Pss 42:3; 144:7, LXX. A similar note is struck in Cleanthes' famous *Hymn to Zeus:* "O Zeus, all-bountiful, whose dazzling lightning / Splits Thy black clouds, rescue mankind from wretched / Ignorance, scatter darkness from their minds, / Give them that wisdom by which Thou dost steer / All things in justice" (translation of F. H. Sandbach, *The Stoics,* [Cambridge, 1975]: 111).

majestic throne. Cf. Jer 17:12, LXX.

11. *magnificence.* Cf. Isa 58:8; Sir 6:31. Goodrick translates: "with her good repute."

XVIII. DIVINE WISDOM BROUGHT MEN SALVATION
(9:13–18)

9   13 For what man can comprehend the plan of God,
or who can grasp what the Lord wills?
14 The reasonings of mortals are wretched,
and our devices precarious;
15 for a perishable body weighs down the soul,
and this tent of clay encumbers a mind full of cares.
16 We barely make inferences concerning what is on earth,
and laboriously discover what is at hand;
who, then, has tracked out what is in the heavens?
17 Who was privy to your design, unless you gave him Wisdom,
and sent your holy spirit from on high?
18 Thus it was that the paths of earthlings were set aright,
and men were taught what pleases you,
and were saved by Wisdom.

NOTES

9:13. *what man can comprehend.* The same idea is found in Isa 40:13–14; 55:8. Cf. Prov 30:2–4; Sir 1:1–10; 18:1–7; 24:28–29; I Bar 3:29–37; *Sib Or* Frag. 3:15; I Enoch 93:11–14 [a sapiential poem, constructed in the form of rhetorical questions, concerning the transcendence of God]: "For who is there of all the children of men that is able to hear the voice of the Holy One without being troubled? And who can think his thoughts? And who is there that can behold all the works of heaven? And how should there be one who could behold the heaven, and who is there that could understand the things of heaven . . ."; II Bar 14:8–9; IV Ezra chap. 4. A similar note had already been sounded in the Babylonian poem *Ludlul Bēl Nemēqi* 36–38: "Who knows the will of the gods in heaven? Who understands the plans of the underworld gods? Where have mortals learnt the way of a god?" (Lambert 1960:41). Cf.

Saggilkīnam-ubbib *The Babylonian Theodicy:* XXIV 256–257: "The divine mind, like the center of the heavens, is remote; knowledge of it is difficult; the masses do not know it" (Lambert:87; *ANET* Supp., p. 604). For further discussion, see Introduction: Gilbert 1971:145–166; M. E. Stone, "Lists of Revealed Things in the Apocalyptic Literature," In *Magnalia Dei,* ed. F. M. Cross (New York, 1976):414–452.

15. The adverse influence of body on soul is advanced with the greatest fervor in Plato's *Phaedo.* At 66B, Plato says that "so long as we have the body, and the soul is contaminated by such an evil, we shall never attain completely what we desire, that is, the truth. For the body keeps us constantly busy by reason of its need for sustenance." The image of the body weighing down the soul recurs persistently in the writings of the Platonists and Roman Stoics, and although the later Platonic dialogues, particularly the *Republic,* modify this doctrine considerably, there are nevertheless passages where the human body continues to be regarded as something which hampers the soul's activity. In *Rep.* 611C the soul is described as marred (*lelōbēmenon*) by association with the body, and at *Tim.* 43BC we are given a picture of the soul in infancy assailed by physical motions which pass into it through the body and violently upset its various circuits.

weighs down the soul. A widespread Platonic motif. Cf. *Phaedo* 81C: "And such a soul is weighed down (*barynetai*) by this and is dragged back into the sensible world." According to the Pythagorean Ecphantus, man on earth is "an exiled creature weighed down by a large portion of earth (*polla ta ga barynomenon*)" (Thesleff:79). This image is fairly common in Philo: "But those which bear the burden of the flesh, oppressed by the grievous load (*barynomenai kai piezomenai*), cannot look up to the heavens as they revolve, but with necks bowed downwards are constrained to stand rooted to the ground like four-footed beasts" (*Gig.* 31; cf. *LA* 3.152; *Det.* 16). Cf. *CH, Asclepius* 9.17 (*mole corporis resederunt*); Plotinus 6.9.8.16; Plutarch *Is. et Os.* 353A: "but they want their bodies to be compact and light around their souls and not to oppress (*piezein*) or weigh down (*katathlibein*) the divine part with a mortal element which is strong and heavy"; Seneca *Ep.* 65.16: "For this body of ours is a weight upon the soul and its penance (*pondus ac poena est*); as the load presses down, the soul is crushed and is in bondage, unless philosophy has come to its assistance;" Jos. *J.W.* 7.8.7: "But it is not until, freed from the weight (*barous*) that drags it down to earth and clings about it, the soul is restored to its proper sphere."

tent of clay. For *skēnos,* cf. Democritus DK, B.187; Hippocrates *Peri Kardiēs* (*On the Heart*) 7; Ps-Plato *Axiochus* 366A; Timaeus Locrus 104d; *Par.Jer.* 6:6; II Cor 5:1,4; Job 4:19. It is very frequent in the Neopythagorean writings (see Thesleff 1965:43,21; 49,9; 70,9; 80,2; 124,18; 143,19; 145,2; etc.).

encumbers. brithō is another *vox Platonica*. Cf. *Phaedrus* 247B: "the horse of evil nature weighs down (*brithei*) their chariots, pulling heavily toward the earth any charioteer who has not trained him well"; *Phaedo* 81C: "we must believe that the corporeal is burdensome (*embrithes*) and heavy and earthly and visible"; Philo *Spec.* 4.114: "For the natural gravitation of the body pulls down with it those of little mind (*brithousa tous oligophronas*); *Plant.* 25; *Her.* 295. At *Phaedo* 66B, Socrates eloquently describes the contaminating influence of body over mind: "So long as we have the body and the soul is contaminated by such an evil, we shall never attain completely what we desire, that is, the truth. For the body keeps us constantly busy by reason of its need of sustenance. . . . And the body fills us with passions and desires and fears. . . . Because of all these things we have no leisure for philosophy. But the worst of all is that if we do get a bit of leisure and turn to philosophy, the body is constantly breaking in upon our studies and disturbing us with noise and confusion, so that it prevents our beholding the truth, and in fact we perceive that, if we are ever to know anything absolutely, we must be free from the body and must behold the actual realities with the eye of the soul alone."

16. We have here a widespread conceit. Cf. IV Ezra 4:11: "What belongs to thee . . . thou art incapable of understanding: how then should thy vessel be able to comprehend the way of the Most High?" (cf. 4:21); *Test. Job* 8:19–23: "If thou hast not understood even the exits of the body, how canst thou understand the celestial circuits?"; Judith 8:14; Ps-Callisthenes *Life of Alexander* 1.14; Philo *Somn.* 1.23, 54: "And why, treading as you do on earth, do you leap over the clouds? And why do you say that you are able to lay hold of what is in the upper air, when you are rooted to the ground?"; *BT Sanh.* 39a: "You know not what is in heaven." Cf. also John 3:12: "If you disbelieve me when I talk to you about things on earth, how are you to believe if I should talk to you about the things of heaven?"; II Enoch 40:2–3. Gregg (1909) notes: "For *ta en chersin*, א reads *posin*, 'at his feet,' which causes a singular resemblance between this passage and D.L. 1.8.34: 'If Thales cannot see the things at his feet, does he expect to learn the things in the heavens?'" Cf. also D.L. 6.28: "And he [Diogenes] would wonder . . . that the mathematicians should gaze at the sun and the moon, but overlook matters close at hand (*ta d'en posi*)." See also Isa 55:9; Job 38:31; Prov 30:4; Philo *Conf.* 3 (*tōn en chersi kai para podas*). For *eksichniazō* (=*eksichneuō*), which occurs only in LXX (and later in Patristic Greek), cf. Sir 1:3; 18:4,6; 24:28.

18. *the paths of earthlings were set aright*. Cf. Prov 4:26. This verse marks the culmination of the author's emphatic teaching in this chapter concerning man's complete dependence on God's gift of his spirit of Wisdom for the achievement of a righteous existence. The same idea is

eloquently expressed in 1QH 4.31 in almost the same words: "Righteousness, I know, is not of man, nor is perfection of way of the son of man: to the Most High God belong all righteous deeds. The way of man is not established (*lô' tikkôn*) except by the spirit which God created for him to make perfect a way for the children of men." See D. Flusser, "The Dualism of Flesh and Spirit in the Dead Sea Scrolls" (Hebrew), *Tarbiz* 27 (1958): 158–165. The word *esōthēsan* which occurs here for the first time in this work, announces the theme for the rest of the book. It will occur again in 10:4; 14:4,5; 16:7,11; 18:5.

XIX. FROM ADAM TO MOSES
(10:1–14)

10   1 It was Wisdom who closely guarded
    the first-fashioned father of the world, created alone;
    she extricated him from his own blunder,
  2 and gave him the power to master all things.
  3 A wicked man, however, who shunned her in his anger,
    perished through a fit of fratricidal rage.
  4 When the earth was flooded on his account, Wisdom once
      again came to the rescue, piloting the righteous man
      on a plain wooden hulk.
  5 It was she who when the nations in their single-minded
      wickedness were put to confusion,
    recognized the righteous man and kept him blameless
      before God,
    and steeled him against pity for his child.
  6 It was she who rescued a righteous man when the ungodly
      were perishing,
    and he escaped the fire that descended on the Five Cities,
  7 which were turned into a smoking waste
    as a testimony of their wickedness;
    with plants that bear fruit before they ripen,
    and a pillar of salt standing there as a memorial of an
      unbelieving soul.
  8 For having passed Wisdom by,
    they were not only distracted from a knowledge of the
      good,
    but also left behind for the world a monument of their folly,
    so that they were unable to go undetected in their failure.
  9 But Wisdom rescued her servants from troubles.
  10 It was she who guided a righteous man, fugitive from his
      brother's wrath, on the straight path;

she showed him the kingdom of God
and gave him knowledge of holy things;
she prospered him in his toils
and multiplied the fruits of his labors.

11 When men in their greed tried to get the better of him, she
        stood by him and made him rich.
12 She sedulously guarded him from his enemies,
and secured him from ambush;
she gave him victory in a hard contest,
that he might know that godliness is more potent than all
        else.
13 It was she who would not abandon a righteous man sold
        into slavery,
but rescued him from sin;
14 she descended into the dungeon with him,
and when he was in chains she did not leave him,
until she brought him imperial sovereignty
and authority over his masters;
she gave the lie to those who found fault with him
and she bestowed on him everlasting honor.

NOTES

10:1–21. Wisdom's saving and punishing power is here illustrated by
the enumeration of seven righteous heroes and their wicked counterparts,
although the contrast is not consistently carried out. We have Adam-Cain;
Noah-generation of the Flood; Abraham-the nations confounded in their
wickedness; Lot-Sodomites; Jacob-Esau; Joseph-his critics; Israel under
Moses-the Egyptian oppressors under Pharaoh. Of the seven, only Adam
is not called *dikaios.* "The idea of Wisdom's repeated efforts among men
through her envoys," writes M. J. Suggs, "is elaborated in Wisd 10–11
into a new interpretation of *Heilsgeschichte,* in which Israel's history is
seen as determined by Sophia's providential guidance of the people
through chosen vessels in each generation" (1970:21). "The old *Heilsgeschichte* with its idea of miraculous divine eruption in history is rein-
terpreted. What is now described is the providential ordering of Israel's
history through Sophia's generation-by-generation election of holy servants" (pp. 40–41). Cf. Collins: "The events in question are not ascribed

to the direct intervention of God but to the constant activity of wisdom in the world. Revelation does not take place by theophanies, but by the constant mediation of wisdom" (1977:127). For a similar list of seven paradigmatic righteous men, cf. *Ps-Clementine Homilies* 18.14 which alludes to the "seven pillars of the world who were able to please the most just God" (cf. *BT Ḥag.* 12b). In the preceding chapter (18.13) six of them are enumerated: Adam, Enoch, Noah, Abraham, Isaac, and Jacob. In 17.4 the list is completed with the addition of Moses. (In *Ps-Clementine Recognitions* 3.61, some of these are included in an elaborate grouping of ten pairs of evil and good men.) The author of Wisd had already singled out Enoch in 4:10, and so here substitutes Lot for the latter, and instead of Isaac he prefers Joseph as affording an opportunity for a more elaborate description. (For a different list of seven righteous men, cf. *BT Suk.* 52b.) The author has constructed his Ode by the use of anaphora, introducing Wisdom with the emphatic pronoun *hautē* which marks off six sections each of which contains the word *dikaios* once. The word *sophia* occurs at the end of the first (v. 4), third (twice: vv. 8 and 9), and sixth (v. 21) sections. There are also two inclusions: *diephylaksen/ephylaksen* (vv. 1 and 5), and *errysato* (vv. 6 and 9) (Reese 1965:392). In Heb 11 we have a long list of exemplary heroes of faith, with which we may compare the much shorter list in IV Macc 16:20–21 (cf. also I Macc 2:49–64). An encomiastic review of Israel's heroes on a much broader scale had already been provided in Ben Sira 44–50. See W. Staerk, "Die sieben Säulen der Welt und des Hauses der Weisheit," *ZNW* 35 (1936) 232–261; R. Neudecker, "Die alttestamentliche Heilsgeschichte in lehrhaft-paränetischen Darstellung. Eine Studie zu Sap 10 und Hebr 11" (Diss. masch., Innsbruck, 1971); Von Armin Schmitt, "Struktur, Herkunft und Bedeutung der Beispielreihe in Weish 10," *BZ* 21 (1977) 1–22 cites Greek models for this use of *exempla* or *paradeigmata,* e.g. *Iliad* 5.381–402; Isocrates *Antidosis* 231–235; Lycurgus *Against Leocrates*). Cf. Philo *Virt.* 198–205; *Praem.* 67ff (and Colson's note to 78). See also H. Thyen, *Der Stil der jüdisch-hellenistischen Homilie* (Göttingen 1955): 111–116; T. R. Lee, "*Studies in the Form of Sirach 44–50*" (Dissertation, Graduate Theological Union 1979). Lee has pointed out that the repeated use of the pronominal suffix 1 in CD 2:17 – 3:12 is similar to the recurrent use of *pistei,* by faith, in Heb 11 and the recurrent *hautē* in Wisd 10.

10:1. *It was Wisdom.* The emphatic pronoun *hautē* is used for Wisdom throughout the chapter. Cf. Acts 7:35–38, where each sentence begins with the emphatic *touton* or *houtos.* Norden has pointed out that this is one form of the encomium to the gods in Greek literature (1913:163–165, 223–224). Similar repetition of the personal pronoun is a feature of Hellenistic aretalogies or hymns of praise discovered in Egypt (see A. J. Festugière, "Le Style de la 'Kore Kosmou,'" *Vivre et Penser* 2 [1942] 50–53; *CH* 23 [*Korē Kosmou*] 65–68, eleven *houtoi* follow each other). See also Y. Grandjean, *Une nouvelle Arétalogie d'Isis à Maronée* (Leiden, 1975) 17–18, where we find *hautē* three times in succession, after which the invocations continue in the second person. See Aristides *Encomium on Zeus* 43.29*f*; Philo *Legat.* 144*ff*; *PGM* 5.135.

first-fashioned. See NOTE on 7:1.

father of the world. I.e. Adam. For Wisd's omission of the proper names of Israel's heroes, see NOTE on 4:10.

monon ktisthenta. Either "created alone" or "the alone created." For the latter, cf. Philo *Op.* 140: "Such was the first man created, as I think in body and soul, surpassing all the men that now are, and all that have been before us. For our beginning is from men, whereas God created him, and the more eminent the maker is, so much the better is the work . . . The man first fashioned (*prōtos diaplastheis*) was clearly the bloom of our entire race." For the former translation we may quote *M. Sanh.* 4.5: "Therefore was a single man only [first] created to teach thee that if anyone destroy a single soul . . . Scripture charges him as though he had destroyed a whole world, and whoever rescues a single soul . . . Scripture credits him as though he had saved a whole world. And a single man only was first created for the sake of peace in the human race, that no man might say to his fellow, 'My ancestor was greater than thy ancestor.'" *Targ.Yerush.* on Gen 3:22: "Man, whom I created alone in the world, just as I am alone in the heavens . . ."; *BR* 21.5 (Th-Alb:200): "'Now that the man has become like one of us' (Gen 3:22), R. Judah b. Simon said, 'like the "Only One" of the world.'" (Cf. Philo *Decal.* 37; *Dēnkart* 268.3–8 (see Zaehner 1972:453*ff*); Quran 4:1.

from his own blunder. The threat to Adam's existence was not that of an external menace, but was rather a product of his own blundering, and the only antidote for it was the directive power of Wisdom; cf. *Apocryphon of John* (*CG* II) 20 (Plate [8]) 17–28. We read of Adam's repentance in *Vita Adae; BT Erubin* 18b; *BR* 20.11; 24.6; Irenaeus *Adv. Haer.* 3.23; Tertullian *De Paenitentia* 12.

3. *A wicked man.* I.e. Cain.

a fit of fratricidal rage. I.e. by murdering his brother in a fit of rage, he thereby destroyed himself. The phrase, as Bauermeister long ago noted, has an Aeschylean ring. Philo thrice applies the adjective *adelphoktonos* to Cain (*Cher.* 52; *Fug.* 60; *Praem.* 68; cf. Jos. *Ant.* 1.2.2). Philo explains Cain's punishment as follows: "Cain has been done away with by himself. . . . For the soul that has extirpated from itself the principle of the love of virtue and the love of God, has died to the love of virtue" (*Det.* 47). Ginzberg has suggested that Philo seems to be explaining allegorically a legend according to which Cain never died (1954:5. 147). For rabbinic legends concerning Cain's death, see *Tanḥ. Bereshit* 11. (According to Jub 4:31, Cain was killed by a stone when his house caved in on him.)

4. *on his account*. Cain, as the first murderer, serves as a paradigm of human wickedness, so that the cause of the Flood can be ascribed to him. Cf. *PRE* 22: "From Cain arose and were descended all the generations of the wicked, who rebel (cf. Ezek 20:38) and sin, who rebelled against their Rock, and they said, "We do not need the drops of thy rain (perhaps an allusion to the flood which came as a punishment for their sins), neither to walk in thy ways, as it is said, 'Yet they said unto God, Depart from us' (Job 21:14)" (Stein).

piloting. The verb *kybernaō* was employed by the Stoics to describe the guiding power of Logos (*SVF* 3.390; M. Aurel. 7.64; cf. *Dox*. 335, line 15). In this they were following the presocratics (Anaximander DK, A.15; Diogenes of Apollonia, DK, B.5) and Plato *Critias* 109C; *Euthydemus* 291D; *Rep*. 590D; *Phaedrus* 247C; *Laws* 963A (noun *kybernētikon*); *Theages* 123D. Philo is particularly fond of the collocation *kybernan kai hēniochein* both in reference to the guidance of human reason (*Op*. 88, 119; *LA* 3.80; *Det*. 53) and of divine providence (*Ebr*. 199; *Mut*. 16; *Abr*. 84; *Jos*. 149; *Decal*. 155; *Praem*. 34). According to *BR* 34.8 (Th-Alb:323), the sun, moon, and stars did not function during the period of the Flood, thus implying that Noah's ark was piloted by God. *kybernētis* is a title of Isis (*P. Oxy*. xi 1380,69). Cf. also Pseudo-Phocylides 131 (*FPG*: 153): *agrous kai polias sophiē kai nēa kyberna:* "Wisdom directs the course of lands and cities and ships."

the righteous man. I.e. Noah, the first man in the Bible to be called *ṣaddîq*. Cf. Philo *Congr*. 90.

on a plain wooden hulk. Wisdom's power is such that she could pilot Noah to safety though limited in means to his crudely built wooden hulk. Cf. Philo *Mos*. 1.112, where it is pointed out that God's power is so great that he can provide the slightest (*eutelesi*) and the smallest with irresistible and invincible powers and through them wreak vengeance on the evildoers.

5. *single-minded*. Cf. Gen 11:1: "All the earth had the same language and the same words." Ps-Jonathan and *Targ. Yerush*. translate the latter phrase "of one mind."

put to confusion. Cf. Gen 11:7,9, LXX.

the righteous man. Here, Abraham. According to *BR* 38.6 (Th-Alb:354), Abraham was a contemporary of the generation of the Tower of Babel and was harshly described by them as a barren jennet unable to give birth. (In *Seder Olam R*. 1 we read that Abraham was forty-eight years old at the time of the confounding of the nations.) Cf. *LAB* 6.

blameless. Cf. Gen 17:1, LXX.

against pity for his child. Cf. IV Macc 14:20: "But sympathy for her offspring did not move the mother of the youths, whose soul was like Abraham's." Cf. 15:28–29, where the martyr mother is addressed as "victor in the contest of the heart" (*tou dia splangchnōn agōnos athlophore*).

6. *that descended. katabasion.* Found only here (though it appears again in Patristic Greek).

the Five Cities. The five cities of the plain are Sodom, Gomorrah, Admah, Zeboiim, and Zoar (Gen 10:19; 14:2). The last was actually spared for the sake of Lot. An earlier tradition, however, apparently spoke of the destruction of all five (cf. *BR* 51.4, Th-Alb:536; and *Ency.Bib.* 5:1001). "In one of the famous Ebla tablets, the full list of the five cities is given, the same names in the same order as in Gen 14. This is the first non-biblical confirmation of the Cities of the Plain, and the date of the tablets must be somewhere around 2500 BCE give or take a century. The tablet in question is a trading document, and naturally attests the existence of the cities at that time. But there is now significant evidence that the period is not far from the time of Gen 14, and that we must look for the setting of the story in Gen 14 in the same pre-Sargonic period of history, namely the third millennium" (David N. Freedman, private communication). For Philo, the five cities represent the five senses (*Abr.* 147).

7. *turned into a smoking waste as a testimony of their wickedness.* The literal translation is: "of which, yet as a testimony of its wickedness, a smoking waste has come into being." Philo similarly writes: "And to this day it goes on burning, for the fire of the thunderbolt is never quenched but either continues its ravages or else smoulders. And the clearest proof is what is still visible, for a monument (*mnēmeion*) of the disastrous event remains in the smoke which rises ceaselessly and the brimstone which the miners obtain." Cf. *Mos.* 2.56: "and to the present day the memorials to the awful disaster are shown in Syria, ruins and cinders and brimstone and smoke, and the dusky flame still arises (*eti anadidomenē*) as though fire were smouldering within"; Jos. *J.W.* 4.8.4: "and in fact vestiges of the divine fire and faint traces of five cities are still visible." An analogous phenomenon may be seen in the Greek mystery cult of Dionysus. The demolished home of Semele, the ruins of which the Euripidean Dionysus still sees smoking on his return to his native city of Thebes, was still being shown to marveling foreigners in the late centuries of antiquity (Euripides *Bacchae* 6–11; Pausanius 9.12.3; Aristides 1:72, Keil).

plants that bear fruit before they ripen. (Literally, "plants that bear fruit before their seasons are complete.") There was apparently an early tradition that the fruit of Sodom had become accursed, although there is only a vague allusion to it in Scripture (Deut 32:32, "Ah! The vine for them is from Sodom, From the vineyards of Gomorrah; The grapes for them are poison, A bitter growth their clusters. Their wine is the venom of asps, The pitiless poison of vipers." See *Ency.Bib.* 5:1001). Josephus writes: "Still, too, may one see ashes reproduced in the fruits, which from their outward appearance would be thought edible, but on being plucked with the hand dissolve into smoke and ashes" *J.W.* 4.8.4). Similarly, Tacitus: "In fact, all the plants there, whether wild or cultivated, turn black, become sterile, and seem to wither into dust, either in leaf or in flower, or after they have reached their usual mature form. Now, for my part, although I shall grant that famous cities were once destroyed by fire from heaven, I still think that it is the exhalations from the lake that infect the ground and poison the atmosphere about this district, and that this is the reason that crops and fruits decay, since both soil and climate are deleterious" (*Historiae* 5.7). In the twelfth century, the French chronicler Fulcher of Chartres could still make a similar report in his *Historia Hierosolymitana* (2.4, Migne), one of the most trustworthy sources for the history of the First Crusade. He speaks of apples within which he found upon breaking their rind something like black powder which gave off an empty smoke. C. Geikie writes: "The 'osher' of the Arab is the true apple of Sodom. Its fruit is like a large smooth apple or orange. . . . When ripe it is yellow and looks fair and attractive, and is soft to the touch, but if pressed, it bursts with a crack, and only the broken shell and a row of small seeds in a half-open pod, with a few dry filaments, remain in the hand" (*The Holy Land and the Bible* [New York, 1888] 2.117. Quoted by H. St. J. Thackeray in his Loeb translation of Josephus, 3. 144, note a). Cf. also *BR* 51.4 (Th-Alb: 536): "Until this day [says R. Joshua b. Levi], if one gathers rainwater from the atmosphere of Sodom and introduces it into another garden-bed, it will not produce growth."

a pillar of salt. Cf. Gen 19:26. Josephus writes: "I have seen this pillar of salt (*stēlēn halōn*) which remains to this day" (*Ant.* 1.11.4). The rabbis even prescribed a blessing to be recited upon seeing Lot's wife (*BT Ber.* 54a). "Jebel Usdum ('Mount of Sodom'), a mountain about five miles long and over seven hundred feet high, largely a mass of crystalline salt, is situated along the south end of the west side of the Dead Sea. The erosion of this salt mountain over the centuries has caused pinnacles to stand out, which ancient and modern writers have likened to Lot's wife" (J. P. Harland, *IDB* 4. 396). We read in *PRE* 25: "And she stands even now. All day the oxen lick it and it decreases up to her feet, and in the morning (the pillar of salt) grows afresh." Cf. Irenaeus *Adv. Haer.* 4.31.3; Clement of Rome *Epistle to the Corinthians,* chap. 11. The famous Jewish traveler Benjamin of Tudela (in Navarre) also tells us in his *Sefer ha-Massa'ot* (*Book of Travels*) (second half of twelfth century) that he had seen the salt pillar.

an unbelieving soul. Our author sees the cause of her punishment in her lack of belief in God, i.e. he has made Lot's wife a symbol of the untrusting soul. St. Augustine's interpretation is as follows: By being turned into salt she "provided a solemn and sacred warning that no man who has set his foot on the path of salvation ought to yearn again for what he has left behind" (*Civ.Dei* 10.8). According to *BR* 51.5 (*Th-Alb:*536; cf. 50.4, Th-Alb:521), she was so punished, because upon being asked by her husband to serve their guests with salt, she responded: "Do you wish to introduce this evil custom (*synētheia*) here too?" In the addition found in the printed texts of *BR,* it is said that it was because she went to her neighbors on the night the angels had arrived, asking for salt for her guests with the sole intention of alerting her fellow townsmen concerning her visitors. (Cf. Ps-Jonathan on Gen 19:26.) It is interesting to note that, according to Philo, if we gave Lot's wife her right name, we might call her 'custom' (*synētheia*), for "her nature is hostile to truth, and if we take her with us, she lags behind and gazes round at the old familiar objects and remains among them like a lifeless monument" (*Ebr.* 164; cf. *Somn.* 1.247–248).

8. *for the world.* For *bios* in this sense, cf. Sext. *Math.* 11.49; *Pyrrhoneae Hypotyposes* 1.211 (LSJ: 316, *bios:* III): IV Macc 17:14. Other translations are: "for human life," or "by their life."

10. *a righteous man.* Here, Jacob.

fugitive from his brother's wrath. See Gen 27:41–45.

the kingdom of God . . . knowledge of holy things. See Gen 28:10ff. There seems to be more implied here than what is found in the Genesis passage. According to *Test.Levi* 9:3, Jacob saw a vision concerning Levi, that he should be a priest unto God, and he rose up early in the morning and paid tithes of all to the Lord through him. (Cf. Jub 32:1, where it is Levi who has the vision). Moreover, at 5:1–2, Levi is privileged with a vision of the heavenly temple and told that he has received the blessings of the priesthood. Burrows conjectured that our author may be alluding to Jacob's vision of the heavenly temple (this is exactly the sense of *ta hagia* in Heb 9:12) and of the heavenly Jerusalem which will one day descend to earth when the kingdom of God is established. For the heavenly temple, cf. NOTE on 9:8. (See Burrows 1939:405–407.) There appears to be a pervasive influence of the *Test.Levi* on Wisd. Cf. Wisd 5:17–19 and *Test.Levi* 8:2; Wisd 2:22; 6:22 and *Test.Levi* 1:10; Wisd 18:4 and *Test.Levi* 14:4 (cf. 18:9); Wisd 2:13,16; 18:13; 14:3 and *Test.Levi* 17:2; Wisd 5:16 and *Test.Levi* 8:10; Wisd 8:21; 1:1 and *Test.Levi* 13:1; Wisd 16:5 and *Test.Levi* 6:11; Wisd 1:12–16; 3:24 and *Test.Levi* 19:1–3. Philo, as is his wont, allegorizes Jacob's dream (*Somn.* 1.146).

11. *greed.* See Gen 31:38ff.

12. *ambush.* Cf. Gen 34:30; 31:24; Jub 37–38.

a hard contest. Undoubtedly a reference to his struggle with the angel

(Gen 32:24ff). The words *ischyros* and *dynatōtera* appear to echo Gen 32:29b, LXX, and Hosea 12:5, LXX. Jacob also appears in the writings of Philo as the athlete of God par excellence, and the Agōn as it appears in Philo is essentially an Agōn of piety (*eusebeia*) or godliness (*Spec.* 2.183; *Mos.* 1.307; 2.136; *Virt.* 45; *Spec.* 1.57) (Pfitzner:56). For *brabeuō*, cf. Jos. *Ant.* 14.9.5: *ei kai polemon rhopas brabeuei to theion;* Philo *Mos.* 1.16 (*brabeuontos kai epineuontos theou*).

that he might know. The story of the struggle with the angel is given a symbolic meaning.

13. *a righteous man.* Here, Joseph.

sold into slavery. See Gen 37:37ff.

14. *dungeon.* Cf. Gen 40:15, LXX, where *lakkos* stands for the dun-(*amemptos*) in v. 5 above (Stein).

XX. THE EXODUS
(10:15–21)

10   15 It was she who rescued a holy people and blameless race
from a nation of oppressors;
16 she entered the soul of the servant of the Lord,
and with signs and wonders withstood dread kings.
17 She rewarded the labors of holy men,
she guided them on a wondrous journey,
and became a covering for them by day
and a blaze of stars by night.
18 She led them across the Red Sea,
and guided them through deep waters;
19 but their enemies she overwhelmed,
then spat them out of the boundless deep.
20 The righteous therefore spoiled the godless,
and hymned your holy name, O Lord,
and praised with one accord your champion might;
21 for Wisdom opened the mouth of the dumb,
and rendered the tongues of infants articulate.

NOTES

10:15. *blameless race*. The seed of Abraham, called blameless (*amemptos*) in v. 5 above (Stein).

16. *she entered the soul of the servant of the Lord*. Cf. Isa 63:11. Much of the saving activity here ascribed to Wisdom had been assigned directly to God in Isa 63:11–14.

the servant of the Lord. I.e. Moses.

kings. Perhaps the allusive plural (Smyth 1107; *BDF* 141; cf. Matt 2:20; Aeschylus *Choephori* 52; *Eumenides* 100), by which one person is alluded to in the plural number. The reference is to Pharaoh.

17. *She rewarded the labors of holy men*. The reference is probably to

the objects of silver and gold which the Israelites "borrowed" from the Egyptians before leaving Egypt (Exod 11:2; 12:35–36). Cf. Ps 105:37; Jub 48:18: "And on the fourteenth we bound him [Mastema] that he might not accuse the children of Israel on the day when they asked the Egyptians for vessels of silver, and vessels of gold . . . in order to despoil the Egyptians in return for the bondage in which they had forced them to serve." Ezekiel the Tragedian similarly wrote that God promises to dispose the Egyptians favorably toward the Israelites when they are ready to leave, so that they will receive gold, silver, and garments, in order that they may be rewarded for the work which they had done (*hin' hōn epraksan misthon apodōsi brotois*) (*FPG:* 213, line 5ff). Moreover, the reason given by Artapanos for the Egyptians' pursuit of the Israelites was their desire to retrieve the property borrowed from them (*FPG:* 195, line 4). A similar explanation was given by the Augustan historian Pompeius Trogus in his *Historiae Philippicae* (see Justinus' Latin epitome 36.2.13), except that for ordinary vessels he substituted holy vessels (*sacra Aegyptiarum*) which the Israelites allegedly stole and the Egyptians sought to retrieve by force of arms but were unsuccessful. (See also *BT Sanh.* 91a for the story of the lawsuit before Alexander the Great.) Among Marcion's many calumnies against the Demiurge was the charge that he induced his people to spoil the Egyptians (see A. von Harnack, *Marcion* [rep. Darmstadt, 1960] 280). These citations all clearly imply that the Israelite borrowing of gold and silver vessels from the Egyptians had been a special target of the polemical and anti-Semitic literature of the Greco-Roman age and that Jewish writers found it necessary to provide some sort of apologetic defense. The matter is clinched, however, by the considerably more explicit defense made by Philo: "For they took out with them much spoil. . . . And they did this not in avarice, or, as their accusers might say, in covetousness of what belonged to others. No, indeed. In the first place, they were but receiving a bare wage for all their time of service; secondly, they were retaliating, not on an equal but on a lesser scale, for their enslavement. For what resemblance is there between forfeiture of money and deprivation of liberty, for which men of sense are willing to sacrifice not only their substance but their life? In either case, their action was right. . . . For the Egyptians began the wrongdoing by reducing guests and suppliants to slavery like captives [cf. Wisd 19:14], as I said before" (*Mos.* 1.140–142).

a covering. skepē is very frequent in LXX, Psalms (e.g. 16:8; 35:7; 90:1; 104:39). Cf. Sir 31:16; Exod 13:21f. Drummond writes: "Although it did not suit the author's plan to enter, like Philo, into a detailed exegesis, it is evident that the pillar of cloud and of fire is allegorised into wisdom" 1969: 1. 185). Cf. Philo *Her.* 203: "For the further pursuit of the sober and God-beloved race by the passion-loving and godless was forbidden by that cloud, which was a weapon of shelter and salvation (*skepastērion kai sōtērion*) to its friends. . . . For in minds of rich soil that cloud sends in gentle showers the drops of wisdom, whose very nature exempts it from all harm"; Sir 24:3–4: "I [Wisdom] came forth from the mouth of the Most High, / And as a mist I covered the earth. / In the high places did I fix my abode, / And my throne was in the pillar of cloud." See also Philo *Mos.* 1.166: "Perhaps indeed there was enclosed within the cloud one of the lieutenants of the great King, an unseen angel, a forerunner on whom the eyes of the body were not permitted to look."

19. *then spat them out.* For *anabrassō*, cf. Aristotle *Meteorologicum* 368b29; Apollonius Rhodius 2.566. Philo uses the similar verb *apobrassō* in the same context: "That doom is evidenced by the corpses which are floated to the top and strew the surface of the sea: last comes a mighty rushing wave, which flings the corpses in heaps (*sōrēdon apebrasthēsan*) upon the opposite shore, a sight inevitably to be seen by the saved, thus permitted not only to escape their dangers, but also to behold their enemies fallen under a chastisement which no words can express, through the power of God and not of man" (*Mos.* 2.255). The rabbis similarly comment on Exod 14:30: "And Israel saw the Egyptians dying upon the seashore": "There were four reasons why the Egyptians had to be dying upon the seashore in the sight of Israel: that the Israelites should not say: As we came out of the sea on this side, so the Egyptians may have come out of the sea on another side. That the Egyptians should not say: Just as we are lost in the sea, so the Israelites also are lost in the sea. That the Israelites might be enabled to take the spoil. . . . That the Israelites, setting their eyes upon them, should recognize them and reprove them" (*Mek. Beshallaḥ,* Lauterbach, 1:250). Cf. *Mek. Shirta* on Exod 15:2: "Thou stretchest out thy right hand, the earth swallowed them": The sea would cast them out to the land and the land would throw them back into the sea. The land said: "Even when I received only the blood of Abel, who was but one individual, it was said of me: 'And now cursed art thou from the ground, etc.' And now how can I receive the blood of all these troops? So that the Holy One, blessed be He, had to swear to it: 'I shall not make you stand trial'" (cf. Ps-Jonathan ad loc.; *PRE* 42, end).

boundless. ek bathous abyssou. abyssos is either the adjective ('bottomless'), as is always the case in Classical Greek, or the substantive *hē abyssos* as in the LXX (Fichtner prefers the former).

20. *spoiled the godless. skyleuō* is to strip or despoil a slain enemy, especially of his arms. Demetrius, the earliest known Greco-Jewish writer (last quarter of third century BCE), had already attempted to find an answer to the question that someone had raised (*epizētein de tina*) as to how the Israelites, who had left Egypt unarmed (deduced from Exod

5:3, despite Exod 13:18, since Demetrius was apparently following the LXX which translated *waḥamusîm* not as 'armed' but 'in the fifth generation,' in spite of Gen 15:16; cf. *MRS* on Exod 13:18: "Some left in the fourth and some in the fifth generation"), somehow managed to obtain arms. "It appears," he writes, "that those who had not been overwhelmed in the sea [i.e. the Israelites], made use of the others' [i.e. the Egyptians'] arms" (*FPG:* 179; Jacoby *FGH:* 3C:670–671). Demetrius' surmise becomes historical fact for Josephus: "On the morrow, the arms of the Egyptians having been carried up to the Hebrews' camp by the tide and the force of the wind setting in that direction, Moses, surmising that this too was due to the providence of God, to ensure that even in weapons they should not be wanting, collected them and, having accoutred the Hebrews therein led them forward to Mount Sinai" (*Ant.* 2.16.6). (See Freudenthal 1875–79:46.)

with one accord. homothymadon is very frequent in the LXX. Cf. II Enoch 19:6; *Ascension of Isaiah* 7:15; 8:18; 9:28 (cf. Rom 15:6). In the *Test. Sol.* 18:2 we read that the thirty-six *kosmokratores* answer Solomon *homothymadon mia phōnē,* and in the description of the celestial *Kedushah* (Isa 6:3) preserved in the *Hekhaloth* texts we read that the Holy Living Creatures sing songs and hymns "with one voice, with one utterance, with one mind, and with one melody." Similarly in one of the oldest hymns introducing the main mystery of the Mass, all kinds of angels, cherubim and serafim praise God's glory, *quia non cessant clamare cotidie, una voce dicentes: Sanctus Sanctus Sanctus Dominus Deus Sabaoth*" (see Scholem:29–30); cf. also *Hypostasis of the Archons* (*CG* II), 145.17–21. This conceit may perhaps be traced to an Iranian source. The Bounteous Immortals (*Ameša Spentas*) are seven beings who are "of one mind, of one voice, of one act; whose mind is one, whose voice is one, whose act is one, whose father and ruler is one, the Creator, Ahura Mazda" (*Yasht.* 19.16–18; cf. *Zatspram* 35.1 [see Zaehner 1972:455]).

champion might. For *hypermachon* cf. 16:17; II Macc 8:36; 14:34; *Sib Or* 3:708–709: the Immortal One himself will be their champion (*hypermachos*) and the hand of the Holy One.

21. *opened the mouth of the dumb.* Cf. Exod 4:10; Philo *Mut.* 56.

tongues of infants. The author is alluding to an early Jewish tradition that even the infants sang God's praises. Cf. *Tosef.Sotah* 6.4: "R. Jose the Galilean says, when the Israelites came up out of the sea, and saw that their enemies were dead corpses lying upon the seashore, they recited a song of praise. When the babe lying on its mother's lap and the suckling at his mother's breast saw the divine presence, the former raised his neck, and the latter let go of his mother's breasts, and they all responded with a song of praise, saying, 'This is my God, and I will glorify him.' R. Meir said, even foetuses in their mothers' wombs sang a song of praise, for it is said, 'In assemblies bless God, the Lord, O you who are from the fountain of Israel' (Ps 68:27)"; *Mek. Shirta* 1, Lauterbach, 2:11 (where Ps 8:3 is quoted by R. Jose); *PT Sotah* 5.4,20a; *BT Sotah* 30b; *Targ.Yerush.* to Exod 15:2: "From their mothers' breasts even the children have given signs with their fingers to their fathers, and said, This is our God, who nourished us with honey from the rock, and with oil from the stone of clay, at the time when our mothers went forth upon the face of the field to give us birth, and leave us there and He sent an angel who washed us and enwrapped us, and now we will praise Him"; *ShR* 23.9; *Mid.Teh.* 8.5, Buber 39a (cf. also Luke 1:41; Augustine *Civ.Dei* 3.31. See Grelot 1961b:49–60); E. Levine, "Neofiti 1: A Study of Exodus 15," *Biblica* 54 (1973) 307.

articulate. For *tranas,* cf. Isa 35:6, LXX.

C. DIVINE WISDOM OR JUSTICE IN THE EXODUS (11–19)

XXI. First Antithesis: Nile water changed to blood, but Israelites obtained water from the desert rock (11:1–14)

Excursus I: Nature and Purpose of Divine Mercy (XXII–XXIV)

XXII. God's Mercy toward the Egyptians and its causes (His Might the source of His Merciful Love) (11:15 – 12:2)

XXIII. God's Mercy toward the Canaanites and its causes (12:3–18)

XXIV. God's Mercy a model lesson for Israel (12:19–22)

XXV. Return to theme of measure for measure and transition to second Excursus (12:23–27)

Excursus II: On Idolatry (XXVI–XXXI)

XXVI. Mindless nature worship (13:1–9)

XXVII. Wretched wooden-image making (13:10 – 14:11)

XXVIII. Origin and evil consequences of idolatry (14:12–31)

XXIX. Israel's immunity from idolatry (15:1–6)

XXX. Malicious manufacture of clay figurines (15:7–13)

XXXI. Folly of Egyptian idolatry (15:14–19)

XXXII. Second Antithesis: Egyptians hunger through animal plague, but Israel enjoys exotic quail food (16:1–4)

XXXIII. Third Antithesis: Egyptians slain by locusts and flies, but Israel survives a serpent attack through the bronze serpent, symbol of salvation (16:5–14)

XXXIV. Fourth Antithesis: Egyptians plagued by thunderstorms but Israel fed by a rain of manna (16:15–29)

XXXV. Fifth Antithesis: Egyptians terrified by darkness, but Israel illuminated with bright light and guided through desert by a pillar of fire (17:1 – 18:4)

XXXVI. Sixth Antithesis: Egyptian firstborn destroyed, but Israel protected and glorified (18:5–25)

XXXVII. Seventh Antithesis: Egyptians drowned in the sea, but Israel passes safely through (19:1–9)

XXXVIII. Retrospective review of God's wonders through which Nature was refashioned for Israel (19:10–12)

XXXIX. Egypt more blameworthy than Sodom (19:13–17)

XL. Transposition of the elements (11:18–21)

XLI. Concluding doxology (19:22)

XXI. FIRST ANTITHESIS: NILE WATER CHANGED TO BLOOD, BUT ISRAELITES OBTAINED WATERS FROM THE DESERT ROCK (11:1–14)

11

1 Their works prospered at the hand of a holy prophet.
2 They traveled through an uninhabited solitude,
and pitched tents in untrodden wastes;
3 they stood their ground against their enemies, and beat off
hostile foes.
4 They thirsted and called upon you,
and water was given them out of a flinty rock,
and quenching of their thirst out of hard stone.
5 For by those very things through which their enemies were
punished, they in their want were benefited:
6 In place of the perennial source of streaming water,
turbid with gore
7 as a reproach for their edict for the slaying of infants,
you gave the Israelites abundant water when all hope was
gone,
8 demonstrating by the thirst they had then endured
how you punished their antagonists.
9 For when they were put to the test, though disciplined
compassionately,
they understood how the godless, brought to trial in anger,
were tormented.
10 Your own people you made trial of like a reproving father,
but those others you scrutinized like a stern king passing
sentence.
11 Both at home and abroad, they were equally devastated:
12 for a twofold pain overtook them,
and a groaning over memories of things bygone.
13 When they learned that through their own punishments
the others were being benefited, they took note of the Lord.

14 The castaway whom formerly during the exposure of
        infants they had scornfully disowned,
     they came in the event to admire,
     having thirsted in a manner unlike the righteous.

NOTES

11:1-14. Introductory narrative, in which we are told of the successful
advance of the Israelites through the desert.

11:1. *Their works prospered. eusdoō* is frequent in the LXX as a transitive verb. Cf. Gen 24:40; Sir 15:10. It is also used intransitively in Isa
54:17; Jer 12:1; and II Chron 18:14, LXX; and in Theophrastus *De
Causis Plantarum* 5.6.7. Grimm (followed by Fichtner) connects this
verse with the end of chap. 10, taking *euodoō* transitively and making
Wisdom its subject, but Reese has argued (1965:392) that this is contrary to the structure of the poem. After introducing Wisdom six times
with the emphatic *hautē,* our author would hardly abandon this rhetorical
device at the climax. Reese, therefore, retains the verse with Ziegler at the
beginning of chap. 11, and translates it as follows: "Their works succeeded at the holy prophet's hand." (He also notes that the word play
euodōsen/diōdeusan links 11:1-2.) Wright (1967c:176), on the other
hand, considers Reese's translation unlikely. "The holy prophet," he
writes, "is clearly Moses and he appears precisely in the role of instrument in 10:16*ff.* In chaps. 11–19 God acts directly and Moses appears
only secondarily (11:14 and 18:5). So 11:1 would provide a discordant
introduction to 11–19 but goes quite naturally with what precedes as a
summary: 'She made their affairs prosper through the holy prophet.' If
the word play *euodōsen/diōdeusan* links 11:1-2 it is as a mot crochet."
Wright's objection, however, does not seem to me to carry much weight.
It would be well in keeping with the style and thought of the author of
Wisd to move almost imperceptibly from the attribution of certain historical events to the instrumentality of Wisdom (or the prophet she inspires)
to their attribution directly to God, since with him, as with Philo, Wisdom
is in reality the Divine Mind, and therefore virtually synonymous with
the Deity. Philo's discourse about nature, similarly, at times passes over
almost unconsciously into speech about God, a usage almost equivalent to
Spinoza's famous locution: *Deus sive Natura (Sacr.* 98*ff; Mig.* 128; Goodenough 1969:51). As to Reese's main point, however, it can be argued
that if the verse is only a summarizing conclusion one should not in that
case expect the emphatic *hautē.* Yet this verse does seem either unnec-

essary or out of place at the end of chap. 10, and I therefore prefer Reese's rendition.

at the hand of. A common Hebraism. Cf. Neh 9:14; Ps 76:20.

a holy prophet. I.e. Moses. Cf. Hosea 12:14.

2. *tents.* See Lev 23:43.

3. *enemies.* I.e. the Amalekites (Exod 17:8–16), Arad, Siḥon, and Og (Num 21), and the Midianites (Num 31:1–12).

4. *They thirsted and called upon you.* An idealized picture suggested by Ps 107:6. Compare the positive tradition of the wilderness which appears especially in such passages as Deut 32:10*ff;* Hosea 2:16; 11:1*ff;* 13:4*ff;* Jer 2:1*ff.* B. S. Childs feels that just as Ezekiel used his great freedom in intensifying the negative side of the murmuring tradition, other prophets, such as Hosea and Jeremiah, isolated the positive elements which had always been there for a particular purpose (1974:263).

a flinty rock. akrotomos is the LXX rendering of Hebrew *ḥalamiš* in Deut 8:15; Job 28:9; Ps 114:8; cf. Philo *Mos.* 1.210.

quenching of their thirst. Cf. IV Macc 3:10: *iasasthai tēn dipsan;* Philo *Mos.* 1.211: *akos dipsous; Post.* 138; *Somn.* 2.60.

5. In an elaborate *synkrisis* or 'comparison,' the author employs seven antitheses (the first one here, the other six in 16:1 – 19:22) to illustrate his chosen theme: that Egypt was punished measure for measure, whereas Israel was benefited by those very things whereby Egypt was punished (see Focke 1913:12–15; and for the use of *synkrisis* in Greek literature, his "Synkrisis," 1923:327–368; Stein, 1934:558–574; Heinemann 1948:241–251; *Darke ha-Agadah* [Jerusalem, 1970] 44–55). Definitions of this rhetorical term may be found in the Progymnasmata of Aelius Theon, Hermogenes, Aphthonius, Joannes Sardianus, and Nicolaus. The *synkrisis* is essentially a comparative arrangement of either good or bad persons or things, through which one tries to show that the objects of comparison are either equal, better, or worse. According to Focke, in all *synkriseis,* the weaker side comes first, the winning side last, as also in Wisd. Cf. Isa 65:13, where the order is the reverse. Fichtner has pointed out that already in the biblical account, the contrast between the fate of the Egyptians and the Israelites is clearly spelled out in five of the ten plagues (Exod 8:16*ff;* 9:4*ff;* 9:26*ff;* 10:23; 12:7*ff;* cf. Philo *Mos.* 1.143; "And the strangest thing of all was that the same elements in the same place and at the same time brought destruction to one people and safety to the other." Wisd's comparisons, however, are not at all uniform, and some of them are obviously quite forced. Although there is apparently no rabbinic equivalent to Wisd's particular form of *synkrisis,* it should be noted that the rabbis had elaborate ten-part 'comparisons' contrasting God and man. In *Mek. Shirta* 8 we have a section with the formula "the rule with flesh and flood. . . . But He Who spoke and the World Came to Be." Ten

such statements are made. (Cf. the series of seven contrasts between God and the idols in *MRS* on Exod 15:11.) Similarly, in *Wayyik.R.* 18.5, we have a series of ten antitheses between God and man. As Stein has already pointed out, the last of these antitheses is somewhat reminiscent of Wisd's form of *synkrisis:* "The Holy One blessed be He heals by the same means whereby He smites."

6. *perennial source of streaming water.* I.e. the Nile. According to Philo, "the river changed to blood, but not for the Hebrews; for when they wished to draw from it, it turned into good drinking water" (*Mos.* 1.144; cf. Jos. *Ant.* 2.14.1; *ShR* 9.11; *Midrash Hagadol* 7.24).

turbid with gore. haimati lythrōdei is pleonastic, since *lythrōdēs* means 'defiled with gore'. *lythrōdēs* is first attested here. Cf. *AP* 9.258 (Antiphanes Megalopolitanus, first century CE).

7. *as a reproach.* We find the same notion in *Mishnat R. Eliezer* 19, Enelau:344, where it is stated that God plagued the waters of the Nile because the Egyptians had cast the children of the Israelites into the Nile. In Ps-Jonathan on Exod 2:23 it is stated that Pharaoh was stricken with leprosy and commanded that the firstborn of the Hebrews be slain so that he could bathe in their blood. Cf. *ShR* 1.41 (where there is the further elaboration that Pharaoh's leprosy could not be cured unless 150 Israelite children were slaughtered every morning and 150 every evening so that he could bathe in their blood).

edict for the slaying of infants. nēpioktonos is found only here (it occurs again once in Patristic Greek). Cf. the similar formation *mētroktonos* (Aeschylus *Agamemnon* 1281; Euripides *Orestes* 1649; Plato *Laws* 869B). For *diatagma,* cf. Ezra 7:11, LXX (for Aramaic/Persian *nishtiwan*); Esther 3B:4, LXX (Hanhart); Philodemus *Rhetorica* 2.2895; Diodorus 18.64; Philo (who uses it very frequently): *Sacr.* 88; *Post.* 95; etc. According to Bickerman *diatagma* never occurs in Ptolemaic documents (1976:258, n.41). Cf. Pelletier:280ff (in the Roman period, the imperial decrees are called *diatagmata*).

8. *demonstrating by the thirst they had then endured.* The author here enunciates a principle which recurs at 16:4 (cf. 18:20), to the effect that it was pedagogically necessary that the Israelites should have a taste of their enemies' punishments. There is no analogue to this in our extant versions of the rabbinic writings, but R. Ḥayyim Yoseph David Azulai (known by his acronym Ḥida, 1724–1806) writes in his book *Pene David* 54a: "The rabbis of blessed memory said that all the plagues were visited upon Israel for a little while (*bereg'a katan;* cf. Isa 54:7) but they were immediately delivered, and this was necessary in order for them to realize the power of the plagues" (cited by M. Kasher, *Torah Shelemah,* 10/11:286, with the admission that the source of these words was unknown to him). Kasher further cites R. Yom Tov b. Abraham Ishbili

(known by his acronym Ritba, 1250–1330), Menahem b. Solomon Meiri (1249–1316), and Maimonides as stating in the name of the rabbis that the plague of lice also afflicted the Israelites although it did not pain them (Kasher, 9/10:66,129). Ibn Ezra on Exod 7:24, similarly takes the absence of an explicit notice that the Israelites were exempt from the first three plagues to mean that they affected the Egyptians and Israelites alike, but did little harm. According to Philo, on the other hand, none of the plagues touched the Hebrews (*Mos.* 1.143). Cf. NOTE on 11:6.

9. *put to the test . . . disciplined compassionately.* Cf. Deut 8:2–5; *Mek. Bahodesh* 10; Philo *Spec.* 4.180: "The orphan-like desolate state of his people is always an object of pity and compassion to the Ruler of the Universe whose portion it is." See also NOTE on 3:5.

10. *like a reproving father.* Cf Deut 8:5; Jos. *Ant.* 3.15.1; Ps Sol 13:9.

11. *at home and abroad.* At home, in Egypt, they were afflicted with the plagues, and abroad, in pursuit of the Israelites, they were overwhelmed in the sea. Cf. *Mek. Beshallah* on Exod 14:25: "R. Jose says How can you prove that those Egyptians who had remained in Egypt were smitten with the same plague with which those who were at the sea were smitten, and that the one group even saw the other suffering? It is in this sense that it is said, 'So that the Egyptians said: "Let us flee from the face of Israel, for the Lord fighteth for them in Egypt."'"

12. *a twofold pain.* They were pained both at their own calamity, and the fact that it brought deliverance to the Israelites. For *diplē lypē,* cf. Philo *Mos.* 1.137: *diploun penthos.*

14. *having thirsted in a manner unlike the righteous.* An understated way of describing the much severer form of thirst suffered by the Egyptians. Note the parallel with the belated appreciation of the righteous man in chap. 5.

XXII. GOD'S MERCY TOWARD THE EGYPTIANS AND ITS CAUSES (HIS MIGHT THE SOURCE OF HIS MERCIFUL LOVE)
(11:15 – 12:2)

11   15 In repayment for their wicked and witless reasoning,
     by which they were misled into worshiping brute reptiles
         and worthless beasts,
     you sent against them a swarm of creatures devoid of
         reasoning;
   16 that they might know that by those things through which a
         man sins, through them he is punished.
   17 For your all-powerful hand
     which created the world out of formless matter
     did not lack the means to send upon them an army of bears
         or brazen lions
   18 or unknown monsters newly created, filled with fury,
     either snorting out blasts of fiery breath,
     or scattering thunderous fumes,
     or flashing fearful sparks from their eyes,
   19 who could utterly annihilate them not only by the harm
         they might inflict,
     but could destroy them by their terrifying appearance
         alone.
   20 Even without these they might have been laid low by a
         single breath,
     pursued by justice
     and scattered by the breath of your power,
     but you ordered all things by measure and number and
         weight.
   21 To exert supreme force is at all times your option,
     and who could resist the might of your arm?

22 For in your sight the entire cosmos is as a turn of the scale,
and as a dewdrop in the dawn alighting on the earth.
23 But you have compassion over all, because you can do all,
and you overlook the sins of men with a view to their
repentance.
24 For you love all that exists,
and loathe nothing which you have created;
for if you had hated anything you would never have
fashioned it.
25 How could anything have endured, had it not been your
will,
or that which was undesignated by you have been
preserved?
26 But you spare all because they are yours, O Sovereign
Lord, lover of all that lives;

12 1 for your imperishable spirit is in them all.
2 For this reason you correct those that err little by little,
and jogging their memories by means of the very things
in which they go wrong you admonish them,
so that they may be released from their vicious ways and
put their trust in you, O Lord.

NOTES

11:15–12:2. The Egyptians could have been smashed with one fell blow, had the Deity so wished. God, however, never acts arbitraily, but always according to the laws of his own being. His omnipotence guarantees the unbiased character of his all-embracing love. The act of creation is itself a manifestation of this love, and precludes the possibility of divine hatred toward any of his creatures. The deity therefore compassionately overlooks the sins of men with a constant view to their repentance, and his punishments are at first only pedagogic.

11:15. *brute reptiles and worthless beasts*. The collocution *herpeta kai knōdala* is found in Ps-Aristeas 138: "What need even to speak of other infatuated (*polymataiōn*) people, Egyptians and their like, who have put their reliance in wild beasts and most creeping creatures and animals (*herpetōn . . . kai knōdalōn*) and worship these, and to these offer sacrifice, whether alive or dead?" Cf. Ps-Aristeas 169; *Sib Or* Frag. 3:22–28, 30.

On Egyptian animal worship, see Philo *Decal.* 76–80: "Strangers on their first arrival in Egypt before the vanity of the land has gained a lodgement in their minds are like to die with laughing at it, while anyone who knows the flavor of right instruction, horrified at this veneration of things so much the reverse of venerable, pities those who render it and regards them with good reason as more miserable than the creatures they honor, as men with souls transformed into the nature of those creatures, so that as they pass before him, they seem beasts in human shape." Cf. Herodotus 2.65–74; Cicero *Tusc.* 5.78; *ND* 1.43: "the insane mythology of Egypt"; 3.39; Strabo 17.1.38–40, 47; Juvenal 15.1–15; Plutarch *Is. et Os.* 380AB; Eusebius *PE* 3.2.3; Aristides *Apologia* 12. Both Cicero and Juvenal exhibit a mocking attitude toward Egyptian animal worship. Octavian, when asked if he would like to visit the Apis bull, remarked: "My custom is to worship gods, not cattle" (Dio Cassius 51.16.5).

creatures devoid of reasoning. alogon zōon is a technical expression in Greek philosophy for brute animals, and is very frequent in Philo (see Leisegang, Index, s.v. *alogos* [vols. 7:1 and 7:2 in the Cohn-Wendland edition of Philo's works constitute Leisegang's Index]); cf. IV Macc 14:14, 18; Jos. *Ag.Ap.* 2.213. The Stoics made a sharp distinction between nonrational animals and men (*SVF* 2.725–726) (also simply *aloga,* "brutes": Democritus DK, B.164; Plato *Protagoras* 321C).

16. We have in this verse an explicit statement of the principle of talion, which forms such a central thread of the author's elaborate *synkrisis.* According to G. R. Driver and J. C. Miles, "talion was a fundamental principle of early law and was only gradually replaced by a system of fixed composition" (*The Babylonian Laws* [Oxford, 1960] 1. 408). "It has been pointed out, however," writes R. Yaron, "that the Code of Urnammu, preceding the Laws of Eshnunna and the Code of Hammurabi by centuries, is based on a system of fixed penalties, in silver. It is even possible that talion may have been introduced by Hammurabi himself. To the present-day observer talion appears as 'primitive, archaic, barbaric.' One may readily accept all these attributes as perfectly correct, but they should not be allowed to distort the true perspective. Talion is not primary, original: on the contrary, it cannot be disputed that within the sources at present available pecuniary penalties constitute the earlier system" (*The Laws of Eshnunna* [Jerusalem, 1969] 174–175). Cf. the interesting remarks of Thucydides 3.45.3; A. S. Diamond, "An Eye for an Eye," *Iraq* 19 (1957) 151–155; *The Evolution of Law and Order* (London, 1951) 288–300; J. J. Finkelstein, "Ammisaduqa's Edict and the Babylonian Law Codes," *JCS* 15 (1961): 98; B. S. Jackson, *Theft in Early Jewish Law* (Oxford, 1972) 153. See also *The Instruction for King Merikare:* "A blow is to be repaid with its own like. That is the application of all that has been done" (*ANET:*417). The law of retaliation occurs three times in the Penta-

teuch (Exod 21:23*ff;* Lev 24:18*ff;* Deut 19:21), and appears frequently in the Apocrypha and Pseudepigrapha. Cf. Jub 4:31–32; 48:14; II Macc 4:38; 13:8; 5:10; 15:32*ff;* Test.*Gad* 5:10; *LAB* 44:10; 43:5; 45:3; Matt 7:2. The rabbis were equally fond of elaborating this principle. Cf. *M.Sotah* 1.7–9: "With the kind of measure that a man measures they shall mete [out] to him: she [the faithless wife] adorned herself for transgression, the Almighty reduced her to shame; she exposed herself for transgression, the Almighty laid her bare; with her thigh did she first begin transgression, and then with the belly, therefore shall the thigh be stricken first and afterward the belly. . . . Samson went after his eyes, therefore the Philistines gouged out his eyes. . . . Absalom glorified in his hair, hence he was suspended by his hair; and because he copulated with the ten concubines of his father, therefore they thrust ten javelins into him . . . and since he stole three hearts—the heart of his father and the heart of the court and the heart of Israel, therefore three darts were thrust into him"; *Tosef. Sotah,* where two full chapters (3–4) laboriously elaborate our theme; *BT Sotah* 11a; *BR* 9.11; *Mek. Shirta* 4 (where we get five consecutive examples of our principle, with two more in chs. 5–6); *Lament.R., Petiḥ.* 21; *PT Ḥag.* 2.2, 77d. Lieberman has shown that section 39 of the *Apocalypse of Paul* is dependent on rabbinic material (1974:35). See also Philo *Spec.* 3.181–183; *Flac.* 170–175, 189; *Mos.* 2.202; *QG* 1.77; Jos. *Ag.Ap.* 2.143; *Ant.* 11.6.11; *J.W.* 1.36; 2.18.1; (cf. I. Heinemann, *Philons griechische und jüdische Bildung* [Breslau, 1932] 349–383).

17. *formless matter.* For *amorphou hylēs,* see Aristotle *Physica* 191a,10: *hē hylē kai to amorphon;* Plato *Timaeus* 50D; Posidonius: *tēn tōn holōn ousian kai hylēn apoion kai amorphon einai* (F 92, Kidd; Philo *Spec.* 1.328–329). For a detailed analysis, see Introduction and Winston 1971.

bears or brazen lions. Philo raises exactly the same question as the author of Wisd and his first answer is similar to that given here in v. 23: "Someone perhaps may ask why he punished the land through such petty and insignificant creatures, and refrained from using bears and lions and panthers and other kinds of savage beasts. . . . First, God wished to admonish the inhabitants of the land rather than to destroy them. . . . And after this the inquirer shall be taught a further lesson. . . . When men make war, they look round to find the most powerful auxiliaries to fight beside them . . . but God, the highest and greatest power, needs no one. But if, at any time, he wills to use any as instruments for his vengeance, he does not choose the strongest and the greatest . . . but provides the slightest and the smallest with irresistible and invincible powers. So it was in this case. For what is slighter than a gnat? Yet so great was its power that all Egypt lost heart, and was forced to cry aloud: 'This is the finger of

God'; for as for his hand not all the habitable world from end to end could stand against it" (*Mos.* 1.109–112).

18. *snorting out blasts*. Cf. the description of Leviathan in Job 41:10–13: "His sneezings flash forth light . . . out of his mouth go burning torches, and sparks of fire leap forth. Out of his nostrils goeth smoke, as out of a seething pot and burning rushes."

19. *who could utterly annihilate them*. Cf. Exod 9:15: "I could have stretched forth My hand and stricken you and your people with pestilence, and you would have been effaced from the earth." *synektripsai* is found only here.

20. *by a single breath*. Cf. Job 4:9; Ps 18:16; Isa 11:4.

justice. Cf. IV Macc 4:13.

by measure and number and weight. God's actions are never arbitrary or random, but always follow the mathematical laws by which he governs the entire cosmos. Disproportionate punishments such as those described in vv. 17–19 are therefore inevitably ruled out. Cf. Job 28:25; Isa 40:12; IV Ezra 4:36–37: "For he has weighed the age in the balance, and with measure has measured the times, and by number has numbered the seasons." Philo, who had a very strong affinity for the Neopythagorean tradition, placed special emphasis on this notion. *Somn.* 2.193: "But Moses held that God . . . is the measure and weighing scale and numbering of all things (*stathmēn kai metron kai arithmon tōn holōn*)"; *Prov.*, ap. Eusebius *PE* 7.21.336b[626]: "For it would be monstrous to suppose that while particular craftsmen when framing something, especially anything costly, estimate (*stathmēsasthai*) what material is just sufficient, He who invented numbers, measures (*arithmous kai metra*) and equality in them had no thought for what was adequate"; *Her.* 152: "As for proportional equality, we find it practically in everything great or small, throughout the whole world"; *Her.* 156: "They judge that the master art of God by which He wrought all things is one that admits of no heightening or lowering of intensity (*oute epitasin oute anesin;* cf. Wisd 16:24) but always remains the same and that through its transcendent excellence it has wrought in perfection each thing that is, every number and every form that tends to perfectness being used to the full by the Maker"; *Her.* 143: "God alone is exact in judgment and alone is able to 'divide in the middle' things material and immaterial, in such a way that no section is greater or less than another by even an infinitesimal difference." Cf. also *Test.Naphtali* 2:3: "for by weight and measure and rule (*stathmō kai gar metrō kai kanoni*) was all the creation made"; I Enoch 43:2; Ps Sol 5:6; Sophocles Frag. 432; Gorgias *Palamedes,* DK, B.11a,30; Plato *Rep.* 602D; *Laws* 575B: "the equality determined by measure, weight, and number (*tēn metrō isēn kai stathmō kai arithmō*);" *Philebus* 55E; *Euthyphro* 7BC; Xenophon

Mem. 1.1.9; Claudianus Mamertus *De Statu Animae* 2.3. See Genzmer, 1952:469–494. (Wisd 11:20 is quoted by Augustine *Civ.Dei* 11.30.)

22. *a turn of the scale.* Cf. Isa 40:15, where the Hebrew *šaḥaq mō'znayim* ('dust on a balance') is translated in the LXX by *rhopē zugou.*

as a dewdrop in the dawn. Cf. Hosea 6:4; 13:3.

23. *you have compassion over all, because you can do all.* Cf. 12:16 below; Pss 62:12–13; 145:9; Sir 18:11–13; Ps-Aristeas 192: "God does not smite them according to their shortcomings or according to the greatness of his strength, but he uses forbearance"; 211: "God, to whom nothing is needful, is also gentle"; III Macc 6:2; Philo *Spec.* 1.308: "Yet vast as are His excellences and powers, He takes pity and compassion on those most helplessly in need."

repentance. Cf. Ezek. 33:11; 18:32; Ps-Aristeas 188; *PT Mak.* 2.6, 31d; *BT Yoma* 86b; Rom 2:4–5. Although Philo awards it only the second prize and recognizes the bitterness attached to it (*QE* 1.15), he nevertheless (unlike the Stoics) places repentance among the virtues and considers it the mark of a man of wisdom (*Virt.* 177; *Abr.* 26; *Somn.* 1.91; *Spec.* 1.103; *QG* 2.13).

24. *you love all that exists.* Cf. Ps 145:8–9; Philo *Cher.* 99; *Spec.* 3.36; *Op.* 21; Plato *Tim.* 29E.

and loathe nothing. We read similarly in Sir 15:11: "Say not, 'From God is my transgression,' for that which He hateth made He not." Contrast 1QS 3.25: "He created the spirits of light and darkness, and upon them he founded every work and every action. . . . The one God loves for all eternity, and delights in all its doings forever; the other—its assembly he loathes, and all its ways he hates forever."

25. *How could anything have endured.* A sentiment much emphasized in the Qumran hymns: "and nothing exists except by Thy will . . . what strength shall I have unless Thou keep me upright?" (1QH 1.10 and 6). Philo similarly writes: "and that nothing whose being He had willed would ever be brought to nought" (*Mos.* 2.61).

undesignated. Cf. Isa 41:4; 48:13; Eccles 6:10; *CD* 2:11; IV Ezra 10:57; Rom 8:28; 4:17.

26. *yours.* Cf. Ezek 18:4.

lover of all that lives. philopsychos in Classical Greek means 'loving one's life,' with the collateral sense of 'cowardly' (Euripides *Hecuba* 348). The favorable sense of the word is only found again in Patristic Greek. Cf., however, Xenophon *Mem.* 1.4.7: "The handiwork of a wise and loving (*philozōou*) creator." One of the recurring prayers in the Jewish High Holy Day liturgy expresses this sentiment well: "Remember us unto life, O King who desires life, and inscribe us in the book of life."

12:1. *is in them all.* The universal nature of God's compassion is also emphasized by Ben Sira: "The mercy of man is (exercised upon) his own kin, But the mercy of God is (extended) to all flesh, Reproving, and chastening, and teaching, And bringing them back as a shepherd his flock" (18:13). The rabbis, too, speak of God's compassion for the Egyptians: "The ministering angels wanted to chant their hymns, but the Holy One blessed be He said, 'The work of my hands is being drowned in the sea, and shall you chant hymns?'" (*BT Meg.* 10b). Cf. *PRK.*, Suppl. 2.8, Braude-Kapstein: "Why does Scripture give no command to rejoice during Passover? Because the Egyptians died during Passover. Therefore, though we read the entire Hallel on each of the seven days of Sukkot [an entirely joyful feast], on Passover we read the entire Hallel only on the first day and on the night preceding it, because of what is said in the verse which Samuel loved to quote, 'Rejoice not when thine enemy falleth' (Prov 24:17)" (cf. *M. Aboth* 4.19). See J. Heinemann, *Aggadah and Its Development* (Hebrew) (Jerusalem, 1974):175–178.

in them all. Cf. *Sib Or* Frag. 1.5: "the Creator who has planted his sweet spirit in all and made him a guide to all mortals."

2. *trust in you. pisteuein* with prepositions is not Classical, but found in the LXX and New Testament.

12   3 The ancient inhabitants, too, of your holy land, 4 who were hateful to you for their loathsome practices, acts of sorcery and licentious mystery rites; 5 ruthless slayers of their children, and entrail-devouring banqueters of human flesh, initiates from the midst of a Dionysian blood revel, 6 and parents, murderers of helpless souls, it was your will to destroy at the hand of our forefathers, 7 so that the land which is of all lands most precious in your eyes might receive a worthy migration of God's children. 8 Yet these too you spared as being men, and sent wasps as the advance guard of your army to exterminate them gradually. 9 It was not through inability to subject the godless to the righteous in pitched battle, or with cruel beasts or a relentless word to wipe them out at once, 10 but judging them gradually you gave them space for repentance, not unaware that their seed was evil, and their viciousness innate, and that their mode of thought would in no way vary to the end of time, 11 for their race was accursed from the very first. Nor was it out of wariness of anyone that you granted them amnesty for those things in which they sinned; 12 for who shall say to you, "What have you done?" or who shall take issue with your decision? Who shall bring a charge against you for having destroyed nations of your own making? Who shall come as an avenger of the unrighteous to plead their cause before you? 13 For neither is there any God beside you who cares for all to induce you to demonstrate that your verdict was not unjust, 14 nor is there king or ruler who shall be able to defy you in regard to those whom you have punished. 15 But being just you manage all things justly, counting it out of keeping with your power to condemn one who is not deserving of punishment. 16 For your might is the source of justice, and it is your mastery over all which causes you to spare all. 17 You exhibit your power when there is disbelief in the perfection of your might,

and the insolence of those well aware of it you put to confusion.
18 But while disposing of might, you judge in fairness, and govern us
with great forbearance, for the power is yours whenever you will.

NOTES

12:3–18. There is a clear intent in this section to justify the Israelite
conquest of Canaan. In Jewish-Hellenistic apologetics, this issue occupied
no small place as may easily be inferred from the author of Jubilees' brazen rewriting of Genesis in order to prove that the land of Canaan was
from the beginning allotted to Shem and illegally seized by Canaan (Jub.
8:8–11; 9:14–15; 10:29–34; cf. *BR* 56.14, Th-Alb:608; *Mid.Teh.* 76.3,
where Melchizedek is identified with Shem, thereby indicating that Palestine is his heritage), and Philo's openly apologetic account of the conquest
of Canaan. The latter sheepishly suggests that perhaps the Israelites "were
unwarlike and feeble, quite few in numbers and destitute of warlike equip-
ment, but won the respect of their opponents who voluntarily surrendered
their land to them" (*Hypothetica* 356). (See the excellent discussion in
Johanan Levy, *Studies in Jewish Hellenism* [Hebrew] [Jerusalem, 1960]
60–78.)

12:3. *holy land.* For this designation, cf. Zech 2:16; II Macc 1:7; *Test.
Job* 33:5; Ps-Philo LAB 19:10; *Sib Or* 3:267; II Bar 63:10; 84:8; Philo
Her. 293. According to S. Zeitlin, the term 'the Holy Land' was "used
only by Jews who lived outside Judaea. Neither in Josephus nor in 'tannaitic' literature do we find it applied to Judaea" (see the note to II Macc
1:7 in his edition of *The Second Book of Maccabees* [New York, 1954]).

4. *acts of sorcery.* Cf. I Enoch 7:1, where it is said that the angels
taught their human wives *pharmakeias kai epaoidas kai rhizotomias.*

licentious mystery rites. anosios in the LXX translates Hebrew *zimmāh.*
There is considerable evidence that some of the mystery cults, especially
that of Dionysus, involved sexual licentiousness. Livy, for example, tells us
regarding the Bacchanalia: "When wine had influenced their minds, and
night and the mingling of males with females, youth with age, had destroyed every sentiment of modesty, all varieties of corruption first began
to be practised, since each one had at hand the pleasure answering to that
to which his nature was more inclined" (*History of Rome* 39.8–18). We
find that the LXX had already used mystery terminology in translating
various biblical verses dealing with unchastity connected with idolatry
(Num 25:3: *kai etelesthē Israēl tō Beelphegōr,* i.e. they were consecrated

or initiated into the mysteries of Baal Peor; 25:5; Deut 23:17; Philo clearly understood these words as referring to initiation into the mysteries (*Spec.* 1.319–320); cf. Amos 7:9: *aphanisthēsontai bōmoi tou gelōtos kai hai teletai tou Israēl erēmosthēsontai.* *Gelōs* or *deus Risus* was associated with Dionysus: Philostratus *Imagines* 1.2; Plutarch *Lycurgus* 25.2. See Gutman 1963 1. 144–145).

5. *ruthless slayers of their children.* The sacrifices to Moloch described in the Bible (Lev 18:21; 20:2–5; Deut 12:31; 18:10; Jer 32:35; II Kings 23:10; Ezek 16:21; 20:31; 23:37; Ps 106:37–38) are certainly identical with the 'molk' sacrifices in North Africa, and they are, in Israel, something borrowed from the Phoenicians. Both archaeology and written texts indicate that the sacrifices of children were a current practice in the cult of Baal Hammon in North Africa and that they were kept up for a very long time (Quintus Curtius Rufus 4.3.23; Plutarch *Moralia* 552A, 171C, 175A; Diodorus 13.86.3; 20.14.4–6; Tertullian *Apologeticus* 9.2–4). These Punic sacrifices (also offered in the Punic dependencies of the Mediterranean, where excavations have revealed urns at Nora in Sardinia and at Motya in Sicily) were a heritage of the Phoenician country of origin (Porphyry *De Abstinentia* 2.56; Eusebius *PE* 4.6.16). (See R. de Vaux, *Studies in Old Testament Sacrifice* [Cardiff, 1964] 73–90; M. Weinfeld, "The Worship of Molech and the Queen of Heaven and Its Background," *UF* 4 [1972] 133–154; and Morton Smith's rejoinder, "A Note on Burning Babies," *JAOS* 95:3 [1975] 477–479.) It should also be noted that there is evidence of human sacrifice in Egypt during the Roman period, as practiced, for example, by the *Boukoloi,* a robber band of the Nile Delta. In Lollianos' romance *Phoinikika,* recently recovered from papyrus finds (*Cologne Papyrus* inv.3328), we have a gruesome description of the ritual murder of a child by a robber band, during which they remove the heart, roast it in the fire, and then after seasoning it, have the initiates consume it and take an oath while still holding a part of it in their hands. Moreover, the mystery meal in the cult of Dionysus-Zagreus apparently consisted of a dramatic representation of the consumption of this god's flesh and the drinking of his blood by the initiates. This would readily explain our author's allusion to the Dionysian revel band. See Albert Henrichs, *Die Phoinikika des Lollianos* (Bonn 1972) 28–79; J. G. Griffiths, "Human Sacrifices in Egypt: The Classical Evidence," *Annales du Service des Antiquités de l'Egypte* 48 (1948) 409ff.

entrail-devouring. splangchnophagon, an Aeschylean-type compound (for others cf. 10:3; 14:23), is first attested here. It occurs again only in Ps-Plutarch *Fluviis* 5.3. Cf. Aeschylus *Agamemnon* 1221; Plato *Rep.* 565D; Diodorus 22.5; Dio Cassius 27.30.3; 71.4.1.

banqueters of human flesh. "Since *phoneas* is supported by *mystas* and *authentas goneis,* it is better not to emend it to *phonas,* and to understand *thoinan* to signify by metonomy 'banqueters'" (see Holmes *APOT* 1 554). If, however, *thoinan* as the metonymical equivalent of *thoinatores* is unacceptable, we should then have to read *phonas* instead of the *phoneas* of the manuscripts and translate as follows: "ruthless slayings of children, and cannibal banquets of human flesh." The charge of cannibalism is an exaggeration (cf., however, Ezek 16:20), and turns the tables on those who (like Damocritus and Apion) had hurled this charge against the Jews. Apion accused the Jews of annually immolating a Greek victim, *gustare ex eius visceribus,* and swearing an oath of hostility to the Greeks (Stern: 1976:531, 412. Flusser [cited below] points out the similarity between Damocritus' account and the description of human sacrifice known from the Dionysiac cult, in Porphyry *De Abstinentia* 2.55). Cf. Tcherikover-Fuks 1957: 2. 437; Dio Cassius 68.32. See E. Bickermann, "Ritualmord u. Eselkult," *MGWJ* 71, N.F.35 (1927) 171–187; F. J. Dölger, "Sacramentum infanticidii," *Antike und Christentum* 4 (Münster, 1934): 188*ff.* David Gill has suggested that the author of Wisd simply got caught up in the similarities beween the Canaanites and the Greeks and absentmindedly exaggerated them. Alternatively, his use of the language of the tragedies may have been intentional, and he could be saying in effect that what applies explicitly to the Canaanites also applies by implication to the Greeks. His admonitions may indeed be directed at Hellenized Jews who took part in pagan mystery cults. (Gill 1965: 383–388.) Cf. III Macc 2:30–33; Grimm ad loc.; Cerfaux 29–88, esp. pp. 51–53; Philo *Spec.* 1.319*ff* (where he inveighs against the mysteries). It should also be noted that the ancient Canaanite religions were apparently still flourishing in Palestine in the first century CE. See D. Flusser, "Paganism in Palestine," in *The Jewish People in the First Century,* eds. S. Safrai and M. Stern (Philadelphia, 1976) 2. 1069–1079.

initiates from the midst of a Dionysian blood revel. With Reese (1970:27), we divide 12:5c as follows: *kai haimatos ek mesou mystas thiasou.* Cf. *Sib Or* 3:36: "O race that delights in blood."

6. *murderers.* Phrynichus explains *authentēs* by *autocheir phoneus,* "one who murders with his own hand." Cf. Aeschylus *Eumenides* 212; *Agamemnon* 1572. *Authentēs* is found in Herodotus, Thucydides, Euripides, and Apollonius Rhodius. It appears again in late prose but with the meaning 'perpetrator,' 'author' (Polybius 22.14.2; Diodorus 16.61) or 'master' (whence Turkish 'effendi') (*P. Mag. Leid. W.* 6.46: *authenta hēlie;* Hermas *Similitudes* 9.5.6). This usage was condemned by the Atticist Phrynicus (96). A. Dihle has deduced from this that Wisdom was written in the first century CE: "My point is that in this book the word *authentēs* is used in the meaning of 'murderer,' and this is the Attic meaning of the word which no Hellenistic writer would have applied in the first century BCE" (Colloquy 10 of the center for Hermeneutical Studies

[1974] 50). Cf. *Sib Or* 3:761–764: "Rear thine own offspring and slay it not"; Philo *Spec.* 3.110; *Virt.* 131; Jos. *Ag.Ap.* 2.202; Hecataeus of Abdera, in Stern: 29,33.

7. *most precious.* For the prevalence of this conceit in ancient Jewish literature, see Ginzberg 5. 14*ff;* W. D. Davies, *The Gospel and the Land* (Berkeley and Los Angeles, 1974) 15–74.

a worthy migration. The Canaanites had polluted the land (Lev 18:24–30) and were therefore spewed out of it, as being unworthy of living in the land owned by Yahweh and in which he dwelt. *apoikia* is here used in the sense of 'migration' rather than 'colony.' Cf. Philo *Mig.* 176; *Her.* 98; etc.

8. *wasps.* Cf. Exod 23:28. Aelianus (*De Natura Animalium* 11.28) reports that a swarm of wasps drove out the people of Phaselis (on the east coast of Lycia).

9. *at once.* For *hyph hen,* cf. Sext. *Math.* 10.123–124.

10. *judging them gradually.* Cf. Exod 23:29; Judg 2:29.

you gave them space. A Hebraism. Cf. Sir 4:5. (Goodrick thinks that it is a translation from the Latin, and cites Livy 24.26; 44.10: *poenitentiae relinquens locum.*) Frequent in Hellenistic Greek (Heb 12:17; Rom 12:19; Eph 4:27); cf. IV Ezra 9:12, Philo *Spec.* 1.58: *anachōrēsin eis metanoian; LA* 3.106: *chronon eis metanoian; LA* 105: "For it is God's property to hold out good things and to be beforehand in bestowing them, but to be slow to inflict evil things." A similar notion is found in Greek religious thought. The statue of the Delian Apollo held the graces in his right hand and bow and arrow in his left. This gave rise to an allegorical-ethical interpretation, namely, that the god holds the bow in his left hand "because he is slower to chastise if man repents" (Callimachus Frag. 114.8–11, Pfeiffer) (cf. Apollodorus' *Peri Theōn, FGH,* 244 F 15; Philo *Legat.* 95). See R. Pfeiffer, *Ausgewählte Schriften* (München, 1960): 55*ff*.

their seed was evil. A similar notion is found in IV Ezra 4:30: "For a grain of evil seed was sown in the heart of Adam from the beginning." In our text, however, it is applied only to the Canaanites.

11. *was accursed.* The reference is obviously to the curse laid upon Canaan (Gen 9:25–27), but there is no hint in the biblical text of a curse which entails moral degeneracy. Cf. Wisd 3:12; Sir 33:12: "Some he cursed (*katērasato*) and abased"; Jub 22:20–21: "Canaan erred, and all his seed shall be destroyed from off the earth . . . and none springing from him shall be saved on the day of judgment."

12. *"What have you done?"* Cf. Job 9:12; Eccles 8:4; Sir 36:8; 1QS 11:18: "There is none beside Thee to dispute Thy counsel or to understand all Thy holy design"; Dan 4:32; Rom 9:20.

take issue with your decision. For *antistēsetai,* cf. Job 9:19: *tis oun krimati autou antistēsetai;* Job 41:2; Jer 27:44, LXX; Nah 1:6, LXX; Ps 75:8, LXX; Judith 16:14: *kai ouk estin hos antistēsetai tē phonē sou;* Wisd 11:21.

Who shall bring a charge against you . . . ? We find a similar mode of argumentation in *BR* 1.2, Th-Alb:4, where it is stated in the name of R. Levi (early fourth century CE) that the reason for the inclusion of the creation narrative in the Torah was to neutralize the Gentiles so that they could not accuse Israel of piracy because of their possession of the land of Canaan. Israel could thus counter that the Canaanites were themselves not the original inhabitants of Palestine (Deut 2:23), and that the entire world belonged to God who, when he so wished, gave the land to the Canaanites and when he wished he took it away from them and gave it to the Israelites. This is the significance of the verse, "He revealed to his people his powerful works, in giving them the heritage of nations" (Ps 111:6), he revealed to them the 'beginning,' i.e. "In the beginning God created."

14. *defy you. antophthalmeō* is not attested before Polybius 18.46.12.

15. *you manage all things justly.* It is quite clear that for Philo, too, the formula "all things are possible to God" which recurs so frequently in his writings, does not include what is not "what law and right demand" (*kata nomon kai dikēn: Op.* 46; *Spec.* 1.14; cf. *Tanḥ.* Buber, *Wayyera* 49a). God as the wise 'manager' (*dioikētēs*) of the orderly universe is a common theme in the Hellenistic literature on the ideal king. For *diepeis,* cf. Ps-Aristotle *De Mundo* 399a18: *diepontos theou.*

out of keeping with your power. For *allotrion tēs sēs dynameōs,* cf. Philo *Abr.* 258: *allotrion hēgēsamenos sophias* ("holding [mourning] to be out of keeping with wisdom"). The virtues mentioned in vv. 15–19 and their order are the same as found in Ps-Aristeas 206–208: *dynamis, epieikeia* (v. 18), *philanthrōpia* (v. 19). Both are dependent on Ptolemaic "kingship tracts." See Festugière 2. 301–309; Reese 1970:75.

16. *your mastery over all . . . causes you to spare all.* Similarly, according to R. Joshua b. Levi, God's omnipotence reaches its culmination in the repression of his wrath and in his long suffering with the wicked (*BT Yoma* 69b). So, too, we find in Ps-Aristeas 253–254, that when the king asks how he might be beyond outbursts of wrath, he is admonished to realize that he has power over all things, and that when all men were his subjects, to what end should he fall into a rage? Furthermore, he must realize that God governs the whole world with kindliness and without any passion, and he should follow that example. Cf. Sir 16:11 (*dynastēs eksilasmōn,* "he shows his power in forgiveness").

XXIV. GOD'S MERCY A MODEL LESSON FOR ISRAEL
(12:19–22)

12   19 By such acts you taught your people that the righteous man
must be humane, and rendered your sons cheerful in that you grant
repentance for sins. 20 For if your children's enemies who deserved to
die, you punished with such care and indulgence allowing them time
and space to work free from their wickedness, 21 how conscientiously
did you pass judgment on your sons, to whose fathers you gave sworn
covenants full of good promise! 22 We, then, are thus chastened, but
our enemies you scourge ten thousandfold, so that, when sitting in
judgment, we may meditate on your goodness, but when judged ourselves we may look for mercy.

NOTES

12:19–22. According to Stein (1936), the author is here addressing
himself to a question which would at this point inevitably arise in the
reader's mind. If God, as the author himself testifies, knew that the seed of
the Canaanites was evil and that "their mode of thought would in no way
vary to the end of time," and that the Egyptians would stubbornly resist a
change of heart (cf. 19:1–4), why did he go through the empty charade of
giving them space for repentance? The answer is that God wished to provide a model lesson for his beloved people in order to teach them that they
should practice humanity in their relations with others, and that repentance is always available to the sinner. It would seem, however, that our
original *aporia* has by no means been resolved, for if the Canaanites were
in reality foredoomed, how would the empty gesture of the mere appearance of a chance for a fundamental change in their case hold any persua-
siveness for Israel? The answer, I believe, lies in the author's conviction
(shared by many religious thinkers of the ancient Near East) that God has
bestowed on man the privilege (or burden) of moral choice, and only in
very rare instances does he ever interfere with this process. (The author

indeed deliberately chooses to ignore an example of such interference in the case of the Egyptians, namely, God's hardening of Pharaoh's heart.) Thus even in the extreme case of the Canaanites, whose viciousness was innate and whose doom was sealed in advance, God did not bypass their capacity to make choices in spite of its futility. The Canaanite example thus serves as a vivid illustration of the fact that no man is merely a mechanical link in the universal causal chain. The more recalcitrant problem raised by God's ultimate determination of the way in which choice is exercised is generally relegated to the realm of divine mystery which no human mind can hope to penetrate, and usually remains dormant unless it is blasted out of this protective shell by the force of catastrophic events. For further discussion, see Introduction, VII.8.

12:20. *care and indulgence. diesis* literally means 'discharge,' 'letting through,' and hence 'indulgence.' (According to LSJ *Suppl.*, it means 'sifting,' 'careful investigation.')

21. *sworn covenants.* See NOTE on 18:22.

22. *ten thousandfold. myriotēs* is found only here. The usual form is *myrias.* Vanhoye has made a strong case for reading *metriotēti* (originally suggested by G. Kuhn in 1931) instead of *myriotēti*, which hardly fits the context. We should thus render 22b as follows: "but our enemies you scourge with measured deliberation"; cf. 11:20. See Vanhoye 1962:530–537. Vanhoye quotes J. Ziegler's response to his conjecture: "Hätte ich sie [=die Aüsfuhrungen] vor einem Jahr bereits erhalten, dann hätte ich wohl Ihre Konjektur als Textlesart aufgenommen."

XXV. RETURN TO THEME OF MEASURE FOR MEASURE AND TRANSITION TO SECOND EXCURSUS (12:23–27)

12 ²³ It is for this reason, too, that those who in their wickedness lived thoughtless lives you tormented with their own abominations. ²⁴ For they strayed far beyond the ordinary paths of error, taking for gods those which even among animals are the most despicable of loathsome things, deluded like foolish infants. ²⁵ Therefore as to unreasoning children you sent your judgment as a mockery; ²⁶ but those who do not take warning from such derisive castigation will experience a judgment worthy of God. ²⁷ For through those animal deities at whom they were indignant by reason of their own suffering, punished by means of those very creatures whom they deemed gods, they came to recognize the true God, perceiving him whom they had formerly denied knowing. Thus did the utter limit of judgment descend upon them.

NOTES

12:23. *abominations. bdelygma* is the LXX rendering of Hebrew *gillûlîm* ('dung pellets'), *šiqqûs* ('detested thing'), *tôʻēbâ* ('abomination').

24. *like foolish infants.* Cf. Philo *Mos.* 1.102; *Decal.* 69; *Iliad* 17.32; Hesiod *Op.* 218. The adverbial accusative *dikēn* is not found elsewhere in the LXX or Apocrypha. It is Classical and occurs also in late prose (Ps-Aristotle *De Mundo* 395b22).

25. *as a mockery.* The mocking judgments were the earlier and lighter plagues. Cf. Exod 10:2: "That you may recount in the hearing of your sons and of your sons' sons how I made a mockery of the Egyptians" (LXX: *hosa empepaicha tois Aigyptiois*).

27. *at whom. eph hois.* sc. *zōois.*

they came to recognize the true God, perceiving him whom they had formerly denied knowing. eidenai . . . epegnōsan. The verbs *eidenai* and *epegnōsan* are technical. The idiom *eidenai theous* is unattested before the Hellenistic period. See A. Henrichs, "The Atheism of Prodicus," *Cronache Ercolanesi* 6 (Naples, 1976) 18–19. On *theon gignōskein,* see E. Norden, *Agnostos Theos* (Leipzig, Berlin, 1913) 87*ff.* On the related term *theous enomisan* (Wisd 13:2), see W. Fahr, *Theous nomizein. Zum Problem des Atheismus bei den Griechen* (New York, 1969) (Spudasmata. Bd. 26).

the utter limit of judgment. I.e. death of the firstborn and the drowning of the Egyptian host.

Exercursus II: On Idolatry (XXVI–XXXI)

XXVI. MINDLESS NATURE WORSHIP
(13:1–9)

13 1 Born to mindlessness were all those who were [inherently] ignorant of God, and unable to perceive the Existent One from visible goods, nor recognize the Artificer, though intent on his works. 2 But either fire, or breath, or swift air, or starry heaven, or torrential water, or the celestial lights, cosmic lords, they accounted gods. 3 If through delight in the beauty of these things they took them to be gods, let them know how much superior is the Master of these things, for it was the primal author of beauty who created them. 4 If it was through amazement at their dynamic operations, let them apprehend from these how much more powerful is he who shaped them. 5 For from the greatness and beauty of created things, is their author correspondingly perceived. 6 Yet little blame attaches to these, for they too perhaps err in spite of their search for God and their desire to find him. 7 For they are engaged in searching out his works, and are persuaded by visual impressions, since what they see is beautiful. 8 Yet even they are not to be excused, 9 for if they were so resourceful as to be able to infer the 'Universe,' how is it they did not sooner discover the master of these things?

NOTES

13–15. "From Herodotus onwards," writes Nock, "ancient historians were fond of digressions and one type was the retrospect giving the antecedents of the situation of the moment" (1972:860). Polybius defended his regular use of digression as follows: "For hard workers find a sort of rest in change of the subjects which absorb and interest them. And this, I think, is why the most thoughtful of ancient writers were in the habit of giving their readers a rest in the way I say, some of them employing digressions dealing with myth or story and others digressions on matters of fact" (38.6.1).

13:1–9. The theme of Egyptian animal worship with which chap. 12 has ended, now leads the author to a long excursus on idol worship. The major components of his account are clearly discernible in the analogous passages of Philo (*Decal*. 52*ff; Spec.* 1.13*ff; Cont.* 3*ff; Congr.* 133), and although it may be that both derive from a common Jewish-Hellenistic apologetic tradition, it is equally likely that the one is directly dependent on the other. (See Ricken 1968:54–86; cf. P. Wendland, *Die Therapeuten und die philonische Schrift vom beschaulichen Leben* [Leipzig, 1896] 706–708; Geffcken, 1907). The striking similarities between them may be briefly summarized. Both provide a sharp distinction between the worship of the natural elements or the celestial bodies and that of manufactured idols or animals [thus following a Stoic schema which distinguished three forms of religious worship: the mythical or *genos mythikon,* the philosophical or *genos physikon,* and the legislative or *genos nomikon:* Augustine *Civ.Dei* 6.10; *SVF* 2. 1009. Aristobulus also mentions this threefold schema: *FPG:* 217, 20–25. See K. Praechter, *Die Philosophie des Altertums* (Basel, Stuttgart, 1957) 477; Pépin: 276*ff.* The Stoic schema is an expansion of Prodicus' twofold theory of the origins of cult: cf. A. Henrichs, *HSCP* 79 (1975):109–113)], and indicate that the offense of the former is less than that of the latter, although it is not to be excused (*Decal.* 66; Wisd 13:6–10; cf. *Ep.Jer.* 59–63). The nature worshipers (from Philo *Decal.* 54, it is clear that it is the Stoics who are being referred to) are afflicted with a fundamental ignorance or error (*Spec.* 1.15; *Decal.* 52, 59, 69; Wisd 13:1; 15:14), and misled by the beauty and dynamic operations of nature, they have failed to draw the proper analogy which would have revealed to them the Charioteer or Prime Author of its marvels (*Decal.* 60–61; *Spec.* 1.14–20; Wisd 13:3–5). The manufacturers of idols, on the other hand, worship wood and stone but recently shapeless, hewn away from their congenital structure by quarrymen and woodcutters, while pieces from the same original source have become urns and footbasins and other less honorable vessels (*Cont.* 7; Wisd 15:7*ff;* 13:11*ff*). Moreover, sculptors and painters have idealized their subjects, thereby beguiling the senses of the multitudes and deceiving them. The utter absurdity of image worship is easily discerned from the fact that it entails the worship of what is soulless or dead by those who are endowed with soul, and the addressing of prayers to creations inferior to the craftsmen who made them (*Cont.* 69; Wisd 15:17; 13:17–19; 14:18–20). It should be noted that the author presents the three forms of false worship in the form of a *klimaks:* the nature worshipers are described as *mataioi* or mindless (13:1), the idolators as *talaipōroi* or wretched (13:10), and the Egyptian animal worshipers as *aphronestatoi* or most foolish of all (15:14). Finally, there is a description of the vast damage or corruption caused by idolatry and a depiction of the Egyptians as worshipers of irrational animals who are most hateful or of the utmost savagery (*Decal.* 66; Wisd 14:12,21,27; *Decal.* 78; Wisd 15:18). It will be apparent from the commentary that in this long excursus the author has followed certain well-known biblical patterns, but has freely made use of Hellenistic and more especially Jewish-Hellenistic themes.

13:1. *mindlessness. mataioi* often characterizes the idols in the LXX, translating Hebrew *hebel:* e.g. Jer 2:5; 8:19; 10:15; II Kings 17:15. Less frequently it characterizes those who made them: e.g. Isa 44:9; Ps 62:10. Cf. Ps-Aristeas 138, 134; *Sib Or* 3:29; III Macc 6:11; Rom 1:21. The adjective denotes emptiness and nothingness. See Bauerfeind, *TDNT* 4. 525–528.

[*inherently*] *ignorant.* Cf. 12:10; Philo *Decal.* 59: *adidaktō tē physei; Jos.* 81; Plato *Sophista* 267B (where *gnōsis* is contrasted with *agnōsia*). Cf. also Job 35:16: *mataiōs anoigei to stoma, en agnōsia rhēmata barynei;* I Cor 15:34.

the Existent One. ton onta is derived from Exod 3:14: *egō eimi ho ōn.* Cf. Jer 1:6, 14:13, 39:17, LXX; *Sib Or* 1:137; Rev 1:4, 8; 4:8. See J. Whittaker. "Moses Atticizing," *Phoenix* 21 (1967) 196–201. In contrast to Philo who makes frequent use of both the personal *ho ōn* and the impersonal *to on,* Wisd employs only the former (cf. Philo *Mos.* 1.75; *La* 2.1; *Post.* 168, 28; *Abr.* 80. See Leisegang's Index in NOTE on 11:15, above).

from visible goods. Philo similarly writes: "They suppose that there is no invisible and conceptual cause (*aoraton kai noēton aition*) outside what the senses perceive" (*Decal.* 59–60). Cf. Rom 1:20: "Ever since the creation of the world his invisible nature, namely, his eternal power and deity, has been clearly perceived in the things that have been made. So they are without excuse (*anapologētous*)." (See v. 8 below.)

nor recognize. For *ouk ischysan eidenai,* cf. Philo *Decal.* 60: *ischysan theasasthai.*

Artificer. technitis is applied to Wisdom in 8:6. The title 'craftsman' or 'artificer' is never used of God in the Hebrew Bible, although the image of the divine potter is well known (and *technitēs* is used of a potter in C. C. Edgar, *Zenon Papyri,* 4 vols. (1925–31) 500.2.3: third century BCE). On the other hand, the Stoics had defined *physis* as "an artistically working fire, going on its way to create" (*pyr technikon hodō badizon eis genesin.* D.L. 7.156; cf. *SVF* 2. 411; 1.120), and Anaxagoras' *nous* is called *technitēs* (DK, A.46, line 6). In Philo, *technitēs* is very frequently applied to God (*Deus* 30; *LA* 3.99, 102; *Op.* 20, 135; *Cher.* 32, 128; *Plant.* 31; etc.; cf. Heb 11:10). A very similar argument to that found in this verse may be found in Epictetus 1.6.7: "Assuredly from the very structure of all made objects we are accustomed to prove that the work is certainly the product of some artificer (*technitou tinos*) and has not been constructed at random. Does, then, every such work reveal its artificer (*ton technitēn*), but do visible objects (*ta d'horata*) and vision and light not reveal him?" According to the Stoic view, the universe is God's *fabrica*, 'workshop' (=*ergastērion*): Cicero *ND* 1.20.53.

2. For the worship of the elements, see Philo *Decal*. 52–53: "A great delusion (*planos tis*) has taken hold of the larger part of mankind in regard to a fact which properly should be established beyond all question in every mind. . . . For some have deified the four elements, earth [for earth Wisd has substituted *pneuma*], water, air and fire, others the sun, moon, planets and fixed stars, others again the heaven by itself, others the whole world." (Cf. *Cont*. 3; *Conf*. 173; Plato *Cratylus* 397D: "I think the earliest men in Greece believed only in those gods in whom many foreigners believe today—sun, moon, earth, stars, and sky.")

swift. tachinon is poetic and late prose for *tachys*. Cf. Theocritus 2.7; Callimachus *Hymns* 1.56; *Cat.Cod.Astr*. 1.137.

celestial lights. phōstēras is late prose (*SVF* 2.1026), and is also found in the LXX (Gen 1:14; I Esd 8:79; Sir 43:7). Cf. *Test.Levi* 14:3; Philip 2:15.

cosmic lords. prytanis is often applied to the gods, but our author appears to be the first to apply it to the sun and moon. Philo implies the same notion and also uses the verb *prytaneuō* in a similar context: "But Moses held that the universe was created and is in a sense the greatest of commonwealths, having magistrates (*archontas*) and subjects; for magistrates, all the heavenly bodies. . . . The said magistrates, however, in his view have not unconditional powers, but are lieutenants of the one Father of All, and it is by copying the example of his government exercised (*prytaneuontos*) according to law and justice over all created beings that they acquit themselves aright" [the variant *prytaneuontas* is adopted by Heinemann, in which case it would refer to the sun and moon, but Colson reminds us of *Spec*. 1.207, where *prytaneuetai* refers to God's governing] (*Spec*. 1.13). We read in Plutarch *Moralia* 601A: "This [the boundless aethēr] is the boundary of our native land, and here no one is either exile or foreigner or alien; here are the same fire, water, and air, the same magistrates (*archontes*) and procurators (*dioikētai*) and councillors (*prytaneis*)—Sun, Moon, and Morning Star." This citation from Plutarch, as Gilbert has pointed out, makes it more than likely that *prytaneis kosmou* in our verse is not to be taken in apposition with *theous* but rather with *phōstēras ouranou* (1973:17–20). Cf. Gen 1:16, LXX: *eis archas tēs hēmeras;* Cicero *Somnium Scripionus De Re Publica* 6.17) (where the sun is called the lord, chief, and ruler of the other lights).

3. The argument of vv. 3–5 is compressed. The author appears to be saying that from the beauty and power of the universe we could both readily deduce the existence of the Designer and First Cause of all things, and equally come to realize how vastly superior he is to all that he has created.

primal author of beauty. genesiarchēs is first attested here. Used of the sun by Julianus Laodicensis in *Cat.Cod.Astr.* 1.136.2 (and occurs again in Patristic Greek). For *kallous,* cf. Sir 43:9: "The beauty (*kallos*) of the heaven, the glory of the stars"; 43:11: "Look upon the rainbow, and praise him that made it, very beautiful it is in the brightness thereof"; Plotinus 1.6.9.42: "but the Good is that which is beyond, the spring and origin of beauty." Philo *Spec.* 3.189: "The mind, drawn by its love of knowledge and beauty and charmed by the marvellous spectacle, came to the reasonable conclusion that all these were not brought together automatically by unreasoning forces, but by the mind of God."

4. *amazement.* Philo uses virtually the same word (*ekplagentes*) in a similar context: "Struck with admiration and astonishment (*thaumasantes kai kataplagentes*) they arrived at a conception according with what they beheld, that surely all these beauties (*kallē*) and this transcendent order has not come into being automatically but by the handiwork of an architect and world maker" (*Praem.* 42). Cf. Diodorus 1.11.1: "Now the men of Egypt, they say, when ages ago they came into existence, as they looked up at the firmament and were struck with both awe and wonder (*kataplagentas te kai thaumasontas*) at the nature of the universe, conceived that two gods were both eternal and first, namely, the sun and the moon." (The ultimate source for the theory that religion is the result of anxiety over celestial phenomena seems to have been Democritus. See A. Henrichs, *HSCP* 79 [1975] 102–106.) Cicero *ND* 2.90: "So it would have been the proper course for the philosophers, if it so happened that the first sight of the world perplexed them (*eos conturbaverat*), afterwards when they had seen its definite and regular motions, and all its phenomena controlled by fixed system and unchanging uniformity, to infer the presence not merely of an inhabitant of this celestial and divine abode, but also of a ruler and governor, the architect as it were of this mighty and monumental structure."

dynamic operations. Cf. NOTE on 7:17; M. Aurel. 12.28: "So then from the continual proofs of their power (*tēs dynameōs autōn*) I am assured that Gods also exist"; *SVF* 2.311: "So then the power (*dynamis*) which moves matter and subjects it to ordered forms of generation and change is eternal. Consequently this power will be God"; Ps-Aristotle *De Mundo* 398b21; *SVF* 2. 318, 848; *CH* 10.22; 1.14; II Macc 3:29.

5. *greatness and beauty.* Cf. *SVF* 2. 1009: "The world is beautiful. This is evident from its shape, color, and magnitude (*tou megethous*), and the

diversity (*poikilias*) of the stars surrounding it"; Xenophon *Cyropaedia* 8.7.22: "then at least fear the gods, eternal, all-seeing, omnipotent, who keep this ordered universe together, unimpaired, ageless, unerring, indescribable in its beauty and its grandeur (*hypo kalous kai megethous adiēgēton*)"; Cicero *ND* 2.93: "This elaborate and beautiful world." Plotinus 5.1.4.1*ff*: "Admiring the world of sense as we look out upon its vastness and beauty (*to megethos kai to kallos*) and the order of its eternal march, thinking of the gods within it, seen and hidden, and the celestial spirits and all the life of animal and plant, let us mount to its archetype, to the yet more authentic sphere"; Iamblichus *De Vita Pythagorica* 12.59. Cf. also Ps-Aristeas 56.

author (*genesiourgos*). First attested here. Cf. *CH* 13.4; Julian *Contra Galilaeos* 100c.

correspondingly. The adverb *analogōs* is rare. Cf. Sext. *Pyrrhoneae Hypotypōsēs* 1.88; Alex.Aphr. *In Metaphysica* 156.5. Virtually the same term, however, is employed by Philo in a somewhat similar context: "For I am straightway compelled to think of the artificer of all this texture as the inventor of the variegator's science (*poikiltikēs epistēmēs*), and I do homage to the inventor, I prize the invention, I am dumbfounded (*katapeplēgmai*) at the result, and that though I am incapable of seeing even the smallest part of it, but from the part brought within the range of my vision, if indeed it has been brought, I form in detail a conjecture about the whole on the strength of what analogy leads me to expect (*to holon eikazōn analogias elpidi*) (*Somn*. 1.204)." Moreover, at *Decal*. 60, in a context more similar to that of Wisd here, Philo speaks of the soul as something from which one can by analogy (*kata metabasin*) form a concept of God. It is more elaborately stated in *Abr*. 71*ff*: "The great is often known by its outlines as shown in the smaller, and by looking at them the observer finds the scope of his vision infinitely enlarged. . . . For it cannot be that while in yourself there is a mind appointed as your ruler . . . the world, the fairest (*kalliston*), and greatest (*megiston*), and most perfect work of all . . . . is without a king who holds it together . . . that the king is invisible need not cause you wonder, for neither is the mind in yourself visible" (cf. Xenophon *Cyropaedia* 8.7.17: "for not even in this life have you seen my soul, but you have detected its existence by what it accomplished"; Ps-Aristotle *De Mundo* 399b15). Although it is a feature of Plato's style to confirm by analogies the conclusions arrived at through a process of dialectic (e.g. *Rep*. 442E*ff;* 433E; *Philebus* 55A; 64D*ff; Laws* 903B; *Gorgias* 497D; *Phaedo* 78B*ff; Alcibiades I* 116B: see P. Shorey, *What Plato Said* [Chicago, 1933] 173, 528; P. Grenet, *Les origines de l'analogie philosophique dans les dialogues de Platon* [Paris, 1948]), it is only with Epicurus that argument from analogy becomes a fundamental principle of philosophical method. According to Sextus Empiricus (*Math*. 9.45), the

Epicureans in general made use of analogy (*metabasis* or *analogia:* Epicurus *Peri Physeōs* 26.30.2–3, Arrighetti; D.L. 10.32) to explain our knowledge of the gods. We form an idea that God is immortal and imperishable and complete in happiness by drawing an analogy from mankind (*kata tēn apo tōn anthrōpōn metabasin*). (See J. M. Rist, *Epicurus* [Cambridge, 1972] 143.) For the Stoic use of analogy, see *SVF* 2.87, 269. (They did not apply it, however, to knowledge of God.) The Middle Platonist Albinus also speaks of knowledge of God *kata analogian* (*Did.* 10.5, Louis). See also H. Lyttkens, *The Analogy Between God and the World* (Uppsala, 1953).

perceived (*theōreitai*). Cf. Ps-Aristotle *De Mundo* 399b22: "because though he is invisible (*atheōretos*) to every mortal thing he is seen through his deeds (*ap' autōn tōn ergōn theōreitai*)." The author of Wisd has here reproduced the teleological and cosmological arguments for the existence of God which had already been elaborated by Plato, Aristotle, and the Stoa. For the teleological argument, see Diogenes of Apollonia, DK, B.3; Plato *Laws* 886A; *Philebus* 28E; Aristotle Frag. 12a, Ross; Cicero *ND* 2.37–39, 15–19; Epictetus 1.6; Ps-Aristotle *De Mundo* 399b–400a; Xenophon *Mem.* 1.4.2–19; Seneca *Beneficiis* 4.6; Albinus *Did.* c.10; Apuleius *De Mundo* 22, 24, 35; Galen, *De Usu Partium* 17.1; 1.8; *CH* 5.5–8, 11, 6–14. Philo similarly expounds the teleological proof (*LA* 3.97–103; *Praem.* 41–42; *Spec.* 1.33*ff; 3.187–189; *QG* 2.34). For the cosmological argument, see Plato *Tim.* 28AC; *Laws* 891–899; Aristotle *Metaphysica* 9.8.1049b24*ff; 12.7.1072b*ff; Philo *Fug.* 12; *Post.* 28, 167 ("from the powers that range the universe, and from the constant and ceaseless motion of his ineffable works"); *Mut.* 54. See A. S. Pease, "Caeli Enarrant," *HTR* 34:3 (1941) 163–200. Jubilees 12:17 implies that Abraham arrived at the knowledge of the existence of God through celestial observations. (It is not quite clear whether the "word which came into his heart" is a divine revelation or the voice of his own reason.) According to Josephus (*Ant.* 1.7.1), he inferred it "from the changes to which land and sea are subject, from the course of the sun and moon, and from all the celestial phenomena; for, he argued, were these bodies endowed with power, they would have provided for their own regularity (*eutaksias*), but, since they lacked this last, it was manifest that even those services in which they cooperate for our greater benefit they render not in virtue of their own authority, but through the might of their commanding sovereign." Indeed, Hecataeus of Abdera, by attributing to Moses the teaching that identified God with the Heaven that surrounds the earth (*ton periechonta tēn gēn ouranon*) and rules the universe (Stern 1976:28), thereby implied that Moses came to a knowledge of God's existence by studying the heavens.

6. *little blame.* Philo makes the very same distinction: "But while all who

give worship and service to sun and moon and the whole heaven and universe or their chief parts as gods most undoubtedly err by magnifying the subject above the ruler, their offense is less than that of the others who have given shape to stocks and stones and silver and gold" (*Decal.* 66). The reluctance of our author to attach much blame to the nature-worshipers, without, however, completely excusing them, since they ought to have advanced further than they did, is somewhat reminiscent of Philo's attitude toward the 'literalists' whom he would not censure (*ouk an aitiasamenos*) though he would exhort them not to remain at the 'literalist' level but press on to allegorical interpretations (*Conf.* 190). Heinemann (1968:148) traces the distinction made here back to Posidonius, but though this may well be correct, the evidence for it is inconclusive.

search for God and their desire to find him. That which softens the author's censure of those who worship the natural elements as gods is their genuine search for the deity (cf. Acts 17:26–27). A similar sentiment is voiced by Philo in regard to the so-called 'Heaven-born,' who, unlike the God-born, reach only to either of the two polar principles of the Divine Logos but not to the one Logos itself. "God cannot suffer injury," writes Philo, "and therefore he gladly invites all who set themselves to honor him under any form whatsoever, and in his eyes none such deserves rejection. . . . For, however different are the characters which produce in them the impulses to do my pleasure, no charge (*ouk aitiateon*) shall be brought against them, since they have one aim and object to serve me" (*Abr.* 124–30; *Gig.* 47–60; *Deus* 60–69; cf. the four different types of devotees in the *Bhagavad Gita* 7.16–19). Similarly, we may recall the beautiful verses of the Jewish philosopher and poet Ibn Gabirol (eleventh century) in his famous poem *The Royal Crown:* "Thou art God, and all creatures are thy servants and worshipers; and thy glory is undiminished in spite of those who worship aught save thee—for the aim of all is to reach unto thee. But they are as blind ones, their faces are set eagerly on the King's Highway, but they have lost their way" (stanza 8). In Islam, the Ikhwān As-Safā (tenth century) held that there was an element of truth in every religion, and therefore believed that everyone should be left free to embrace the religion he chooses (*Rasā' il,* 3:86–90; 4:54–65). This trend of thought had already been a distinctive characteristic of the *Bhagavad Gita* (between fifth and second centuries BCE). The Supreme Being, according to the Hindu view, permits and takes benign delight in all the different illusions that beset the beclouded mind of man: "Whatever form [whatever God], a devotee with faith desires to honor, that very faith do I confirm in him [making it] unswerving and secure. Firm-established in that faith he seeks to reverence that [god] and thence he gains his desires, though it is I who am the true dispenser" (7.21–22, trans. Zaehner [Oxford, 1969]). Cf. the remark of Maximus of Tyre (second century CE): "If a Greek is stirred to the remembrance of God by the art of Phidias, an Egyptian by paying worship to animals, another man by a river, another by fire—I have no anger for their divergences; only let them know, let them love, let them remember" (2:10; p. 29.9 Hobein).

7. *persuaded by visual impressions.* The nature-worshipers are overly impressed by what is visible, whereas the ultimate reality is invisible. Plato has given us a very vivid description of the so-called "Battle of Gods and Giants": "One party is trying to drag everything down to earth out of heaven and the unseen, literally grasping rocks and trees in their hands; for they lay hold upon every stock and stone and strenuously affirm that real existence belongs only to that which can be handled and offers resistance to the touch. . . . Their adversaries are very wary in defending their position somewhere in the heights of the unseen, maintaining with all their force that true reality consists in certain intelligible and bodiless Forms. In the clash of argument they shatter and pulverize those bodies which their opponents wield, and what those others allege to be true reality they call, not real being, but a sort of moving process of becoming" (*Sophista* 246AB. The materialists to whom Plato is referring are undoubtedly the Atomists). Cf. Philo *Abr.* 69: "Thus they [the Chaldeans] glorified visible existence (*tēn horatēn ousian*), leaving out of consideration the intelligible and invisible"; *Testament of Orpheus* 4–5 (*FPG:* 164): "Let not the [natural] appearances which formerly filled your mind deprive you of dear life, but look unto the Divine Logos and wait upon Him." Our author, of course, may simply be referring to the invisible nature of the deity which is thus missed. On the other hand, he has indeed vaguely alluded to an ideal or intelligible reality. In 9:8 he hinted at a primordial form of the holy tabernacle, and in 9:9 he referred to the preexistent Wisdom of God, which presumably contained the paradigmatic forms of all things ("Wisdom who knows your works"). In the manner of Philo, and very likely other Middle Platonists, he may have transferred the realm of Platonic 'Forms' to the Mind of God. There is frequent mention in II Enoch of the creation of "visible things from invisible" (24:2; 30:10; 48:5; 51:5; 65:1,6), but the sources of that book appear to be primarily Iranian rather than Greek (see Winston 1966:199). Cf. also *Joseph and Asenath* 12:2: "Lord God of the ages . . . who brought the invisible (*ta aorata*) out into the light, who made all things and made manifest things that did not appear (*phanerōsas ta aphanē*)"; Heb 11:3.

searching out (*diereunōsin*). The active form of *diereunōsin* appears only once in Plato (*Sophista* 241B), where it means 'to track down.' In its more general sense of 'search,' 'examine,' it appears only in late prose (*CH* 8.25; Julian *Orationes* 7.222c). It is quite frequent in Philo (*Plant.* 79: *hoi tēn tōn ontōn physin diereunōntes; Ebr.* 165; *Congr.* 63; *Mos.* 1.10; *Spec.* 1.8, 283; 3.117; *Virt.* 27; *Praem.* 26: *tēn horatēn hotan hapasin physin diereunēsē . . . pros tēn asōmaton kai noētēn euthys meteisin;* etc.).

8. *to be excused.* When used of persons *syngnōstos* appears only in late prose (Philostratus *VS* 1.8.3; Plutarch *Coriolanus* 36; Philo *Jos.* 53: *syngnōstos . . . tēs agan apaideusias*). Lieberman has pointed out that the rabbis were more lenient toward the worshipers of the astral bodies than to those who adored other objects (1950:138, n.8).

9. *to infer the 'Universe.'* I.e. after inferring the existence of a 'Universe,' they need only have gone one step further to infer the Creator of this 'Universe.' (Cf. Smith 1949:287–290). Philo similarly writes: "For they have learned to rise above the ninth, the seeming deity, the world of sense, and to worship Him who is in very truth God, who stands above as the tenth" (*Congr.* 103–105). At *Praem.* 43, Philo speaks of those who apprehend God through his works as advancing from down to up by a sort of heavenly ladder (cf. Plato *Symp.* 211C) and conjecturing (*stochasamenoi ton dēmiourgon*) his existence through plausible inference. Even more to the point is Philo's explanation as to why the heavenly bodies were not created until the fourth day: "For being aware beforehand of the ways of thinking that would mark the men of future ages, how they would be intent on what looked probable and plausible (*stochastai tōn eikotōn kai pithanōn*), with much in it that could be supported by argument, but would not aim at sheer truth; and how they would trust phenomena rather than God, admiring sophistry more than wisdom; and how they would observe in time to come the circuits of sun and moon . . . and would suppose that the regular movements of the heavenly bodies are the causes of all things that year by year come forth. . . . That there might be none who owing either to shameless audacity or to overwhelming ignorance should venture to ascribe the first place to any created thing, 'let them,' said He, 'Go back in thought to the original creation of the universe, when, before sun or moon existed, the earth bore plants of all sorts' . . ." (*Op.* 45). Cf. *Op.* 58: *ta apobēsomena stochazontai* ("men conjecture future issues"); *Her.* 224; *Mos.* 1.16; Sir 9:14. Augustine makes the same point in regard to Varro: "When he says that only those who believe God to be the soul which governs the world have discovered that he really is, and when he thinks that worship is more devout without images, who can fail to see how near he comes to the truth! If he had the strength to resist so ancient an error, assuredly he would have held that one God should be worshiped, by whom the world is governed, and worshiped without an image. And being found so near the truth, he might perhaps have yielded easily to correction in regard to the mutability of the soul, so that he would perceive that the true God is rather an unchanging being, who also created the soul itself" (*Civ.Dei* 4.31).

For *aiōn* as 'world,' cf. Hippocrates *Epistulae* 17.34; Aelius Aristides 20.13K=21, 434D; Maximus of Tyre 115e; Exod 15:18, LXX. The word recurs at 14:16 and 18:4 below. "The sense of *aiōn* as 'time or course of the world' can easily pass over into that of the 'world' itself. Cf. Mark 4:19; I Cor 1:30; 2:6; 3:19. The equation of *aiōn* and *kosmos,* also found in the Hellenistic mysteries (Ditt. *Syll.*[3] 1125, 8), is to be explained in the New Testament by Jewish linguistic usage. Only at a later stage did Hebrew develop the concept of the universe, and for it, in addition to the paraphrase 'heaven and earth,' it fashioned the terms *hakkōl* and *'ōlām.* In IV Ezra the spatial significance is just as definite as the temporal, as in expressions like *habitantes saeculum* (3:9), or *qui in saeculo seminati sunt* (8:41). Both meanings are also found in the Greek version of Syriac Baruch (II Baruch). In the rabbinic writings there is only sparse attestation for *'ōlām* or *'ālmā'* in the sense of the spatial world prior to the first century CE, but there are several examples later. The plural *aiōnes* shares the change of meaning. Hence the *aiōnes* of Heb 1:2 and 11:3 are to be understood spatially as 'worlds' or 'spheres'" (*TDNT* 1. 203–204. The author of this article, Sasse, however, takes Wisd 13:9 to mean "to search out the course of the world"; 14:6: "left seed to the later time of the world"; 18:4: "to the course of the world"). LSJ take *stochasasthai* here to mean 'survey', 'explore' (as in Deut 19:3, LXX). The author of Wisd may also be alluding here to the Hellenistic deity *Aiōn,* god of Eternity, whose mysteries are known to have been celebrated in Alexandria from about 200 BCE (Ps-Callisthenes 1.30.6; 1.33.2; Epiphanius *Panarion* 51.22). "A late inscription dedicated to Zeus Helios Great Sarapis Aion illustrates the syncretistic development of the Sarapis figure. Aion was also equated with Sarapis on an amulet addressed to Aion Herpetes Lord Sarapis. Before the second century CE, Aion was more a flexible philosophical concept than a well-defined god with established cults—Nock listed eight distinct conceptions, starting with Plato's, through various Orphic and magical interpretations, ending with the establishment of a cult of Aion as a personal god, at Alexandria in the second century CE. Pseudo-Callisthenes (1.30.6; 1.33.2) called Sarapis 'Plutonian Eternity, himself ruling on the five-ridged peaks of Alexandria and turning round the endless cosmos'" (John E. Stambaugh, *Sarapis under the Early Ptolemies* [Leiden 1972] 84–85; Nock 1972:375–400; Festugière 1950 4. 152–199). More important is Philo's report that "time is considered a god by the wicked among men, who would conceal the really existing One. For which reason Scripture says, 'The time of all mankind has come against me,' inasmuch as they made a god of human time and oppose it to the true God" (*QG* 1.100). (For the philosophical sources of the concept of *aiōn,* see Plato *Tim.* 37D*ff;* Parmenides DK, B.8.5; Aristotle *De Caelo* 283b26*ff;* 279a23*ff*).

XXVII. WRETCHED WOODEN-IMAGE MAKING
(13:10 – 14:11)

13 10 But wretched are they and on dead things are their hopes, who designated as gods the works of human hands, gold and silver artfully contrived, and animal representations, or useless stone, a product of ancient craftsmanship. 11 For granting some skilled worker in wood has sawn a ready tree, skillfully scraped off all the bark, and with cunning art shaped a vessel for everyday use, 12 while the castings of his manufacture he used up for the preparation of his food and had his fill. 13 But taking one of these useless castings, a crooked piece of wood streaked with knots, he diligently carved it in his spare moments, fashioned it with leisurely skill and made it into the likeness of a human image; 14 or else he likened it to a worthless creature, coating it with vermilion, dyeing its surface red, and smearing over every blemish in it. 15 Then making for it a worthy shrine, he fixed it in a wall and secured it with iron, 16 thus taking precautions that it might not fall, in the knowledge that it is powerless to fend for itself, for it is an image and in need of help. 17 Yet praying to it about his possessions, his marriage, and his children, he feels no shame in addressing this lifeless object; for health he invokes that which is feeble; 18 for life he prays to a corpse, for succor he beseeches one totally inexperienced, for a journey, that which is incapable of using its legs; 19 for means of livelihood, business, and success of his handiwork, he asks for strength from that whose hands are entirely impotent.

14 1 Again, one setting out on a voyage and about to travel through savage seas, cries out for aid to a piece of wood more unsound than the craft that carries him. 2 For the latter was invented by the drive to obtain a livelihood, and Wisdom the Artificer built it. 3 But it is your providence, Father, that pilots it, for you have made a road through the sea and a safe path through the waves, 4 showing that you can save from all, so that even without [navigational] skill a man may put to sea. 5 It is your will that the works of your wisdom not lie idle; and therefore men trust their lives to the flimsiest plank, and passing through the surf on a raft come safely through. 6 For in the beginning, too, while haughty giants were perishing, the hope of the world escaped on a raft and, piloted by your hand, bequeathed to the world the germ for a [new] generation. 7 For blessed is the plank through which righteousness has survived; 8 but the idol made by hand is itself accursed and he that made it—he because he made it, the other because, though perishable, it was called a god. 9 For equally hateful to God are both the godless man and his godlessness; 10 both the deed and the perpetrator will be punished. 11 Divine judgment will therefore also overtake the idols of the nations, for though part of God's creation they have become an abomination, a stumbling for men, and a snare for the feet of fools.

NOTES

13:10. *dead things*. Cf. Ps 105:28, LXX; *Ep.Jer.* 27: "but the offerings are set before them, as if they were dead men (*hōsper nekrois*)."

the works of human hands. Cf. Deut 4:28; Ps 115:4.

contrived (emmeletēma). First attested here. Cf. *AP* 6.83.

representations (apeikasmata). Elsewhere only in Plato *Cratylus* 402D; 420C.

useless stone. Cf. Euripides *Iphigenia in Taurus* 977; Acts 19:35; *Pausanias* 1.44.2; 2.9.6; 10.24.6; 9.24.3 ("There [in Hyettus] is an image not carefully carved, but of unwrought stone after the ancient fashion": *lithon de argon kata to archaion*); Tacitus *Historiae* 2.3. See Albert (M.-J.) Lagrange, *Études sur les religions semitiques* (Paris, 1905): 158–216; H. Vincent, *Canaan d'après l'exploration récente* (1907):102–123; 144*ff.* Philo of Byblos defined the bethels (in Greek transliteration: *baityl*) (rough stones regarded as the residence of a god) as *lithoi empsychoi* or 'animate stones' (*FGH* 790, f2=Eusebius *PE* 1.10.23). "They became in time the origin both of altars and of iconic statues, passing through gradations of rude shaping. At first unshaped single rocks or cairns, we find them developed in the majority of earlier Aegean cult-scenes into pillars, monolithic or built up" (*ERE* 1.143). Aphrodite Astarte was worshiped in the shape of a conical stone at Paphos, and a black aerolite covered with projections and depressions to which a symbolic meaning was attributed represented Elagabal (the Baal of Emesa in Syria) and was transferred from Emesa to Rome by the fourteen-year-old Emperor Elagabalus in 219 (Dio Cassius 79; *S.H.A. Helio-gabalus;* cf. Dio Chrysostomus 12.61: *asēmous lithous;* F. Cumont, *Oriental Religions in Roman Paganism* [New York, 1956] 114–116; F. Lenormant, in Ch. Daremberg and E. Saglio, *Dictionnaire des antiquités grecques et romaines d'après les textes et les monuments* [1877–1919] s.v. *Baetylia:* 642–647). See also Carl F. Graesser, "Standing Stones in Ancient Palestine," *BA* 35 (1972) 34–63. For further bibliography, see Nock (1966):xlviii, n.47. The animate quality mentioned by Philo of Byblos was magnetism, very common in meteorites (T. Hopfner, "Lithika," PW, XIII [1927]:756–757; see also W. Gundel, "Sternschnuppen," PW, IIIA [1929]:2439–2449). According to J. Goldstein, Antiochus IV had ordered meteorites to be affixed to the temple altar as objects to be worshiped (see his edition of I Maccabees, AB 41 [New York, 1976] 145*ff*); cf. also Pausanias 7.22.4: "[At Pharae in Achaia, close to the image of Hermes], stand square stones, about thirty in number. These the people of Pharae adore, calling each by the name of some god. At a more remote period all the Greeks alike worshiped uncarved stones instead of images of the gods" (cf. J. G. Frazer, *Pausanias' Description of Greece* (London, 1898) 4. 154); Lucian *Alexander* 30.

11. The apodosis of *ei de kai tis* is found only at the end of v. 13. Verses 11–19 are inspired by Isa 44:9–20 (see Gilbert 1973:64–75). Cf. Jer 10:3; *Ep.Jer.;* Archias *AP* 10.8 (on a rough-hewn image of Priapus, patron of fishermen): "Small to look at, I, Priapus, dwell on the breakwater by the beach, head pointed, feet wanting, such as the sons of toiling fishermen might carve on deserted shores. Yet if any fisher with net or line calls me to help him, swifter than the wind I rush . . . truly it is from their deeds, not from their shapes that the character which spirits have is recognized" (*The Garland of Philip,* eds. A. S. F. Gow and D. L. Page [Cambridge, 1968] 1. 418–419); Horace *Satirae* 1.8.1: "Once I was a fig-wood stem, a worthless log, when the carpenter, doubtful whether to make a stool or a Priapus, chose that I be a god."

some skilled worker in wood. The *tis* in *tis hylotomos tektōn* is scornful —any common workman (Farrar [1888]).

has sawn (ekprisas). More precisely, "after sawing down one tree out of a number" (Grimm; Farrar).

a ready tree. eukinēton means 'easily moved,' i.e. easy to handle or manage.

a vessel for everyday use. For *chrēsimon skeuos,* cf. *Ep.Jer.* 59: "It is better to be a vessel in a house profitable (*ei skeuos en oikia chrēsimon*) for that whereof the owner shall have need, than such false gods." For the literary structure of vv. 11–19, see Gilbert 1973:55–63.

12. *castings. apoblēmata* is first attested here. Cf. Scholia on Aristophanes *Equites* 412.

for the preparation of his food and had his fill. Cf. Isa 44:16, LXX; *Apoc. Abraham* 5: Abraham is commanded by his father: "Take and collect the splinters of the wood out of which I made gods of pinewood before thou camest; and make ready for me the food of the midday meal." While collecting the splinters Abraham finds a little god called Barisat (probably *bar 'ishta*, 'son of fire') and throws him too into the fire with instructions to pay careful attention that the fire not die down until he returns. Cf. *Deut.R.*, Lieberman: 56; *Mek. Baḥodesh*, on Exod 20:3: "R. Eliezer says: 'Other God'—For every day they make for themselves new gods. How so? If one has an idol of gold and then needs the gold, he makes the idol of silver. If he has one of silver and then needs the silver, he makes the idol of copper . . ."; Clem.Alex. (*Prot.* 4.46) similarly writes: "Dionysius the tyrant, the younger, having stripped off the golden mantle from the statue of Jupiter in Sicily, ordered him to be clothed in a wooden one, remarking facetiously that the latter was better than the golden one, being lighter in summer and warmer in winter. And Antiochus of Cyzicus, being in difficulties for money, ordered the golden statue of Zeus to be melted, and one like it, of less valuable material, plated with gold, to be erected in place of it"; cf. 2.24: "Another, taking an image of Herakles made of wood (for he happened most likely to be cooking something at home), said, Come now, Herakles; now is the time to undergo for us this thirteenth labor . . . and so cast it into the fire as a log of wood"; Epicharmus Frag. 77, Olivieri.

13. *streaked with knots*. For *sympephykos*. Cf. Philo *Cont*. 7: *tēs symphyias*.

carved it. For *eglypsen*. Cf. Isa 44:9–10; Hab 2:18, LXX.

and made it into the likeness of a human image: or else he likened it . . . For *apeikasen auto eikoni anthrōpou . . . hōmoiōsen auto*. Cf. Deut 4:16, LXX: *glypton homoiōma pasan eikona;* Isa 40:18,19; Gen 1:26, LXX.

14. *coating it with vermilion*. Cf. *Sib Or* 3.589 (*miltochrista*); Pliny the Elder *NH* 33.36; Pausanias 2.2.6 (the faces of the wooden images of Dionysus are ornamented with red paint); Virgil *Ecl*. 10.26–27; Ovid *Fasti* 1.415; Tibullus 2.1.55; Herodotus 4.19. See E. Wunderlich, *Die Bedeutung der roten Farbe im Kultus der Griechen und Römer* (Giessen, 1925); J. G. Griffiths, "The Symbolism of Red in Egyptian Religion," *Ex Orbe Religionum* (Leiden, 1972) 1.81–90.

15. *with iron*. Cf. Isa 41:7; 40:19–20, LXX; Jer 10:4.

16. *might not fall*. Cf. *Ep.Jer*. 27; Isa 46:7.

17. *praying to it*. Cf. Isa 44:17, LXX; Philo *Decal*. 72.

lifeless object. Cf. Ps 134:17. Criticism of images as lifeless is already implied in the famous utterance of Heraclitus, DK, B.5. Timaeus of Tauromenium used the adjective *apsychos* as a term of reproach for statues of the gods (*FGH* 566, F 32). Philo similarly writes: "Let no one, then, who has a soul worship a soulless thing (*apsychō tini*)" (*Decal.* 76). Cf. Plato *Laws* 931A: "but of other gods we set up statues as images, and we believe that when we worship these, lifeless though they be (*apsychous ontas*), the living gods beyond feel great good-will towards us and gratitude"; Epictetus 2.8.20: "And the Athena of Pheidias, when once it had stretched out its hand and received the Nike upon it, stands in this attitude for all time to come, but the works of God are capable of movement, have the breath of life (*empnoa*), can make use of external impressions and pass judgment upon them." Philo *LA* 1.6: "For whereas things produced by human art when finished stand still and remain as they are, the products of divine skill, when completed, begin again to move."

It should be noted that the Egyptian view of their idols was considerably more sophisticated than it would appear from our author's polemical description. A ritual of "opening the mouth" was performed on the statues while they were still in the sculptor's workshop (the "gold house"), as a result of which the work of human hands was thought to come alive. The deity was thought to be in the heavens, and only to take up a temporary residence in his image after the necessary rite had been performed (see S. Morenz, *Egyptian Religion* [London, 1973] 155–156). Cf. Bevan, 1940:31–39; *ERE* 7. 144–145, 113, for other examples of rituals for the animation of images among the Hindus, the Africans of the West Coast, the New Zealanders, etc.; R. Wilhelm, *The Soul of China* (New York, 1928) 314, where it is observed that in Chinese temples the images of the gods are ordinarily treated with no respect. "These pictures are not gods at all. They are merely places which they enter if they are called upon in the right way. When the god is there, then the presence in his image is a stern and holy matter. When he is not there, then his image is a piece of wood or clay." The *Suda* has preserved a fragment of Damascius which tells us of an Alexandrian philosopher, Heraïskos (fifth century CE), who "had a natural gift of discernment in regard to sacred images, whether they were alive or not. The moment he looked at one, if it was alive, he felt a stab of peculiar feeling go through his heart. . . . If, on the other hand, he felt no such emotion, the image was a lifeless one, destitute of any divine spirit. It was in this way that he knew, by what may be truly called a mystical union with the deity, that the awful image of Aion was inhabited by the god whom the Alexandrians worshipped, and who is Osiris and Adonis in one" (Bevan 1940:34–35). Still, the very notion that the idols were capable of being vitalized through the performance of some sort of ritual would have been sufficient to arouse our author's contempt. It may be observed that even a philosopher like Plotinus, who would deny that a god may himself descend into an image, could yet seek to defend the use of statues with the following arguments: "I think, therefore, that those ancient sages, who sought to secure the presence of divine beings by the erection of shrines and statues, showed insight into the nature of the All; they perceived that, though this Soul is everywhere tractable, its presence will be secured all the more readily when an appropriate receptacle is elaborated, a place especially capable of receiving some portion or phase of it, something reproducing it, or representing it and serving like a mirror to catch an image of it" (4.3.11).

17b–19. We have here a very effective series of rhetorical contrasts.

18. *for succor*. Pausanias speaks of Apollo *epikourios* (8.41.7). Cf. Dittenberger, *SIG* 1015, 25–35 (third century BCE); Philo *Flac.* 191; *Virt.* 45. In the Hellenistic period, gods are often designated as *boēthoi* (Callimachus *Hymns* 4:27; Theocritus *Idyls* 22:23; Isyllus of Epidaurus *IG* IV² 128.60).

19. *strength*. *eudraneia* is first found here, and elsewhere only in a Phrygian inscription of second/third centuries CE, in which vigor (*eudraniē*) is attributed to Artemis. Cf. Ps-Aristeas 134: "Though they are themselves much more powerful than the gods they vainly revere." Note the double polyptoton: *cheirōn . . . chersin . . . adranestaton . . . eudraneian*.

14:1 The argument of the first two verses of chap. 14 may be stated briefly. The idolator calls to his aid a piece of wood artlessly fashioned by a simple woodcutter, while sailing aboard a vessel which was at least artfully contrived by a well-motivated shipwright. The idol whose aid is invoked is thus clearly inferior to the ship it is called upon to protect.

setting out on a voyage. Cf. Philo *Decal.* 14: *hoi stellomenoi makron ploun* (*stellesthai* has same sense in active. Cf. Sophocles *Ajax* 1045; *Philoctetus* 911).

cries out for aid to a piece of wood. Cf. Herodotus 3.37: "The Phoenician Pataici which the Phoenicians carry on the prows of their triremes" (they were in the form of dwarfs); Horace *Odes* 1.3.2; Acts 28:11: "We set sail on an Alexandrian ship . . . its figurehead was the Sign of the Twins [Castor and Pollux]." (Cf. M. Nilsson, *History of Greek Religion* [Oxford, 1949] 35.) Cyril of Alexandria on Acts 28:11 says it was especially an Alexandrian custom to have pictures of the twins to right and left of the ship's prow. Cf. also Epictetus 2.18.29: "Call upon God to help you and stand by your side, just as voyagers, in a storm, call upon the Dioscuri"; Ovid *Amores* 2.11.29.

2. Antithetical notions shaped the ancients' attitude toward man's ability to navigate the seas. The primitivists, who idealized man's early existence and characterized it as a life of innocent bliss and carefree abundance which was forfeited in the course of time, naturally looked askance at the newfangled sophistication which launched men upon the open seas, and

attributed it to their greed. Cf. Hesiod *Op*. 236: "They flourish continually with good things and do not travel on ships"; Ps-Plato *Axiochus* 368AB: "for terrestrial man casts himself upon the sea as though he were an amphibian, entirely at the mercy of Chance"; Horace *Odes* 13:21–40: "Vain was the purpose of the god in severing the lands by the estranging main, if in spite of him our impious ships dash across the depths he meant should not be touched. . . . Daedalus essayed the empty air on wings denied to man. . . . No ascent is too steep for mortals. Heaven itself we seek in our folly"; *Odes* 3.24.40*ff;* Propertius 1.17.13; 3.7.31–38: "Earth was too small for death, we have added the waves: by our craft have we enlarged the cruel paths of fortune . . . Nature with guile hath made the sea a path for greed"; Virgil *Ecl*. 4.32: "yet shall some few traces of olden sin lurk behind, to call men to essay the sea in ships"; *Ecl*. 38–39: "even the trader shall quit the sea, nor shall the ship of pine exchange wares, every land shall bear all fruits"; Ovid *Amores* 2.11; Statius *Silvae* 3.2; *AP* 9.29 (Antiphilus sees *tolma* or 'audacity' as inventor of ships); Seneca *Ep*. 90.24*ff:* "Reason did indeed devise all these things, but it was not right reason. It was man, but not the wise man, that discovered them; just as they invented ships, in which we cross rivers and seas" (cf., however, his *De Beneficiis* 4.28.3: "it was to the common good that traffic on the sea should be open to all, and that the kingdom of mankind should be enlarged"); *CH* 23 (*Korē Kosmou*):45. The antipodal view held that man once lived like a wild beast, and only by a gradual ascent with the aid of the arts achieved a more humane and abundant life. From this point of view, seafaring is but one further step forward in man's slow ascent. Cf. Euripides *The Suppliant Women* 201–213; Sophocles *Antigone* 332*ff:* "Wonders are many, and none is more wonderful than man; the power that crosses the white sea, driven by the stormy south-wind, making a path under surges that threaten to engulf him"; Aeschylus *Prometheus Bound* 467–468; *Lucretius* 5:330–333; *Test.Zebulun* 6:1: "I was the first to make a boat to sail upon the sea, for the Lord gave me understanding and wisdom therein." The author of Wisd clearly follows the latter view, and the greed or avarice which the former saw as the chief motive for seafaring is softened by him into the drive to obtain a livelihood.

Wisdom the Artificer built it. Philo's "champions of mind" are similarly impressed with the powers of the human mind: "It is mind which constructed a ship (*ho naun kataskeuasas*), and by devices admirable beyond description turned what was naturally dry land into a waterway, opened up in the sea routes whose many branches serve as highways to the havens and roadsteads of the different states, and made the inhabitants of the mainland and those of the islands known to each other, who would never have met if a vessel had not been built" (*Spec*. 1.335). It may also be noted that Athene, goddess of wisdom, patroness of arts and crafts, and known in such connections by her title *Erganē,* 'the work-woman' (Pausanius 1.24.3), is said to have supervised the construction of the Argo. She is said to have inserted into its prow an oak branch from Dodona, endowed with the power of prophecy (Apollonius Rhodius 1. 113–114; Ps-Apollodorus 1.9.16*ff*). Cf. Aelius Aristides *Oration* 2: "She [Athena] alone has the names of Craft-worker (*Erganē*) and Providence, having assumed the appellations which indicate her as the savior of the whole order of things" (Bevan, 1927:160).

3. *your providence . . . that pilots it.* Platonic and Stoic terminology. For *diakybernaō,* see NOTE on 10:4. We find a similar cooperation between God and human art in the following passage of Plato: "God controls all that is, and Chance and Occasion cooperate with God in the control of all human affairs. It is, however, less harsh to admit that these two must be accompanied by a third factor, which is Art. For that the pilots' art should cooperate with Occasion—verily I, for one, should esteem that a great advantage" (*Laws* 709B). Cf. *Tim.* 42E; *Philebus* 28D; and for *pronoia: Tim.* 30C, 44C; *SVF* 2.1157, 1107–1108, 1029; Herodotus 3.108; Xenophon *Mem.* 11.4.2; III Macc 4:21; IV Macc 9:24; 13:19. *Pronoia* is very frequent in Philo (*Op.* 9: *Deus* 29; *Decal.* 58; etc.), and even forms the subject of a special treatise (the *De Providentia,* preserved only in an Armenian translation and some Greek fragments). Cf. also Ps-Aristotle *De Mundo;* Jos. *Ant.* 10.11.7 (278); Taylor's commentary on *Tim.* 42E3. Except for Wisd and II Macc 14:9, *pronoia* in the sense of Divine Providence is absent from the LXX. See Freudenthal 1890:217.

Father. The earliest invocation of God as 'Father' is in Sir 23:1, and it appears again in III Macc 6:3. Cf. Isa 63:15; Sir 4:10, 51:10; Tobit 13:4; *Apoc. Moses* 35:3; Mark 14:36; Rom 8:14–15; Gal 4:6; *Apostolic Constitutions* 7:24; Jos. *Ant.* 2.6.8; Philo *Jos.* 2.65; *Sacr.* 68 (see Drummond 2. 63, note); *BT Ta'an.* 23b: "When the world was in need of rain the Rabbis would send to him [Ḥanan ha-Neḥba] school children and they would take hold of the hem of his garment and say to him, Father, Father, give us rain. Thereupon he would plead with the Holy One, Blessed be He, Master of the Universe, do it for the sake of those who are unable to distinguish between the Father who gives rain and the father who does not"; 23a: "Thereupon Simeon b. Shetaḥ sent this message to him [Ḥoni the Circle-Drawer], 'Were it not that you are Ḥoni I would have placed you under the ban . . . but what shall I do unto you who actest petulantly before the Omnipresent and He grants you your desire, as a son who acts petulantly before his father and he grants his desires; thus he says to him, Father, take me to bathe in warm water, wash me in cold water, give me nuts, almonds, peaches, and pomegranates and he gives them unto him. Of you Scripture says, 'Let thy father and thy mother be glad, and let her that bore thee rejoice'" (Prov 23:25). The invocation of the deity as 'Father' was common in Greek literature from Homer on. Two Hellenistic examples are Cleanthes' *Hymn to Zeus* 30, and Aratus *Phaenomena* 15 (cf. Aristotle *EN* 8.1160b24). See Kohler, *JE* 1. s.v. Abba; Marchel:77–84, and *passim*. It should be noted that as in Philo and Josephus, the term 'Father' is employed by our author in a universal context.

a road through the sea. Cf. Isa 43:16; 51:10; Ps 77:20 (alluding to the passage through the Reed Sea: see Gilbert 1973:104–109); Ps 107:22–30; Philo *Spec.* 4.155: "By observing the courses of the stars he [the skilful navigator] has been able to open up in the pathless waste highroads where none can err, with this incredible result, that the creature whose element is land can float his way through the element of water"; Isis Aretalogy, Kyme 13, 37, 41, 48; *P. Oxy.* xi 1380, 61, 69 (*kybernētin*), 15 and 74 (*hormistria*), 121–123.

4. *without [navigational] skill.* The reference is apparently to Noah. Cf. 10:4 and NOTE; also v. 6 below.

5. *that the works of your wisdom not lie idle.* Without God's special providence man's shipbuilding and navigational art would not have sufficed to make a safe path for him through the seas. The deity, however, who does not wish that "the works of his wisdom lie idle," supplements man's limited resources, thus allowing him to hazard a path through trackless seas. Similarly, it was God's piloting hand that brought Noah through the Flood. Most commentators, however, understand the words *mē arga einai* to mean that God wishes to allow for a better distribution of nature's products, thereby avoiding unnecessary waste and affording a fuller utilization of earth's riches. The same notion is suggested by Euripides: "and commerce over sea, that by exchange a country may obtain the goods it lacks" (*The Suppliant Women* 209). Very likely both ideas are in the author's mind (cf. Deane's comment: "God wills that men should employ the faculties which he gives them, and use the products of sea and land which he has provided for them" [1881]. So, too, Heinisch [1912]).

arga . . . erga represent an etymological play on words (*argos* comes from *afergos*). Cf. Aristotle *EN* 1097b30: "Are we then to suppose that, while the carpenter and the shoemaker have definite functions (*erga tina*) or businesses belonging to them, man as such has none, and is not designed by nature to fulfill any function (*argon pephyken*)?"

the flimsiest plank. A common literary theme. Cf. Anarcharsis' remark, after ascertaining that the ship's side was four fingers' breadth in thickness, "That the passengers were just so far from death" (D.L. 1.103); *Iliad* 15.624–628; Aratus *Phaenomena* 299: "and only a thin plank staves off death"; Horace *Odes* 1.3; Seneca *Ep.* 49.11: "You are mistaken if you think that only on an ocean voyage there is a very slight space [i.e. the timbers of the ship] between life and death"; *Medea* 301: "Too venturesome the man who in frail barque first cleft the treacherous seas and, with one last look behind him at the well-known shore, trusted his life to the fickle winds; who, ploughing the waters on an unknown course, could trust to a slender plank, stretching too slight a boundary between the ways of life and death"; 364: "Now, in our time, the deep has ceased resistance and submits utterly to law; no famous Argo, framed by a Pallas' hand . . . is sought for; any little craft now wanders at will upon the deep." In the *Life of Secundus* 14, a boat is described as "a ready-made tomb, a floating death, or death in prospect," and a sailor as "a neighbor to death."

on a raft come safely through. diesōthēsan is a Gnomic Aorist. For *schedia* cf. *Odyssey* 5.160*ff*, where the goddess Calypso bids Odysseus "hew with the axe long beams, and make a broad raft (*schediēn*), and fasten upon it cross-planks for a deck well above it, that it may bear thee over the misty deep." Cf. MacDonald:97.

6. *in the beginning. archēs* is a genitive of time; used with a preposition in Attic.

haughty giants. Cf. Judith 16:6: *hypsēloi gigantes* (probably 'proud' rather than 'tall,'); Sir 16:7; Bar 3:26; Jub 7:22; I Enoch 7:5; III Macc 2:4 ("the giants who trusted in strength and boldness"); Ps-Eupolemus, ap. Eusebius *PE* 9.18.2 (*FPG:* 198); Jos. *Ant.* 1.31 (73) (*hybristas . . . paidas*); 1.3.8 (100) (*eksybrizon*); *BR* 31.12.

the hope of the world. Cf. IV Macc 15:31: "The ark of Noah bearing the universe"; Virgil *Aeneid* 12.168: *Ascanius, magnae spes altera Romae.*

the germ for a [new] generation. Cf. Philo *Mig.* 125; *Mos.* 2.60: *spermata hypoleipomenos; QG* 1.96: "as the seed and spark of the new generation of men that was to be." The Sumerian counterpart to Noah, *Ziusudra,* is similarly called the "preserver of the seed of mankind" (*ANET:*44).

7. *plank.* The reference is to Noah's ark. It was natural that the Church Fathers should apply this verse either directly or symbolically to the cross, which is often called *ksylon* in the New Testament (Acts 5:30; Gal 3:13; etc.). Graetz (1888: 3. 613) considered this verse a Christian interpolation. See Gilbert 1973: 114–124.

8. *made by hand.* In the LXX, *cheiropoiēta* renders the Hebrew *'elîlîm. accursed.* Cf. Deut 27:15.

11. *the idols of the nations.* Cf. Exod 12:12; Jer 10:15; 46:25.

abomination . . . stumbling. Cf. Josh 23:13: *esontai hymin eis pagidas kai eis skandala;* Judg 2:3; 8:27, LXX; Ps 105:36, LXX.

part of God's creation. Cf. *M. A.Z.* 4.7: "[Some Romans] asked the elders in Rome, 'If God have no desire for idolatry, why does he not abol-

ish it?' They replied to them, 'If they worshipped a thing for which the
world has no need, he would abolish it; but, behold they worship the sun,
and the moon, and the stars and the planets, shall he then destroy his
world because of fools?' They said to them, 'If so, let him put an end to
that which the world does not need and leave what the world does need.'
[The elders] answered them, 'We should on our part only strengthen
the contention of those that worship them since they would say, "Know
that these are [true] deities, for, lo, they have not been destroyed." ' "

XXVIII. ORIGIN AND EVIL CONSEQUENCES OF
IDOLATRY
(14:12–31)

14   12 For the invention of idols is the beginning of fornication, and their discovery is life's ruin. 13 They did not exist from the beginning, nor will they exist forever. 14 For they came into the world through the empty illusions of men, and therefore a sudden end was devised for them. 15 A father consumed with untimely grief, having made an image of the child so swiftly taken from him, now honored as a god what was once a human corpse, and handed down to his dependents mysteries and initiation rites. 16 Then confirmed by the passage of time, the impious custom was maintained as a law. Again, at the command of rulers graven images came to be worshiped. 17 When men were unable to do honor to these princes in their presence because of the remoteness of their dwelling, they formed a likeness of the distant face, and made a palpable image of the king they wished to revere, so that they might earnestly flatter the absent one as though present. 18 But the ambition of the artist impelled even those who had no knowledge of the matter to a higher pitch of worship. 19 For he, in his desire perhaps to please the ruler, skilfully forced the likeness into a more beautiful form; 20 but the masses, drawn by the charm of his workmanship, now took for an object of worship him who was but lately honored as a man. 21 And this became a trap for human life, that men enslaved either by misfortune or tyranny bestowed on stocks and stones the name that may not be associated with others. 22 And so they were not content to err concerning the knowledge of God, but though living in the midst of a great war rooted in their ignorance, they call such monstrous evils peace. 23 For either performing ritual murders of children or secret mysteries or frenzied revels connected with strange laws, 24 they keep neither their lives nor marriages pure, but one either slays his neighbor insidiously or pains him by adultery. 25 All is confusion—bloody murder, deceitful theft, corruption, treachery, tumult, perjury, agitation of decent men, 26 ingratitude, soul defilement, interchange of sex roles, irregular marriages, adultery and

debauchery. [27] For the worship of the unspeakable idols is the beginning, cause, and end of every evil. [28] For they either make merry to the point of madness, or prophesy lies, or live unrighteously or readily perjure themselves. [29] Placing their trust in lifeless idols, they expect no punishment when swearing falsely. [30] On both accounts will justice pursue them, because in their devotion to the idols they thought wrongly about God, and in their contempt for religion swore deceitful lies. [31] For it is not the power of those by whom they swear, but the judgment of them that sin, that ever proceeds against the transgression of the wicked.

NOTES

14:12–31. To bolster his attack on idolatry, the author argues that it did not exist from the beginning but arose in the course of time through human error. Two different explanations are adduced for its origins. The first, based to some extent on a widespread religious phenomenon of the Greco-Roman world, refers to a father, who, stricken with grief for the untimely death of his child, sets up an image of it to be accorded divine honors. The second refers to the statues of rulers whose beauty has been enhanced by skillful artists intent on flattery, and subsequently become objects of divine worship by the masses. Similar explanations for the rise of idolatry were later given by Minucious Felix (fl. 200–240 CE) in his dialogue *Octavius* (20.5), and by Lactantius (ca. 240–320 CE), in his *Divine Institutions* 2.2.3). See Geffcken:xxii, n.2. Although they are somewhat reminiscent of Euhemerus' theory of the origin of the gods [expounded in his *Hiera Anagraphē* or *Sacred Record,* ca. 300 BCE], which held that Uranus, Cronus, and Zeus had been great kings in their day who were later worshiped as gods by their grateful subjects, they do not derive directly from it, but probably from a later "Euhemeristic" source (see NOTE on v. 15 below), for the author of Wisd is more narrowly interested in explaining the origins of idolatry, whereas Euhemerus was concerned with the larger question regarding the origins of the gods of Greek mythology. A more direct use of Euhemerus' theory by Jewish writers, on the other hand, may be found in the so-called *Letter of Aristeas* and in the *Sibylline Oracles.* In his attack on idolatry (134–137), Ps-Aristeas first ridicules the senselessness of the stone and wooden images, and then, in direct allusion to Euhemerus' view, argues that it is foolish to deify men because of some invention they had contrived, since "such persons only took things already created and put them together and showed that they possessed further usefulness, but they did not themselves create the objects." (Stambaugh has suggested that it was Aristeas of Argos, an adviser at the court of Ptolemy II, who served as the prototype of Ps-Aristeas, for we are told by Clement of Alexandria [*Strom.* 1.21.106] that according to Aristeas, Sarapis was a deified form of an Argive king named Apis. "The climate was congenial to Euhemerism in Egypt where the line between divinity and royal humanity had always been vague, and where Osiris was widely viewed as a mortal king who had been deified [Plutarch *Is. et Os.* 359D–360B; Diodorus 1.13.4; Apuleius *De deo Socratico* 153–154]" (J. E. Stambaugh, *Sarapis under the Early Ptolemies* [Leiden, 1972]: 68–74.) According to the third *Sibylline Oracle* (ca. 140 BCE) (108–113), "Cronos, Titan and Iapetos were kings, the goodliest children of Gaia and Ouranos, whom men called Earth and Heaven, dubbing them so because they were the first of all articulate men" (cf. 3.723, and 522–555). According to Fraser (1.299), it is not likely that the Sibyl derived this directly from Euhemerus, since he evidently referred to the Jews at some point in his work in what was regarded by Josephus (*Ag.Ap.* 1.215–217) as a disparaging manner, and if he applied the same theology to Yahweh as he did to Zeus, that will not have recommended him to the Sibyl. For the Euhemeristic elements in Artapanus' account of Moses, see Gutman: 2. 120–126. Ps-Eupolemus, probably writing in Palestine in the first half of the second century BCE, had already identified Nimrod with the Babylonian Bel and Greek Kronos. The only one of the 'giants' to have been rescued from the great Flood, he founded Babylon and built the famous Tower (*FGH* 724: F 1 and 2). See Freudenthal 1875–79:35–82; Hengel: 1.89; B. Wacholder, *Eupolemus* (New York, 1974):194–205. Fraser asserts that, "there can be little doubt that Euhemerus was led to his reformation of myth above all by the example of the contemporary deification of Alexander and the Diadochi by various Greek cities [a suggestion already made by J. Kaerst in an article entitled "Alexander der Grosse und der Hellenismus," *Historische Zeitschrift* 74 (1895):226], even if he may have been aware of the occasional deification of certain classes of mortals—successful athletes, notable physicians, and others—at a much earlier date, to say nothing of the accepted mortal origin of Asclepius and other gods. . . . In official quarters his work was probably well received as providing a theological system into which the deified rulers fitted as by right" (1. 294).

14:12. *beginning of fornication.* For the close connection between fornication and idolatry, cf. *Test.Reuben* 4:6: "For a pit unto the soul is the sin of fornication, separating it from God (cf. Wisd 1:3), and bringing it near to idols. . . . 11: For if fornication overcomes not your mind, neither can Beliar overcome you"; *Test.Simeon* 5:3; *Sifre Deut.* 171, Finkelstein

218: "'who consigns his son or daughter to the fire' (Deut 18:10), this refers to one who has intercourse with a heathen woman, and begets from her a child hostile to God"; *BT Sanh.* 82a: "R. Hiyya b. Abuiah said: He who is intimate with a heathen woman is as though he had entered into marriage relationship with an idol, for it is written, 'and hath been intimate with the daughter of a strange god': hath then a strange god a daughter? But it refers to one who cohabits with a heathen woman"; *BT Shab.* 17b: "They decreed against their bread and oil on account of their wine, and against their wine on account of their daughters, and against their daughters on account of 'the unmentionable' (literally, 'something else,' i.e., idolatry)"; *BT Meg.* 25a; Ps-Jonathan on Lev 18:12; *Ket.* 13b: "most of the idolators are unrestrained in sexual matters." In Philonic allegory, the son of a whore is a polytheist, "being in the dark about his real father, and for this reason ascribing his begetting to many, instead of to one" (*Mig.* 69).

13. *from the beginning.* For the rise of idolatry in the time of Serug (Hebrew *sur*=turn aside) under the influence of Mastema, see Jub 11:4ff. "This view is entirely unknown to the older rabbinic literature (although it is frequently found among the Church Fathers, e.g. Minucius Felix *Octavius* 26.7; Justin *Apologia* 2.15; *Pseudo-Clementine Recognitions* 4.13–15; Tatian *Oratio ad Graecos* 8; Lactantius *Divinae Institutiones* 2.16, and later in the Kabbalah). The beginning of idolatry according to the older rabbinic sources, based on their interpretation of Gen 4:26, took place in the time of Enosh (*Sifre Deut.* 43, Finkelstein 97; *Mek. Baḥodesh* 6, Lauterbach, 2.239; *Mid. Tannaim* 20 and 195; *BR* 2.3; *Wayyik.R.* 23.3; *BT Shab.* 1186) According to Maimonides (very likely on the basis of older sources), Enosh himself was an idolator (*M.T. Avodat Kokhavim* 1.1; cf. *Guide* 1.36; 3.29, 37; *Letter on Astrology*). In the *Pseudo-Clementine Homilies* 9.4–6, Nimrod is identified with Zoroaster, and is designated as the one 'who chose, giant-like, to devise things in opposition to God, and who, after his death by fire, was worshipped by the ignorant populace. This was the beginning of the worship of idols. Subsequent rulers demanded similar adoration to that which was accorded to Nimrod'" (Ginzberg, 5. 150–151). It should also be noted that according to St. Augustine, Varro claimed that, "for more than one hundred and seventy years the ancient Romans worshipped the gods without an image. 'If this usage had continued to our own day,' he says, 'our worship of the gods would be more devout.' And in support of his opinion he adduces, among other things, the testimony of the Jewish race." (Augustine *Civ.Dei* 4.31). Cf. Strabo 16.2.35: "[Moses] taught that the Egyptians were mistaken in representing the Divine Being by the images of beasts and cattle, as were also the Libyans; and that the Greeks were also wrong in modelling gods in human form; for, according to him, God is this one thing alone that encompasses us all . . ." (see P. Boyancé, "La Théologie

de Varron," *Revue des Études anciennes* 57 [1955] 57–84; Nock
1972:860–865. Nock suggests that the excursus in Strabo may reproduce
the creation of a Jew familiar with the ideas of Posidonius). Heinemann
(1968:147–150) maintained that Wisd's theory as to the origin of idolatry is derived from Posidonius, since a similar theory is to be found in
Lactantius and Minucius Felix, who are known to have drawn on Seneca's
lost work *De Superstitione,* and Seneca in turn is known to have drawn
from Posidonius. This argument is inadequate, since Seneca is known to
have drawn much from Epicurean sources, and the 'Euhemeristic' explanation of idolatry found in Minucius Felix and Lactantius is part of a
much larger criticism of anthropomorphic gods, which apparently derives
from a lost Epicurean source of ca. 150 BCE, and is also echoed in Cicero
ND, in Josephus (*Ag.Ap.* 2.242ff (esp. 250–254), in Philodemus *On
Piety,* and many other authors. See Geffcken:xxiiff.

nor will they exist forever. Cf. Isa 2:18; Zech 13:2; Ezek 30:13; Micah
5:12; *Ep.Jer.* 50ff.

14. *empty illusions. kenodoksia* is an Epicurean term. We read in *K.D.*
30: "Such pleasures are due to idle imagination (*kenēn doksan*) and it is
not owing to their own nature that they fail to be dispelled, but owing to
the empty imaginings (*kenodoksian*) of the man" (i.e. a mental picture of
some object, which does not really contribute to pleasure, causes us to
desire it. Cf. *K.D.* 15 and 29; Usener:456). Cf. Ps-Aristeas 8; IV Macc
2:15; 8:19; Philo *Mut.* 94–96; *Jos.* 36; *Legat.* 114; *Praem.* 100; *Virt.* 7;
QG 3.47; *Somn.* 1.255; 2.105. Moreover, *kenodoksia* is a philosophical
term with deep roots in Epicurus' epistemology, for the latter had especially cautioned against the use of *kenoi phthongoi* or words devoid of
meaning (*Epistulae* 1.38; *K.D.* 37; Cicero *Fin.* 2.48; *Tusc.* 5.73). It was
therefore an eminently apt term for the biblical conception of idolatry,
which, as Kaufmann had pointed out long ago, was a fetishistic one and
therefore saw in the idols objects completely empty and devoid of meaning. On the day when the nations repent of the sin of idolatry they will say,
"Our fathers inherited naught but lies, vanity and things wherein there is
no profit. Shall a man make for himself gods, they being no gods?" (Jer
16:19). When men stop worshiping fetishistic 'no-gods' idolatry shall
come to an end (see Y. Kaufmann, *The Religion of Israel* [Chicago,
1960] 15). Wisd's words now take on a more poignant meaning. Since
the origin of the idols, he argues, is rooted in *kenodoksia* or total vacuity,
"a sudden end was devised for them," i.e. the moment their vacuous character is disclosed idolatry will immediately evaporate into thin air and
completely disappear, almost as if it had never existed.

15. *untimely grief.* The grief may by hypallage be called "untimely" because the child's death is premature (Farrar [1888]). Cf. Prov 10:6:
penthos aōron; Sir 16:3: *penthei aōrō;* Euripides *Alcestis* 168. As Cumont

has pointed out, the masters of sidereal divination were much preoccupied with the calculation of life-spans and the types of death predetermined by the stars, writing long chapters on this subject (*peri chronōn zōēs:* Ptolemy *Tetrabiblos* 3.2; Vettius Valens 9.8*ff*). An individual's natural end could be hastened through the intervention of a murderous star (either Saturn or Mars), which, under certain conditions, causes sudden death. At times the maleficent planets carry away a nursing child from its mother's breast before a single revolution of the sun has been accomplished: these are the *atrophoi* or *non nutriti* (those left unnourished), alluded to by Virgil (*Aeneid* 6.426–429; cf. Plato *Rep.* 615C). The enormous rate of infant mortality in the Roman world focused great attention on the fate of the *aōroi* or *inmaturi* (those who died before reaching maturity). (On the very high infant mortality rate in Egypt, see M. Hombert and C. Préaux, *Chronique d'Égypte* [1945] 139*ff*.) At other times, they cut children off in their adolescence, before marriage could assure them posterity: these are the *agamoi* or *innupti* of Tertullian (*De Anima* 55.4*ff*; cf. O. J. H. Waszink's commentary [Amsterdam, 1947] ad loc.). (For the Babylonian origin of the superstitious views concerning the *aōroi* as well as the *biaiothanatoi* or those who died a violent death, see E. Ebeling, *Tod und Leben nach den Vorstellungen der Babylonier* [Berlin, 1931] 1:131*ff*; 145*ff*. Moreover, Cumont points to a passage in Ptolemy's *Tetrabiblos* [4.9.12] where one finds grouped together three of the four classes of *biothanati* mentioned by Virgil [*Aeneid* 6.430, 435, 479], thus demonstrating that astrology was the source of the aforementioned superstitions. Nock, however, has questioned this interpretation [1973:712–719].) It was further believed that these unfortunate souls, obedient to Fate, had to linger on earth until their appointed time was accomplished, and became demons who lent their aid to diviners and sorcerers. Feeling and reason, at the same time, protested against the cruel doctrine which relegated guilty and innocent alike to long torture. When accident or illness caused the death of a beloved son, could his parents be reconciled to the belief that he would suffer undeserved chastisement? More humane doctrines soon aligned themselves against these cruel superstitions. According to the Pythagoreans, the age of reason did not begin before puberty or sixteen, and until then the soul was exempt from virtue as well as from vice, so that the *aōroi* could not deserve any punishment. Indeed, according to some thinkers, "the souls that are quickly released from intercourse with men find the journey to the gods above most easy, for they carry less weight of earthly dross" (Seneca *De Consolatione ad Marciam* 23.1; cf. Plutarch *Consolatio ad uxorem* 611E). It is hard to determine to what degree these moral ideas had penetrated the popular mind. Religion, however, offered a remedy for the ill to which it had itself lent persuasion. The custom of initiating children to the mysteries became a means of preserving them from the fatal lot which threatened them, and of ensuring their happiness in the other life. Above all, the influence of astral cults, added to that of philosophy, persuaded those parents who were inclined to believe it, that these innocent creatures ascended to the starry heavens. An epitaph of Thasos speaks of a virgin, flower-bearer probably of Demeter and Kore, who was carried off at the age of thirteen by the inexorable Fates, but who, "living among the stars, by the will of the immortals, has taken her place in the sacred abode of the blessed," and a relief from Copenhagen shows the bust of a little girl within a large crescent surrounded by seven stars, thus indicating that she has risen toward the moon, the abode of blessed souls. (Cumont 1942:282, n.3, 242). Transported thus to heaven, these loved beings were transformed by the tenderness of their relatives into protectors of the family in which their memory survived. Whether they were called 'heroes' in Greece, or as elsewhere 'gods,' they were always conceived as guardian powers who acknowledged by benefits the worship rendered them. Thus in the middle of the second century the familia of a proconsul of Asia, C. Julius Quadratus, honored a child of eight years as a hero, at the prayer of his father and mother; and at Smyrna the parents of a dearly loved child of four, raised a tomb to this baby as their tutelary god (*IGR* 4.1377; Kaibel:314). Lieberman (1974:263) writes: "The author of *Sapientia Salomonis* informs us that when a heathen father was afflicted with untimely mourning, he used to make an image of the child and would worship it as a god. This was a good consolation to a heathen father. The Jew comforted himself in a Jewish manner. The rabbis assert that the Lord himself teaches Torah to the babies who died in their infancy (*BT A.Z.* 3b). According to another version (Gemara to minor tractate *Kallah* 2) the angel Metatron teaches them." We do find, however, that the grief of fond parents, who with great admiration had followed the blossoming mind of their precocious child taken away from them too soon, sought comfort in the idea that the studies in which he had distinguished himself would assure him a favorable lot in the hereafter. A series of sarcophagi, which reproduce the career of a child prematurely dead, show him being instructed by his teacher and then elevated to the rank of hero or raised heavenward on a chariot leading to his deification (Cumont, 1942:344*ff*). In a letter to Marcellinus, Pliny the Younger eulogizes the daughter of his friend Fundanus: "She was scarce thirteen and already had all the wisdom of age and sedateness of a matron" (*Epistulae* 5.16). Her tomb was discovered in Rome, and it carries at its top the eagle which symbolizes deification (*CIL* 6.16331). (For all this, see Cumont 1949:303–342, whose detailed discussion has here been briefly summarized.)

Wisd's explanations for the origin of idolatry are undoubtedly etiological, but it is likely that the background of the author's theory lay in certain religious practices of the Greco-Roman age (such as those noted above), which were then projected backward either by him or by his source (just as Euhemerus was probably influenced by the contemporary deification accorded to Alexander and to the Diadochi by various Greek cities). Moreover, even if children who died young were never actually worshiped and no cult-images were ever made of them, the evidence cited by Cumont (however it is interpreted) could easily have served as a sufficient stimulus for the etiology of idol worship expounded in 14:14–16. Guillaumont (1959), Heuten, and Gilbert have noted the close analogy to Wisd's first explanation provided by Firmicus Maternus' 'Euhemeristic' version of the myth of Dionysus-Zagreus (*De errore profanarum religionum* 6), in which Liber or Dionysus is the son of a Cretan king named Jupiter. Since Dionysus is the product of an adulterous union, the king's wife Juno, in her fury, has the infant murdered in the absence of the king by henchmen known as Titans. Upon his return, the father, *acerbi luctus atrocitate commotus* (=*penthei trychomenos patēr*), and utterly disconsolate, has an image made in the likeness of his son and institutes a cult. This parallel and the Fulgentius passage quoted immediately below, may well go back to a pagan Hellenistic source, a highly rationalized 'Euhemeristic' account of the origins of idol cult. (See G. Heuten's edition with commentary of Firmicus Maternus *De errore profanarum religionum* [Bruxelles, 1938] 152–157; Gilbert 1973:153–155; J. Geffcken, "Der Bilderstreit des heidnischen Altertums," *ARW* 19 [1919] 292–293.)

having made an image. Fabius Planciades Fulgentius (ca. 467–532 CE, probably identical with the famous bishop of Ruspe), quoting from the *Antiquities* of one Diophantus of Sparta, tells of an Egyptian named Syrophanes, who, overcome with grief for the loss of his son, erected a statue of him in his house (*in aedibus*). To please the master of the house, the members of the family decked it with flowers, and slaves even fled to it for sanctuary. Thus the statue gradually became an idol. (*Mitologiarum* 1.1, ed. Helm [Teubner] 15–17. Cited by R. Holkot, *In Librum Sapientiae praelectiones* [Venice, 1509]: 139 verso, col. a.) We have an interesting reference to such an Egyptian custom in *Mek.Pisha* on Exodus 12:30 (Lauterbach, 1:100): " 'For there was not a house where there was not one dead.' R. Nathan says: Were there not houses in which there was no first-born? It means simply this: when the first-born of one of the Egyptians died, they would make an image (*eikonion*) of him and set it up in the house. On that night such images were crushed, ground and scattered. And in their eyes that day was as sad as though they just then buried their first-born" (cf. *PRK,* Mandelbaum: 127; *Mid. Hagadol,* on Exod 12:30, p. 209). A. Calmet has cited Apuleius *Metamorphoses* 8.7, where we are told that Charite, on the death of her beloved husband Tlepolemus, "spent whole days and nights in miserable longing, and there was an image of her husband, which she had made like unto Bacchus, unto which she rendered divine honors and services, so that she grieved herself even by her consolation." This motif is already found in Euripides *Alcestis* 348*ff*, though in a non-religious context. In the seventeenth century many commentators had already noted Cicero's intention to set up a shrine for his lost daughter Tullia (Cicero *Ad Atticum* 12:35–36; Lactantius *Divinae Institutiones* 1.15, 16–20). Heinisch (1912) cites the decree of Canopus, discovered in 1865, from which we learn that in 237 BCE, the synod of this town accorded divine honors not only to Ptolemy III Euergetes and his spouse Berenice II, but also to their daughter, likewise named Berenice, who had died at the tender age of eight, proclaiming her queen of virgins, and establishing an annual festival to commemorate her death. Recently, Dulière (1960) has insisted that the reference here is to Hadrian's favorite Antinous, who had drowned in Egypt in 130, and in whose honor Hadrian had instituted cultic mysteries and initiation ceremonies which, according to Dio Cassius (69.11.3), had spread almost throughout the inhabited world. Dulière concluded that the entire pericope of 14:12–16 was an interpolation. Actually, as Gilbert has pointed out, Dulière had already been anticipated by Jansenius of Ypres (1644), Gutberlet (1874), Deane (1881), and Farrar (1888), though they did not absolutize the matter as he had done. Most scholars, however, have rightly rejected this hypothesis. Finally, Scarpat (1967, following Motzo [1924]) has suggested that the allusion here is to the cult rendered by the incestuous Caligula to his sister Drusilla, confused by the author of Wisdom with Caligula's daughter of the same name (see Gilbert 1973:146–157).

what was once a human corpse. Cf. *Sib Or* 3:721–723: "But we had gone astray from the path of the Eternal and with foolish heart worshiped the works of men's hands, idols and images of men that are dead."

16. *at the command.* *epitagē* is late Greek prose. Cf. 18:16; 19:6; III Macc 7:20; Polybius 13.4.3; Diodorus 1.70. Many commentators place the period after *glypta* rather than after *ephylachtē*, for, as Grimm (1860) pointed out in v. 17 speaks of a freely adopted honoring of images rather than one commanded by princes. The author would then be saying that what began as a family custom ended as a state ordinance. Having mentioned rulers, however, he is then naturally led to his second cause of the rise of idolatry, without explicit indication of this transition. If, finding it difficult to begin a new explanation with the relative pronoun, we place the period with Ziegler (1961) after *ephylachtē*, we should then have to understand the passage as follows: Graven images came to be worshiped at the command of rulers, inasmuch as their demand for official expressions of honor led their distant subjects to the production of images exaggerating their beauty, which then led to their awed worship by the masses.

came to be worshiped. *ethrēskeueto* is the inchoative imperfect.

17. *formed a likeness. anatypoō* is first attested here. Cf. 19:6; Plutarch *Moralia* 329B. It is used only once by Philo (*Plant.* 27).

a palpable image. emphanē is perhaps an allusion to the epithet of Ptolemy V and Antiochus IV, and Nero's title *emphanēs theos kaisar*. Cf. Lactantius *Divininae Institutiones* 1.15; Minucius Felix *Octavius* 20.5 (Gilbert 1973:156).

18. *who had no knowledge*. I.e. "even those who did not know whom the statues represented, or how they originally came to be worshiped" (Farrar).

worship. thrēskeia is found in Herodotus 2.18, 37 and inscriptions in the sense of "ritual" or "cult." For the meaning "religion," "service of God," cf. Philo *Legat.* 232, 298; *Fug.* 41 (in *Det.* 21 it is used in the bad sense of "religious formalism"); Acts 26:5; *CH* 12.23. It appears three times in Symmachus' version of the Bible: Jer 3:19; Ezek 20:6,15; Dan 2:46. J. Van Herten has pointed out that *thrēskeia* is not found in literary texts after Herodotus, but reappears in inscriptions in the period of Augustus ("Thrēskeia, Eulabeia, Hiketēs, Bijdrage tot de Kennis der religieuze terminologie in het grieksch" [Diss. Amsterdam, 1934] 2–27). The most up-to-date account of this word is given by L. Robert, *Études épigraphiques et philologiques* [Paris, 1938] 226–235; Robert asserts: "Le mot n'est certainement pas hellénistique; l'argument e silentio est ici très fort; tant et tant d'inscriptions de l'époque hellénistique traitent du culte et louent la piété; on n'y rencontre jamais *thrēskeia.*" He also concludes that Wisd was written in the Imperial Age; idem, *Hellenica* 2 (1946):132–133; cf. A. Pelletier, *Flavius Josèphe Adapteur de la Lettre d'Aristée* [Paris, 1962] 33).

19. *forced*. Cf. Plutarch *Timoleon* 36. See H. P. L'Orange, *Apotheosis in Ancient Portraiture* (Oslo, 1947); H. G. Niemeyer, *Studien zur statuarischen Darstellung der römischen Kaiser* (Monumenta Artis Romanae VI, Berlin, 1969).

20. *by the charm*. Philo similarly writes: "Further, too, they have brought in sculpture and painting to cooperate in the deception, in order that with the colors and shapes and artistic qualities wrought by their fine workmanship they may enthrall the spectators and so beguile the two leading senses, sight and hearing" (*Spec.* 1.29). Cf. *Her.* 69; *Gig.* 59; *Decal.* 66, 156; Cicero *ND* 1.42: *ipsa suavitate nocuerunt* (of the poets); Seneca *Ep.* 88.18; Dio Chrysostomus 12.50*ff;* Clem.Alex. *Prot* 4: "In Rome, the historian Varro says that in ancient times the *Xoanon* of Mars—the idol by which he was worshipped—was a spear, artists not having yet applied themselves to this specious pernicious art; but when art flourished, error increased." Discussing the deified Antinous, Clement says: "And why should you enlarge on his beauty?" (*Prot.*). Cf. also Cicero *ND* 1.77: "These notions, moreover, have been fostered by poets, painters and artificers, who found it difficult to represent living and active deities in the likeness of any other shape than that of man."

20. *an object of worship*. *sebasma* is late Greek prose, first attested in D.H. 1.30; cf. 15:17 below; Bel and the Snake 27; Acts 17:23; Jos. *Ant.* 18.345. If our author is thinking of any of the colossal statues of emperors, like that of Augustus at Ancyra, the word *sebasma* would recall the name "Augustus" (=*Sebastos*), a word apparently coined at the time (27 BCE) of the bestowal on Octavian of the title Augustus for use in the eastern half of the empire. Herod refounded Samaria under the name Sebaste, where he built a splendid temple of Augustus. "In fact he built shrines of the emperor in many cities of his kingdom, refraining only in the cities of Judaea. He went so far in bestowing honors that he felt it necessary to make apologies to his subjects for his violation of national customs, and declared that he acted under orders" (*eks entolés kai prostagmatōn* [cf. 14:16] [Jos. *J.W.* 1.403–415; *Ant.* 15.328–330]); (L. R. Taylor:160, 171).

21. *enslaved*. *Douleusantes* is joined by zeugma both to *symphora* and *tyrannidi*.

that may not be associated with others. Cf. Isa 42:8; Philo *Ebr.* 110: "but they even allowed irrational plants and animals to share the honor which belongs to things imperishable"; Numenius, Frag. 56 (where it is said that the God of the Jews was *akoinōnētos*, and disdained that anyone should share in his honor).

22. *midst of a great war . . . they call such monstrous evils peace*. Cf. Jer 6:14; Tacitus *Agricola* 30: "To plunder, butcher, steal, these things they misname empire; they make a desolation and they call it peace"; Philo *Gig*. 51; *Conf*. 46: "For all the deeds of war are done in peace. Men plunder, rob, kidnap, spoil, sack, outrage, maltreat, violate, dishonor and commit murder sometimes by treachery, or if they be stronger without disguise." This theme of war-in-peace was common in the Cynic-Stoic diatribe literature of the first century CE. Cf. Ps-Heraclitus *Epistle* 7: "In peace you make war with words; in war you deliberate with iron. . . . Give me an opportunity for laughter in peacetime, when you do not do battle in the law courts with weapons on your tongues, after committing frauds, seducing women, poisoning friends, spoiling temples, procuring, being found faithless in your oaths. . . ." (See Attridge:73, line 17; 69, lines 21–25); Ps-Diogenes *Epistle* 28: "nor even in peace, but in war do you grow old throughout life" (Hercher, *Epistolographi graeci* [Paris, 1873]:242). (See Gilbert 1973:161–164.)

23. *secret mysteries*. Cf. NOTE on 12:4. Philo inveighs against the mysteries with equal vigor: "Furthermore, he banishes from the sacred legislation the lore of occult rites and mysteries (*teletas kai mystēria*) and all such imposture and buffoonery. He would not have those who were bred in such a commonwealth as ours take part in mummeries and clinging on to mystic fables despise the truth and pursue things which have taken night and darkness for their province, discarding what is fit to bear the light of

day" (*Spec.* 1.319). Cf. Ps-Heraclitus *Epistle* 4: "Where is God? Is he shut up in temples? You are a fine sort of pious man, who set up God in darkness!" (See Attridge:59.)

frenzied revels. Cf. II Macc 6:4; Philo *Flac.* 4: "The sodalities and clubs, which were constantly holding feasts under pretext of sacrifice in which drunkenness vented itself in political intrigue, he dissolved" (for *eksallōn thesmōn,* cf. Philo *Virt.* 219: *ekthesmōn ethōn*).

ritual murders of children. Cf. 12:5 and 11:7 (*nēpioktonos*). *teknophonous* is found only here. (*teknophoneō* in *A.P.* 9.345.) Cf. the epithet *brephoktonos* applied to Palaimon. Ino, Dionysus' mother's sister, is said to have killed her own infant son, Melikertes, in a fit of madness (Apollodorus 3.4.3). This son of Ino's was worshiped on the island of Tenedos as Palaimon, and since children were sacrificed to him, he was called the "child-killer" (Lycophron 229, and scholia. See W. F. Otto, *Dionysus* [Bloomington and London, 1965] 106).

24. *by adultery. notheuōn.* s.c. *autou gamon.* Cf. Philo *Jos.* 45.

25. For the catalogue of crimes in vv. 25–26, cf. Philo *Conf.* 46 (quoted in NOTE on v. 22); Jer 7:9; Hos 4:2; III Bar 4:17; *Sib Or* 2.256; Rom 1:29–31; Gal 5:19–21; I Tim 1:9–10; Mark 7:21; Matt 15:19; *Didache* 5:1. See S. Wibbing, *Die Tugend-u. Lasterkataloge im N.T.* (Berlin, 1959); Anton Vögtle, *Die Tugend-u. Lasterkataloge im N.T.* (Münster, 1936); A. Dieterich, *Nekyia* (Leipzig, 1893) 163*ff;* A. Deissmann, *Light from the Ancient East* (New York, 1922) 315–318; Bultmann:19, n.3.

apistia, tarachos. Cf. Philo *Decal.* 172; *Jos.* 143.

26. *ingratitude. amnēstia* is found only once in Plato *Menexenus* 239C. Cf. Ps-Heraclitus *Epistle* 2; Plutarch *Moralia* 612D.

defilement. miasmos. In moral sense, first attested here and in *Test.Benjamin* 8:2–3 (cf. *Levi* 17:8). In I Macc 4:43 it refers to physical defilement. Cf. Plutarch *Moralia* 393C.

interchange of sex roles. geneseōs enallagē. Cf. Philo *Cher.* 92: *physeōs ergōn enallagē; Test.Naphtali* 3:4: "that ye become not as Sodom; which changed the order of nature" (*enēllakse taksin physeōs autēs*); Rom 1:26: "their women exchanged (*metēllaksan*) natural relations for unnatural." *geneseōs,* as Goodrick (1913) remarks, is the wrong word. We would expect *genous.*

irregular marriages. gamōn ataksia. The adjective *ataktos* is used of sensual excess, and may mean "irregular," "inordinate": Plato *Laws* 840E (*atakton Aphroditēn*).

27. *unspeakable.* Euripides describes the Furies as *anōnymoi* (*Iphigenia in Taurus* 944; cf. Sophocles *Oedipus at Colonus* 128). *anōnymoi,* however, may also mean 'not to be named,' 'unspeakable': Aristides *Oration* 50.8. Cf. Exod 23:13.

30. *will justice pursue them.* Cf. IV Macc 18:22: *hē theia dikē metēlthen kai meteleusetai,* Esther 8:13, LXX.

15 1 But you, our God, are good and true, slow to anger, and governing all with mercy. 2 For even if we sin, we are yours, since we are cognizant of your might; but knowing that we are reckoned yours, we will not sin. 3 For to know you is the sum of righteousness, and to recognize your power is the root of immortality. 4 For neither did the malicious inventiveness of men lead us astray, nor the sterile labor of painters, a shape splashed with varied colors, 5 the sight of which excites fools to lust for the unbreathing form of a dead image. 6 In love with evil and worthy of such hopes, are they who make these things, they who long for them, and they who worship them.

NOTES

15:1. For the four divine attributes enumerated in this verse, see Exod 34:6 (cf. Num 14:18). The Hebrew *rab-ḥesed we'ĕmet* is translated in the LXX as *polyeleos kai alēthinos,* where *alēthinos* undoubtedly means "trusty" or "faithful." The new Jewish Publication Society translation renders it "rich in steadfast kindness." In our context, however, which seeks to contrast the true God over against the false gods of the heathen, *alēthēs* carries an additional connotation to that which *'emet* bears in Exod 34:6. Cf. Jer 10:10; Wisd 12:27. For *chrēstos,* cf. 8:1; Pss 99:5; 85:5; 144:8, LXX.

2. *we are yours.* Cf. Exod 34:9; Jer 3:22, LXX; *PRK* 16.9, Mandelbaum: 278: "Said Moses before the Holy One, blessed be He: Master of the Universe, when they sin they are mine, but when they are meritorious they are yours; but rather whether they are sinful or meritorious they are yours, as it is written, 'Yet they are your very own people' (Deut 9:29)"; *Sifre Deut.* 96, Finkelstein: 157: "'You are children of the Lord your God' (Deut 14:1). R. Judah says, if you behave like children, then you

are children, but not otherwise. R. Meir says in either case you are children of the Lord your God"; *Sifre Deut.* 308, Finkelstein: 346): according to R. Meir (commenting on Deut 32:5), "even when they are full of blemishes they are called children"; Philo *Spec.* 4.181.

cognizant of your might. Cf. 12:16. Aware of God's infinite power, we know that he will not abandon us in our sins, but this sense of confidence in God will actually prevent us from sinning in the first place.

3. *sum of righteousness.* For *holoklēros,* cf. IV Macc 15:17 (*eusebeian holoklēron*).

your power. With the power of God we may compare the powerlessness of Death's domain (17:14) and his impotence on earth (1:14; cf. 13:17–19, where the author presents by way of a series of pointed contrasts a vivid picture of the total impotence of the idols). See Murphy:88–93. The rabbis similarly see the special manifestation of God's power in his ability to resurrect the dead (the second benediction of the *Amidah,* known as *gĕbûrôt* or "mighty deeds," concludes with "Blessed art Thou, O Lord, who revives the dead"). See *M. Ber.* 5.2; *BT Ber.* 33a. Cf. John 17:3.

4. The writer is thinking of his own period. The consensus among the rabbis of the third century was that all idolatrous impulses had been eradicated from Israel as early as the beginning of the Second Temple period (*BT Yoma* 69b; *Sanh.* 64a; *Arakhin* 32b). For this view there is parallel evidence in Judith 8:18: "For there has not risen in our generations, nor is there today, a tribe, a family, a clan or a city that worships idols made by human hands, as there was once in olden times." Hecataeus of Abdera praises Moses for his non-anthropomorphic notion of God: "But he [Moses] had no images whatsoever of the gods made for them, being of the opinion that God is not in human form" (Stern:28). Tacitus grudgingly allows that Jewish worship is free of idolatry (*Historiae* 5. 5: "The Jews conceive of one god only, and that with the mind alone: they regard as impious those who make from perishable materials representations of god in man's image; that supreme and eternal being is to them incapable of representation and without end. Therefore they set up no statues in their cities, still less in their temples; this flattery is not paid their kings, nor this honor given to the Caesars").

sterile labor of painters. The choice of the word *skiagraphos* is deliberate, since *skiagraphia* is "painting with the shadows so as to produce an illusion of solidity at a distance" [LSJ], and is frequently used to refer to what is illusory or unreal. Cf. Plato *Critias* 107D; *Rep.* 365C; *Phaedrus* 69B; Aristotle *Metaphysica* 1024b23; *Protrepticus* B104, Düring: "For one will find that all the things men think great are mere scene-painting." *skiagraphos* is found only here. Epiphanius (fourth century CE) connected the beginnings of idolatry with painting or shadow-sketching (*skiagraphia*): "With Serug, idolatry and paganism (*Hellēnismos*) took their start amongst men. It was, however, so far, not a matter of images and the graving of stones or of wood, or of figures fashioned in silver or any other substance: it was only in the way of color-painting and pictures that the mind of man devised for itself evil." With Serug's son Terah, however, "there began the fashioning of statues from moulded mud by the craft of the worker in clay, according to the art of this same Terah" (*Panarion* 3.4–5). In his *Ancoratus* (102.1), he actually uses the word *skiagraphia* in this connection: "When this innovation was made by men through the evil work of demons, the idols were first drawn in shadow-sketches (*en skiagraphiais*). Next, everybody passed on to his children, for their homage, the products of the particular art which he himself exercised, and by which he got his living. In the material with which his particular craft dealt each man fashioned gods; the potter in clay, the carpenter in wood, the goldsmith in gold, and so forth." This notion seems to be based on the Greek legend regarding the origin of the art of modeling images in clay. It began, says Pliny, with Butades of Sicyon, whose daughter, "when her lover was going abroad, drew in outline on the wall the shadow of his face thrown by a lamp. Her father pressed clay on this and made a relief, which he hardened by exposure to fire with the rest of his pottery" (*NH* 35.151. See Bevan 1940:51–54). The story is repeated by Athenagoras: "Relief modelling was discovered by the Corinthian maid: she fell in love with someone and traced the outline of his shadow on the wall (*periegrapsen . . . en toichō tēn skian*) as he slept; then her father, a potter, delighted with so precise a likeness, made a relief of the outline and filled it in with clay . . ." (*Legatio ad Graecos* 17.3, Oxford Early Christian Texts Series, ed. W. R. Schoedel, 1972). See Geffcken 1907:xxii, n.2. It is interesting to note that in rabbinic literature a distinction was made between engraving and relief: "A ring bearing an idolatrous emblem may not be used if it is in relief (*boletet*), but may be used if it is not in relief" (*Tosef. A.Z.* 5.2; *BT Rosh HaShana* 24b).

colors. Cf. Plato *Rep.* 420C. "That the surface of archaic statues was regularly painted is now no longer doubtful. During the best period, in the case of marble or other polished surfaces, the painting was regularly confined to the eyes, eyelids, eyebrows, hair, and the like" (J. Adam, commentary on Plato's *Republic,* ad loc.).

5. We have in this verse (imperfect) iambic rhythms. Cf. Heb 12:13–14; James 1:17 (Farrar [1888]).

to lust for the unbreathing form. Grimm cites the story of Pygmalion, legendary king of Cyprus, who having fashioned an ivory statue of a woman fell in love with it (Ovid *Metamorphoses* 10.243–297; Arnobius *Adversus Nationes* 6.22, contains a much cruder version of the story). Cf. Alexis 40, Edmonds, 2:393; Pliny *NH* 36.21: "There is a story that a man once fell in love with it [Praxiteles' Venus at Cnidos] and hiding by night embraced it, and that a stain betrays this lustful act"; Lucian *Imagines* 4; Ps-Lucian *Amores* 13–16; Philostratus *Vita Apollonii* 6.40.

6. *make these things.* The context requires *drōntes* to mean "make," but such a usage seems to be unparalleled. Schleusner quotes Hesychius: *drōntes, poiountes, ergazomenoi* (Deane [1881]).

XXX. MALICIOUS MANUFACTURE OF CLAY
FIGURINES
(15:7–13)

15 7 For a potter, laboriously tempering soft clay, molds each single article for our service, but out of the selfsame clay he fashions those vessels which serve for clean purposes and the contrary sort, all alike; but what shall be the use of each vessel of either class, the worker in clay decides. 8 With misspent toil he molds a nothing-god out of the same clay, he who but shortly before came into being out of the earth and shortly after returns whence he was taken, when the life that was lent him is demanded back. 9 But his concern is not that his health is likely to fail or that his life will shortly end, but he vies with goldsmiths and silversmiths, and emulates molders of bronze and considers it high honor to fashion counterfeits. 10 His heart is ashes, his hope meaner than dirt, and his life more ignoble than clay, 11 because he knew not the one who fashioned him and infused him with an active soul and breathed into him a vital spirit. 12 He rather counts our existence a game, and our life a holiday bargain fair, for one must earn a living, he says, from whatever source, however foul. 13 For this man knows more than any other that he is doing wrong, fabricating from earthen stuff frail vessels and carved images.

NOTES

15:7. *for clean purposes and the contrary sort.* This theme is reminiscent of the story about Amasis narrated by Herodotus 2.172 (cf. Aristotle *Politica* 1259b8; Ps-Plutarch *De Nobilitate* 3.924), and often quoted by Christian writers (Athenagoras *Legatio ad Graecos* 26; Minucius Felix *Octavius* 22.4: see Geffcken, XXVII, n.1. For rabbinic allusions to this story, see Lieberman 1950:122–126). Philo, too, refers to this theme: the images' substance "is wood and stone, till a short time ago completely shapeless, hewn away from their congenital structure by quarrymen and woodcutters while their brethren, pieces from the same original source, have become urns and footbasins or some others of the less honorable vessels which serve the purposes of darkness rather than of light" (*Cont.* 7; cf. Gilbert 1973:205–207). Cf. Rom 9:21: "Has the potter no right over the clay, to make out of the same lump one vessel for beauty and another for menial use?"; Epicharmus Frag. 131, Kaibel: "Out of any piece of wood the yoke of a plough may be made and out of the same piece, a god." See Walzer:164–174.

what shall be the use of each vessel of either class. Cf. *Test.Naphtali* 2:4: *kathaper oiden ho kerameus henos hekastou tēn chrēsin.* The "potter" is here contemptuously used to include a sculptor in clay (Farrar [1888]). Moreover, whereas the woodworker was depicted as at least a believer in his wooden idols, the potter appears as a mere mercenary (v. 12), and is much more vehemently denounced. Work in faience was indeed particularly popular in Alexandria, and it included statuettes of native deities (see Fraser: 1. 140).

the worker in clay. The substantive *pēlourgos* is first attested here (adjective found in *Lyrica Alexandrina Adespota*, ed. J. U. Powell, *Collectonea Alexandrina* (1925) 7.16). Cf. Lucian *Prometheus Es in Verbis* 2.

8. *With misspent toil.* kakomochthos is found only here. Cf. *eumochthos Epigr.Gr.* 239; *IG* 3.758a.

returns. For *poreuetai* see NOTE on 3.3. Cf. Plato *Menexenus* 236D; *Phaedo* 67B; 113D.

the life that was lent him is demanded back. We have here a Platonic image that had become very popular. In fashioning the mortal parts of man, the young gods, according to Plato, "imitating their own Maker, borrowed (*daneizomenoi:* cf. Wisd 15:16) from the Cosmos portions of fire and earth and water and air, as if meaning to pay them back" (*Tim.* 42E). Cf. Ps-Plato *Axiochus* 367b2: "Nature is like a small moneylender; if we do not repay the debt (*chreos*) of life promptly, she comes down on us and takes sight or hearing, or often both, as pledges for a settlement." These words are very similar to those of Bion of Borysthenes: "Just as we move out of a house when the landlord, failing to collect his rent, removes the door, or the tiling, or shuts up the well, so do I quit the body when landlady Nature (*misthōsasa physis*) takes away eyes, ears, hands or feet" (O. Hense, *Teletis Reliquiae* [rep. Hildesheim, New York, 1969] 15–16. Cf. also his statement: "Fortune does not give to the rich, it lends" [*dedaneiken*] [Stobaeus 4.41]). Cf. Alexis (Middle and New Comedy poet): "Because the life we have is not ours: God takes it back from each one lightly when he thinks fit" (*P. Berol.* 11771); Serbian inscription: "We shall make a monument for our life and that which we have unknowingly received we shall return. That's that" (see Nock 1966:23–24). Lydian Inscription, second century CE: "I did not receive this life as my own, stranger. I borrowed it from time and now return it to time as to my creditor" (Peek, 1960: no. 260). Lucretius 3.971: "Life is granted to none for freehold (*mancipio*), to all on lease (*usu*)"; Euripides *The Suppliant Women,* 534; *Phoenician Women* 555; Cicero *Ad Familiares* 7.29.1; 7.30.2; Accius, Frag. 422; Heraclitus *Homeric Allegories* 22.10: "The debt which Nature gave us as a loan in the beginning (*ha dedaneiken en archē chrea*), she takes back in the end; Cicero *Tusc.* 1.93; Plutarch *Moralia* 106F: "Wherefore it is said that life is a debt to destiny (*moiridion chreos*), the idea being that a loan which our forefathers contracted (*edaneisanto*) is to be repaid by us;" Ps-Phocylides 106 (*FPG:* 152); Sextus *Sentences* 21 (Chadwick: 14, line 21); Vettius Valens *Anthologiae,* ed. W. Kroll (Berlin, 1908): 330, 33; Jos. *J.W.* 3.8.5 (372–374); Luke 12:20: "Fool, this night they shall demand back (*apaitousin*) from thee thy soul." Philo is particularly fond of this image: *Abr.* 257; *Post.* 5; *Her.* 104; *Cher.* 118; *Spec.* 1.295; *ShR* on Exod 22:24 (God lends the soul without interest, taking back only the capital; cf. Seneca *De Consolatio ad Polybius* 10.4–5: "If anyone should be angry that he has had to pay back borrowed money—especially that of which he had the use without paying interest—would he not be considered an unfair man? Nature gave your brother his life. . . . If she has required from him from whom she wanted it an earlier payment of her loan, she has but used her own right"); Hermas *Mandates* 3.2; *Similitudes* 9.32.2; *ARN* 14; *Tanḥ Shophetim* 12 (Hadrian's wife said to him, when he proposed to make himself God, that he might do so after returning to God his deposit, his soul); Eccles 12:7; *Mid. Mishle* 31.10. See D. Daube, "Josephus on Suicide and Liability of Depositee," *The Juridical Review* 3 (1964): 1–13. Cf. also *Life of Secundus the Philosopher,* ed. B. E. Perry (Ithaca, 1964):8, where man is described as *gēs apaitēma*.

whence he was taken. Cf. Gen 3:19, LXX.

9. *will shortly end. brachytelē.* Found only here (but reappears in Patristic Greek).

goldsmiths. chrusourgos first attested here. Cf. Pollux 7.97.

silversmiths. argyrochoos found only here (but reappears in Patristic Greek).

molders of bronze. chalkoplastos found only here (but reappears in Patristic Greek).

counterfeits. Earthen figures, colored and glazed, or varnished to look like metal (Deane [1888]).

10. *His heart is ashes.* Based on a mistranslation of Isa 44:20 in LXX.

11. *a vital spirit.* Erasistratus of Alexandria had distinguished between a *pneuma zōtikon* and a *pneuma psychikon,* and our author, with Gen 2:7 in mind, readily adopted this Greek formulation (see Verbeke 1945:224–225; cf. Gilbert 1973:213). It should be noted that the LXX, untouched by Greek philosophical influence, translated Hebrew *nepeš* in Gen 2:7 not with the Greek *psychē,* but with *pnoē.* Cf. Prov 24:12;

20:27, LXX; Ps 150:6, LXX; IV Ezra 16:62. See Freudenthal 1890:210–212.

12. *a game.* For this metaphor, cf. Plato *Laws* 644D, where it is suggested that man may be an ingenious puppet of the gods, contrived by them by way of a toy (*paignion*) or for some serious purpose; Aristotle *Politics* 1337b35; *EN* 1176b27; Cicero *Off.* 1.103: "for Nature has not brought us into the world to act as if we were created for play or jest, but rather for earnestness"; Suetonius *Divus Augustus* 99.1; Palladas (fourth century CE): "The world's a stage and life's a toy" (*paignion*); (*AP* 10.72); *Life of Secundus* 8 (where man is described as *Tychēs paignion*); Quran 57:19: "The life of this world is but a sport, and a play and a gaud."

a holiday bargain fair. panēgyrismon. Life as a festival is another widespread motif. Cf. Alexis, Frag. 219: "I've myself no doubt that all man's doings are madness out and out, and those now living are visitors to this light, allowed a holiday (*eis panēgyrin tina*) from death and night, And whoever laughs, drinks, loves, and, if he can, Dines out, the most, goes home the happiest man" (Edmonds 2:4801); Menander *Reliquiae* II, ed. Koerte, n.416,8; Menander *Sententiae,* ed. Jaekel, 627; Vettius Valens, ed. Kroll, 246.2 (life is mere farce [*paignion*], error [*planē*], and *panēgyris*); Epictetus 4.1.105: "Are you not willing, then, for so long as has been given you, to be a spectator of his pageant and his festival (*panēgyrin*) . . . but the festival has come to an end"; 3.5.10: "And now it is thy will that I leave this festival; I go, I am full of gratitude to Thee that Thou hast deemed me worthy to take part in this festival with Thee"; *Teletis Reliquiae,* ed. Hense: 15.10; Ps-Longinus *On the Sublime* 35.2; Methodius *Symposion* 8.1.171; D.L. 8.8; Cicero *Tusc.* 5.9: "Pythagoras replied that the life of man seemed to him to resemble the festival which was celebrated with most magnificent games before a concourse collected from the whole of Greece; for at this festival some men . . . sought to win the glorious distinction of a crown, others were attracted by the prospect of making gain by buying or selling . . ."; *BT Erub.* 54a: "hurry on and eat, hurry on and drink, since the world from which we must depart is like a wedding feast."

from whatever source, however foul. Another commonplace. Cf. Sophocles *Antigone* 312: "and learn that it is not well to love gain from every source"; Xenophon *Mem.* 2.9.4; Chilon, ap. D.L. 1.70; Horace *Epistulae* 1.1.65: "Make money, money by fair means if you can, if not, by any means money"; Juvenal 14.204: "The smell of gain is good whatever the thing from which it comes. . . . Let this maxim be ever on your lips: 'no matter whence the money comes, but money you must have' "; Philo *Prob.* 65: "As it is, for the sake of money we ransack every corner and open up rough and rocky veins of earth"; *Praem.* 11: "In hope of gain the tradesman arms himself for the manifold forms of money getting."

15   ¹⁴ But most foolish of all, and sorrier than blind infants are the enemies and oppressors of your people, ¹⁵ for even all the idols of the nations they accounted gods, though they have neither use of eyes for seeing, nor nostrils for drawing breath, nor ears to hear, nor fingers for feeling, and their feet are ineffectual for walking. ¹⁶ It was a man who made them, and one who borrowed his breath shaped them; for no human has the power to fashion a god like himself. ¹⁷ But being mortal, he makes a lifeless thing with his lawless hands; for he surpasses the objects of his worship, in that he had life, but they never did. ¹⁸ Moreover, they worship the most hateful beasts, who compared for brutishness are worse than all the rest. ¹⁹ Nor do they chance to have a trace of beauty, so as to make them objects of desire, to the extent that this is possible with a beastly appearance; but they have escaped both the approval of God and his blessing.

NOTES

15:14. *than blind infants.* Cf. NOTE on 12:24.

15. Cf. Pss 115:4*ff;* 135:15*ff;* Philo *Decal.* 74.

for drawing breath. Cf. *Test.Reuben* 2:5: "The fourth is the sense of smell, with which taste is given to draw air and breath (*eis synolkēn aeros kai pnoēs*) (this verse is a late addition to the text, undoubtedly first made in the Greek version. See *Test.XII,* ad loc.). *synolkē* is first attested here. Cf. Hierocles 62A; Ps-Dioscorides *Peri Dēlētēriōn Pharmakōn* (*On Noxious Poisons*) 14; Galen 2.266C.

17. *he surpasses the objects of his worship.* Philo makes the same point: "In their general ignorance they have failed to perceive even that most obvious truth which even 'a witless infant knows' [cf. *Iliad* 17.32; Hesiod *Op.* 218], that the craftsman is superior to the product of his craft both in time, since he is older than what he makes and in a sense its father, and in

value, since the efficient element is held in higher esteem than the passive effect. And while if they were consistent in their sin, they should have deified the sculptors and painters themselves . . . they leave them in obscurity . . . while they regard as gods the figures and pictures made by their workmanship" (*Decal.* 69).

18. *compared for brutishness.* Philo similarly writes: "But actually the Egyptians have gone to a further excess, and chosen the fiercest and most savage of wild animals, lions and crocodiles and among reptiles the venomous asp. . . . For after ransacking the two elements given by God to man for his use, earth and water, to find their fiercest occupants, they found on land no creature more savage than the lion nor in water than the crocodile and these they reverence and honor" (*Decal.* 78; cf. *Cont.* 8; Jos. *Ag.Ap.* 2.6).

19. *nor do they chance to have a trace of beauty* (*oud'* . . . *kala tyngchanei*). sc. *onta.* Cf. Philo *Cont.* 9: "They render worship to them, they the civilized to the uncivilized and untamed, the reasonable to the irrational, the kinsfolk of the Godhead to ugliness unmatched even by a Thersites." Plutarch, on the other hand, attempts to find a justification for animal worship (see *Is. et Os.* 382).

so as to make them objects of desire (*hoson epipothēsai*). A good classical construction (it equals: *epi tosouton hōste*), but it does not seem to occur in Hellenistic Greek (Goodrick [1913]).

escaped both the approval of God and his blessing. This is certainly not a Jewish teaching, and the author appears to be alluding to one of the characteristic doctrines of Zoroastrianism. "All that is aggressive or repulsive," writes M. Boyce, "is classed as *daēvic;* and in time a whole double vocabulary developed for good and evil creatures. Daevic creatures were naturally considered as unclean in themselves, and to slay them was a positive merit; for there is no sin in bringing death to the creatures of him who created death. The generic Avestan term for them, *khrafstra,* used by the prophet himself (Yasna 28.5; 34.5) [Bailey suggested a derivation of the word from Indo-European verbal base *skrep—meaning "bite, sting, pierce"]), occurs in Middle Iranian as *khrafstar,* or dialectically *frestar.* It was applied particularly to insects and reptiles, but could also be used of beasts of prey. . . . Destroying such creatures amounted, in Zoroastrian eyes, to eliminating sources of evil and corruption, and so seemed unquestionably good as does the destruction of disease-germs and microbes to the rationalist today. This practice continued down the ages, being first noticed by Herodotus (1.140), and till the mid-19th century the Zoroastrians of Kerman kept up an annual observance called *kharastar-kōšī,* when members of the community went out into the plains around the city and slew as many *kharastars* as they could, such as scorpions, tarantulas, lizards, snakes, ants, and all else that crept and crawled, pricked, bit or stung, and seemed hideous and repulsive" (pp. 298–299; see also Winston 1966:209, n.72). In the two millennia of Ōshētar and Ōshētarmāh, which are the prelude to the *Frashkart* or Final Rehabilitation, the noxious beasts created by Ahriman, that is, the wolf and cat tribes on the one hand, and reptiles and poisonous insects on the other, are destroyed (*Selections of Zatspram*, chap. 34, translation in Zaehner 1972:354). Cf. Virgil *Ecl*. 4.24: "The serpent, too, shall perish, and the false poison-plant shall perish" (Nicander *Theriaca* 8*ff* quotes Hesiod for the view that snakes sprang from the spilt blood of the Titans).

XXXII. SECOND ANTITHESIS: EGYPTIANS HUNGER THROUGH ANIMAL PLAGUE, BUT ISRAEL ENJOYS EXOTIC QUAIL FOOD
(16:1–4)

16 ¹ Therefore they were duly chastised by similar creatures, and tormented by swarms of beasts. ² In lieu of such punishment, you exhibited kindness to your people and prepared for the satisfaction of their fierce craving an exotic delicacy of quail food; ³ so that those others, though desiring food, might turn away even from their necessary craving through the hideousness of the creatures sent against them, while your people, only briefly made to want, might partake of an exotic dish. ⁴ For it was necessary that an inexorable famine overtake the oppressors, but for your people only to be shown how their enemies were tortured.

NOTES

16:1. *Therefore.* I.e. because they worshiped "the most hateful beasts (15:18).

swarms of beasts. The plagues included frogs, lice, locusts, and either "a mixture of wild beasts" (Jos. *Ant.* 2.14.3) or dogflies (LXX: *kynomuia* (cf. *ShR* 11.4).

2. *quail food. ortygomētra* is the LXX translation of Hebrew *šĕlāw,* but rendered in LSJ as "a bird which migrates with quails, perhaps, corncrake, landrail, Rallus crex." Cf. Exod 16:9–13; Num 11:10–32; Pss 78:26–29; 105:40.

3. *craving.* For *oreksis,* cf. Sir 18:30; 23:6. It is an Aristotelian term: *De Anima* 414b2. Cf. Epicurus *K.D.* 26; Frags. 45 and 60, Bailey.

hideousness. eidechtheia is found only here (but occurs again in Patristic Greek). (In Philo *Op.* 158, the editor, L. Cohn, has removed the word.) For *eidechthēs,* see Theophrastus *Characteres* 28.4; Polybius

36.15.1; Philo *LA* 3.62; *Jos.* 101; *Aet.* 56. The author has adapted the biblical version of this event to serve his own peculiar exegesis, by omitting all mention of the people's murmuring and gluttony and God's furious anger which culminated in the destruction of many of them (a characteristic feature of encomiastic writing).

XXXIII. THIRD ANTITHESIS: EGYPTIANS SLAIN BY LOCUSTS AND FLIES, BUT ISRAEL SURVIVES A SERPENT ATTACK THROUGH THE BRONZE SERPENT, SYMBOL OF SALVATION (16:5–14)

16   5 Even when the terrible fury of beasts came upon them, and they were perishing through the bites of tortuous serpents, your anger did not abide to the end; 6 only for a while were they thrown into disarray as a warning, possessing as they did a symbol of your salvation to remind them of the commandment of your law. 7 For whoever turned towards it was saved not by the sight beheld, but through you, the savior of all. 8 And by this you convinced our foes that you are the one who delivers from every evil. 9 For those men were slain by the bites of locusts and flies, and no remedy was found for their life, since they deserved to be punished by such creatures. 10 But your sons were not overcome by the fangs of venom-spraying serpents, for your compassion came forth to their aid and healed them. 11 It was to remind them of your oracles that they were sharply prodded and quickly delivered so that they might not fall into a deep forgetfulness and become complacent through your kindness. 12 For it was neither herb nor emollient that cured them, but your word, O Lord, that heals all. 13 For you have the power of life and death; you lead down to the gates of Hades and bring back up again. 14 Man indeed slays in his wickedness, but he does not bring back the expired life breath nor release the soul embraced by death.

NOTES

16:5. *tortuous serpents.* Cf. Isa 27:1: *ton drakonta ophin skolion;* Virgil *Aen.* 2.204.

to the end. Cf. 19:1; I Thess 2:16; *Test.Levi* 6:11.

6. *a symbol of your salvation.* I.e. the bronze serpent. Cf. Num 21:9.

(Ms אA reads *symboulon,* which is reminiscent of Philo *Agr.* 97, where the serpent of Eve or 'pleasure' is described as *symboulon anthrōpou.* Cf. *Agr.* 95. F. H. Colson (the translator of Philo in the LCL), however, suggests the reading *epiboulon* in that passage.) Philo similarly interprets the serpent of Moses as a symbol of steadfast endurance (*karteria*), which explains, he says, "why it is represented as being made of very strong material like brass." "He, then, who has looked with fixed gaze on the form of patient endurance, even though he should perchance have been previously bitten by the wiles of pleasure, cannot but live; for, whereas pleasure menaces the soul with inevitable death, self-control (*engkrateia*) holds out to it health and safety (*sōtērion*) for life" (*Agr.* 98). Cf. *LA* 2.79–81; Justin *Apologia* 1.60: "Moses, by the inspiration and influence of God, took brass, and made it into the figure of a cross, and set it in the holy tabernacle, and said to the people, 'If ye look to this figure (*typō*), and believe, ye shall be saved thereby' "; John 3:14.

7. *was saved not by the sight beheld.* The author seeks to replace the principle of homeopathic magic which appears to be operative in Num 21:8–9 with a spiritual conception. (See B. A. Levine, *In the Presence of the Lord* [Leiden, 1974]:85–86.) We find a similar interpretation in *M. Rosh Hashanah* 3.8: "But could the serpent kill or could the serpent keep alive? But rather, whenever Israel looked on high and subjected their heart to their Father in heaven were they healed, but if not, they perished." It may be noted that the rabbis explained the punishment of the Israelites by means of serpents on the talion principle, a conceit to which, as we have already seen, both they and the author of Wisd were equally attached. See *Tanḥ. Ḥukat* 45: "Let the serpent who began with slander come and exact punishment from those who utter slander. . . . Let the serpent who eats all kinds of food and yet enjoys only one taste (cf. *BT Yoma* 75a), come and exact punishment from those who eat only one kind of food and yet enjoy the taste of many kinds." Cf. *Targ.Yerush.* and Ps-Jonathan on Num 21:6: "And the *bath-kol* fell from the high heaven and thus spoke: I made manna come down for them from heaven, yet now they turn and murmur against me. Yet, behold, the serpent whom, in the days of the beginning of the world, I doomed to have dust for his food, hath not murmured against me. Now shall the serpents who have not complained of their food come and bite the people who complain."

9. *slain.* The only allusion to deadly effects of the locusts is in Exod 10:17, where Pharaoh calls the locusts 'this death.' Josephus, on the other hand, tells us that the Egyptians perished miserably both through the attacks of the lice and "the wild beasts of every species and kind" (*Ant.* 2.14.3–4). For a vivid description of the ferocious dog-fly, see Philo *Mos.* 1.130–132.

10. *venom-spraying.* For *iobolōn,* cf. Aristotle *Historia Animalium*

607a28; Philo *Op.* 156; *Agr.* 95; *Ebr.* 223; etc. For Philo the reptiles are a symbol of poisonous passions (*iobolōn pathōn*): *QG* 2.56.

came forth to their aid. (*antiparēlthen*). In the sense of "come up and help" found only here.

11. *to remind them of your oracles.* Cf. Ps-Aristeas 158: "He has ordained for us that we place the chapters (*ta logia*) 'upon our doorposts and gates' to serve as a remembrance (*mneian*) of God."

prodded. enkentrizō in the sense of 'goad,' 'spur on,' used only here (but occurs again in Patristic Greek).

complacent. For *aperispastos,* cf. Epictetus 3.9.19; 2.21.22 ("free from distraction"; here, in the sense of complacency).

12. *neither herb nor emollient that cured them.* Cf. Philo *Sacr.* 70: "When anything befalls them which they would not, since they have never had any firm faith in God their savior, they first flee to the help which things created give, to physicians, herbs (*botanas*), drug-mixtures, strict rules of diet, and all the other aids that mortals use."

word. Cf. Ps 107:20.

13. *power of life and death.* Cf. Deut 32:39; I Sam 2:6.

lead down . . . and bring back. Cf. I Sam 2:6; Tobit 13:2: "He leads down (*katagei*) to Hades below the earth. but he delivers (or brings up: *anagei*) from the great Abyss." For the gates of Hades, cf. Isa 38:10; Job 38:17; III Macc 5:51; Pss 9:14; 107:18.

14. *he does not bring back the expired life breath.* A basic sentiment. Cf. *Iliad* 9.408–409: "but that the spirit of man should come again when once it hath passed the barrier of his teeth, neither harrying availeth nor winning."

XXXIV. FOURTH ANTITHESIS: EGYPTIANS PLAGUED BY THUNDERSTORMS, BUT ISRAEL FED BY A RAIN OF MANNA
(16:15–29)

16   15 But from your hand flight is impossible; 16 for godless men who denied knowing you were scourged by the might of your arm, pursued by unusual downpours and relentless hail and thunderstorms, and utterly wasted by fire. 17 Most incredible of all, in water which quenches everything, fire was the most dynamic force, for the cosmic order champions the righteous. 18 At one moment the flame was tempered, so that it might not burn up the beasts sent against the godless, the better for them to see and perceive that it was by God's judgment that they were pursued; 19 at another, even amid the water it flared up beyond the ordinary force of fire, to destroy the fruits of an unrighteous land. 20 By contrast, you spoonfed your people with angel food, and unwearyingly furnished them from heaven bread already prepared, equivalent to every pleasure, and suited to every taste. 21 For your sustenance displayed your sweetness toward your children, and serving the desire of him that tasted it, changed its nature in accordance with what anyone wished. 22 But the snow and ice[-like food] endured fire and did not melt, that they might know that fire destroyed the fruits of their enemies, flaming in the hail and flashing in the storm; 23 and this fire again has forgotten even its own power, in order that the righteous be fed. 24 For creation, serving you its maker, tenses itself for punishment against the unrighteous, and slackens into benevolence on behalf of those who trust in you. 25 Therefore, at that time, too, changing into all things, it served your all-nurturing bounty in accordance with the wish of those who were in want, 26 that your sons whom you love, O Lord, might learn that it is not the varieties of fruit which nourish a man, but that your word preserves those that trust in you. 27 For that which was not destroyed by fire, melted straightaway when warmed by a fleeting sunbeam, 28 so that men might know that one must rise before the sun to give

you thanks, and make petition at the crack of dawn. 29 For the hope
of the ungrateful will melt away like the winter's frost, and drain off
like water that goes to waste.

NOTES

16:15. *from your hand flight is impossible.* Cf. Tobit 13:28: "There is
nothing that can escape his hand" (*ouk estin ouden ho ekpheuksetai tēn
cheira autou*).

16. *unusual downpours.* Philo highlights this fact: "We must remember
that Egypt is almost the only country, apart from those in southern lati-
tudes, which is unvisited by one of the year's seasons—winter. . . . Such
was the condition of the land, enjoying springtime at mid-winter, the
seaboard enriched by only slight showers, while the parts above Memphis,
where the royal palace of Egypt was, experienced no rainfall at all, when
suddenly a complete change came over the air, and all the visitations
which belong to severe winter fell upon it in a body" (*Mos.* 1.114, 118).

17. *fire was the most dynamic force.* See Exod 9:24. Philo similarly
writes: "These last [flashes of lightning and thunderbolts] provided a most
marvellous spectacle, for they ran through the hail, their natural antago-
nist, and yet did not melt it nor were quenched by it, but unchanged
coursed up and down and kept guard over the hail" (*Mos.* 1.118). Cf.
ShR 12.6: "a miracle within a miracle."

18. Cf. 19:21. The author appears to be assuming that the plagues of
frogs, flies, lice, locusts and hail were coterminous, thus contradicting the
biblical narrative. Although there were varying traditions concerning both
the number and order of the plagues, and we find Artapanus, for example,
combining locusts, lice, and frogs into one plague (*FPG:* 194, lines
17–20), there is no known parallel to our author's particular scheme.

20. *spoonfed.* For *epsōmisas,* cf. Deut 8:3: *epsōmise se to manna.*

angel food. Cf. Ps 78:25, LXX, where *leḥem abbîrîm* is translated *arton
angelōn; BT Yoma* 75b, where this interpretation is maintained by
R. Akiba. His colleague R. Ishmael, however, strongly objects to the view
that angels partake of food, and interprets *leḥem abbîrîm* as bread which
is absorbed by the 248 parts [*ēbārîm*] of the body (cf. *Tanḥ.* Buber,
Beshallah 34; *Targ. Yerush* on Ps 78:25; IV Ezra 1:19 [*panem
angelorum*]; *Vita Adae* 4:2).

unwearyingly. For *akopiatōs,* cf. *SVF* 1.549: *tēn akamaton kai akopiaton pronoian* (the adverbial form is found in Philodemus *De Pietate* 15).
The translation 'without their laboring for it' is grammatically unjustified

(see Fichtner [1938], ad loc.), though it ties in well with Philo's designation of the manna as *tēn aponon kai atalaipōron trophēn* (*Congr.* 173; *Mos.* 2.267).

suited to every taste. Cf. *Mek.Wayassaʿ* 5.41, on Exod 16:23: "R. Joshua says, if one liked it baked, it would become baked for him; if one liked it cooked, it would become cooked for him. R. Eliezer of Modiʿim says, if one liked to eat something baked, he could taste in the manna the taste of any kind of baked things in the world; if one liked to eat something cooked, he could taste in it the taste of any dish in the world"; *Sifre Num.* 89; *BT Yoma* 75a: "R. Akiba said: [Do not read *le-šad* (cake), but *šad* (breast)] i.e. Just as the infant finds very many a flavor in the breast, so also did Israel find many a taste in the manna as long as they were eating it. Some there are who say: [*"Le-šad"* means] a real demon, even as the demon changes into many colors, so did the manna change into many tastes"; *ShR* 25.3, on Exod 16:4.

21. *sustenance.* Others translate 'substance,' referring either to God's substance as the power working in the manna (Grimm [1860]) or to the manna itself (Farrar [1888]; Heinisch [1912]). "Many commentators take it to refer to the Person of the Logos, as Heb 1:3 (*charaktēr tēs hypostaseōs autou*), but the corresponding clause ('and serving the desire of him that tasted it') shows that it refers to the manna" (Deane [1881]). In Philo's allegorical interpretation, the manna refers to the Logos: "Manna is the divine Logos, eldest of all existences, which bears the most comprehensive name of 'somewhat' (*to genikōtaton ti*). Out of it are made two cakes, the one of honey, the other of oil. These are two inseparable and all-important stages in education, at the outset causing a sweetness to flow from what knowledge opens, and afterwards causing a most brilliant light to flash from them on those who handle in no fickle and perfunctory way the subjects which they love, but lay hold of them strongly and firmly with a persistence that knows no slackness of intermission" (*Det.* 118).

changed its nature. metakirnaō (=*metakerannymi.* Cf. Pausanius 9.28.4) is found only here (but occurs again in Patristic Greek).

22. *snow.* Cf. 19:21. Exod 16:14 merely speaks of the manna as "small as the hoar frost on the ground" but the comparison to snow occurs already in Artapanus: *chioni paraplēsion tēn chroan* (*FPG:* 195, lines 23–24), and again in Josephus (*Ant.* 3.1.6). Cf. Philo *Mos.* 1.200.

did not melt. I.e. in ordinary fire, since it did melt under sunlight (see v. 27 below). Cf. Philo *Mos.* 1.118; Plato *Phaedo* 106A.

flaming in the hail. Cf. Exod 9:24, LXX.

flashing. diastraptō is found only here (but occurs again in Patristic Greek) (classical form is *astraptō*).

24. *serving you its maker.* Philo uses virtually the same language in a

similar context: "But God has subject to him not one portion of the universe, but the whole world and its parts, to minister as slaves to their master (*hōs despotē doula hypēretēsonta*). So now it has seemed good to him that the air should bring food instead of water" (*Mos.* 1.201).

tenses itself . . . and slackens. The intent of this verse is that the elements of fire and water, through a heightening or lowering of their *tonos* ('tension'), underwent a sufficient inner transformation to account, on the one hand, for the miracle of the ice-like manna which "endured fire and did not melt," and, on the other hand, for the punishment of the Egyptians by fire "flaming in the hail and flashing in the storm." Cf. 19:6,18–20, with commentary. The correlative notions of *epitasis* and *anesis* may be traced back to Plato: *Rep.* 442A; *Phaedo* 86C, 94C. For the Stoics, see *SVF* 3.92, 525, where we are told that Virtue and the Good admit neither of *epitasis* nor *anesis,* and in this differ from the *technai* which do admit of such variations and gradations. According to Chrysippus each virtue was a different state of the pneuma which constituted the psyche: *SVF* 3.259. The health of the soul was equated with the right tension or *eutonia,* and its sickness with wrong tension or *atonia: SVF* 3.471. Sleep was thus seen by the Stoics as a slackening (*anesis*) of the soul's perceptive pneuma and death as its total slackening: *Dox.* 436a10ff. Philo similarly describes the diseased or healthy state of the soul in terms equivalent to the Stoic *atonia* and *eutonia* (*Conf.* 166; *Virt.* 13; *Ebr.* 95, 122), and suggests that perhaps Moses indicates by the bow which God sets in the clouds (Gen 9:13–17); that "in the laxness and force (*anesin kai epitasin*) of earthly things there will not take place a dissolution by their being completely loosened to the point of incongruity nor will there be force up to the point of reaching a break" (*QG* 2.64; cf. *Deus* 162; *Her.* 156; *Mut.* 87).

into benevolence (*eis euergesian*) Cf. Philo *Congr.* 173: *ep' euergesia tōn chrēsomenōn.*

25. *changing.* For *metalleuomenē* see NOTE on 4:12.

into all things (*eis panta*). Heinisch [1912] translates 'completely,' insisting that it did not change into everything, but that it simply adapted itself to each individual's taste.

all-nurturing (*pantotrophō*). Cf. Philo *Confr.* 174: *tou pantotrophou geumatos sophias.*

26. An adaptation of Deut 8:3 (*rhēma* is the LXX rendering of Hebrew *môtza' pî*). Cf. Philo *LA* 3.162–163: "You see that the soul is fed not with things of earth that decay, but with such words as God shall have poured like rain out of that lofty and pure region of life to which the prophet has given the title of 'heaven'"; *Fug.* 137; *Mut.* 259; *Her.* 191.

27. *melted.* See Exod 16:21. We read in *Mek. Wayassa'* on Exod 16:21: "As soon as the sun shone upon it, it began to melt and formed rivulets

which flowed into the great sea. Harts, gazelles, and roebuck, and all kinds of animals would come and drink from them. The nations of the world then would hunt these animals and eat them and taste in them the taste of the manna that came down for Israel" (cf. *Targ.Yerush.* on Exod 16:21, where we find a slightly different version).

28. *rise before the sun.* Cf. Pss 87:13, LXX; 77:34; 62:1; 56:8; Job 8:5, LXX; *Test.Joseph* 3:6.

at the crack of dawn. Cf. Sir 39:5; *BT Ber.* 9b: "The *watikin* (i.e. those 'strong' in their piety) used to finish it [the recital of the *Shema*] with sunrise"; Jos. *J.W.* 2.8.5: "Before the sun is up they [the Essenes] utter no word on mundane affairs, but offer to him certain prayers which have been handed down from their forefathers, as though entreating him to rise." Cf. M. Smith, "Essenes in Josephus and the Philosophumena," *HUCA* 29 (1958) 288, n.55 (quotes Lieberman as saying that Josephus' account misinterprets the use of Isa 60:1, known from Genizah fragments to have been recited in morning prayers). Philo writes of the Therapeutae: "They stand with their faces and whole body turned to the east and when they see the sun rising they stretch their hands up to heaven and pray for bright days." Cf. also Ezek 8:16; *M. Suk.* 5.4. For further examples, see Festugière 1950:4. 245, n.3. Cf. Hengel 1:236; 2:159, n.821. We have here another example of our author's eagerness to uncover the symbolic meaning behind physical events whenever he is able to do so.

XXXV. FIFTH ANTITHESIS: EGYPTIANS TERRIFIED BY DARKNESS, BUT ISRAEL ILLUMINATED WITH BRIGHT LIGHT AND GUIDED THROUGH DESERT BY A PILLAR OF FIRE
(17:1 – 18:4)

17 ¹ Great and inexplicable are your judgments; therefore did untrained minds go astray. ² For though lawless men thought to lord it over a holy people, themselves shackled by darkness and captives of the long night, they lay locked in under their roofs, fugitives from eternal providence. ³ Thinking to remain unnoticed in their secret sins, cloaked by dark oblivion, they were scattered in fearful dismay and terrified by phantoms. ⁴ For even the cranny that confined them did not shield them from fear, but terrifying noises crashed all around them, and gloomy grim-faced apparitions appeared. ⁵ No fire had force enough to give them light, nor did the brightly blazing stars avail to illumine that hideous darkness. ⁶ Only a terrifying self-kindled flaming mass opened a path of light for them, but terrified when the sight was no longer visible, they considered what they had seen more terrible than ever. ⁷ Their magical shams proved ineffectual and their pretension to wisdom was contemptuously unmasked, ⁸ for they who were pledged to drive out terror and tumult from sick souls were themselves diseased with a ridiculous timorousness. ⁹ For even if nothing disturbing alarmed them, they were panicked by the prowling of beasts and the hissing of reptiles, ¹⁰ and perished stricken by convulsions and refusing so much as to look upon the dark haze from which there was no escape. ¹¹ For wickedness [self-]condemned testifies to its innate cowardice, and when anguished by conscience always increases its pain. ¹² Fear is nothing but the abandonment of reason's aid, ¹³ and the vanquished expectation within accounts its ignorance of greater concern than the cause through which its torment comes. ¹⁴ But they, all through a night in reality powerless, inasmuch as it came upon them out of the recesses of the powerless infernal realm, entranced by a death-like sleep, ¹⁵ were now plagued by phantom monsters, now paralyzed by the betrayal of their own minds, for sudden and unexpected fear poured over them. 16 Thus, whosoever fell down there was held bound, locked in a prison without bars. 17 Farmer or shepherd or troubled laborer in the desert he was overtaken and awaited the inescapable fate; 18 for all were bound by one chain of darkness. Whether it was a whistling wind, or the tuneful song of birds in spreading branches, or the cadence of violently onrushing water, 19 or the harsh din of avalanching rocks, or the unseen racing of bounding animals, or the roar of savage beasts, or an echo reverberating from a hollow in the hills—it paralyzed them with terror. 20 For the whole world was illuminated with bright light and went about its tasks unhindered; 21 over them alone there stretched oppressive night, an image of the darkness which was to receive them; yet they were to themselves more burdensome than darkness.

18　　1 But for your holy ones there was light supreme. The enemy who could hear their voices though not discover their shapes, deemed them happy because they had not suffered like themselves, 2 and were thankful that they did not harm them though wronged first, and begged the favor of their being parted. 3 In contrast you provided your people with a blazing pillar as a guide for their uncharted journey, a benign sun to accompany them on their glorious pilgrimage. 4 But well did those others deserve to be deprived of light and imprisoned in darkness, since they kept your sons captive, through whom the imperishable light of the Law was to be given to the world.

NOTES

17:1 – 18:4. In this elaborate antithesis, the author employs all his rhetorical skill to provide his readers with a living impression of the psychological terror occasioned by the plague of darkness. As is his wont, he deftly and almost imperceptibly moves from the physical contrast between darkness and light to the spiritual one which sees in the Egyptians moral villains obsessed with a bad conscience, and in Israel ethical heroes destined to illumine the world with the light of the Torah. Although his language lapses occasionally into virtual obscurity, it is not lacking in either power or pathos, and his vivid description of the paralyzing fear which had gripped the Egyptians, though rhetorically effusive, is not unimpressive. It has been pointed out that the author was undoubtedly influenced by the literary genre known as *katabaseis* or 'descents into Hades' (our best surviving example is Virgil's *Aeneid,* book 6), which includes a graphic description of the terror that paralyzed the guilty. The rabbis had similarly identified the darkness which plagued the Egyptians as coming from Gehenna (*ShR* 14.2, where in support of this R. Naḥman quotes Job 10:22). See Cumont 1949:64–65, 221*ff*; T. F. Glasson, *Greek Influence in Jewish Eschatology* (London, 1961) 8–11; Reese 1970:101–102.

17:1. *inexplicable dysdiēgētoi* is found only here (but occurs again in Patristic Greek). Cf. Isa 40:13–14; Rom 11:33.

2. *For. gar.* It has been remarked that the use of the particle *gar* here is very loose, and that eight out of the first twelve verses of this chapter begin with *gar* (Gregg). Such a loose use of particles was also characteristic of the early diatribe.

lawless men. I.e. the Egyptians.

the long night. Cf. Exod 10:22: "Thick darkness descended upon all the land of Egypt for three days." Cf. Philo *Mos.* 1.123: "What else could it seem but a single night of great length (*mian nykta makrotatēn*) equivalent to three days and the same number of nights?" Some rabbis further exaggerated the length of the darkness: "There were seven days of darkness. How so! During the first three days, whoever was seated and wished to stand up could do so, and vice versa, and concerning these three days it is said, 'Thick darkness descended upon all the land of Egypt for three days, people could not see one another.' During the other three days, he who was seated could not get up, he who was standing could not be seated, and he who was lying down could not stand erect, and concerning them it is said, 'and for three days no one could get up from where he was.' These were the six days of darkness in Egypt, whereas the seventh day of darkness was at the sea, as it is said, 'and there was the cloud with the darkness and it lit the night,' Thus did the Holy One blessed be He send cloud and darkness upon the Egyptians while illuminating Israel, as he did for them in Egypt, and concerning this it was said, 'The Lord is my light and my help'" (Ps 27:1) (*ShR* 14.3).

fugitives. Cf. Empedocles, DK, B.115: *phygas theothen,* 'a fugitive from heaven.'

3. *in their secret sins.* Another example of the principle of talion (cf. NOTE on 11:5): they sought to conceal their sins in darkness, and were therefore plagued by darkness. In *ShR* 14.2, Hizkiah similarly explains that "because 'the works of the wicked are in the dark' (Isa 29:15), therefore the Holy One blessed be He covers them over with the deep (*tehom*) which is darkness, for it is said, 'and darkness over the surface of the deep' (Gen 1:2), this refers to Gehenna." Cf. *Tanḥ.* Buber, *Bo* 5, 21a: "What-

ever the Egyptians planned against the Israelites, the Holy One blessed be He brought upon them. . . . They planned to imprison them, therefore He brought darkness upon them."

cloaked by dark oblivion. parakalymma: First attested in the comic poet Antiphanes (fourth century BCE), 167, and occurs again later in Philo *Decal.* 39; Jos. *Ant.* 16.8.1; Plutarch *Moralia* 654D.

scattered. I.e. they were sundered from one another by the solid darkness.

by phantoms. indalma is used in Jer 27:39, LXX, in the sense of 'idol,' but is first attested here in the sense of 'appearance' or 'hallucination.' Cf. Aelianus *De natura animalium* 17–35; *IG* 3.1403; Lucian *Gallus* 5; *Indalmoi* is the title of one of the writings (Aretaeus *SD [On the Causes and Symptoms of Chronic Diseases]* 1.6) of the skeptic Timon of Phlius (ca. 320–230 BCE) (D.L. 9.65, 105). By *indalmoi* he probably meant the deceptive images or appearances of wisdom brought forward by philosophers. Cf. Philo *Somn.* 2.133: "The sunless region of the impious where deep night reigns and endless darkness, and innumerable tribes of spectres and phantoms (*eidōlōn kai phasmatōn*) and dream illusions."

4. *crashed all around them. perikompeō* is first attested here, and in the sense 'sound round about' only here (though it occurs again in Patristic Greek). Cf. Jos. *J.W.* 1.25.2 (where it means 'declare loudly').

5. *No fire had force enough.* Philo similarly writes: "The light of artificial fire (or 'fire of common use') was partly quenched by the prevailing storm wind, and partly dimmed to the point of disappearance by the depth of the darkness," cf. Jos. *Ant.* 2.14.5: "darkness so thick that their eyes were blinded by it and their breath choked." "From the fact that the darkness could be felt it has been supposed that it consisted of something of cloudlike density—moderns have thought of dense hamsin sandstorms" (M. Greenberg, *Understanding Exodus* [New York, 1969] 165, n.1). ['Hamsin,' from the Arabic, 'hot wind, heat-wave.']

6. The meaning of this verse is unclear. Goodrick [1913], following à Lapide [1627], gives the likely meaning: "Every now and then an electric flash lit up the darkness and showed the Egyptians the spectral forms of objects for a moment; when the flash ceased they exaggerated in the darkness the things they had for an instant beheld." For *automatē pyra,* cf. Nonnus *Dionysiaca* 40.474: *automaton pyr.*

7. *magical shams.* Cf. Exod 7:11; 8:14. *ephybristos* is first attested here, although the adverb is found in Posidonius, F 59, Kidd. For the adjective, cf. Vettius Valens 71.18; Herodian 2.4.2, but in the passive sense of 'contemptible,' found only here.

8. *timorousness. eulabeia* in bad sense of 'overcaution,' 'timidity,' first attested here. Cf. Plutarch *De Fabio Maximo* 1.3; *Aretaeus Medicus CA (Remedy of Acute Diseases)* 1.2.

10. *the dark haze from which there was no escape* (*mēdamothen pheukton aera*). Grimm notes the suggestion that *aēr* may mean darkness, but although it may signify cloudy, and therefore murky, dark air in Homer, he doubted that it could mean darkness (*skotos*). Deane (1881) added that "it is hardly likely that, after the harrowing description of the darkness given above, the author should apply to it the mild term *aēr* in a sense almost unknown to later writers." The fact is, however, that the Homeric conception of *aēr* would fit our passage very well indeed, and that this term was so employed in literature quite familiar to our author. "*Aēr*," writes Kahn, "is closely related in sense to 'cloud,' as well as to darkness, conceived not as a privation of light, but as a positive reality. This is brought out very clearly in the battle scene around the body of Patroclus. In order to protect the corpse from the Trojans, Zeus 'poured an abundant *aēr* about the helmets' of the Achaean warriors standing around it (*Iliad* 17.268*ff*). Their view was so obstructed in consequence that 'one would say that neither sun nor moon was safe and sound; for they were oppressed by *aēr*,' while the other warriors continued to fight at ease 'under a clear sky' (366*ff*). Unable to see the field around him, Ajax calls upon father Zeus: 'Deliver the sons of the Achaeans out from under the *aēr*; make the sky bright and grant us to see with our eyes. Yea, destroy us in the light, if such is now thy pleasure' (645*ff*). Zeus had pity on his prayer and his tears, 'and straightway scattered the *aēr* and pushed away the mist' (649). The *aēr* thus dispelled by Zeus is plainly a kind of 'suspension' like haze or fog. Moreover, the haze in which Apollo hides Hector is described as 'deep' or thick, and Achilles strikes it three times with his spear (20.446). Such a haze is even conceived as capable of supporting objects belonging to the gods. Thus Ares, when he rests from battle, deposits his spear and chariot in an *aēr* (5.356)" (see Charles H. Kahn, *Anaximander and the Origins of Greek Cosmology* [New York, 1960] 140–145). Plato similarly writes: "And so with air: there is the brightest and clearest kind called aether, and the most turbid called 'murk' (*homichlē*) and 'gloom' (*skotos*)" (*Tim*. 58D). The same conception is found in Stoic physics. According to Chrysippus the air "is naturally murky" (*physei zopheron* [*SVF* 2.429]). Expounding Stoic doctrine, Plutarch writes: "It follows, then, that in nature the primordially dark is also the primordially cold; and that it is air which is primordially dark does not, in fact, escape the notice of the poets since they use the term 'air' for 'darkness' (*skotos*). (There follow quotations from *Odyssey* 9.144–145; Hesiod *Op*. 255; *Iliad* 17.649–650.) They also call the lightless air *knephas*, being as it were *kenon phaous;* and collected and condensed air has been termed *nephos* or cloud because it is a negation of light. Flecks in the sky and mist and fog and anything else that does not provide a transparent medium for light to reach our senses are merely variations of air; and its invisible and colorless part is called Hades and Acheron"

(*SVF* 2.430). Philo, too, in describing the creation of the intelligible world, writes: "First, then, the Creator made an incorporeal heaven, and an invisible earth, and the idea of air and of void. He called the one darkness, since air is black by nature" (*Op.* 29; cf. *Spec.* 1.85, 94; *Mos.* 118). Cf. also Ps-Aristotle *De Mundo* 392b6: *ho aēr . . . zophōdēs ōn.*

anguished by conscience. For *synechomenē tē syneidēsei,* cf. *Test. Reuben* 4:3: "My conscience (*syneidēsis*) causeth me anguish (*synechei*) on account of my impiety." The notion of conscience had already appeared in the writings of the Greek poets and popular moralists, such as Euripides and Menander (Eur. *Orestes* 396; Men *Monostichi* 654, Frags. 145, 522, 531; Prologues to *Samia* and *Misoumenos;* Terence *Eunuchus* 119; *Adelphoe* 348; Plautus *Mostellaria* 544; Cicero *Pro Cluentio* 159; *Tusc.* 4.45), and above all, in the Epicureans' constant stress on the pangs of conscience suffered by the guilty sinner (Lucretius 3.1011*ff; Seneca Ep.* 97.15; 105.9). The closest verbal anticipation of Philo's notion of conscience is found in Polybius (18.43.13), and virtually the same philosophical conception appears in the writings of the Late Stoa (Posidonius F 187, Kidd; Epictetus 1.14.11–14; 2.8.13–14; M. Aurel. 3.6.2; 5.27; 2.17; 3.16.2–4; Seneca *Ep.* 41), although there is a hint of Cicero *ND* 3.85, that it had already appeared in the Stoic writings of the first century BCE. "To express the concept of conscience, Philo uses two main terms, either singly or in combination, *elenchos* and *syneidos.* The latter, more frequently in the form *synesis* or *syneidēsis* (or their cognates) is the normal Greek term for conscience (cf. Stobaeus *Anthology,* chap. 24). The former, on the other hand, does not appear to be found in precisely this sense before Philo. As a legal or philosophical term, it connotes interrogation or cross-examination and has sometimes the further sense of proof, refutation, or conviction. And while the parallel, and sometimes the contrast, is drawn in contemporary philosophical literature between conviction by an external court or accuser and by the inner voice of conscience (Cicero *De Legibus* 1.40; *elenchos* appears five times in a similar context in chap. 1 of Wisd), Philo's use of the term to mean conscience as such still seems to be original (cf. Philo *Virt.* 206; *Jos.* 47–48). The most complete description of the function of the *elenchos* comes at *Det.* 22–32 (cf. *Fug.* 117–118, 131; *QE* 2.13; *Deus* 50, 126; 135–138; 182–183; *Decal.* 17; *Op.* 128; *Post.* 59). (See R. T. Wallis, "The Idea of Conscience in Philo of Alexandria," Colloquy 13 of the *Center for Hermeneutical Studies in Hellenistic and Modern Culture,* ed. W. Wuellner [Berkeley, 1975]) 2; cf. V. Nikiprowetzky, "La Doctrine de l'elenchos chez Philon," *Colloques nationaux du CNRS* (Paris, 1967) 255–273; Bréhier:295*ff;* W. D. Davies, "Conscience," *IDB,* A–D (1962) 671–676; A. Pelletier, "Deux Expressions de la notion de Conscience," *REG* 80 (1967) 363–371. C. Maurer, *Synoida, syneidēsis, TDNT* 7 (1971) 898–919; D. E. Marietta, "Conscience in Greek Stoicism," *Numen* 17 (1970):176–187. For the question of whether conscience in Philo's view is a transcendent power or one immanent within man, see my discussion "Philo's Ethical Theory" in *ANRW* (forthcoming).

11. *innate cowardice*. For *deilon,* 'a cowardly thing' see NOTE on 7:24. Cf. Menander Frag. 522, Körte: "When anyone has something on his conscience, even the bravest man is transformed into a coward by that conscience."

12–13. The meaning of these verses is unclear, although they possess the earmarks of a sententious pronouncement culled from some Alexandrian philosophical handbook. Cf. Plutarch *Moralia* 165D: "But fear alone, lacking no less in boldness than in power to reason (*ouch hētton ōn tolmēs endeēs ē logismou*), keeps its irrationality impotent, helpless, and hopeless." Our author appears to be saying that those who, in their desperation, have abandoned reason as a key to the understanding of their lives, find their greatest source of misery to lie in their ignorance of the causes which lead to their various troubles.

13. *expectation*. *Scilicet* of reason's aid (*prosdokia,* sc. *tōn apo logismou boēthēmatōn*). *prosdokia* usually appears in Stoic definitions of fear. Cf. Philo *Mut.* 163: "The presence of evil produces grief, and its expectation (*prosdokia*) fear"; D.L. 7.112. Heinisch (1912) translates 12a as follows: "but if the fear within is less," taking prosdokia as *prosdokia kakōn,* the Stoic definition of fear.

14. *out of the recesses of the powerless infernal realm*. Cf. *ShR* 14.2, quoted in NOTE on 17:3. Sheol is a land of the silent and utterly weak (Pss 88:12; 115:17; Isa 38:18–19; 14:9–11,18). For *mychos* in connection with Hades, cf. Hesiod *Theogonia* 119; Euripides *The Suppliant Women* 926; *AP* 7.213.6. On their return voyage, the Argonauts encounter a sudden and total darkness which makes navigation impossible. In his description of it, Apollonius of Rhodes connects it with the darkness of Hades: "But straightway as they sped over the wide Cretan Sea night scared them, that night which they name the Pall of Darkness; the stars pierced not that fatal night nor the beams of the moon, but black chaos descended from heaven, or haply some other darkness came, rising from the nethermost depths (*mychatōn barathrōn*). And the heroes, whether they drifted in Hades or on the waters, knew not one whit . . ." (*Argonautica* 1694–1700). Callimachus, a contemporary of Apollonius and perhaps his source, described the same incident in his *Aetia,* but only a few lines of his description survive (Frag. 17–18, Pfeiffer). One of the extant lines mentions *aēr:* "if you [Apollo] would drive away from the ship the misty *aēr* . . ." (Frag. 18.8; cf. Wisd 17:10).

entranced by a death-like sleep. *ton auton hypnon* means the same sleep that characterizes the inhabitants of Hades. Cf. 17:21.

15. *phantom monsters.* For *phantasmatōn.* Frequent in Plato for 'appearances' or 'images' (*eidōla*). Cf., for example, *Tim.* 71A: "bewitched for the most part both day and night by images and phantasms (*eidōlōn kai phantasmatōn*)"; *Rep.* 584A. It is a technical term in Aristotles' psychology for the percept persisting as an after-image. "So also in sleep," writes Aristotle, "the images (*phantasmata*) or residuary movements that arise from the the sense-impressions are altogether obscured owing to the aforesaid movement when it is too great and sometimes the visions appear confused and montrous (*teratōdeis*), and the dreams are morbid" (*De Divinatione per Somnia* 461a18). Cf. *De Anima* 431a17. It is also used by the Epicureans and Stoics; cf. Epicurus *Epistulae* 2.88, 102, 110; 1.75; *SVF* 2.55 (*phantasma* is *dokēsis dianoias*); Ps-Aristotle *De Mundo* 395a29.

sudden and unexpected fear. For *aiphnidios . . . kai aprosdokētos.* Cf. Aeschylus *Prometheus Bound* 680: *aprosdokētos d'auton aphnidios moros tou zēn apesterēsen.*

16. *prison without bars.* For *asidēron heirktēn,* cf. Euripides *Bacchae* 1104: *asidērois mochlois.*

17. *or troubled laborer in the desert.* The commentators have been puzzled by this curious reference. "What could a man, not a shepherd," asks Goodrick, "be toiling at in the desert? It is probably another instance of the wrong word. Very likely Pseudo-Solomon meant *kat' ēremian,* 'in peace'—a mechanic quietly working in his shop at his trade: we have then a pretty complete enumeration of the working class." There may, however, be a simple explanation, which involves the economic conditions in Egypt under the domination of the Ptolemies and of Rome. "It often happened," writes Festugière, "that the peasants, crushed by taxes and tolls, left their village to withdraw (*anachōrein, ekchōrein*) either to a place of asylum or to some village where they might be hidden, or even to swamps or the desert (*anachōrein eis tēn ksenēn, eis ten erēmian*), where they led the life of outlaws. These flights, which could be isolated or collective, constituted a kind of strike, which the government tolerated while it did not sanction it as a right." (R. P. Festugière, *Personal Religion among the Greeks* [Berkeley and Los Angeles, 1954] 57–58; cf. Claire Préaux, *Économie royale des Lagides* [Brussels, 1939]; M. Rostovtzeff, *Social and Economic History of the Hellenistic World* [Oxford, 1941]; *The Social and Economic History of the Roman Empire* [Oxford, 1957], index, s.v. *anachōrēsis*). "But while in the Ptolemaic period," writes N. Lewis, "these flights often partook of the nature of strikes, which ended with the return of the fugitive upon the removal of the injustice against which the flight was a protest, under the increased and ever-increasing fiscal oppression which the Roman domination brought for the Egyptian people these 'strikes' became definite departures, with no intention of return. Under the

Romans fugitives became also more numerous, and flights more frequent and widespread. Already Philo, writing under the first Emperors, describes the brutal treatment which the impoverished suffered at the hands of ruthless tax-collectors, their despairing flight, and the resultant depopulation of villages and towns" (*Spec.* 3.159). For the village of Philadelphia, we know from *P. Corn.* 24 that the number "of poor people who fled in the first year of Nero (54/5) and whose whereabouts are unknown, was 44" (N. Lewis, "Merismos Anakechorēkotōn: An Aspect of the Roman Oppression in Egypt," *JEA* 23 [1937] 63–75).

18. *bound by one chain of darkness. mia gar halysei . . . edethēsan.* Cf. Dio Chrysostomus 30.17: *en halysei mia dedemenous.*

inescapable (*dysalykton*). First attested in Nicander (second century BCE) *Alexipharmaca* 251.537.

"It is plain," writes Goodrick (1913), "here as elsewhere, that the darkness is conceived as only covering the Egyptians, while the birds were singing in the trees around, and all natural noises still going on." The suspension-like haze referred to in our NOTE on 17:9 would fit this state of affairs well.

21. *an image of the darkness.* Cf. *Test.Reuben* 3:1: "Besides all these there is an eighth spirit of sleep, with which is brought about the trance of nature and the image of death (*eikōn tou thanatou*)"; *Iliad* 14.231: "There she [Hera] met Sleep, the brother of Death."

18:1. *light supreme.* See Exod 10:23. Cf. *Mishnat R. Eliezer,* 19: "When an Israelite approached an Egyptian in order to borrow from him, the light accompanied him, and when he left, the light exited along with him."

had not suffered. Grimm explains the pluperfect (*epepontheisan*), instead of the expected imperfect, as referring to the moment at which the plague of darkness had struck the Egyptians.

2. *of their being parted.* Cf. Exod 11:8; 12:33; Ps 105:38. Others translate: "and asked forgiveness for their past ill will" (Fichtner, *JB*).

3. *a blazing pillar.* Cf. Exod 13:21, LXX. According to the rabbis, the Israelites were constantly accompanied by seven clouds of glory during their sojourn in the desert, four hovering in front, behind, and at the two sides of them, one suspended above them, to keep off rain, hail, and the rays of the sun, and one under them [or alternatively, one for the Divine Presence which was among them]. The seventh cloud preceded them, and prepared the way for them, making a pathway, exalting the valleys and making low every mountain and hill, killing the snakes and scorpions, and burning away brambles and thorns. That a difference might be made between day and night, a pillar of fire took the place of the cloud in the evening. (*Tosef. Sotah* 4.2; *BR,* Th-Alb:487; *Sifre Num.* 83; *Mek. Beshallaḥ* on Exod 13:31; *BT Shab.* 23b; *MRS* Epst-Mel: 47; Ps-

Jonathan on Exod 12:37). Cf. Philo *Mos.* 1.165–166: "A cloud shaped like a tall pillar, the light of which in the daytime was as the sun and in night as flame, went before the host, so that they should not stray in their journey, but follow in the steps of a guide who could never err. Perhaps indeed, there was enclosed within the cloud one of the lieutenants of the great King, an unseen angel, a forerunner on whom the eyes of the body were not permitted to look." For Wisdom dwelling in a cloud, cf. Sir 24:4; I Bar 3:29; *On the Origin of the World* (*CG* II) 106, 5–6.

a benign sun. Cf. Ps 121:6. We find a similar notion in *MRS,* Epst-Mel: 47: (commenting on Exod 13:21 "That they might travel day and night") "He compares their journey by day to their journey by night . . . just as during their journey by night 'they suffered neither hunger nor thirst and hot wind and sun did not strike them' (Isa 49:10), so during their journey by day, they suffered neither hunger nor thirst and hot wind and sun did not strike them."

4. *deserve to be deprived of light.* Another example of measure for measure. The rabbis made a similar spiritual contrast between Egypt and Israel: "Said the Holy One blessed be He, let the darkness which is distinguished from light come and exact punishment from the Egyptians who sought to annihilate a nation distinguished from the Canaanites who worshipped idols, which were called darkness, as it is said, 'Behold! Darkness shall cover the earth. . . . But upon you the Lord will shine. . . . And nations shall walk by your light' (Isa 60:2)" (*Midrash Yelamdenu,* cited by *Yalkut Shimeoni:* see M. Kasher, *Torah Shelemah,* v. 10/11, p. 16. Cf. *Tanh. Bo,* 796; *PRK,* 7.12, Mandelbaum: 134).

imprisoned. phylakizō is first attested here and *Test.Joseph* 2:3; cf. Acts 22:19. It occurs again in Patristic Greek.

through whom the imperishable light of the law was to be given to the world. Cf. Isaiah 2; Deutero Isa 42:1–6. Both in Jewish-Hellenistic and in rabbinic literature, we find an attempt to interpret Israel's acceptance of the Torah as including the obligation to spread Torah's teachings to the Gentile nations. Thus we read in *Test.Levi* 14:4: "That if ye be darkened through transgressions, what, therefore, will all the Gentiles do living in blindness? Yea, ye shall bring a curse upon our race, because the light of the law which was given to lighten every man (we have variant readings here: *to phōs tou kosmou* [*nomou; kosmou kai nomou*], *to dothen en hymin eis photismon pantos asthrōpou*), this ye desire to destroy by teaching commandments contrary to the ordinances of God." Cf. II Bar 48:40; 59:2; IV Ezra 7:20–24; 14:20; *Test. Orpheus* 3: "Who flee the laws of the righteous, though God established them for all men [reading: *theioio tithentos pasin homou*] (*FPG:* 164); *Mek. Bahodesh* 5.65, 100, on Exod 20:2, Lauterbach, 2:234–237: "And it was for the following reason that the nations of the world were asked to accept the Torah: in order that they should have no excuse for saying: Had we been asked we would have accepted it for behold they were asked and they refused to accept it. . . . To three things the Torah is likened: to the desert, to fire, and to water. This is to tell you that just as these three things are free to all who come into the world, so also are the words of the Torah free to all who come into the world"; *Sifre Deut.* 343; *BT A.Z.* 2b. (Cf. also John 1:9, Isa 42:6; 49:6; Micah 4; Tobit 13:13). It is most interesting to observe Philo's reformulation of the biblical doctrine of election under the impact of his ideal of *philanthrōpia* or 'humanity,' rooted as that was in a universalistic conception of man. At every possible opportunity, Philo emphasizes the universal aspects of Jewish particularism. The Jews are indeed "the nation dearest of all to God," but it "has received the gift of priesthood and prophecy on behalf of all mankind" (*Abr.* 98; cf. *Spec.* 1.168). "Out of the whole human race God chose Israel and called them to his service," but it is only because they are "in a true sense men" (*Spec.* 1.303). Israel's function is "to offer prayers on behalf of the whole human race that it may be delivered from evil" (*Mos.* 1.149), and the High Priest "makes prayers and gives thanks not only on behalf of the whole human race but also for the parts of nature, for he holds the world to be his country" (*Spec.* 1.96–97). The Sabbath becomes for Philo "a festival of the universe" and belongs to all people as the birthday of the world (*Op.* 89). Israel stands out as a model for all other peoples, "not for its own glory, but for the benefit of the beholders. For to gaze continuously upon noble models imprints their likeness in souls which are not entirely hardened and strong" (*Praem.* 114; cf. *QE* 2.42, where Israel's law is described "as a law for the world (*kosmikon nomon*), for the chosen race is a likeness of the world"). Through proselytism, moreover, Philo sees the possibility of the participation of all nations in the universal religion of Judaism "as pilgrims to truth" who have abandoned the "mythical fables and multiplicity of sovereigns" to honor the "One who alone is worthy of honor" (*Spec.* 4.178; 1.309; 1.51–52; *Mos.* 244). See my "Philo's Ethical Theory" (in *ANRW,* forthcoming).

XXXVI. SIXTH ANTITHESIS: EGYPTIAN FIRSTBORN DESTROYED, BUT ISRAEL PROTECTED AND GLORIFIED
(18:5–25)

18   5 When they resolved to slay the infant children of your holy ones—though one child had been exposed and saved—you bereaved them of the multitude of their children for their discomfiture and destroyed them as one in the violent waters. 6 That night was made known in advance to our fathers, so that having sure knowledge of the nature of the plighted compacts in which they trusted they might be cheered. 7 Your people expected the deliverance of the righteous and the destruction of their enemies, 8 for by the same means whereby you punished our antagonists, you summoned us to your side and glorified us. 9 For secretly did the devout children of virtuous folk make sacrifice and with one mind set forth the divine law that the holy ones should share alike in both blessings and dangers, while already raising a chant of the praises of the fathers. 10 But the discordant cry of their enemies echoed in response and the pitiable sound of lamentation for their children was spread abroad. 11 Slave and master were punished together with the same penalty, commoner and king suffered a like fate: 12 united by a common death, all had corpses past counting, for the living were not even sufficient to bury the dead, since in a single moment their most precious offspring had perished. 13 Wholly incredulous thanks to their magical enchantments, at the destruction of their firstborn they acknowledged your people to be God's son. 14 While all things were enveloped in peaceful silence and night was midway through her swift course, 15 your all-powerful Logos, out of the heavens, from the royal throne, leaped like a relentless warrior into the midst of the land marked for destruction, 16 bearing your unambiguous decree as a sharp sword. Standing it filled all things with death; it touched the heavens, yet stood poised upon the earth. 17 At once nightmarish visions terrified them, and unexpected fears beset them, 18 and one here, another there, flung down half dead, made known the cause of his dying. 19 For the dreams that

bewildered them indicated this in advance, so that they should not die without knowing the reason they suffered so terribly. 20 But the righteous, too, were touched by an experience of death, and a mass slaughter took place in the wilderness, though the divine wrath did not long abide. 21 For a blameless man pressed forward to fight as their champion, introducing the armor of his ministry, prayer and atoning incense. He withstood the wrath and set a limit to the disaster, showing that it was you whom he served. 22 He overcame the divine anger not by bodily strength, nor by force of arms, but by word he subdued the chastiser, by recalling the oaths and covenants of the fathers. 23 For when the dead already lay fallen upon one another in heaps, he interposed and checked the divine anger, cutting off its line of advance toward the living. 24 On his full-length robe there was a representation of the entire cosmos, and the glories of the fathers upon his four rows of carved stones, and your splendor on the diadem upon his head. 25 To these the destroyer gave way, these he feared; for the single taste of his wrath was enough.

NOTES

18:5. *one child.* I.e. Moses.

destroyed them . . . in the violent waters. The author returns to his favorite theme of measure for measure. The Egyptians who had slain the children of the Israelites were first bereaved of their firstborn and later were all drowned in the sea. We similarly read in *Tanḥ.* Buber, *Bo* 5, 22a: "Whatever the Egyptians intended against Israel, the Holy One blessed be He brought against them. . . . They intended to kill the Israelites, the Holy One blessed be He killed their firstborn, as it is said, 'The Lord struck down all the firstborn in the land of Egypt' (Exod 12:29); they intended to submerge the Israelites in the water, the Holy One blessed be He likewise submerged them in the water, as it is said, 'Who hurled Pharaoh and his army into the Sea of Reeds' (Ps 136:15)." Cf. *Mek.* on Exod 14:26 (Lauterbach 1:243): " 'That the waters may come back upon the Egyptians.' Let the wheel [of fortune] turn against them and bring back upon them their own violence. For with the same device with which they planned to destroy Israel I am going to punish them. They planned to destroy my children by water, so I will likewise punish them only by water"; *Mid.Yelamdenu* on Exod 11:4: "Said the Holy One blessed be He, I will go forth among the Egyptians in the middle of the night, and I will exact punishment of the Egyptians who sought to destroy a nation who are the children of my friend Abraham who deployed against them at night in order to destroy his enemies, as it is written, 'at night, he deployed against them' (Gen 14:15); and because they cast my firstborn son into the Nile, behold I shall slay your firstborn son; and because of the ten trials which Abraham had undergone and was found perfect, I therefore smote them with ten plagues." (See M. Kasher, *Torah Shelemah,* vol. 10/11 [New York, 1941], 32). There is a similar notion in Jub 48:14: "The Lord our God cast them into the midst of the sea, even as the children of Egypt had cast their children into the river. He took vengeance on one million of them, and one thousand strong and energetic men were destroyed on account of one suckling of the children of thy people which they had thrown into the river." Goodrick (1913) notes that "on the strength of this verse in Jubilees Charles would translate here 'in retribution (*eis elengchon*) for even a single child that was exposed thou didst take away a multitude': but it is more than doubtful if *elengchos* would bear this meaning."

6. *That night.* I.e. the well-known night on which the firstborn of the Egyptians were slain. Cf. Exod 12:42.

our fathers. "Either the Israelite heads of families, who were forewarned of the death of the firstborn (Exod 6:6; 11:4), or the patriarchs, to whom the deliverance from bondage was revealed (Gen 15:14)" (Gregg [1909]). We read in *Mek. Pisḥa* 16 (on Exod 13:4): "R. Eleazar the son of Azariah says: Because of the merit of our father Abraham did God bring Israel out of Egypt, as it is said: 'For He remembered His holy word unto Abraham his servant,' and, 'And He brought forth His people with joy' (Ps 105:42)." Cf. *PT Ta'anith* 1.1; *MRS* to Exod 6:2. The intimate connection between the night during which God gave his oath to Abraham and the night of Passover is confirmed by *Targ.Yerush.* on Exod 12:42: "Four nights are there written in the Book of Memorials before the Lord of the world. Night the first, when He was revealed in creating the world; the second, when He was revealed to Abraham; the third, when He was revealed in Miṣraim, His hand killing all the firstborn of Miṣraim, and His right hand saving the firstborn of Israel; the fourth, when He will yet be revealed to liberate the people of the house of Israel from among the nations." See Jaubert 1963:356; R. Le Déaut, *La Nuit Pascale* (Rome, 1963) 287–298.

be cheered. epeuthymeō is attested only here and in Aristaenetus *Love Letters* 2.14 (fifth century).

8. *by the same means.* The redemption of Israel through the smashing blow delivered upon the Egyptian firstborn by Yahweh marked the beginning of Israel's national life as God's elect. The author may also be alluding to the consecration of Israel's eldest born in consequence of God's slaying the Egyptian firstborn while sparing the former (Exod 13:15).

9. *secretly*. Goodrick thinks this is justified by Exod 12:46, but privacy is not secrecy (cf. Exod 8:22; 12:22). Philo, however, had allegorized the biblical phrase *engkryphias azymous* (Exod 12:39, LXX: "cakes baked in the ashes or over charcoals"), interpreting it as "buried unleavened cakes." "The Israelites kneaded the savage untamed passion with the aid of reason that softened it as though it were food. And the method by which they softened it and wrought it to something better was revealed to them by divine inspiration, and they did not utter it aloud, but treasured it in silence" (*Sacr.* 64; cf. 16.59). J. B. Segal has hesitatingly suggested that it is perhaps this phrase *engkryphias azymous* that lay behind our author's reference to the Paschal sacrifice as having been done *kryphē* (*The Hebrew Passover* [London, 1963] 25, n.6). It may also be noted that there is a theory that there was an early tradition which knew the story of a secret escape from Egypt, and perhaps connected with this tradition was the notion of a secret sacrifice of the Paschal Lamb (see M. Noth, *Exodus, A Commentary* [Philadelphia, 1962] 111). Another possibility is that our author, writing in a milieu in which the mysteries of Isis and Osiris were very prominent, wished to present the paschal ceremony in the guise of a mystery, and felt that Exod 12:46 readily lent itself to such an interpretation. Jacobson (1976:204) suggests that a slight emendation yields a satisfactory text. Read: *tryphē*, "with joy" (Theodotion translates Isaiah's "if you call the Sabbath a day of joy" [58:13] by *tryphē hagian*. Wisd uses *tryphē* at 19:11.

with one mind. Cf. Philo *QE* 1.10: "And he decided that there is nothing more beautiful than that the divine cult [the reference here is to the Paschal sacrifice] should be performed by all in harmony."

the divine law. For *theiotētos*. Cf. Ps-Aristeas 95. See also A. J. Festugière, *Epicurus and his Gods* (Oxford, 1955) 70, n.64.

raising a chant of the praises of the fathers. *proanamelpontes* is found only here. The writer is attributing to those who partook of the first Passover a practice which grew up in later days. Cf. II Chron 30:21; 35:15; Jub 49:6: "And all Israel was eating the flesh of the paschal lamb, and drinking the wine, and was lauding and blessing, and giving thanks to the Lord God of their fathers, and was ready to go forth from under the yoke of Egypt, and from the evil bondage" (wine appears here for the first time as an accompaniment of the meal, and there appears to be an oblique reference to the psalmody mentioned by the Chronicler). Philo is more explicit: "but to fulfill with prayers and hymns the custom handed down by their fathers" (*Spec.* 2.148). Cf. *BT Pesaḥ.* 117a.

10. *the discordant cry of their enemies echoed in response*. The rabbis draw exactly the same contrast: "R. Jonathan says (in explanation of Ps 68:7: 'God . . . sets free the imprisoned, safe and sound (*bakoŝarot*)': *Bakoŝarot* means: There were those who wept and those who

sang (understanding *bakośarot* as *bekî wĕširôt*). The Egyptians wept, as it is said: 'While the Egyptians were burying' (Num 33:4). The Israelites sang, as it is said, 'The voice of rejoicing and salvation is in the tents of the righteous. . . . The right hand of the Lord is exalted' (Ps 118:15–16), because the Lord was exalted over the Egyptians" (*Mek. Pisḥa* 16, Lauterbach, 1:140; cf. *Mid. Lekaḥ Tov,* Shemot 13.17).

11. *Slave and master.* See Exod 11:5; 12:29.

12. *united* (*homothymadon*). Cf. Philo *Mos.* 1.136: "And so, since in this general disaster the same emotion drew from all a united cry (*athroōs homothymadon ekboēsantōn*), one single dirge of wailing resounded from end to end of the whole land."

by a common death (*en heni onomati thanatou*). *onoma* may be used in periphrastic phrases. See LSJ, s.v. meaning iv.

not even sufficient to bury the dead. Perhaps a rhetorical amplification of Num 33:3–4. Cf. Philo *Mos.* 1.100: "A great multitude of men, killed by thirst, lay in heaps at the cross-roads, since their relatives had not the strength to carry the dead to the tombs" (Gregg).

in a single moment. Cf. I Enoch 99:9 "Therefore in an instant (*epi mias*) shall they perish."

13. *God's son.* An amplification of Exod 12:31. Cf. Exod 4:22–23; Hosea 11:1; IV Ezra 6:58; Ps Sol 18:4 *PT Pesaḥ.* 5.5: "What did Pharaoh say! Up, depart from among my people, in the past you were Pharaoh's servants, henceforth, you are the servants of the Lord." A similar acknowledgment is found in Wisd 5:5; cf. I Enoch 62:5–9; Esther 8E:16, LXX (Hanhart); III Macc 6:28; *Joseph and Asen* 5–6 (see Nickelsburg:83, 91–92). Cf. also Ps-Aristeas 140: "Whence the priests who are the guides of the Egyptians, who have looked closely into many things and are conversant with affairs, have named us 'men of God,' a title applicable to no other but only to men who revere the true God. The rest are men of food and raiment, for their whole disposition has recourse to those things." (In II Maccabees, the Jews are called "sons of heaven" in the presence of the persecuting Syrian king. See Gutman 2. 115.)

15. *all-powerful Logos.* The description of the Logos here is strikingly similar to that of Sophia earlier in the book. Both are all-powerful (cf. 7:23); descend from the heavenly throne (cf. 9:4,10,17); and carry out God's commandments (cf. 7:21; 8:4) (Fichtner).

leaped like a relentless warrior. Athena, the personification of *phronēsis,* is similarly described in the Hymn to Athena 5–9: "From his awful head wise Zeus himself bare her arrayed in warlike arms of flashing gold. . . . But Athena sprang quickly from the immortal head and stood before Zeus . . . shaking a sharp spear." For the Stoic allegorization of Athena's birth, see *SVF* 3. Diogenes Babylonius 33; Cicero *ND* 1.41. Cf. *Pseudo-Clementine Homilies* 6.8, where we are told that the aether is in ceaseless palpitation which begets intelligence, and is called on that account Pallas (*pallesthai*). "And this is artistic wisdom, by which the aetherial artificer wrought out the whole world." The Stoics also tried to connect Athena with the conception of immortality, explaining Athena as *athanatos* (*Pseudo-Clementine Recognitions* 10.33). See Harris 1922–23:56–72; A. Henrichs, "Towards a New Edition of Philodemus' Treatise on Piety," *GRBS* 13 (1972) 96, n.97. A whole catalogue of poetic descriptions of Athena's birth from the head of Zeus (including her "leaping" [*hallesthai* was believed to underlie her epithet Pallas] and her armor) can be found in *P. Oxy.* 2660 (Vol. 20, 1952). The poets quoted include Ibycus (Frag. 298, Page, *Poetae Melici Graeci*), Stesichorus (Frag. 233, Page), and Callimachus (Frag. 37, Pfeiffer). The papyrus is a fragment of Apollodorus, *Peri Theōn* (ca. 150 BCE). Callimachus used the same verb as the author of Wisd: "From your father's divine head you [Athena] leaped (*hēlao*) in full armor" (Frag. 37, Pfeiffer).

The imagery of leaping or springing forth recurs in the Gnostic writings. In the system of Simon Magus, First Thought or Wisdom (or Holy Spirit) is described as "leaping forth" (*exsilientem*) from God (Irenaeus *Adv. Haer.* 1.23.2). See G. Lüdemann, *Untersuchungen zur simonianischen Gnosis* (Göttingen, 1975):58. Similarly, according to the Barbelognostics, *Sophia,* seeking a partner and not finding one, extended herself downwards and made a leap (Irénaeus *Adv. Haer.* 1.29.1–4). Cf. Valentinus, Irenaeus *Adv. Haer.* 1.2.2: *proēlato . . . hē Sophia; CH* 1.5 (and 10), where the Logos leaps (*ekesepēdēsen*) like a flame from the moist nature upwards into the light.

16. *bearing your unambiguous decree as a sharp sword.* According to Orphic tradition, Athena springs from the head of Zeus "gleaming with arms, a brazen glory to behold," and becomes the "accomplisher of his will" (Kern, *Orphicorum Fragmenta* 21, 174, 176). Philo employs the fiery sword of the Cherubim as a symbol of the Logos (*Cher.* 28; cf. 35: "behold the armed angel, the reason of God"); *Mut.* 108. Cf. Isa 49:2; Judg 3:19–21; Heb 4:12: "for the word of God is living and active, sharper than any two-edged sword"; Eph 6:17; Rev 1:16; 2:16; 19:15. In *PGM* 4.1717, an incantation is described as "the sword of Dardanus," a formula employing seven archangels. See M. Gaster, "The Sword of Moses," in *Studies and Texts* (rep. New York, 1971) 288–337; M. Margaliot, *Sefer Ha-Razim* (Jerusalem, 1966) 29–30.

it filled all things with death. The author of Jubilees (49:2) ascribes the slaying of the firstborn to all the powers of Mastema whereas Ezekiel the Tragedian ascribes it to a "fearful angel" (*deinos angelos*) (*FPG:* 213, line 1). In *Targ.Yerush.* on Exod 12:29, it is the Word (*memra*) of the Lord which slew them. The *memra* of the Targum, however, is only a reverent circumlocution for God, and is, as Moore (1. 419) puts it, "purely a phenomenon of translation, not a figment of speculation." The rabbis, on the other hand, emphasized that God did not employ either an angel or a messenger for this task. Cf. *Mek. Pisḥa* 7 and 13, Lauterbach, 1:53, 97; *PT Sanh.* 2.1; *Horayot* 3.1. Philo's position in this matter is not quite clear, but it would appear that when he writes that three of the plagues (the dog-fly, murrain, and the death of the Egyptian firstborn) were accomplished by God or were "self-wrought" (*autourgētheisai: Mos.* 1.97, 130–135; cf. *ShR* 12.4), he only wishes to say that they were not, as the other seven, carried out either by Aaron or Moses or both in common, but rather by himself, without any human partnership. This is not necessarily to deny, however, that God, as is his wont, inflicted these punishments through his regent or punitive power rather than by himself directly. Our author's position would appear to be similar to that of Philo, and is thus somewhere between the view of the author of *Jubilees* who assigns this plague to Mastema and that of the rabbis who emphatically deny that God employed any intermediary whatever. Still, since the Logos is in reality God himself in one of his aspects, our author's position is almost identical with that of the rabbis. (The words *wĕlō' 'al yĕdê haddābār,* "and not through the word," are a later addition to the Passover Haggadah in the version of Saadiah Gaon and in the Genizah fragments. See D. Goldschmidt, *Haggadah Shel Pesah* (Jerusalem, 1960) 44, n.60; Kasher:45; J. Goldin, "Not by Means of an Angel and not by Means of a Messenger," in *Religions in Antiquity,* ed. J. Neusner (Leiden, 1968) 412–424).

it touched the heavens, yet stood poised upon the earth. The author is employing a well-known Homeric image. We read in *Iliad* 4.443: "She [Discord] plants her head in heaven, while her feet tread on earth" (*ouranō estērikse karē kai epi chthoni bainei*). This was imitated by Virgil in *Aeneid* 4.177: "she [Rumor] mounts up to heaven, and walks the ground with head hidden in the clouds." We find a similar image in *Testament of Orpheus* 33–34: "God is firmly set in brazen heaven on his golden throne, and plants his feet upon the earth" (*chalkeion es ouranon estēriktai . . . gaiē d'hypo possi bebēke*) (*FPG:* 166). Very likely, I Chron 21:16 was also in our author's mind: "[David] saw the angel of the Lord standing between the earth and the heaven, having a drawn sword in his hand stretched out over Jerusalem". Cf. the description of the angel Sandalfon as "standing on earth with his head reaching to the Heavenly Living Creatures [Ḥayot]" (*BT Hag.* 13b).

18. *half dead.* We find the same notion in *PRK* 7.5, Mandelbaum 1:126–127: "The firstborn received the deathblow in the evening, struggled convulsively through the night, and died in the daytime." The midrash is attempting to reconcile two apparently conflicting verses: "In the middle of the night the Lord struck down all the firstborn" (Exod 12:29)—"On the day that I smote every firstborn in the land of Egypt" (Num 3:13).

20. *a mass slaughter took place in the wilderness.* See Num 17:6–15.

For *thrausis,* cf. Num 16:47–50, LXX, where it translates Hebrew *maggēpa* and *negep;* II Kings 17:9; 18:7; 24:15, LXX.

21. *pressed forward.* See Num 17:12; cf. IV Macc 7:11.

the armor of his ministry. For prayer as the righteous man's weaponry, cf. *Mek. Beshallaḥ* on Exod 14:10: " 'Moreover, I have given to thee one portion above thy brethren, which I took out of the hand of the Amorite, with my sword and with my bow' (Gen 48:22). And did he really take it with his sword and his bow? Has it not already been said: 'For I trust not in my bow, neither can my sword save me' (Ps 47:7)? Hence, what must be the meaning of the words, 'with my sword and with my bow'? With prayer." (*beqaštî* read as *baqqāšâti.* Cf. *MRS* on Exod 14:10, Epst-Mel: 53: *ûbĕqašti zû baqqāšâ; BT B.B.* 123a; *Targum* to Gen 48:22) (Stein [1936]).

prayer. Cf. *Targ.Yerush.* on Num 17:12: "Aaron stood in the midst with prayer" (derived from the verb *wayya 'ămod; 'āmîda* in rabbinic literature signifies 'prayer').

atoning incense. Cf. IV Macc 7:11 (*tō thymiatēriō kathōplismenos*); *Mek.Wayassaʿ* on Exod 17:5, Lauterbach, 2.131: "The Israelites used to say: This incense is but a means of punishment. It was this that killed Nadab and Abihu. For it is said: 'And Nadab and Abihu took,' etc. (Lev 10:1). Therefore the people should know that it was really a means of atonement, as it is said, 'And he put on the incense, and made atonement for the people' " (Num 17:12).

22. *the divine anger. cholon.* Bauermeister's emendation of the Manuscripts' *ochlon* has been adopted by most commentators. Cf. Aquila on Ps 6:2: *en ochlō* instead of *cholō* (translating Hebrew *baḥamatka*). See Grimm's detailed discussion. "Gregg's suggestion *ton ochlounta* (the 'harasser') from Tobit 6:8, where it is used of the troublings of an evil spirit, does not seem likely, it would not have been altered; but his second suggestion, that *angelon* may have been originally read, is better. A copyist finding that the word was elsewhere studiously avoided, may have altered it here" (Goodrick). Cf. IV Macc 7:11, where the destroyer is called 'angel of fire': *empyristēn angelon.*

by word. Cf. Philo *Her.* 201: "I marvel too when I read of that sacred Word (*hieron logon*), which ran in impetuous, breathless haste 'to stand between the living and dead.' " In the light of this Philonic passage, Goodenough translates "by Logos" (1969:275).

the chastiser. In Philo's writings, the *kolastikē dynamis* or Punitive Power (also called 'Regent' or 'Legislative Power') is one of the two primary Powers of God (the other being the *poiētikē dynamis,* the 'Creative' or 'Beneficent Power') which constitute the dynamic polar principles of the Logos' activity (see, for example, *Her.* 166).

the oaths and covenants of the fathers. Cf. 12:21 above, where *diathēkē* is replaced by *synthēkē*. In II Macc, *synthēkē* is exclusively employed for treaties between men, whereas *diathēkē* is reserved for God's covenant. See Jaubert 1963:311–315. According to some rabbinic texts, it is because of the convenant with the fathers that Israel was released from Egypt (*ShR* 1.36; 15.4). When Israel worshiped the golden calf, Moses uttered ever so many prayers and supplications and he was not answered. Indeed, his pleading for Israel lasted not less than forty days and forty nights, but all in vain. Yet when he said, "Remember Abraham, Isaac, and Jacob thy servants" (Exod 32:13), his prayer was heard at once (*BT Shab.* 42a; cf. *ShR* 44.1. See Schechter 1936:170–198).

23. *in heaps. sōrēdon.* Cf. Philo *Mos.* 1.100: *polys ochlos . . . diaphthareis ekeito sōrēdon epi tōn triodōn;* .255; *Prob.* 119. The word is first attested in Polybius 1.34.5.

24. *full-length robe. podērēs* is used alone in the LXX of the High Priest's robe (Exod 25:6, 28:4, LXX; cf. Ps-Aristeas 96; *Test.Levi* 8:2; Philo *Mos.* 2.118), translating Hebrew *ephod, ḥoshen, bad,* or *me'il.*

the entire cosmos. We have here a fleeting allusion to a notion which was especially widespread in Stoic and Cynic writings of the first century CE, namely, that the true temple is the universe itself. We read, for example, in the fourth epistle of Ps-Heraclitus: "You ignorant men, don't you know that God is not wrought by hands and has not from the beginning had a pedestal, and does not have a single enclosure! Rather the whole world is his temple, decorated with animals, plants, and stars" (Attridge 1976:59; cf. 13–23, where the same idea is quoted from an Egyptian shard. See J. and L. Robert *REG* 64 [1951] 210). Cf. Euripides Frag. 968; Seneca *Ep.* 90.28; *Benficiis* 7.7.3; Plutarch *Moralia* 477c; Chrysippus, ap. Cicero *ND* 3.10.26; *De Republica* 3.14; 6.15.15. An exact parallel, however, to our author's allusion may be found in Philo *Spec.* 1.66–97, where we are told that the truest temple of God is the whole universe, with heaven for its sanctuary, the stars for its votive ornaments, and the angels for its priests. The high priest's "long robe" is in its very complicated formation a likeness and copy (*apeikonisma kai mimēma*) of the universe: "It is a circular garment of a dark blue color throughout, a tunic with a full-length shirt (*podērēs chitōn*), thus symbolizing the air, because the air is both naturally black and in a sense a full-length robe stretching from the sublunar region above to the lowest recesses of the earth. Secondly on this is set a piece of woven work in the shape of a breastplate, which symbolizes heaven. . . . Then on the breast there are twelve precious stones of different colors, arranged in four rows (*tetrastoichei*) of three each, set in this form on the model of the zodiac, for the zodiac consisting of twelve signs makes the four seasons of the year by giving three signs to each." This sacred vesture thus "expresses the wish first that the high priest should have in evidence upon him an image of the All, that so by constantly contemplating it he should render his own life worthy of the sum of things, secondly that in performing his holy office he should have the whole universe as his fellow-ministrant." Cf. *Mos.* 2.117–135; *Cher.* 100; *QE* 2.73, 76, 91; *Somn.* 1.214–215; Jos. *Ant.* 3.7.7; 3.7.5; *J.W.* 5.5.4–5; Plutarch *Is. et Os.* 77 (382C). A good analogy to the cosmic symbolism of the high priest's garments is the shield of Achilles, in the forging of which, according to Heraclitus the Rhetor (as also Crates of Mallos), Homer depicted [in its metallic components] the genesis of the cosmos and its elements (*Quaestiones Homericae* 43). It may also be noted that Demetrius Poliorcetes wore a robe on which were figured the hosts of heaven. Cf. also Bar 3:24; Targum on Isa 40:22. See also R. Eisler, *Weltenmantel und Himmelszelt,* 2 vols. (München, 1910); and NOTE on 9:8.

four rows of carved stones. tetrastichou lithōn glyphēs. Cf. Exod 28:17–21, LXX.

on the diadem. See Exod 28:36–38. Cf. *BT Shab.* 63b: "The ZIZ was a kind of golden plate two fingerbreadths broad, and it stretched round [the forehead] from ear to ear, and upon it was written in two lines 'yod he' above and 'Holy "lamed"' below (i.e. the Divine Name on the upper line and 'Holy unto' on the lower line). But R. Eliezer son of R. Jose said: I saw it in the city of Rome, and 'Holy unto the Lord' was written in one line." Philo interprets it as follows: "Above the turban is the golden plate on which the graven shapes of four letters, indicating, as we are told, the name of the Self-Existent, are impressed, meaning that it is impossible for anything that is to subsist without invocation of Him: for it is His goodness and gracious power which join and compact all things" (*Mos.* 2.132).

25. *the single taste of his wrath was enough.* Cf. Philo *QG* 2.54: "For it is enough to be resentful and embittered this one time and to exact punishment of sinners."

XXXVII. SEVENTH ANTITHESIS: EGYPTIANS DROWNED IN THE SEA, BUT ISRAEL PASSES SAFELY THROUGH (19:1–9)

19 ¹ But the godless were hounded to the very end by pitiless anger, for God knew beforehand what they were yet to do: ² how after permitting their departure, and urgently escorting your people out, they would change their purpose and pursue them. ³ While they were still engaged in their mourning, and stood lamenting beside the graves of their dead, they adopted another mad scheme, and pursued as fugitives those whom they had beseeched to leave. ⁴ For a condign fate drew them on to this denouement and made them forget what had happened, so that they might fill in the one penalty still lacking to their torments, ⁵ and that your people might accomplish an incredible journey, while their enemies might bring upon themselves a bizarre death. ⁶ For the whole creation was fashioned over again in its original nature, submitting to your commands, so that your children might be preserved unharmed. ⁷ One could see the cloud overshadowing the camp, the emergence of dry land out of what before was water, an unimpeded way out of the Red Sea, and a leafy plain in place of the violent surf, ⁸ through which, sheltered by your hand, the whole nation passed after gazing at amazing marvels. ⁹ They were like horses at pasture, they skipped like lambs, as they praised you, O Lord, their deliverer.

NOTES

19:1. *the godless*. I.e. the Egyptians.

to the very end. Until their final annihilation in the Reed Sea.

God knew beforehand. Philo, too, places great emphasis on divine providence: "God employs the forethought and foreknowledge (*promētheia kai pronoia*) which are virtues peculiarly his own, and suffers nothing to escape his control or pass outside his comprehension. For not even about the future (*tōn mellontōn*) can uncertainty be found with him, since nothing is uncertain or future to God" (*Deus* 29). Cf. Ps-Philo *LAB* 22:7.

2. *after permitting their departure. epitrepsantes . . . tou apeinai.* The genitive is surprising even if we read with Swete *epistrepsantes* and translate either "having thought anxiously over their departure" (Grimm) or "having changed their minds about their departure" (*RV*). See, however, BDF 400.7: "Elsewhere *tou* is pleonastically prefixed to any sort of infinitive after the pattern of LXX (=Heb *lě*), at least by Luke (especially in Acts) and sporadically by James (Acts 10:25; 23:15; James 5:17)." *tou apeinai* is a concise form of *tou apienai kai apeinai* (Grimm).

urgently. Cf. Exod 12:33, LXX.

escorting. We find the same notion in *Mek. Beshallah* on Exod 13:17: "'When Pharaoh had let the people go': Letting go (*šillûah*) means escorting, as it is said, 'And Abraham went with them to bring them on the way' (Gen 18:16). The mouth that had said: 'And moreover I will not let Israel go' (Exod 5:2), that same mouth said: 'I will let you go.' What was the reward for this? 'Thou shalt not abhor an Egyptian' (Deut 23:8)."

3. *and stood lamenting. prosodyromenoi.* Found only here.

another mad scheme. According to Ps-Jonathan on Exod 14:9, Pharaoh believed that the Egyptian deity *Baal-Zephon* had "shut the Israelites in close upon the desert." Cf. *Mek.* on same verse: "*Baal-Zephon* alone was left of all the deities, to mislead the minds of the Egyptians. To him applies the scriptural passage: 'He misleadeth the nations and destroyeth them'" (Job 12:23).

4. *a condign fate.* Cf. *Sib Or* 3:184: "And straightway a fated ungodliness (*asebeias anangkē*) shall fall upon them." In *Jub* 48:12, *Mastema* urges the Egyptians to pursue the Israelites. "In *aksia anangkē*," writes Reuss, "we have a flat contradiction in terms. 'Fatality' implies predestination; 'deserving' implies the free will of man" (cited by Goodrick [1913]). In the literature of the ancient world, however, 'worthy' need have no such implication. The 'worthy' may simply be those whom God in his infinite wisdom has predetermined to be his chosen ones, for good or for ill. Philo, for example, writes: "God has not fashioned beforehand any deed of his, but produces him [Melchizedek] to begin with as such a king, peaceable and worthy of His own priesthood" (*LA* 3.79). Similarly, we read in Sir 1:14: "To fear the Lord is the beginning of wisdom, and with the faithful was she created in the womb." For the rabbinic explanation of God's hardening of Pharaoh's heart, see *ShR* 13.4.

6. *the whole creation was fashioned over again.* The author employs a Greek philosophical principle in order to make the notion of miracles more plausible. The Presocratics had already taught the material interchange of the elements (D.L. 8.25). The principle behind this doctrine was stated with especial clarity by Diogenes of Apollonia (DK, B.2). By

the Hellenistic age it was a commonplace of Greek philosophy that the stuff of which the world is made is *apoios hylē,* and that therefore the elements were mutually interchangeable (D.L. 7.150; 8.25; Epictetus 3.24; Frag. 8 (*auta ta tettara stoicheia anō kai katō trepetai kai metaballei*) *SVF* 2.405–411). The Stoics, in their attempt to explicate divination and the various miracle stories it involved, made especial use of this principle to show that the gods could accomplish anything without violating the laws of nature (Cicero *ND* 3.39.92. See Winston 1971).

7. *the cloud overshadowing the camp.* Cf. Num 9:18, LXX: *pasas tas hēmeras en hais skiazei hē nephelē epi tēs skēnēs, parembalousin hoi huioi Israēl.* Since the author is here invoking the motif of a new creation, the cloud overshadowing the camp, rather than interposing itself between the Israelites and the Egyptians as in Exod 14:19, may perhaps be an allusion to the darkness over the deep in Gen 1:2. See Guillaumont 1959, ad loc., and especially Beauchamp 1964:502*ff.*

of what before was water (*proüphestōtos hydatos*). *proüphistamai,* usually in Aorist 2 and Perfect Active, meaning 'exist before' is first attested here. Cf. Plutarch *Moralia* 570F.

the emergence of dry land. Continues the motif of a new creation. Cf. Gen 1:9: *kai ophthētō hē ksēra. anadysis,* in the sense of 'emergence,' first attested here. Cf. Jos. *J.W.* 7.2.2; Scholia on *Odyssey* 5.377.

a leafy plain. Probably a legendary elaboration of the biblical narrative. Gutmann quoted from a Hebrew prayer for the last day of Passover (*ōmeṣ gebûrōtêkā mî yemallēl*): "and he rebuked the Red Sea, and the raging waters dried up, so that they walked through abysses as on paved roads; on either side rose trees laden with fruit, and he caused sweet springs to gush out for them in the abyss, and perfume of sweet spices to spread its scent before them" (Moses Gutmann, *Die Apokryphen des alten Testaments* [Altona, 1841] 39, note) (Grimm). "The 'green field,'" writes Goodrick, "is possibly a fantastic description of the actual bottom of the Red Sea." Cf. Pliny *NH* 13.135: "Shrubs and trees also grew at the bottom of the sea—those in the Mediterranean being of smaller size, for the Red Sea and the whole of the Eastern Ocean are filled with forests [mangroves]. The Latin language has no name for what the Greeks call *phykos* [seaweed], as our word alga denotes a herbaceous sea-plant, whereas the *phykos* is a shrub. It has a broad leaf and is colored green." If we see in the leafy plain a continuation of the creation motif (cf. Gen 1:11–13: "Let the earth sprout vegetation . . ."), then the sequence becomes perfectly clear. For *chloēphoron,* cf. Philo *Op.* 40: *keleuei gar autēn chloēphorein.*

8. *the whole nation. panethnei.* Elsewhere only in Strabo 5.1.6.

9. *like horses.* Cf. Isa 63:13.

they skipped. dieskirtēsan. First attested here. Cf. Plutarch *Eumenes* 11; and 17:18 above. For the imagery, see Ps 114:4.

XXXVIII. RETROSPECTIVE REVIEW OF GOD'S WONDERS THROUGH WHICH NATURE WAS REFASHIONED FOR ISRAEL
(19:10–12)

19 10 They still recalled their experiences during their sojourn in a foreign land: how instead of cattle the earth brought forth lice, and instead of aquatic creatures, the river disgorged a swarm of frogs. 11 But later they also witnessed a new mode of bird production, when driven by appetite they demanded delicacies, 12 and quails came up from the sea for their relief.

NOTES

19:10. *instead of cattle.* Cf. NOTES on 19:6 and 18.

brought forth. For *eksēgagen.* Cf. Gen 1:24, LXX (and 1:20): *eksagagetō hē gē.*

lice. For *sknipa.* Cf. Exod 8:16, LXX.

disgorged. For *eksereugesthai,* cf. Exod 8:3; Pss 44:1; 118:171, LXX.

12. *quails came up from the sea.* "Quails in the Mediterranean area winter in Africa and migrate northward in vast flocks in the spring. . . . This is an exhausting flight and is done in stages. When the birds alight to refresh themselves, they are easily caught. Presumably it was a cloud of migrating quails that came down on the Hebrew encampment (cf. Aristotle *Historia Animalium* 8.579b)" (McCullough, *IDB,* s.v.).

19   13 On the sinners, however, punishments rained down, not unheralded by violent thunderbolts; justly did they suffer from their own misdeeds, since they practiced such cruel hostility toward strangers. 14 Others refused to welcome strangers who visited them, but these enslaved guests and benefactors. 15 And that was not the sum of it—indeed their final reckoning is yet to come—for the former received strangers with hostility [from the start], 16 whereas the latter, after a festal welcome, oppressed with hard labor men who had already shared with them equal rights. 17 But they were struck with blindness too, as were those at the doors of the righteous man, when encompassed by an immense darkness each went groping for his own doorway.

NOTES

19:13. *by violent thunderbolts.* Cf. Ps 77:16ff. We read in *Mek. Beshallah* on Exod 14:25, Lauterbach, 1.241: "R. Nehemiah says: By the repercussion of the thunder above, the pins of the wheels below flew off, as it is said: 'The voice of thy thunder was upon the wheel, the lightnings lighted up the world' (Ps 77:19)"; and on Exod 14:27: "When the last of the Israelites came out from the sea, the last of the pursuing Egyptians entered into the bed of the sea. The ministering angels then began hurling at them arrows, great hailstones, fire and brimstone." Cf. *Targ.Yerush.* on Exod 14:24: "The word of the Lord looked forth upon the host of the Egyptians and cast upon them pitch and fire and hailstones." Josephus tells us that "rains fell in torrents from heaven, crashing thunder accompanied the flash of lightning, aye and thunderbolts were hurled" (*Ant.* 6.16.3).

hostility toward strangers. misoksenia is found only here, but *misoksenos* occurs in Diodorus 34.1; 40.3; Jos. *Ant.* 1.11.1. In styling the conduct of the Egyptians as *misoksenia,* the author is reversing the very charge made against the Jews by his pagan contemporaries. Even the friendly Hecataeus of Abdera claimed that Moses introduced "a form of life encouraging seclusion from humankind and a hatred of aliens" (*apanthropon tina kai misoksenon bion:* Diodorus 40.3.4), although he was prepared to explain it away as the result of their own expulsion from Egypt. There is a fragment from the thirty-fourth book of Diodorus' history which deals with the struggle between Antiochus VIII Sidetes and the Jews (134–132 BCE), and which relates that the anti-Semitic advisers of the victorious Seleucid king suggested that he should storm Jerusalem and "wipe out completely the race of the Jews, since they above all nations avoided dealings with any other people and looked upon all men as their enemies. They pointed out, too, that the ancestors of the Jews had been driven out of all Egypt as men who were impious and detested by the gods. . . . Having organized the nation of the Jews they made their hatred of mankind into a tradition, and on this account had introduced utterly outlandish laws: not to break bread with any other race, nor to show them any good will at all. . . . They reminded him that Antiochus, called Epiphanes, on defeating the Jews [in 169 BCE] had entered the innermost sanctuary of the god's temple. . . . Finding there a marble statue of a heavily bearded man seated on an ass, with a book in his hands, he supposed it to be an image of Moses . . . the man who had ordained for the Jews their misanthropic and lawless customs" (Jos. *Ag.Ap.* 2.79*ff*. The common view that this passage derives from Posidonius is based mainly on the prevalent opinion that Diodorus' narrative from the thirty-third book on derives from Posidonius. See Stern:142. For Lysimachus' similar report, see 16.1.309). According to Pompeius Trogus, the Jews anxiously avoided all contact with aliens. The original reason for this was fortuitous, but Moses made of it a religious institution (Justinus 36.2; Stern 1976:332–343). At the beginning of the third century CE, Philostratus wrote: "The Jews have long been in revolt not only against the Romans, but against humanity, and a race that has made its own life apart (*bion amikton*) and irreconcilable, that cannot share with the rest of mankind in the pleasures of the table nor join in their libations or prayers or sacrifices, are separated from ourselves by a greater gulf than divides us from Susa or Bactra in the most distant Indies" (*Vita Apollonii* 5.33; cf. Tacitus *Historiae* 5.5.2). Philo not only inveighs directly against these charges (*Spec.* 3.110, 113; 2.167), but accuses the ancient Egyptians in words very similar to those of our author: "So, then, these strangers, who had left their own country and came to Egypt hoping to live there in safety as in a second fatherland, were made slaves by the ruler of the country. . . . And in thus making serfs of men who were not only free but guests, suppliants, and settlers, he showed no shame or fear of the God of liberty and hospitality and of justice to guests and suppliants" (*Mos.* 1.36; cf. J. N.

Sevenster, *The Roots of Pagan Anti-Semitism in the Ancient World* [Leiden, 1975] 89–94).

14. *Others*. I.e. the Sodomites. Cf. *Mek. Shirta* 2 (Goldin:91–93).
guests. See Gen 45:17.
benefactors. A reference to Joseph's services. Some see in v. 14 an allusion to the condition of the Jews in Egypt during the author's own period (Gregg; Goodrick). The degrading *laographia,* or poll tax, imposed by the Romans 24/23 BCE) only on those who were not Greek citizens was a strong incentive for the Jews of Alexandria to strive to attain Greek citizenship. The Greeks and Egyptians, however, violently opposed this attempt. In the words "men who had already shared with them equal rights" (v. 16), it is tempting to see a reference to the fact that in the Ptolemaic period many Alexandrian Jews had indeed succeeded by irregular means in gaining access to the gymnasium and thus to Greek citizenship, whereas in the Roman period the gates were tightly shut before them. See Tcherikover-Fuks 1957:1. 59–65. See also NOTE on 10:17.

15. The meaning of this verse remains obscure. Goodrick translates: "And not only so, but whatever allowance (*hētis episkopē*) there be shall be theirs." I have in my own rendering adopted Swete's reading $\hat{\eta}$ ('in truth'). Cf. IV Ezra 15:11–12.

16. *a festal welcome*. Cf. Gen 43:31–34. *heortasma* is found only here, but *heortasmos* occurs in Plutarch *Moralia* 1101E.
shared with them equal rights. Cf. Gen 45:17–20 ("for the best of the land of Egypt will be yours").

17. *blindness*. The reference is to Exod 14:20: "And there was the cloud and the darkness." Cf. *Mek. Beshallaḥ,* ad loc.: "The cloud upon Israel and the darkness upon the Egyptians. Scripture tells that the Israelites were in the light and the Egyptians were in the dark. . . . 'And the one came not near the other all night.' Scripture tells that if an Egyptian was standing he could not sit down, if he was sitting he could not stand up; if he was unladen he could not load, if he was laden he could not unload, because he was groping in the darkness." For *aorasia* cf. Philo *Somn.* 1.114.
the righteous man. I.e. Lot.
immense darkness. *achanēs* in this sense first attested here. Cf. Plutarch *Moralia* 866B; M. Aurel. 12.32.

XL. TRANSPOSITION OF THE ELEMENTS
(19:18–21)

19   18 For as the notes of a psaltery vary the beat [key] while holding to the melody, so were the elements transposed, as can be accurately inferred from the observation of what happened. 19 For land animals became aquatic, and things that swim migrated to the shore. 20 So fire retained its own force in the water, and water forgot its quenching properties. 21 Conversely, flames did not waste the flesh of perishable creatures that walked among them, nor was the easily melted ice-like type of heavenly food dissolved.

NOTES

19:18. *transposed*. For *metharmozomena*, cf. Philo *Post*. 108: "Moreover, just as instruments change their modes (*metharmottetai*) in accordance with the infinite number of combinations of melody. . . ."

beat. *rhythmos*. If we translate *rhythmos* with the English term 'key' (ordinarily rendered in Greek as *tonos* or *tropos*), then the musical analogy employed by the author would be particularly sharpened. He would then be saying (in accordance with Stoic theory) that the *tonos* of the elements was either heightened or lowered through a change in the relative proportions of fire and air constituting their *pneumata* (air currents), just as the *tonos* of a musical mode is varied by the transposition of the notes within it. Both the elements and the modes retain their identity despite the transposition, which only affects their *tonos*. For the author's tendency to view the transformation of nature in terms of a change in *tonos*, see 16:24 above. There is evidence that a variety of modes were in use by Alexandrian Jews in their chanting of the psalms, and Clement of Alexandria, who praised the majestic psalmody of the Alexandrian Jews, singled out one of these modes as the *Tropos Spondeiakos*, apparently a modification of the Dorian mode (*Paedagogus* 2.4). In light of this Jewish familiarity with modes, Wisd's use of a musical analogy referring to the latter is very understandable (see Winston 1971: Appendix). As so often, Philo again provides us with a very close analogy to the author's approach. Just as Wisd explains some of the miracles as involving an interchange of functions between the elements (19:10–12), and sees this as implying a new creation (19:6,18–21), so, too, Philo. In describing the miracle of the manna, he claims that the heavenly food "followed the analogy of the birth of the world; for both the creating of the world and also the raining of the said food were begun by God on the first day out of six. The copy reproduces the original very exactly: for, as God called up His most perfect work, the world, out of not being into being, so He called up plenty in the desert, changing round the elements (*metabalōn ta stoicheia*) to meet the pressing need of the occasion, so that instead of the earth the air bore food for their nourishment, and that without labor or travail for those who had no chance of resorting to any deliberate process of providing sustenance." (Cf. *Mos.* 2.266–267; 1.96; *ShR* 12.4.) Philo appears to be ascribing the redistribution of functions among the various elements to God's absolute power to create out of non-being, but as I have demonstrated elsewhere ("Philo's Theory of Cosmogony", 1975), he is referring only to a 'relative' non-being, and what he has in mind is God's power to bestow form on what is in itself formless and qualityless. He is therefore not resorting to the well-known formulation known later as *creatio ex nihilo,* whose champions invariably view the divine miracles as rooted in God's ability to create something "not out of anything," a negative formula which places them beyond the scope of human reason. For if God's power to create, which serves as a paradigm for all other miracles, is itself inexplicable and unamenable to rational analysis, then the latter too necessarily have the same status. Those, on the other hand, who understand creation as the bestowal of form on some sort of unformed material substratum have theoretically placed the divine miracles in the category of what is rationally explicable. Since it is in their camp that Philo is located, it is very likely that although he makes no explicit reference in this context to the material principles involved (he does refer to them in other contexts), he, too, like the author of Wisd, had the Stoic theory in the back of his mind as the rationale behind the divine miracles. It is instructive, however, to note that the author of Wisd, who is usually regarded as more pious and less philosophically sophisticated than Philo, has gone considerably further than the latter in his attempt to explicate certain well-known biblical miracles by alluding to a specific physical theory well known in Hellenistic philosophy. The psychological explanation for this may perhaps be seen in the fact that Philo's religious philosophy as a whole is in reality considerably more radical than that of the author of Wisd, so that he felt constrained to exercise the greatest caution when discussing something so crucial to biblical tradition as the miracles. We have already seen something analogous to this in the fact that Wisd designated Sophia as an *aporroia* or effluence of God's glory, whereas Philo cautiously restricted the application of that term to emanations of the Logos (see NOTES on 7:25).

19. *land animals became aquatic.* "By passing through the waters, the Israelites momentarily obtained the powers of water-dwellers" (Gregg [1909]).

things that swim. The reference is to the plague of frogs. Cf. Philo *Mos.* 1.103: "a multitude of frogs so numerous that . . . every place, public or private, was filled with them, as though it was nature's purpose to send one kind of aquatic animals to colonize the opposite region" (Gregg [1909]).

20. Cf. 16:17.

21. Cf. 16:18,22.

heavenly food. Cf. 16:20; *Sib Or* Frag. 3:46–49: "But they who honor the true and everlasting God inherit life, throughout the aeonian time dwelling in the fertile garden of Paradise, feasting on sweet bread from the starry heaven"; 3:746; II Bar 29:8: "The treasury of manna shall again descend from on high."

XLI. CONCLUDING DOXOLOGY
(19:22)

19   22 For in every way, O Lord, you exalted and glorified your people, and did not neglect to assist them in every time and place.

NOTES

19:22. Concluding doxologies are common in Jewish religious literature, e.g. Ps 150; Sir 51:30; III Macc 7:23; IV Macc 18:24; Tobit 14:15. Moreover, it was already a common practice in the Tannaitic age for a homily to end with words of consolation. Cf. *Sifre Deut.* 342, Finkelstein: 391: "Since Moses first addressed Israel severely, he later added words of consolation." The following words, for example, were added to the end of *M. Moed Katan* 3.9 (which dealt with the laws of mourning): "But as for the time that is to come, [the Prophet] says: 'He will destroy death forever. My Lord God will wipe the tears away from all faces.'" This type of *peroratio* is known to us from later midrashim as a well-established formula: "In this world it is so, but for the time that is to come." See E. Stein, "Die homiletische Peroratio im Midrasch," *HUCA* 8–9 (1931–32) 353–371.

in every way . . . in every time. kata panta . . . en panti kairō. Cf. III Macc 7:9; II Macc 14:15,34; Philo *Decal.* 178.

neglect. For *hypereides.* Cf. Ps 9:22: *hyperoras.*

to assist them in every . . . place. kai topō paristamenos. Cf. *Test.Joseph* 2:6: *epi pasi de topois paristatai;* Ps 108:31, LXX.

INDEX OF ANCIENT AUTHORS

INDEX OF SUBJECTS

INDEX OF SCRIPTURAL REFERENCES

INDEX OF PSEUDEPIGRAPHA, QUMRAN, AND RABBINIC LITERATURE

(I Enoch)	97:3–6 146
	98:4 107
	99:9 317
	99:14 137
	100:10–13 149
	102–105 125
	102:5 32
	102:6–7 126
	102:6–11 115
	102:11 116
	103:2 120, 159
	103:3–4 32
	103:9 107
	104:2 128
	104:2, 6 147
	104:6 32
	104:7 107
	104:12 121, 159
	108:9 127
	108:15 146

II Enoch	23:45 198
	24:2 255
	25:3 201
	25:4 204
(A)	30:8 201
	30:10 255
(A)	30:12 201
	31 123
	31:3–6 121
	40:2–3 208
	48:5 255
	49:2 127
	51:5 255
	52:2 106
(A)	58:3 201
	61:5 105
	63:2 105
	65:1, 6 255
	66:7 128

IV Ezra	1:19 298
	3:9 257
	3:14 188
	4 206
	4:11 208
	4:36–37 234
	5:10 103
	6:38 201
	6:54 201
	6:58 317
	7 125
	7:20–24 311
	7:36 146
	7:81–87 146
	7:97 128
	7:116 46
	8:41 257

	8:44 201
	8:53 113
	8:60 107
	9:17 129
	10:57 113, 235
	14:20 311
	15:11–12 329
	16:62 288

Joseph and Asen	5–6 317
	6:6 120
	12:2 225
	12:16 181
	13:10 120

Jubilees (Jub)	1:23 48
	2:2 175
	2:8 175
	4:17 159
	4:24 159
	4:31–32 233
	5:12 48
	7:22 267
	7:23 102
	8:8–11 238
	9:14–15 238
	10:29–34 238
	11:4ff 272
	12:4 201
	12:17 253
	19:9 188
	23:31 32
	30:20–21 188
	32:1 217
	37–38 217
	48:12 324
	48:14 233, 315
	48:18 220
	49:2 318
	49:6 316

LAB	6 214
	12:1–3 189
	12:3 48
	18:5 175
	19:10 238
	22:7 324
	43:5 233
	44:10 233
	45:3 233

| Odes Solomon | 6:7 186 |

| Par.Jer. | 5:32 126 |
| | 6:6 207 |

| Prayer of Azariah | 12 188 |

KEY TO THE TEXT